Exploring 3D Modeling with 3ds Max 2019

A Beginner's Guide

Pradeep Mamgain

PADEXI

Exploring 3D Modeling with 3ds Max 2019: A Beginner's Guide

NOTICE TO THE READER

Examination Copies

Textbooks received as examination copies in any form such as paperback and eBook are for review only and may not be made available for the use of the student. These files may not be transferred to any other party. Resale of examination copies is prohibited.

Electronic Files

The electronic file/eBook in any form of this textbook is licensed to the original user only and may not be transferred to any other party.

Disclaimer

No patent liability is assumed with respect to the use of information contained herein. Although every precaution has been taken in the preparation of this book, neither the author, nor PADEXI, and its dealers and distributors will be held liable for any damages caused or alleged to be caused directly or indirectly by this book. All terms mentioned in this book that are known to be trademarks or service marks have been appropriately capitalized. PADEXI cannot attest to the accuracy of this information. Use of a term in this book should not be regarded as affecting the validity of any trademark or service mark.

Book Code: PDX007P

ISBN: 9781723745447

For information about the books, eBooks, and video courses published by PADEXI ACADEMY, visit our website: www.padexi.academy

Contents

Acknowledgments

I would like to express my gratitude to the many people who saw me through this book; to all those who provided support, offered comments, and assisted in the editing, proofreading, and design.

Thanks to:

Parents, family, and friends.

Teachers and mentors: Thank you for your wisdom and whip-cracking--they have helped me immensely.

I am grateful to my many students at the organizations where I've taught. Many of them taught me things I did not know about computer graphics.

Everyone at Autodesk [www.autodesk.com].

Finally, thank you for picking up the book.

This page is intentionally left blank

About the Author

I'll keep this short, I am a digital artist, coder, teacher, consultant, and founder of Padexi Academy [**www.padexi.academy**]. I am self-taught in computer graphics, Internet has been the best source of training for me [thanks to those amazing artists, who share the knowledge for free on YouTube]. I have worked with several companies dealing with animation and VFX. I love helping young aspiring 3D artists to become professional 3D artists. I helped my students to achieve rewarding careers in 3D animation and visual effects industry.

I have more than ten years of experience in CGI. I am passionate about computer graphics that helped me building skills in particles, fluids, cloth, RBD, pyrotechnics simulations, and post-production techniques. The core software applications that I use are: Maya, 3ds Max, CINEMA 4D, Photoshop, Nuke, After Effects, and Fusion. In addition to the computer graphics, I have keen interest in web design/development, digital marketing, and search engine optimization. You can contact me by sending an e-mail to **pradeepmamgain@gmail.com.**

This page is intentionally left blank

Introduction

The **Exploring 3D Modeling with 3ds Max 2019: A Beginner's Guide** textbook walks you through every step of creating 3D models with 3ds Max 2019. This guide is perfect for both novices and those moving from other software to 3ds Max. This book will help you to get started with modeling in 3ds Max, you will learn important concepts and techniques about 3D modeling which you can utilize to create hard-surfaced objects for your projects. This book shares tips, tricks, notes, and cautions throughout, that will help you become a better 3D modeler and you will be able to speed up your workflow.

The first page of the every chapter summarizes the topics that will be covered in the chapter. Every chapter of this textbook contains hands-on exercises which instruct users how things can be done in 3ds Max step-by-step.

Although, this book is designed for beginners, it is aimed to be a solid teaching resource for 3D modeling. It avoids any jargon and explains concepts and techniques in an easy-to-understand manner.

What are the key features of the book?

- Learn 3ds Max's updated user interface, navigation, tools, functions, and commands.
- Polygon, subdivision, and spline modeling techniques covered.
- Detailed coverage of tools and features.
- All modifiers covered.
- Contains **35** hands-on exercises.
- Contains **8** practice activities to test the knowledge gained.
- Additional guidance is provided in form of tips, notes, and cautions.
- Important terms are in bold face so that you never miss them.
- The content under **"What just happened?"** heading explains the working of the instructions.
- The content under **"What next?"** heading tells you about the procedure you will follow after completing a step(s).
- Includes an ePub file that contains the color images of the screenshots/ illustrations used in the textbook. These color images will help you in the learning process. This ePub file is included with the resources.

- Tech support from the author.
- Access to each exercise's initial and final states along with the resources used in the hands-on exercises.
- Quiz to assess the knowledge.
- Bonus hands-on exercises.

Who this book is for?

This book is designed for beginners and intermediate users of 3ds Max 2019.

Prerequisites

Before jumping into the lessons of this book, make sure you have working knowledge of your computer and its operating system. Also, make sure that you have installed the required software and hardware. You need to install 3ds Max 2019 on your system. Most of the hands-on exercises will work in 3ds Max 2017 and 2018 as well.

How this book is structured?

This book is divided into following units:

Unit M1: Introduction to 3ds Max -I, introduces the 3ds Max interface as well as the tools that allow you to transform objects in the viewport.

Unit M2: Introduction to 3ds Max -II, covers the tools and procedures that will help you immensely during the modeling process. You will know about various explorers as well as various precision tools that 3ds Max offers.

Unit M3: Geometric Primitives and Architectural Objects, explains **Standard** and **Extended** primitives and how you can use them to create some basic models. This unit also covers the AEC objects.

Unit M4: Polygon Modeling, introduces you to the polygon modeling tools, concepts, and techniques. This chapter talks about polygons components, selection tools, polygons structure tools, and modeling objects.

Unit M5: Graphite Modeling Tools, describes the tools available in the **Ribbon** interface and how you can use them to improve your modeling workflow.

Unit M6: Spline Modeling, introduces you to the spline modeling tools, concepts, and techniques.

Unit M7: Modifiers, walks you through the various modifiers available in 3ds Max that you can use to sculpt or edit the objects without changing its base structure.

Unit MB: Bonus Hands-on Exercises [Modeling], contains bonus hands-on exercises.

Unit MP: Practice Activities [Modeling], contains some practice activities which you are highly encouraged to complete.

Appendix MA: Quiz Answers [Modeling], contains quiz answers.

Conventions

Icons Used in This Book

Icon	Description
	Tip: A tip tells you about an alternate method for a procedure. It also show a shortcut, a workaround, or some other kind of helpful information.
	Note: This icon draws your attention to a specific point(s) that you may want to commit to the memory.
	Caution: Pay particular attention when you see the caution icon in the book. It tells you about possible side-effects you might encounter when following a particular procedure.
	What just happened?: This icons draws your attention to working of instructions in a hands-on exercise.
	What next?: This icons tells you about the procedure you will follow after completing a step(s).

Given below are some examples with these icons:

Note: The editable poly objects vs editable mesh objects
The editable poly object is similar to the edit mesh object with the only difference is that the edit mesh object comprises of triangular faces whereas the editable poly object comprises of polygons with any number of vertices.

Tip: Dragging a modifier to an object
*To drag a modifier form one object to another object in the scene, select an object that already has a modifier. To copy a modifier without instancing it, drag the modifier name from the stack display to the target object in the scene. If you want to create an instance, **Ctrl+drag** the modifier's name.*

Caution: Preserving the parametric nature of a primitive
*When you convert an object to an editable poly object, you loose all of its creation parameters. If you want to retain the creation parameters, use the **Edit Poly** modifier.*

What just happened?
*The **Detach** tool separates the selected sub-objects and associated polygons as new object or element[s]. When you click **Detach**, the **Detach** dialog box appears. Type the name of the new object in the **Detach as** text box and click **OK** to create the new object with the specified name. The selection is removed from the original object. You can turn on **Detach To Element** to make the detached sub-object selection part of the original object but it becomes a new element. Select **Detach as Clone** to detach the selection as copy of the original selection; the selection remains intact with the original object.*

What next?
Now, we will create a sphere and then conform the splines to the sphere.

Important Words

Important words such as menu name, tools' name, name of the dialogs/windows, button names, and so on are in bold face. For example:

In the **Create** panel, click **Geometry**, and then choose **Standard Primitives** from the drop-down list located below **Geometry**. In the **Object Type** rollout, click **Tube**. Create a tube in the **Top** viewport. Place the tube at the origin. Switch to the **Modify** panel and then in the **Parameters** rollout, change **Radius 1** to **30**, **Radius 2** to **50**, **Height** to **15**, **Height Segments** to **1**, **Cap Segments to 2**, and **Sides** to **24**.

Unit Numbers

Following terminology is used for the unit numbers and appendix:

Unit M1, M2.......M7: M stands for Modeling.
Unit MB: MB stands for Modeling **B**onus hands-on exercises.
Unit MP: MP stands for Modeling **P**ractice Activities.
Appendix MA: MA stands for Modeling Appendix

This approach helps us better organize the units when multiple modules are included in a textbook. For example, texturing units will be numbered as **T1, T2, T3,** and so on; the lighting units will be numbered as **L1, L2,** and so on.

Figure Numbers

In theory, figure numbers are in the following sequence **Fig. 1, Fig. 2,** and so on. In exercises, the sequence is as follows: **Fig. E1, Fig. E2,** and so on. In exercises, the sequence restarts from number **E1** for each hands-on exercise.

LMB, MMB, and RMB

These acronyms stand for left mouse button, middle mouse button, and right mouse button.

Tool

If you click an item in a palette, toolbar, manager, or window and a command is invoked to create/edit an object or perform some action then that item is termed as tool. For example: **Align** tool, **Mirror** tool, **Select and Move** tool.

Quad Menus

The right-click menus or quad menus [see Fig. 1] are the contextual menus in 3ds Max that provide quick access to the commands/functions/tools related to the currently selected entities.

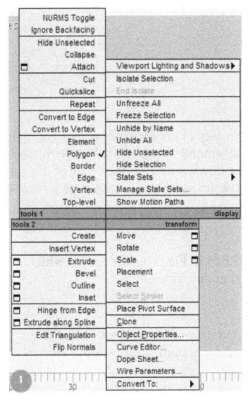

Check Box

A small box [labelled as 1 in Fig. 2] that, when selected by the user, shows that a particular feature has been enabled or a particular option chosen.

Button

The term button (sometimes known as a command button or push button) refers to any graphical control element [labelled as 2 in Fig. 2] that provides the user a simple way to trigger an event, like searching for a query, or to interact with dialog boxes, like confirming an action.

Dialog Box or Dialog

An area on screen in which the user is prompted to provide information or select commands. Fig. 2 shows the **Array** dialog box.

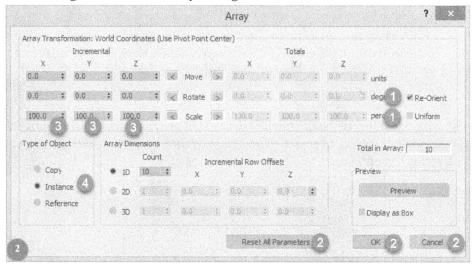

Spinner

Spinners [labelled as 3 in Fig. 2] are controllers that you will touch on regular basis. They allow you to quickly amend numerical values with ease. To change the value in a spinner, click the up or down arrow on the right of the spinner. To change values quickly, click and drag the arrows. You can also type a value directly in the spinner's field.

Radio Button

A radio button [labelled as 4 in Fig. 2] is the one in which a set of options, only one of which can be selected at any time.

Drop-down

A drop-down (abbreviated drop-down list; also known as a drop-down menu, drop menu, pull-down list, picklist) is a graphical control element, similar to a list box, that allows the user to choose one value from a list. Fig. 3 shows the **Workspaces** drop-down list.

Window

A window is a separate viewing area on a computer display screen in a system that allows multiple viewing areas as part of a graphical user interface (GUI). Fig. 4 shows the **Reaction Manager** window.

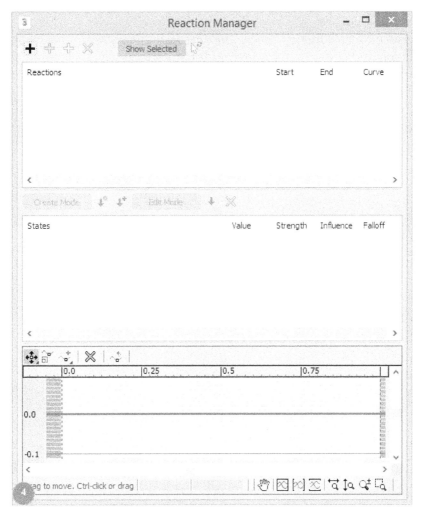

Trademarks

Windows is the registered trademarks of **Microsoft Inc. 3ds Max** is the registered trademarks of **Autodesk Inc.**

Access to Electronic Files

This book is sold via multiple sales channels. If you don't have access to the resources used in this book, you can place a request for the resources by visiting the following link: *http://www.padexi.academy/contact.* Fill the form under the **Book Resources [Electronic Files]** section and submit your request.

Tech Support

At **PADEXI Academy,** our technical team is always ready to take care of your technical queries. If you are facing any problem with the technical aspect of the textbook, please send an email to author at the following address:
pradeepmamgain@gmail.com

Errata

We have made every effort to ensure the accuracy of this book and its companion content. If you find any error, please report it to us so that we can improve the quality of the book. If you find any errata, please report them by visiting the following link: *http://www.padexi.academy/errata*.

This will help the other readers from frustration. Once your errata is verified, it will appear in the errata section of the book's online page.

- Understanding workspaces
- Navigating the workspace
- Customizing the interface
- Understanding various UI components
- Working with the file management commands
- Setting preferences for 3ds Max
- Working with viewports
- Setting preferences for the viewports
- Creating objects in the scene
- Selecting objects
- Using the navigational gizmos
- Moving, rotating, and scaling objects
- Getting help
- Per-view Preferences, Asset Library, and Game Exporter

Unit M1: Introduction to 3ds Max - I

Welcome to the latest version [2019] of **3ds Max**. In any 3D computer graphics application, the first thing you see is interface. Interface is where you view and work with your scene. 3ds Max's interface is intuitive and highly customizable. You can make changes to the interface and then save multiple 3ds Max User Interface [UI] settings using the **Workspaces** feature. You can create multiple workspaces and switch between them easily.

 Note: Interface Customization
*By default, 3ds Max starts with a dark theme [white text on the dark gray background]. This is good for those digital artists who spend hours working on 3ds Max, however, the default theme is not good for printing. I have customized the theme so that the captures appear fine when book is printed. You can easily switch between the custom color themes from the **Choose initial settings for tool options and UI layout** dialog box. To open this dialog box, choose **Custom UI and Default Switcher** from the **Customize** menu.*

The 3ds Max's interface is now **HDPI** [High Dots Per Inch] aware. Now, **Windows** scaling is correctly applied when interface appears on high DPI monitors and laptops. If you are working on a ultra-high resolution monitor, the 3ds Max's icons may appear small. You can scale the interface from the **Windows' Control Panel**. Here's the process on Windows 7.

RMB click on your **Desktop** and choose **Screen Resolution** from the popup menu. In the window displayed, choose **Make text and other items larger or smaller**. Now, you can choose a preset value from the page [see Fig. 1]. If you want to create a custom text size, click **Set custom size (DPI)** from the left of the page [see Fig. 1]. Now, click drag the scale on the **Custom DPI Setting** dialog box to change the scale [see Fig. 2]. Click **OK** to accept the settings.

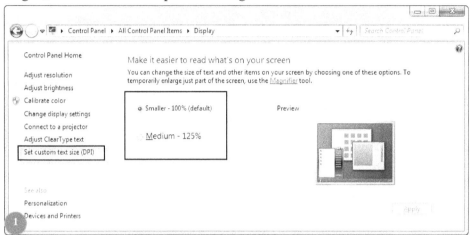

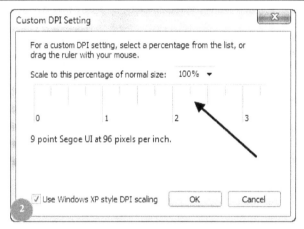

When you first time open 3ds Max, you will see **Welcome Screen**. This screen hosts a slide show designed to inspire as well as provide new users some basic information to get them started.

> *Note: Welcome Screen*
> *If you don't want to see **Welcome Screen** next time you open 3ds Max, clear **Show this Welcome Screen at startup** check box. You can bring back the screen anytime by choosing **Welcome Screen** from the **Help** menu.*

Close **Welcome Screen** to view the default UI of 3ds Max [refer Fig. 3]. Notice, I have marked different components of the UI with numbers to make the learning process easier. In 3ds Max, commands and tools are arranged in groups so that you can find them easily. For example, all viewport navigation tools are grouped together on the bottom-right corner of the interface [marked as 9 in Fig. 3].

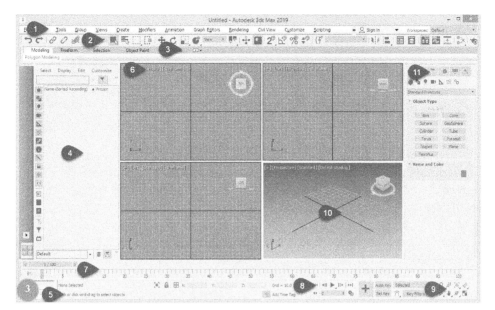

The 3ds Max interface can be divided into 11 sections. I have marked those sections in Fig. 3. Table 1 summarizes the numbers and the sections of the UI they represent.

Table 1: 3ds Max interface overview		
No.	Item	Description
1	Menubar	The menubar provides access to command and tools.
2	Main toolbar	This toolbar consists of many commonly used tools.
3	Ribbon	**Ribbon** contains many tools for modeling and painting in the scene. Also, here you will find tools for adding people to populate a scene.
4	Scene Explorer	**Scene Explorer** lets you view, sort, filter, and select objects in a scene. You can also use it to rename, delete, hide, and freeze objects. It is also used to create and amend object hierarchies.
5	Status Bar	**Status Bar** contains the prompt and status information about the scene. The **Coordinate Transform Type-In** boxes in **Status Bar** let you transform the objects manually.
6	Viewport Label Menus	These menus let you change the shading style for the viewport. They also contain other viewport related commands and features.
7	Time Slider	Allows you to navigate along the timeline.
8	Create and Play Back Animation	These controls affect the animation. This area also contains buttons to playback animation in the viewports.
9	Viewport Navigation	These buttons allow you to navigate your scene [Active Viewport].

10	Viewports	Viewports let you view your scene from multiple angles. They also allow you to preview lighting, shading, shadows, and other effects.
11	Command panel	The **Command** panel is the nerve center of 3ds Max. It contains six panels that you can use to create and modify objects in 3ds Max.

There are some other elements of the interface that are not visible in the default UI. These elements appear when you run a command from the **Main** toolbar or menu, or choose an option from the RMB click menu. Here's is the quick rundown to those elements:

■ **Toolbars**: There are quite a few toolbars available in 3ds Max. To access these toolbars, RMB click on an empty gray area on the **Main** toolbar to open a popup menu [see Fig. 4] containing the options for invoking the toolbars. When I chose **MassFx Toolbar** from the popup menu, the **Mass FX Toolbar** appeared [see Fig. 5].

■ **Quad Menus**: Whenever you RMB click in an active viewport [except on a viewport label], 3ds Max opens a **Quad** menu at the location of the mouse pointer. The **Quad** menu can display up to four quadrants [see Fig. 6] with various commands and allows you to work efficiently because the commands in the menu are context-sensitive. The **Quad** menu is the quickest way to find commands. Fig. 6 shows a **Quad** menu which appeared when I RMB clicked on an **Editable Poly** object in the viewport.

■ **Caddy Controls**: A caddy control in 3ds Max can be described as **"in-canvas"** interface that comprises a dynamic label and an array of buttons superimposed over a viewport. You can use the standard mouse operations such as clicking and dragging to change the values in the spinners. The changes you made are immediately updated in the viewport. The **Chamfer** caddy control shown in Fig. 7 appeared when I selected edges of a box and then clicked **Chamfer**'s settings button in the **Command** panel.

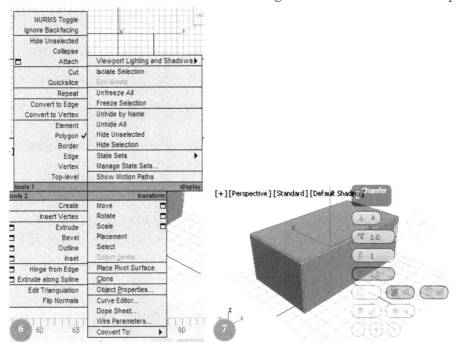

■ **Dialogs, Windows, and Editors**: Some of the commands in 3ds Max opens dialogs, editors, and windows. Some of these elements have their own menu bars and toolbars. Fig. 8 shows **Slate Material Editor**. You can use the **M** hot key to open this editor.

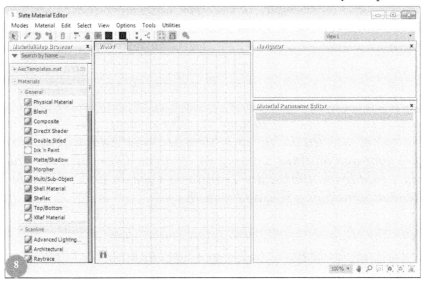

Note: Spinners

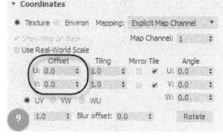

Spinners are found everywhere in 3ds Max [I have marked **U** and **V** spinners with black rectangle in Fig. 9]. Spinners are controllers that you will touch on regular basis. They allow you to quickly amend numerical values with ease. To change the value in a spinner, click the up or down arrow on the right of the spinner. To change values quickly, click and drag the arrows. You can also type a value directly in the spinner's field.

Tip: Fast and slow scroll rate in a spinner

Press and hold **Alt** and then click-drag the spinner's up or down arrow for a slower numerical scroll rate. Hold **Ctrl** for the faster scroll rate. RMB click on a spinner to set it to its default value.

Note: Numerical Expression Evaluator

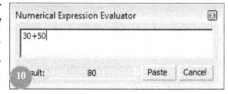

If the type cursor is located inside a spinner and you press **Ctrl+N**, the **Numerical Expression Evaluator** appears [see Fig. 10]. This evaluator lets you calculate the value for the spinner using an expression. For example, if you type **30+50** in this evaluator's field and click **Paste**, **80** appears in the associated spinner.

Note: Modeless dialogs, controls, windows, and editors

Quite a few dialogs in 3ds Max are modeless meaning the dialog box doesn't need to be closed in order to work on other elements of the interface. A good example of modeless dialog box is **Slate Material Editor**. You can minimize the editor and continue working on the scene. Other modeless dialogs that you would frequently use are **Transform Type-In** dialogs, **Caddy** controls, **Render Scene** dialog box, and so forth.

Tip: Toggling the visibility of all open dialogs

You can toggle visibility of all open dialogs by using the **Ctrl+~** hotkeys.

UI Components

You can now easily customize the workspace by floating and docking the window, panels, toolbars, and so forth. You can dock any element of the interface that has a handle. A handle can be on the left or top of the element [see Fig. 11]. To float an element, click drag the handle. As you move around the handle, target dock locations will be highlighted in blue. Drop the element on the blue highlight if you want to dock element in the interface.

Caution: Toolbars
Toolbars can be docked only on the outer edge of the interface.

Caution: Resize Elements
When you move around elements, some of the elements may not automatically resize. In such cases, you will have to resize elements manually.

Note: Docking floating windows
*You can dock a floating window by RMB clicking on the title bar or handle of the window and then choosing **Dock** from the popup menu. Then, you can select available location from the menu displayed.*

Once you are happy with the arrangement of the elements in the interface, you can save the arrangement using the **Workspaces** feature. This feature is available on the right of the menubar. The following section presents what you need to know about 3ds Max UI.

Caption Bar

The **Caption** bar is another name for the **Title** bar. It is the topmost element in the 3ds Max UI. The **Title** bar displays the name of the current 3ds Max file.

Menubar

The menubar is located below the **Caption** bar. The menus in the menubar gives you access to various commands and tools. In the previous release of 3ds Max, Autodesk has removed the **Application** button. All its functionality is included in the **File** menu.

What is the function of the Reset command?

This command clears all data as well as resets 3ds Max settings such as viewport configuration, snap settings, Material Editor, background image, and so on. If you have done some customization during the current session of the 3ds Max, and you execute the **Reset** command, all startup defaults will be restored according to the setting stored in the **maxstrat.max** file. The **Reset** command is available in the **File** menu.

How can I use maxstart.max?

You can use this file to make the changes you would like to see at the startup. Start 3ds Max and make the adjustments. Then, save file in the scenes folder with the name **maxstrat.max**.

Note: Templates

If you reset the scene, it will also affect the template that you had used to open the scene. The template will be reset back to its default settings.

How can I change the undo levels?

You can change it from the **Preferences** dialog box. By default, 3ds Max allows only **20** levels for the undo operations. To change it, choose **Preferences** from the **Customize** menu. In the **General** panel of the dialog box, you can set Levels from the **Scene Undo** group.

What is the use of the Preferences dialog box?

The **Preferences** dialog box contains options that 3ds Max offers for its operations. 3ds Max behaves according to the options you set in the **Preferences** dialog box. You have just seen an example how you can change the undo levels. If you increase the number of levels, you force 3ds Max to obey that setting. The **Preferences** dialog box comprises many panels with many options that you can use.

Tip: The Preferences dialog box

You can also open the **Preferences** dialog box by selecting **Preferences** from the **File** menu.

Can I undo all commands in 3ds Max?

No. You cannot undo commands such as saving a file or using the **Collapse** utility. If you know an action cannot be undone, first hold you scene by choosing **Hold** from the **Edit** menu [Hotkeys: **Ctrl+H**]. When you want to recall, choose **Fetch** from the **Edit** menu [Hotkeys: **Alt+Ctrl+F**].

Why do I need a project folder?

*When you work on a project, you have to deal with many scenes, texture files, third party data, rendering, material libraries, and so forth. If you don't organize the data for the project, it would be very difficult for you to manage the assets for the project. The project folder allows you to organize all your files in a folder for a particular project. You can set a project by using the options available in the **File > Project** menu.*

What is the Workspaces feature?

*This feature allows you to quickly switch between the different arrangement of panels, toolbars, menus, viewports, and other interface elements. Choose **Reset To Default State** from the **Workspaces** drop-down list to rest the workspace to the saved settings of the active workspace. On selecting the **Manage Workspaces** option from the **Workspaces** drop-down list, the **Manage Workspaces** dialog box appears from where you can switch, add, edit, and delete workspaces.*

The menu system follows the standard **Windows** conventions. When you click on a menu item on the menu bar, a pulldown menu appears. You can also open a pulldown menu by pressing the associated menu hot key with **Alt**. The hot key is denoted by an underline in the name of the menu. For example, if you want to open the **Edit** menu, press **Alt+E**. Similarly, for the **Customize** menu, press **Alt+U**.

If a hot key is available for a command, it will appear in the menu next to the command name. You can use these hot keys to execute the command without invoking the menu. For example, to select all objects in a scene, you can press **Ctrl+A**. To execute this command from the menubar, you have to choose **Select All** from the **Edit** menu.

Not all the commands are available all the time, some commands are context-sensitive. If a black triangle appears [for example, the **Selection Region** command in the **Edit** menu] on the next to a menu command, it indicates that a sub-menu exists. Place the mouse pointer on the command to view the sub-menu.

Viewports

In 3ds Max, you will be doing most of the work in the viewports. Viewports are openings into 3D space you work. A viewport represents 3D space using the **Cartesian** coordinates system. The coordinate are expressed using three numbers such as **[10, 10, 20]**. These number represent points in 3D space. The origin is always at **[0, 0, 0]**.

By default, 3ds Max displays a four viewport arrangement: **Top, Front, Left**, and **Perspective**. The **Top, Front**, and **Left** are known as orthographic views. 3ds Max provides many options to change the viewport as well as the layout. Using multiple viewports can help you visualize the scene better.

What do you mean by an Orthographic View?
Most of the 3D designs created using computer relies on the 2D representation of the designs. Some examples of the 2D representations are maps, elevations, and plans. Even to create a character model, you first design it on paper [front, side, and back views] [see Fig. 12] and then create 3D model using these designs.

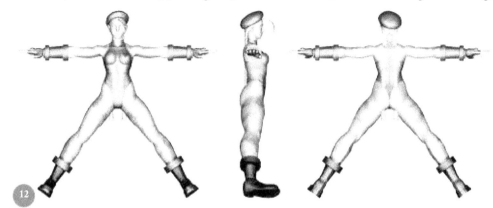

12

Note:
Blueprint Courtesy: *http://www.the-blueprints.com*

In laymen terms, you can think of the orthographic views as flat, or straight on. The orthographic views are two dimensional views. Each dimension is defined by two world coordinate axes. Combination of these two axes produce three sets of orthographic views: **Top and Bottom, Front and Back**, and **Left and Right**. Fig. 13 shows a model in three orthographic views [**Top, Right**, and **Left**] and in the **Perspective** view.

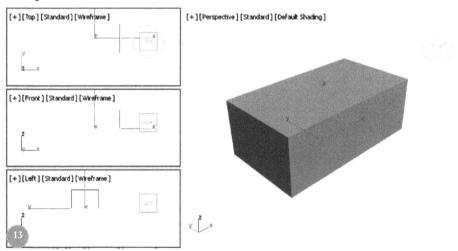

You can change a viewport to various orthographic views using the controls available in the **Point-Of-View (POV)** viewport label menu. The **Perspective** view on the other hand closely resembles with the human view. In 3ds Max there are three ways to create a perspective view: **Perspective** view, camera view, and light view.

Can you tell me little more about Viewport Label menus and how can I change a viewport to the orthographic views?

*Notice on top-left corner of a viewport, there are three labels. Fig. 14 shows labels on the **Perspective** viewport. Each label is clickable [click or RMB click]. When you click on any of the labels, a popup menu appears.*

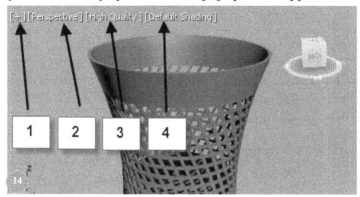

The left most menu is the **General Viewport** label menu [marked as 1], in the middle is the **Point-Of-View [POV]** viewport label menu [marked as 2], and on the right is **Lights and Shadows** viewport label menu [marked as 3]. The right most menu is the **Shading** viewport label menu [marked as 4]. The **General Viewport** label menu comprises controls for overall viewport display or activation. It also gives you access to the **Viewport Configuration** dialog box. The **POV Viewport** label menu provides options mainly for changing the viewports. To switch a viewport, for example, to change the **Top** viewport into the **Bottom** viewport, make sure the **Top** viewport is active and then click or RMB click on the **POV Viewport** label menu. Now, choose **Bottom** from the menu. You can also use the hot key **B**. Table 2 summarizes the hot keys that you can use to change the viewports.

Table 2: The hot keys for switching the viewports	
View	**Hotkey**
Top	T
Bottom	B
Front	F
Left	L
Camera	C
Orthographic	U
Perspective	P

The **Shading Viewport** menu lets you control how objects are displayed in the viewport. I will discuss the options in this menu later in the unit. The **Lights and Shadows** option lets you adjust the behavior of the lights and shadows in the viewport. You can also adjust quality settings from this menu.

What is an active viewport?
An active viewport is where all actions take place in 3ds Max. One viewport is always active in 3ds Max marked with a highlighted border. To switch the active viewport, you can use any of the three mouse buttons. It is recommended that you use the MMB for making a viewport active as LMB and RMB clicks are also associated with other command in 3ds Max.

When viewports are not maximized, you can press the **Windows** key and **Shift** on the keyboard to cycle the active viewport. When one of the view is maximized, pressing **Windows** key and **Shift** displays the available viewports [see Fig. 15] and then you can press **Shift** repeatedly with the **Windows** key held down to cycle among viewports. When you release the keys, the chosen viewport becomes the maximized viewport.

 How can I change the viewport configuration like the one shown in Fig. 13?
*The **Viewport Layouts** bar lets you quickly switch among different types of viewport layouts. This bar generally docked on the left of the viewports [see Fig. 16]. If it is not visible, RMB click on the empty area of the **Main** toolbar and then choose **Viewport Layout Tabs**. To change the layout, click on the arrow on the bar to open a flyout and then click on the desired layout to make it active.*

*You can also change the layout using the **General Viewport** label menu. Click on the label and then choose **Configure Viewports**. The **Viewport Configuration** dialog box appears [see Fig. 17]. Select the **Layout** panel and then choose the desired layout. Now, click **OK** to accept the changes.*

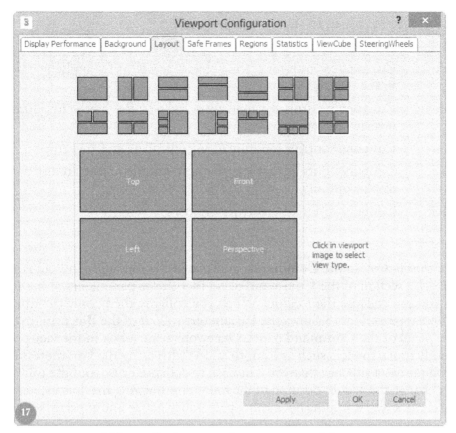

 I can see a grid in each viewport, how can I use it?
The grid you see in each viewport is one of the three planes [along the **X**, **Y**, and **Z** axes] that intersect at the right angles to each other at a common point called origin [**X**=0, **Y**=0, and **Z**=0]. The three planes based on the world coordinate axes are called home grid. To help you easily position objects on the grid, one plane of the home grid is visible in each viewport. The grid acts as a construction plane when you create objects on it.

 Tip: Turning off the grid
*You can turn off the grid in the active viewport by pressing the **G** hot key.*

Command Panel

The **Command** panel is the nerve center of 3ds Max. It comprises of six panels that give you access to most of the modeling tools, animation features, display choices, and utilities. Table 3 summarizes the panels in the **Command** panel.

Table 3: Different panels in the **Command** panel	
Panel	**Description**
Create	Contains controls for creating object such as geometry, lights, cameras, and so forth.

Panel	Description
Modify	Contains controls for editing objects as well as for applying modifiers to the objects.
Hierarchy	Contains controls for managing links in the hierarchy, joints, and inverse kinematics.
Motion	Contains controls for animation controllers and trajectories.
Display	Contains controls that lets you hide/unhide objects. It also contains display options.
Utilities	Contains different utility programs.

Table 3: Different panels in the **Command** panel

Rollouts

Most of the controls in the **Command** panel live inside rollouts. A rollout is a group of controls, a section of the **Command** panel that shows parameters of the selected object. You can collapse the rollouts. When you collapse them, only the title bar of the rollout appears. Fig. 18 shows the **Parameters** rollout of the **Box** primitive in the **Modify** panel of the **Command** panel. Once you create a box in the viewport, you can modify its parameters such as **Length** and **Width** using the **Parameters** rollout. Each rollout has a title bar that you can click to collapse or expand the rollout. You can also change the default position of the rollout by dragging the dots located on the right of the title and dropping on another place when a blue line appears [see Fig. 19].

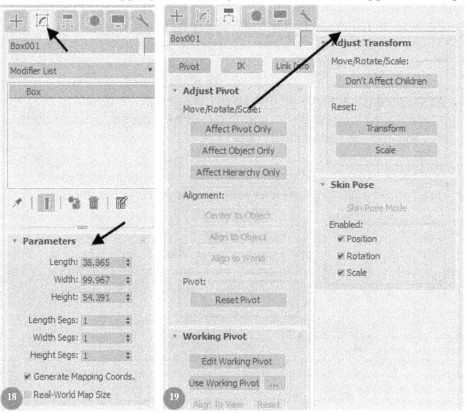

By default, the rollout occupies a single column space in UI. However, you can increase the numbers of columns by dragging the left most edge of the panel. You can create as many columns as you want [see Fig. 19] as long the screen real state is available. Multiple columns are helpful when you are working with an object with which many rollouts are associated.

If you RMB click on a rollout [**on the empty gray area**], a popup menu appears [see Fig. 20]. This popup allows you to open or close all rollouts at once, or close the rollout on which you RMB clicked. In the bottom section of the popup menu, you will see a list of rollouts available for the selected object. No tick appears for the collapsed rollouts.

If you have changed order of the rollouts, you can rest the order by choosing **Reset Rollout Order** from the bottom of the menu. If you have expanded the **Command** panel to more than one column and you RMB click on a rollout, only those rollouts appear on the popup menu that are in the column [see Fig. 21].

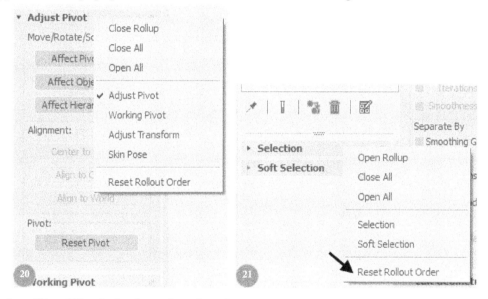

Tip: The default value for the spinners
*The nature of the spinners in 3ds Max is persistence meaning that value specified for the spinners remains set for the current spinners. For example, if you created a **Sphere** primitive with **64** segments.*

*When you create the next sphere, the value **64** will be default for it. To reset spinners to their default values, choose **Reset** from the **File** menu.*

Main Toolbar

The **Main** toolbar comprises commonly used tools and dialog box. Table 4 summarizes the tools available in the **Main** toolbar.

Table 4: The **Main** toolbar interface overview		
Item	Icon	Description
Undo/Redo		**Undo** reverses the last command. **Redo** reverses the last undo command.
Select and Link		Defines the hierarchical relationship [links] between two objects.
Unlink Selection		Removes the hierarchical relationship between two objects.
Bind to Space Warp		Attaches the current selection to a space warp or vice versa.
Selection Filter List		Limits the selection to specific types and combinations of objects.
Select Object		Selects objects and sub-objects. Hotkey: **Q.**
Select by Name		Allows you to select specific objects from a list of objects using the **Select From Scene** dialog box. Hotkey: **H.**
Selection Region Flyout		Allows you to select objects within a region using different methods. You can create different marquee shapes using the options available in this flyout.
Window/Crossing Selection Toggle		Switch between window and crossing methods for selection.
Select and Move		Selects and moves objects. Hotkey: **W.**

Table 4: The **Main** toolbar interface overview		
Item	**Icon**	**Description**
Select and Rotate		Selects and rotates objects. Hotkey: **E**.
Select and Scale		Selects and scales objects. Hotkey: **R** to cycle.
Select and Place Flyout		Position an object accurately on the surface of another object.
Reference Coordinate System	Local ▼ View Screen World Parent Local Gimbal Grid Working Local Aligned Pick	Specifies the coordinate system used for a transformations (Move, Rotate, and Scale).
Use Center Flyout		Specifies geometric centers for scale and rotate transformations.
Select and Manipulate		Selects objects and allows editing of the parameters for certain objects, modifiers, and controllers by dragging "manipulators" in viewports.
Keyboard Shortcut Override Toggle		Allows you to toggle between using only the "Main User Interface" hotkeys or using both the main hotkeys and hotkeys for groups such as **Edit/Editable Mesh**, **Track View**, **NURBS**, and so on.

Table 4: The **Main** toolbar interface overview

Item	Icon	Description
2D Snap, 2.5D Snap, 3D Snap		Specify the snap types. Hotkey: **S** to cycle.
Angle Snap Toggle		Enables angle increment snap for rotation. It allows you to snap rotations to certain angles. Hotkey: **A**.
Percent Snap Toggle		Toggles increments scaling of objects by the specified percentage. Hotkeys: **Shift+Ctrl+P**.
Spinner Snap Toggle		Sets the single-click increment or the decrement value for all of the spinners in 3ds Max.
Manage Selection Sets		Displays the **Edit Named Selections** dialog box, letting you manage named selection sets of sub-objects
Named Selection Sets	Create Selection Se ▾	Allows you to name a selection set and recall the selection for later use.
Mirror		Enables you to move and clone selected objects while reflecting their orientation.
Align Flyout		Gives you access to six different tools for alignment. Hotkeys: **Align [Alt+A]**, and **Normal Align [Alt+N]**.
Toggle Scene Explorer		Toggles **Scene Explorer**.
Toggle Layer Explorer		Toggles **Layer Explorer**.
Toggle Ribbon		Expands or collapses **Ribbon**.
Curve Editor		Opens **Track View - Curve Editor**.
Schematic View (Open)		Opens the **Schematic View** window.

Table 4: The **Main** toolbar interface overview		
Item	Icon	Description
Material Editor flyout		Opens **Material Editor** that provides functions to create and edit materials and maps.
Render Setup		Opens the **Render Setup** dialog box. Hotkey: **F10**.
Rendered Frame Window		Opens **Rendered Frame Window** that displays rendered output.
Render Production		Renders the scene using the current production render settings without opening the **Render Setup** dialog box.
Render Iterative		Renders the scene in iterative mode without opening the **Render Setup** dialog box.
Render in the Cloud		Opens a dialog for setting up cloud rendering with Autodesk A360.
Open Autodesk A360 Gallery		Opens the default browser that displays the home page of the Autodesk A360 image library.

Main Toolbar Flyouts

You might have noticed a small triangle on the lower right corner of some buttons on the **Main** toolbar. Click and hold on such a button to expand a flyout with additional buttons. Fig. 22 shows the **Selection Region** flyout.

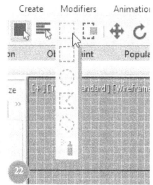

Ribbon

Ribbon [see Fig. 23], is available below the **Main** toolbar. **Ribbon** appears in collapsed state by default. To expand it, double-click on it. You can toggle the display of **Ribbon** by clicking **Toggle Ribbon** from the **Main** toolbar.

It contains many tabs. The content in the tabs is depended on the context. The items displayed may vary according to the selected sub-objects. I will cover **Ribbon** in a later unit. Most of the tools are only visible in the **Ribbon** when you are editing a poly object. You will learn about **Ribbon** and poly modeling techniques in a later unit.

The animation controls are found on the left of the **Viewport Navigation** controls [see Fig. 24]. Two other controls that are vital to animation are **Time Slider** and **Track Bar** [see Fig. 25]. These controls are available below the viewports. The **Time Slider** works with the **Track Bar** to allow you to view and edit animation. The sliders shows the current frame and the total number of frames in the range. The **Track Bar** shows the frame numbers and allows you to move, copy, and delete keys.

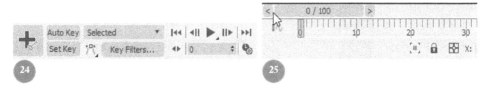

Table 5 summarizes the animation controls.

Table 5: The animation controls

Item	Icon	Description
Auto Key Set Key Set Keys		**Auto Key** toggles the automatic key mode. Hotkey: **N** **Set Keys** allows you to create keys for selected object's individual tracks using a combination of the **Set Keys** button and **Key Filters**. Hotkey: '
Selection List		Provides quick access to **Named Selection Sets** and track sets.
Default In/Out Tangents for New Keys		This flyout provides a quick way to set a default tangent type for new animation keys.
Key Filters		Opens the **Set Key Filters** dialog box where you can specify the tracks on which keys are created.
Go To Start		Moves the time slider to the first frame of the active time segment. Hotkey: **Home**
Previous Frame/Key		Moves the time slider back one frame. Hotkey: **,**
Play Animation Stop Animation		The **Play Animation** button plays the animation in the active viewport. You can stop the playback by clicking on the button again. Hotkey: **/**
Next Frame/Key		Moves the time slider ahead one frame. Hotkey: **.**

Table 5: The animation controls

Item	Icon	Description
Go To End	▶▶|	Moves the time slider to the last frame of the active time segment. Hotkey: **End**
Current Frame (Go To Frame)	38 ↕	Displays the number or time of the current frame, indicating the position of the time slider.
Key Mode	◀▶	Allows you jump directly between keyframes in your animation.
Time Configuration	🕘	Opens the **Time Configuration** dialog box that allows you to specify the settings for the animation.

Viewport Navigational Controls

The **Viewport Navigation Controls** are located at the right end of Status Bar [see Fig. 26]. The controls in the **Viewport Navigational Controls** depend on the type of viewport [**Perspective**, orthographic, camera, or light] active. Some of the buttons have a little black triangle at the right bottom corner. The arrow indicates that there are some hidden buttons exist. To view them, press and hold the LMB on the button. When a button is active, it is highlighted, to deactivate it, press **ESC**, choose another tool, or RMB click in a viewport.

Table 6 shows the controls available for all viewports. Table 7 shows the controls available for the **Perspective** and orthographic views. Table 8 shows the controls available for the camera views. Table 9 shows the controls available for the light views.

Table 6: The viewport navigational controls available for all viewports

Item	Icon	Description
Zoom Extents All / Zoom Extents All Selected	🔲	Allow you to zoom selected objects or all objects to their extent in the viewport.
Maximize Viewport Toggle	↗	It switches any active viewport between its normal size and full-screen size. Hotkeys: **Alt+W**.

Table 7: The viewport navigational controls available for **Perspective** and orthographic views

Item	Icon	Description
Zoom	🔍	Allows you to change the magnification by dragging in a **Perspective** or orthographic viewport. Hot keys: **Alt+Z**. You can also use the bracket keys, [and].

Table 7: The viewport navigational controls available for **Perspective** and orthographic views

Item	Icon	Description
Zoom All		Allows you adjust view magnification in all perspective and orthographic viewports at the same time.
Zoom Extents, Zoom Extents Selected		**Zoom Extents** centers all visible objects in an active perspective or orthographic viewport until it fills the viewport. Hotkeys: **Ctrl+Alt+Z. Zoom Extents Selected** centers a selected object, or set of objects. Hotkey:**Z.**
Field-of-View		**Field-of-View** adjusts the area of the scene that is visible in a viewport. It's only available in the **Perspective** viewport. Hotkeys: **Ctrl+W. Zoom Region** magnifies a rectangular area you drag within a viewport.
Pan View		**Pan View** moves the view parallel to the current viewport plane. Hotkeys: **Ctrl+P.**
Walk Through		Allows you to move through a viewport by pressing arrow keys. Hot key: **Up Arrow.**
Orbit Orbit Selected Orbit Sub-Object		**Orbit** rotates the viewport and uses the view center as the center of rotation. Hotkeys: **Ctrl+R. Orbit Selected** uses the center of the current selection as the center of rotation. **Orbit Sub-object** uses the center of the current sub-object selection as the center of rotation.

Table 8: The viewport navigational controls available for camera views

Item	Icon	Description
Dolly Camera, Target, or Both		This flyout replaces the **Zoom** button when the **Camera** viewport is active. Use these tools to move camera and/or its target along the camera main axis.
Perspective		It performs a combination of FOV and Dolly for target cameras and free cameras.
Roll Camera		Rotates a free camera around its local Z-axis.
Field-of-View Button		Adjusts the amount of the scene that is visible in a viewport
Truck Camera		Moves the camera parallel to the view plane.

Table 8: The viewport navigational controls available for camera views

Item	Icon	Description
Walk Through		Allows you move through a viewport by pressing a set of shortcut keys.
Orbit/Pan Camera		**Orbit Camera** rotates a camera about the target. **Pan Camera** rotates the target about the camera.

Table 9: The viewport navigational controls available for light views

Item	Icon	Description
Dolly Light, Target, or Both		Moves the light or its target or both along the light's main axis, toward or away from what the light is pointing at.
Light Hotspot		Allows you adjust the angle of a light's hotspot.
Roll Light		**Roll Light** rotates the light about its own line of sight (the light's local Z axis).
Light Falloff		Adjusts the angle of a light's falloff.
Truck Light		Moves a target light and its target parallel to the light view, and moves a free light in its XY plane.
Orbit/Pan Light		Rotates a light about the target. **Pan Light** rotates the target about the light.

Interaction Mode Preferences

If you are an **Autodesk Maya** user then it's good news for you that you can change the interaction mode to **Maya**. The **Interaction Mode** panel of the **Preferences** dialog box [see Fig. 27] allows you to set the mouse and keyboard shortcut according to **3ds Max** or **Maya**.

When you set **Interaction Mode** to **Maya**, most of the hotkeys and mouse operations behave as they do in **Autodesk Maya**. Here's the list:

- Pressing **Spacebar** maximizes the viewport that is beneath the mouse pointer.
- **Shift+Click** adds or removes from the selection. **Ctrl+Click** removes from the selection.
- The **Orbit** tools are not available in the orthographic views.
- **Alt+Home** switches to the default **Perspective** view.
- **Alt+LMB** drag to rotate the view. **Alt+MMB** drag to pan the view. **Alt+RMB** drag to zoom in or out in the view.

Table 10 shows a comparison between **3ds Max** and **Maya** hotkeys.

Table 10: The comparison between 3ds Max and Maya hotkeys		
Function	**3ds Max**	**Maya**
Maximize Viewport Toggle	Alt+W	Spacebar
Zoom Extents Selected	Z	F
Zoom Extents All	Shift+Ctrl+Z	A
Undo Viewport Operation	Shift+Z	Alt+Z
Redo Viewport Operation	Shift+Y	Alt+Y
Play Animation	/	Alt+V
Set Key	K	S
Group	None	Ctrl+G
Editable Poly Repeat Last Operation	;	G

Getting Around in 3ds Max

In the previous section, you have seen various components of the 3ds Max's UI. Don't get hung up on all the buttons, commands, menus, and options. It was a quick tour of the interface to get your feet wet. The more time you spent on **Unit M1** and **Unit M2**, easier it will be for you to understand rest of the units.

Creating Objects in the Scene

You can't do much with a blank scene. You need some objects in the scene in order to work on them. 3ds Max offers a wide range of standard objects. Let's start with creating some geometry in the scene.

Start 3ds Max, if not already running. Choose **Reset** from the **File** menu to open the **3ds Max** message box. Click **Yes** to reset the scene. Notice there are several panels in the **Command** panel: **Create, Modify, Hierarchy, Motion, Display**, and **Utilities**. Position the mouse pointer on a panel's icon; a tooltip appears showing the name of the panel. The **Create** panel comprises of the following basic categories: **Geometry**, **Shapes**, **Lights**, **Cameras**, **Helpers**, **Space Warps**, and **Systems**. Each category is farther divided into sub-categories.

Notice in [see Fig. 28] the **Create** panel [marked as 1], the **Geometry** button [marked as 2] is active. Below that button you will see a drop-down list [marked as 3] that contains the **Geometry** sub-categories 3ds Max offers. Notice the **Standard Primitives** is selected by default in the drop-down list.

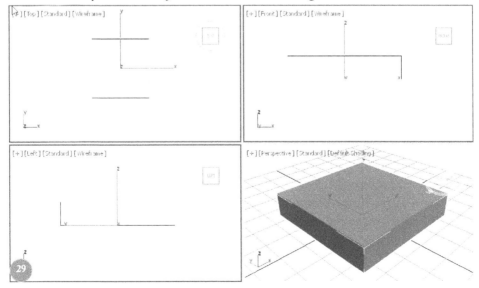

Below the drop-down list there is **Object Type** rollout [marked as 4]. There are eleven buttons in this rollout. When you click on one of the buttons, the corresponding tool gets active and then you can create the corresponding object in the scene interactively using the mouse or by entering precise values using the keyboard.

Let's create an object from the **Standard Primitive** sub-category. Ensure you are in the **Command** panel > **Create** panel > **Geometry** category > **Standard Primitives**. Now, click on **Box** in the **Object Type** rollout. Notice four rollouts appears in the **Create** panel: **Name and Color**, **Creation Method**, **Keyboard Entry**, and **Parameters**.

The **Keyboard Entry** rollout is collapsed whereas the other two are in the expanded state. Expand the **Keyboard Entry** rollout by clicking on the title bar of the rollout. Change **Length** to **50**, **Width** to **50**, and **Height** to **10**. Click **Create**. You need to press **Enter** or **Tab** after typing the values. Congratulations, you have created your first object in 3ds Max [see Fig. 29].

You have not changed values of the **X**, **Y**, and **Z** controls in the **Keyboard Entry** rollout. As a result, the box is created at the origin of the home grid [0, 0, 0].

Also, notice the name of the object [**Box001**] in the **Name and Color** rollout. Every time you create an object, 3ds Max assigns it a default name. Collapse the **Keyboard Entry** rollout. In the **Parameters** rollout, change **Length** and **Width** to **100**.

Notice the box in the viewports resizes as per the new dimensions you have set for the **Length** and **Width** controls. The change occurs because still **Box** is active in the **Object Type** rollout. If you select any other tool, then you would not be able to modify values from the **Create** panel.

Then, how to change the parameters? Well, once you select any other tool, you can change values for controls from the **Modify** panel [panel available on the right of the **Create** panel]. Click the **Modify** panel [see Fig. 30] and notice the **Parameters** rollout appears there. Change **Height** to **20**.

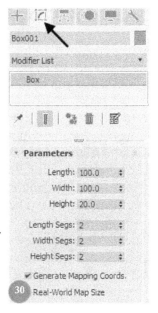

Change **Length Segs**, **Width Segs**, and **Height Segs** to **2** each. Notice the change is reflected on the object in the viewport.

Notice the white brackets around the box in the **Perspective** viewport. These are selection brackets that show the bounding box of the object. I am not a big fan of the selection brackets and don't find them very useful. Press **J** to get rid of the selection brackets. In order to change values for controls of an object from the **Parameters** rollout, the object must be selected in the viewport. I will cover selection methods later in the unit.

Click the **General Viewport** label in the **Perspective** viewport and choose **Configure Viewports** from the popup menu. In the **Viewport Configuration** dialog box that appears, choose the **Layout** tab and then click on the layout button highlighted with white borders in Fig. 31. Now, click **OK** to change the viewport layout [see Fig. 32].

You have just changed the viewport layout. The **Top**, **Front**, and **Left** viewports are stacked over each other on the left and on the right you will see enlarged **Perspective** viewport.

Note: Viewport layout
I frequently change viewport layouts as per my needs. In hands-on exercises, if you find a different viewport layout in captures, this is the place from where you can change it. I have not written this process in hands-on exercises.

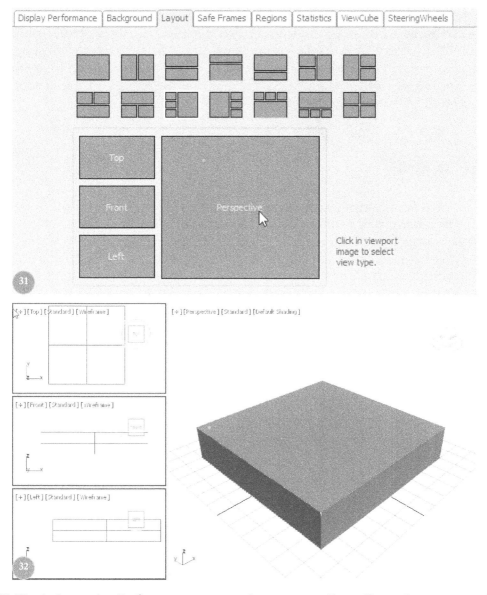

MMB click on the **Left** viewport to make it active. Press **B** to change it to the **Bottom** viewport. Press **L** to change it to the **Left** viewport. As discussed earlier, the options for changing the viewport are available in the **Point-Of-View [POV]** viewport label menu. Now onwards, I will refer **Point-Of-View [POV]** viewport label menu as **POV** viewport label menu.

Notice the text for the **Shading Viewport** label reads **Default Shading**. Click on the **Shading Viewport** label to display the **Shading Viewport** label menu. The options in this menu allow you to define the shading style for the viewport. Choose **Clay** from the menu to display object in the **Clay** shading mode. The **Edged Faces** modes allows you to view object subdivisions in the viewports. **Hidden Line** hides the faces and vertices whose normals are pointing away from the viewport. Shadows are unavailable in this mode.

Wireframe Override displays objects in the wireframe mode. The hotkey for toggling the **Wireframe** mode is **F3**. **Bounding Box** displays the edges of the bounding box of the geometry. **Clay** displays geometry in an uniform terracotta color. Fig. 33 shows the teapot in the **Hidden Line, Wireframe, Bounding Box**, and **Clay** modes, respectively. My favorite shading mode for modeling is **Clay** with **Edges Faces** and I have extensively used it in this book.

Press **Ctrl+S** to open the **Save File As** dialog box and then type the name of the file in the **File name** text box and click **Save** to save the file. Now, if you want to open this file later, choose **Open** from the **File** menu or press **Ctrl+O** to open the **Open File** dialog box. Navigate to the file and then click **Open** to open the file. If you want to save an already saved file with different name, choose **Save As** from the **File** menu.

You can also save a copy to the previous version of 3ds Max, choose **Save As** from the **File** menu to open the **Save File As** dialog box. In this dialog box, choose the appropriate option from the **Save as type** drop-down list [see Fig. 34]. Click **Save** to save the file.

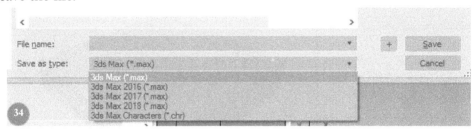

Tip: Incremental Save
*When you are working on a file, I highly recommend that you save different versions of it. If the current version gets corrupt, you can always fall back to a previous version of the file. 3ds Max allows you to save the file incrementally. In the **Save File As** dialog box, click + on the left of **Save** to save the file with a name ending in a number greater than the current number displayed with the file name. For example, if the current name is **x1.max**, clicking + will save file with the name **x02.max**.*

Selecting Objects

Selecting objects is an important process before you perform any action on an object or objects. Selection in 3ds Max works on the noun-verb terminology. You first select the object (**the noun**) and then execute a command (**the verb**). 3ds Max provides a wide variety of tools for selecting objects.

The **Selection** commands and functions are found in the following areas of interface:

- Main toolbar
- Edit menu
- Quad menu
- Tools menu
- Track View
- Display panel
- Modify panel
- Ribbon
- Schematic View
- Scene Explorer

Selecting Objects using Main Toolbar Selection Buttons

The buttons available on the **Main** toolbar provides direct means of selection. These buttons are: **Select Object, Select by Name, Select and Move, Select and Rotate, Select and Scale**, and **Select and Manipulate**. To select an object, click on one of the selection buttons on the **Main** toolbar. Position the mouse pointer on the object that you want to select. The shape of the pointer changes to a small cross if the object is eligible for the selection. Click on the object to select it and de-select any selected object.

 Note: Valid surface for selection
*The valid selection zone for the surface depends on the type of the object you are selecting and shading mode of the viewport in which you are selecting the object. In **Shaded** mode, any visible area of the surface is valid selection zone whereas in the **Wireframe** mode any edge or segment of the object is valid including the hidden lines.*

Adding and Removing Objects from the Current Selection

To extend a selection [adds objects to the existing selection], press and hold **Ctrl** while you make selections. For example, if you have selected two objects and you want to add third object to the selection, press and hold **Ctrl** and click on the third object to add it to the selection. To remove an object from selection, press and hold **Alt** and click on the object that you want to remove from the selection.

Inverting Selection

To invert the selection, choose **Select Invert** from the **Edit** menu. The hot keys for this operation are **Ctrl+I**. For example, if you have total five objects in the scene and three of them are selected. Now, to select the remaining two objects and terminating the current selection, press **Ctrl+I**.

Selecting All Objects

To select all objects, choose **Select All** from the **Edit** menu or press **Ctrl+A**.

Locking the Selection

When the selection is locked, you can click-drag mouse anywhere in the viewport without losing the selection. To lock a selection, click **Selection Lock Toggle** [see Fig. 35] from **Status Bar** or press **Spacebar**. Press **Spacebar** again to unlock the selection.

Deselecting an Object

To deselect an object, click on another object, or click on an empty area of the viewport. To deselect all objects in a scene, choose **Select None** from the **Edit** menu or press **Ctrl+D**.

Selecting by Region

The region selection tools in 3ds Max allow you to select one more object by defining a selection region using mouse. By default, a rectangular region is created when you drag the mouse. You can change the region by picking a region type from the **Region** flyout [see Fig. 36] from the **Main** toolbar.

> ✎ *Note: Using Ctrl and Alt*
> *If you draw a selection region with the **Ctrl** held down, the affected objects are added to the selection. Conversely, if you hold down **Alt**, the affected objects are removed from the selection.*

Table 12 lists the types of region selection. Fig. 37 shows the rectangular, circular, fence, lasso, and paint marquee selections, respectively.

Table 11: The region selection types	
Type	**Description**
Rectangular	Allows you select objects using the rectangular selection region.
Circular	Allows you select objects using the circular selection region.
Fence	Allows you to draw an irregular selection region.

Table 11: The region selection types	
Type	**Description**
Lasso	Allows you to draw an irregular selection region with single mouse operation.
Paint	Activates a brush. Paint on the objects to add them to the selection.

 Note: Changing the Brush Size
*You can change the brush size from the **Preferences** dialog box. RMB on **Paint Selection Region** to open the dialog box. In the **General** panel > **Scene Selection** section, you can set the brush size by specifying a value for the **Paint Selection Brush Size** control. The default value for this control is **20**.*

Specifying Region Inclusion

The **Window/Crossing** button on the right of the **Region Selection** flyout is a toggle button. It allows you to specify whether to include objects touched by the region border. This button affects all region selection methods I have described above. The default state of the button is **Crossing**. It selects all objects that are within the region and crossing the boundary of the region [see Fig. 38]. The other state of the button is **Window**. It selects only those objects that are completely within the region [see Fig. 39].

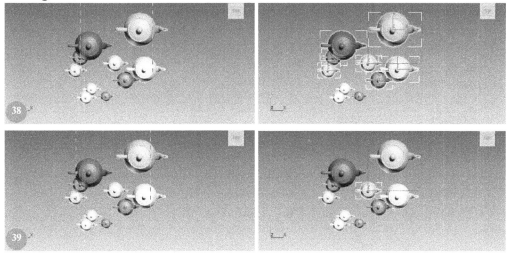

Select By Name

On clicking the **Select By Name** button on the **Main** toolbar, the **Select From Scene** dialog box appears [see Fig. 40]. It allows you to select objects by their assigned names.

To select objects by name, click **Select By Name** on the **Main** toolbar or press **H** to open the **Select From Scene** dialog box. It lists all the objects in the scene. Click on the names of one or more objects to select them and then click **OK** to select the object and close the dialog box and select the highlighted objects. Use **Ctrl+click** to highlight more than one entry in this dialog box.

Tip: Quickly selecting an object
To select a single object, double-click on its name to select it and close the **Select By Name** dialog box.

Named Selection Sets

You can name a selection in 3ds Max and then recall the selection by choosing their name from a list. To assign a name to the selection, select one or more objects or sub-objects in the scene. Click on the **Named Selection** field [see Fig. 41] on the **Main** toolbar to activate a text box and then type a name for your selection set. Press **Enter** to complete the operation.

Caution: Case sensitive names
The names you enter for the selection are case-sensitive.

To retrieve a named selection set, click the **Named Selection Sets** list's arrow. Choose the desired name from the list. The corresponding objects are selected in the viewport. You can also select the selection sets from the **Named Selection Sets** dialog box [see Fig. 42]. To open this dialog box, click **Edit Named Selection Sets** from the **Main** toolbar. Highlight the name of the set in this dialog box and then click **Select Objects in Set** from the **Named Selection Sets** dialog box's toolbar.

Using the Selection Filters

You can use the **Selection Filter** list [see Fig. 43] to deactivate selection of all but a specific category by choosing category from this list. For example, if you select **Lights** from this list, you would be only select the light objects in the scene. To remove filtering, select **All** from this list.

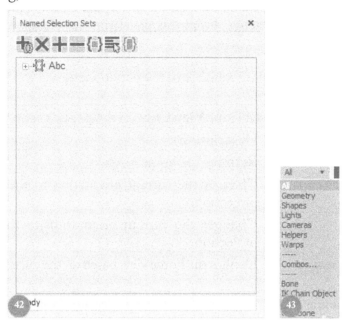

Using the Navigation Controls

3ds Max provides two controls to navigate a viewport: **ViewCube** and **SteeringWheels**. These semi-transparent controls appear on the upper right corner of a viewport and allow you to change the view without using any menu, command, or keyboard.

ViewCube

This gizmo [see Fig. 44] provides a visual feedback to you about the orientation of the viewport. It also lets you quickly switch between the standard and orthographic views. The **ViewCube** does not appear in the camera, light, or shape viewport as well as in the special type of views such as **ActiveShade** or **Schematic**. When the **ViewCube** is inactive, the primary function

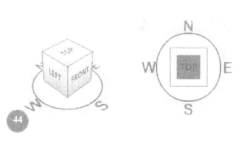

of the **ViewCube** is to show the orientation of the model based on the north direction of the model. The inactive **ViewCube** remains in the semi-transparent state. When you position the mouse pointer on it, it becomes active.

If you hover the mouse pointer on top of the **ViewCube**, you will notice that faces, edges, and corners of the cube are highlighted. Click on the highlighted part of the cube; 3ds Max animates the viewport and orients it according to the clicked part of the cube. Click on the home icon on the **ViewCube** to switch to the default viewport orientation. You can also click and drag the ring to spin model around its current orientation.

To change the **ViewCube's** settings, RMB click on the **ViewCube** and choose **Configure** from the popup menu to open the **Viewport Configuration** dialog box with the **ViewCube** panel active. From this panel you can change various settings for the **ViewCube**.

Table 12 lists the other option available in the popup menu.

Table 12: The options available for **ViewCube** in the popup menu	
Option	**Description**
Home	Restores the home view.
Orthographic	Changes the current orientation to the orthographic projection.
Perspective	Changes the current orientation to the perspective projection.
Set Current View as Home	Defines the home view based on the current orientation.
Set Current View as Front	Defines the front projection based on the current projection.
Reset Front	Resets the front projection to its default view.
Configure	Opens the **Viewport Configuration** dialog box.
Help	Launches the online help system and navigate to the **ViewCube's** documentation.

SteeringWheels

The **SteeringWheels** gizmo [see Fig. 45] allows you to access different 2D and 3D navigation tools from a single tool. When you first start 3ds max, the **SteeringWheels** gizmo is not available. To enable this gizmo press **Shift+W**. When the wheel is displayed, you can activate it by clicking on one of its wedges. If you click drag a wedge, the current view changes. The navigation tools listed in Table 13 support click action.

Table 13: The navigation tools	
Tool	**Function**
Zoom	Adjust the magnification of the view.
Center	Centers the view based on the position of the mouse pointer.
Rewind	Restores the previous view.
Forward	Increases the magnification of the view.

To close a wheel, you can use one of the following methods:

1. Press **Esc**.
2. Press **Shift+W** to toggle the wheel.
3. Click the small **x** button the upper right area of the wheel.
4. RMB click on the wheel.

Tip: Changing wheel's settings
*You can change the **SteeringWheels**' settings from the **SteeringWheels** panel of the **Viewport Configuration** dialog box box.*

There are other versions of the wheels available that you can activate from the **Wheel** menu. To open the menu, click on the down arrow on the bottom-right corner of the wheel. Table 14 lists those options.

Table 14: The options available in the **Wheel** menu.	
Option	**Function**
Mini View Object Wheel	Displays the mini version of the **View Object** wheel [see the first image in Fig. 46].
Mini Tour Building Wheel	Displays the mini version of the **Tour Building** wheel [see the second image in Fig. 46].
Mini Full Navigation Wheel	Displays the mini version of the **Full Navigation** wheel [see the third image in Fig. 46].
Full Navigation Wheel	Displays the big version of the **Full Navigation** wheel [see the fourth image in Fig. 46].
Basic Wheels	Displays the big versions of the **View Object** or **Tour Building** wheel [Fig. 47].
Go Home	Restores the **Home** view.
Restore Original Center	Pans the view to the origin.
Increase Walk Speed	Doubles the walk speed used by the **Walk** tool.
Decrease Walk Speed	Cuts the walk speed by half used by the **Walk** tool.
Help	Navigates you to the online documentation of the steering wheels.
Configure	Opens the **Viewport Configuration** dialog box that allows you set preferences for the wheel.

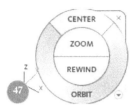 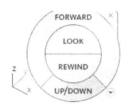

Zooming, Panning, and Orbiting Views using Mouse Scroll

To zoom in and out in the viewport, scroll the mouse wheel. It zooms in or out in steps and is equivalent to using bracket keys, [and]. If you want to gradually zoom, drag the wheel with the **Ctrl+Alt** held down. Press and hold MMB and then drag the mouse pointer to pan the view. You can pan the viewport in any direction. To rotate the viewport press and hold **Alt+MMB** and then drag the mouse pointer.

Moving, Rotating, and Scaling Objects

The transformation tools in 3ds Max allow you to move, rotate, and scale an object[s]. A transformation is the adjustment of position, orientation, and scale relative to the 3D space you are working in. 3ds Max provides four tools that allow you to transform the object: **Select and Move, Select and Rotate, Select and Scale**, and **Select and Place**. The **Select and Move, Select and Rotate**, and **Select and Scale** tools are generally referred as **Move, Rotate**, and **Scale** tools. Now onward, I will use these names.

To transform an object, click the **Move, Rotate**, or **Scale** button from the **Main** toolbar. Position the mouse pointer on the object[s]. If the object[s] is already selected, the shape of the cursor changes to indicate transform. If object[s] is not selected, the shape of the mouse pointer changes to a cross hair. Now, drag the mouse pointer to apply the transform. You can restrict the motion to one or two axes by using the transform gizmos. The transform gizmos are the icons displayed in the viewport. Fig. 48 shows the **Move, Rotate**, and **Scale** gizmos, respectively.

 Tip: Changing size of the gizmos
You can change the size of the gizmos by using the – and = keys on the main keyboard.

When no transform tool is active and you select objects, an axis tripod appears in the viewports [see Fig. 49]. Each axis tripod consists of three lines labeled as **X, Y**, and **Z**. The orientation of the tripod indicates the orientation of the current reference coordinate system.

The point where the three lines meet indicates the current transform center and the highlighted red axis lines show the current axis constraints. Each gizmo indicates axes by using three colors: **X** is **red**, **Y** is **green**, and **Z** is **blue**. You can use any of the axes handles to constrain transformation to that axis.

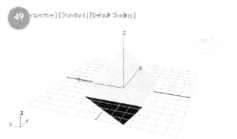

The transform commands are also available from the **Quad** menu. To transform an object using the **Quad** menu, RMB click on the selected object[s], choose the transform command from the **Quad** menu and then drag the object to apply the transform.

 Tip: Cancelling transform
To cancel a transform, RMB click while dragging the mouse.

Using the Transform Type-In dialog box

You can use the **Transform Type-In** dialog box to precisely enter the transformation values. To transform objects using this dialog box, if the **Move**, **Rotate**, or **Scale** tool is active, press **F12** to open the dialog box or choose **Transform Type-In** from the **Edit** menu to open the associated **Transform Type-In** dialog box. Fig. 50 shows the **Move Transform Type-In**, **Rotate Transform Type-In**, and **Scale Transform Type-In** dialogs, respectively. You can enter both the absolute and relative transformation values in this dialog box.

 Tip: Transform Type-In dialog box
You can also open this dialog box by RMB clicking on the tool's button on the ***Main*** *toolbar.*

The controls in this dialog box are also replicated in **Status Bar**. You can use these **Transform Type-In** boxes on **Status Bar** to transform the object. To switch between the absolute and relative transform modes, click the **Relative/Absolute Transform Type-In** button on **Status Bar** [see Fig. 51].

Getting Help

Autodesk provides rock solid documentation for 3ds Max. There are several places in the UI from where you can access different forms of help. The help options are listed in the **Help** menu [see Fig. 52]. Click **Autodesk 3ds Max Help** from the **Help** menu to open the online documentation for 3ds Max. You can also download offline help from the Autodesk website and install on your computer. If you have a slow internet connection, you can download the offline help and use it. To access offline help, download and install it on your system. Press **Alt+U+P** hot keys to open the **Preferences** dialog box [refer Fig. 53].

Choose the **Help** panel from the dialog box and click **Browse** to open the **Browser For Folder** dialog box. In this dialog box, navigate to the directory where you installed help, generally, *C:\Program Files (x86)\Autodesk\Help\3dsmax2019\en_us*. Click **OK** to close the dialog box. Click **OK** from the **Preferences** dialog box to close it. Now, when you press **F1**, 3ds Max will navigate you to the offline help.

Search Command

This feature helps you finding a specific command. For example, if you are looking for the **Sunlight** tool but not sure where it is on the interface. Press **X** to open the **Search Command** text box and then type **Sun; SunLight** System appears in a list. Click on it, 3ds Max takes you to **Systems** category of the **Create** panel in the **Command** panel.

Explore More

Per-view Preferences and Presets

We can define display quality settings for each viewport. For example, you can specify the rendering level [**Basic, Advanced**, and **DX**], Lighting and Shadow settings, ambient occlusion settings, and so forth. The Per-view Preferences and Presets can be accessed from the **Viewport Setting and Preference** dialog box [see Fig. 54]. To open this dialog box, choose **Per-View Preset** from the third viewport label menu or **Per-View Preference** from the fourth viewport label menu.

3ds Max Asset Library

To open the library, choose **Launch 3ds Max Assets Library** from the **Content** menu; 3ds Max opens the **https://apps.autodesk.com/en** page in the default browser. Choose **3ds Max** from the **Product Stores** column on the page and then download the desired app from this browser.

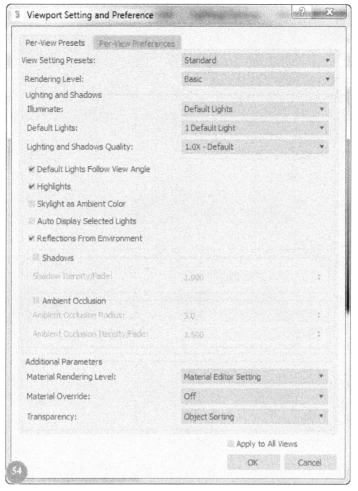

Game Exporter Utility

This utility [see Fig. 55] allows you to export the models and animations clips in **FBX** format to your game engine in a streamlined fashion. This utility is specifically designed for game users to export game assets more efficiently. This utility uses minimal amount of settings, as a result, you can easily export the model without changing too many settings. It also supports animation clips thus allows you to export multiple clips as a single FBX file or as multiple files. You can open this utility from the **File** menu or **Utilities** panel:

- **Utilities** panel > **Utilities** rollout > **More** button > **Utilities** dialog box > **Game Exporter** button
- **File** menu > **Export** > **Game Exporter**

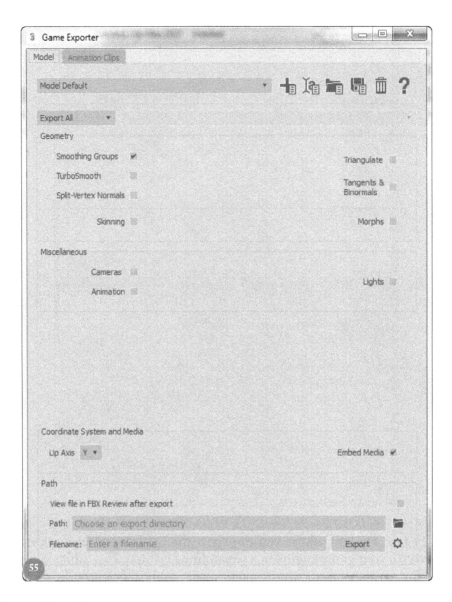

Hands-on Exercise

Before you start the exercise, let's first create a project folder for the hands-on exercise of this unit. You can proceed without creating a project folder but I highly recommend that you create one. The project folder allows you to keep your file organized.

Open **Windows Explorer** and create a new directory with the name **max2019projects** in the **C** drive of your system. Start 3ds Max. From the **File** menu, choose **Reset**. Click **Yes** from the dialog box that opens. From the **File** menu, choose **Project** > **Create Default** to open the **Choose a folder** dialog box. In this dialog box, navigate to the **3dsmax2019projects** directory and then click **New Folder** and then rename the folder as **unit-m1**. Select the folder and then click **Select Folder** to create the project folder. Now, if you navigate to the **\max2019projects\unit-m1** directory, you will see a number of sub-directories [see Fig. E1].

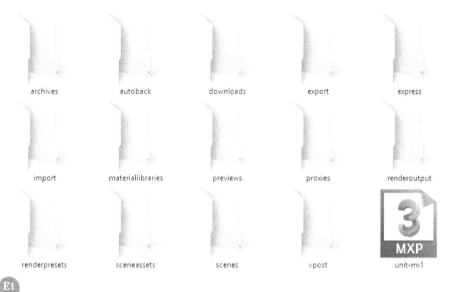

archives   autoback   downloads   export   express

import   materiallibraries   previews   proxies   renderoutput

renderpresets   sceneassets   scenes   vpost   unit-mi1

E1

What just happened?
Here, I have set a project folder for the hands-on exercise of this unit. When you set a project folder for a scene, 3ds Max creates a series of folders such as scenes, sceneassets, and so on. These folders are default locations for certain types of operations in 3ds Max. For example, the scenes folder is used when 3ds Max opens or saves scene files.

Tip: Resetting Scene
*It is a good idea to reset the scene before you start new work because the **Open** command defaults to the folder where the previous scene was saved. After the reset operation, the **Open** command defaults to the **scenes** folder of the current project folder.*

The **unit-m1** folder will contain all the data related to the hands-on exercise of this unit.

Exercise 1: Creating Simple Model of a House

OK, now it is time to work on the first exercise of the book. In this exercise, you will create a simple model of a house using the **Standard Primitives** [see Fig. E2].

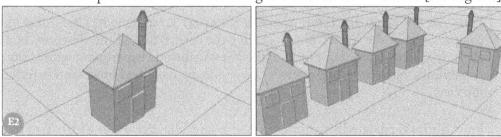

Table E1 summarizes the exercise:

Table E1	
Skill level	Beginner
Time to complete	20 Minutes
Project Folder	**unit-m1**
Final exercise file	**house-finish.max**

1. Start 3ds Max. Choose **Reset** from the **File** menu. Click **Yes** on the **3ds Max** message box to reset the settings. Choose **Unit Setup** from the **Customize** menu to open the **Units Setup** dialog box. Ensure that **Generic Units** in on in this dialog box and then click **OK** to close the dialog box.

2. Click **Box** on the **Object Type** rollout in the **Command** panel and then click-drag in the **Perspective** viewport to define the length and width of the box. Release the mouse button to define the length and width of the box. Release the LMB and then drag upward to define the height. Click to specify the height.

3. Press **J** to turn off the selection brackets and **F4** to turn on the **Edged Faces** mode. Now, click on the **Shading Viewport** label and choose **Clay** from the popup menu.

4. Press **G** To turn off the grid. Press **G** again to turn it on. Drag the mouse pointer with the **MMB+Alt** held down to rotate the view. Drag the mouse pointer with the **MMB** held down to pan the view. Drag the mouse pointer with the **Ctrl+Alt+MMB** held down to zoom in or out of the view. You need to place the mouse pointer on the area for which you want to change the magnification. Next, you will use the brackets keys to change the settings.

5. Place the mouse pointer on the area for which you want to change the magnification settings and then use the bracket keys [and] to change the level of magnification. MMB click on the **Perspective** viewport to make it active, if not already active. Press **Alt+W** to maximize the viewport. Click on the **Home** icon on the **ViewCube** to restore the home view. Alternatively, you can RMB click on the **ViewCube** and then choose **Home** from the **ViewCube's** menu.

6. Press **Alt+W** again to restore the four viewport arrangement. Click drag the compass ring of the **ViewCube** to change the orientation of the viewport. Now, click-drag edges, corners, or faces of the **ViewCube** and experiment with various possibilities that **ViewCube** offers. When done, click on the **Home** icon to restore the view.

7. Press **Shift+Z** repeatedly to undo the scene view changes. Press **Shift+Y** to redo the scene view changes. Click on the **ViewCube's Home** icon to restore the home view.

8. Press **Ctrl+P** to activate the **Pan View** 🖐tool and then drag in the viewport to pan the view. Now, press **Ctrl+R** to activate the **Orbit** tool and drag in the viewport to rotate the view. Press **Q** to deactivate the **Orbit** tool 🔄 and activate the **Select** tool. Press **Shift+W** to activate **StreeringWheels**. Click drag the **ZOOM** wedge to change the magnification level. Similarly, experiment with other wedges of the wheel. Press **Esc** to deactivate **SteeringWheels**.

9. Make sure **Box001** is selected in the viewport and then RMB click on the **Move** ✛ tool to open the **Move Transform Type-In** dialog box. In the **Absolute:World** group of the dialog box, RMB click on the spinners' arrows to set them to their default values which is **zero**. You will notice that the box is now placed at the origin in the viewports. The **Move Transform Type-In** dialog box is a **modeless** dialog box. You don't have to close it in order to work on the model we are creating in this exercise.

10. Choose the **Modify** panel 🗹 in the **Command** panel. In the **Parameters** rollout, change **Length**, **Width**, and **Height** to **80**, **50**, and **70**, respectively, to change the size of the box. Press **Ctr+Shift+Z** to zoom the box to its extents in all viewports [see Fig. E3]. If you press **Z** the box will be zoomed in the active viewport only.

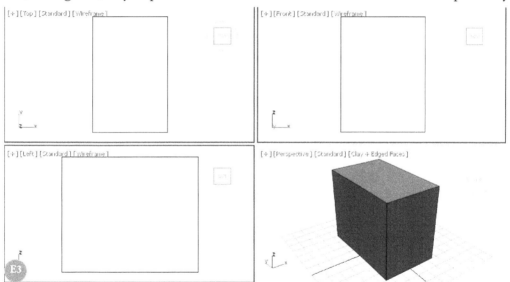

11. Now, let's create door and windows of the house. Create another box in the **Perspective** viewport and then set its **Length**, **Width**, and **Height** to **23**, **6**, and **40**, respectively [see Fig. E4]. Ensure **Box002** as well as the **Move** tool is selected and then enter **-25**, **-2.3**, and **-0.03** in the **Transform Type-In** boxes in **Status Bar** [see Fig. E5].

12. Create two windows using the **Box** primitive. Use the values **23**, **6**, and **18** for the **Length**, **Width**, and **Height** spinners, respectively. Now, align the boxes [see Fig. E6]. Ensure the **Box** tool is active and then turn on **AutoGrid** from the **Object Type** rollout. Position the mouse pointer on the **Box001**, an axis tripod shows up [see Fig. E7]. Create a box on the **Box001**.

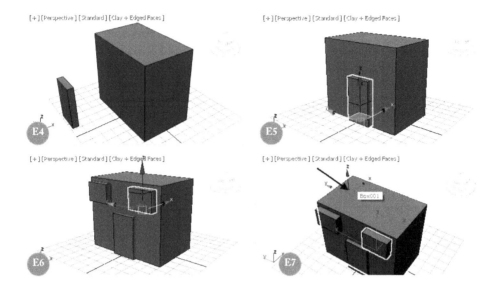

13. Ensure **Box005** is selected and then click **Align** ▤ on the **Main** toolbar. Now, click **Box001** in the **Perspective** viewport to open the **Align Selection** dialog box. In this dialog box, set the values as shown in Fig. E8 and click **OK** to align the boxes.

14. Ensure **Box005** is selected and then choose the **Modify** panel. In the **Parameters** rollout, change **Length**, **Width**, and **Height** to **91, 60,** and **2,** respectively [see Fig. E9]. Choose the **Create** panel and ensure **Auto Grid** is on. Click **Pyramid** on the **Object Type** rollout and then create a pyramid on **Box005**. Align **Pyramid001** with **Box005** using the **Align** tool. Ensure **Pyramid001** is selected and then in the **Modify** panel > **Parameters** rollout, set **Width, Depth,** and **Height** to **60, 90,** and **46,** respectively [see Fig. E10].

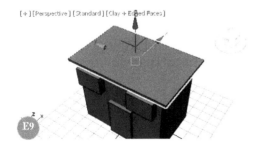

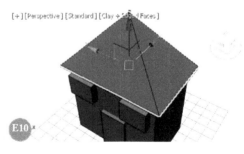

15. Now, let's create a chimney for the house. In the **Create** panel, choose **Cylinder** from the **Object Type** rollout and create a cylinder in the **Perspective** viewport. In the **Modify** panel > **Parameters** rollout, set **Radius** and **Height** to **5** and **60**, respectively. Now, place **Cylinder001** on the roof using the **Move** tool [see Fig. E11]. In the **Create** panel, choose **Cone** from the **Object Type** rollout and ensure **AutoGrid** is on. Create a cone on **Cylinder001**. Align **Cone001** and **Cylinder001**.

16. In the **Modify** panel > **Parameters** rollout, set **Radius 1**, **Radius 2**, and **Height** to **7.5**, **2**, and **13**, respectively [see Fig. E12].

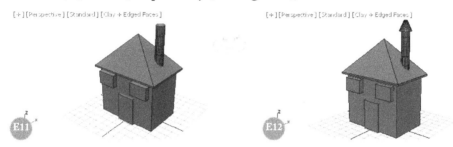

17. Choose **Select All** from the **Edit** menu to select all objects in the scene. Choose **Group** from the **Group** menu to open the **Group** dialog box. In this dialog box, type **House** in the **Group name** field and click **OK** to create a group. Press **Ctrl+S** to open the **Save File As** dialog box. In this dialog box, navigate to the location where you want to save the file. Type the name of the file in the **File name** text box and then click **Save** to save the file.

Quiz

Evaluate your skills to see how many questions you can answer correctly.

Multiple Choice
Answer the following questions, only one choice is correct.

1. Which the following keys is used to for slower scroll rate in a spinner?

   [A] Alt   [B] Ctrl
   [C] Alt+Ctrl   [D] Shift

2. Which of the following keys is used to invoke the **Select Object** tool?

   [A] S   [B] Q
   [C] W   [D] R

3. Which of the following keys is used to switch any active viewport between its normal size and full-screen size?

   [A] Alt+X   [B] Alt+M
   [C] Alt+G   [D] Alt+W

4. Which the following keys is used to lock and unlock the selection?

   [A] Spacebar   [B] L
   [C] Alt+L   [D] Ctrl+L

5. Which of the following hot keys are used to invoke the **SteeringWheel** gizmo?

   [A] Shift+S   [B] Shift+W
   [C] Shift+A   [D] Shift+X

Fill in the Blanks
Fill in the blanks in each of the following statements:

1. Press _____ to open the **Numeric Expression Evaluator** for a spinner.

2. _____ click on a spinner to set it to its default value.

3. The _____ command is used to reset 3ds Max default settings.

4. The _____ hotkeys are used to hold the scene. To recall the scene you can press _____.

5. To select all objects in a scene press _____.

6. The _____, _____, and _____ hotkeys are used to invoke **Select and Move, Select and Rotate**, and **Select and Scale** tools.

7. The _____ hotkeys are used to switch to the default **Perspective** view.

8. To deselect all objects in a scene press _____.

9. You can change the size of the transform gizmos using the _____ and _____ keys.

10. Press _____ to turn off the selection brackets.

11. Press _____ to toggle the wireframe mode.

12. Press _____ to toggle the edges face mode.

True of False
State whether each of the following is true or false:

1. You can use the **Ctrl** key for faster scroll rate in a spinner.

2. Press **Ctrl+~** to toggle the visibility of all open dialogs in 3ds Max.

3. Toolbars can only be docked on the outer edge of the interface.

4. You can press **H** to turn off the grid in the active viewport.

5. The **S** key is used to cycle through snap options.

6. You can press **Ctrl+I** to invert the current selection.

7. The **Shift+Z** and **Shift+Y** hot keys are used to undo and redo the scene view changes, respectively. [T/F]

Summary

The unit covered the following topics:

- Understanding workspaces
- Navigating the workspace
- Customizing the interface
- Understanding various UI components
- Working with the file management commands
- Setting preferences for 3ds Max
- Working with viewports
- Setting preferences for the viewports
- Creating objects in the scene
- Selecting objects
- Using the navigational gizmos
- Moving, rotating, and scaling objects
- Getting help
- Per-view Preferences, Asset Library, and Game Exporter

- Creating clones and duplicates
- Understanding hierarchies
- Working with the **Scene** and **Layer** Explorers
- Understanding the **Mirror, Select and Place**, and **Select and Manipulate** tools
- Working with the **Align** and **Array** tools
- Working with precision and drawing aids
- Understanding modifiers, and normals

Unit M2: Introduction to 3ds Max - II

In the previous unit, I covered the interface as well as the tools that allow you to transform objects in the viewport. In this unit, I will cover the tools and procedures that will help you immensely during the modeling process. You will know about various explorers as well as various precision tools that 3ds Max offers. I have also covered the procedures for creating clones and duplicates.

Creating Copies, Clones, and References

The general terms used for duplicating objects is cloning. To create a duplicate, clone, or reference, transform [move, rotate, or scale] the object with **Shift** held down. This process is generally called **Shift+Transform**. There are some other tools such as the **Mirror** tool available in 3ds Max that allows you to create clones.

 What's is the difference between Copy, Instance, and Reference?
*There are three methods available in 3ds Max to clone the objects: **Copy**, **Instance**, and **Reference**. At geometry level, clones created using any method are identical. However, they behave differently when used with the modifiers such as **Bend** or **Twist**.*

*The **Copy** method allows you to create a completely different copy of the original object. If you modify the original object, it will have no effect on the other. The **Instance** method creates a completely interchangeable clone of the original. If you modify the original or the instance, the change will be replicated in both objects.*

The **Reference** method creates a clone dependent on the original upto the point when the object was created. If you apply a new modifier to the referenced object, it will affect only that object. Depending on the method used, the cloned objects are called copies, instances, or references.

Cloning Techniques

3ds Max provides several techniques for creating clones. You can use any of these techniques on any selection. Here's the list:

- Clone
- Shift+Clone
- Snapshot
- **Array** tool
- **Mirror** tool
- **Spacing** tool
- **Clone and Align** tool
- Copy/Paste (**Scene Explorer**)

Table 1 summarizes these techniques:

Table 1: The list of cloning techniques	
Technique	**Description**
Clone	The easiest method for creating clones is to use the **Clone** command. To create clone using this command, select the object[s] that you want to clone and then choose **Clone** from the **Edit** menu or press **Ctrl+V**. The **Clone Options** dialog box appears. Choose the method you want to use from the **Object** section of the dialog box and then specify a name for the cloned object using **Name** text box and then click **OK** to create a clone. The clone will be superimposed on the original object at the same location. Use the **Move** tool to separate the two.
Shift+Drag	You can use this technique to clone objects while transforming them. This technique is most used technique for cloning objects. To clone and transform objects, click **Move, Rotate,** or **Scale** on the **Main** toolbar and then select an object, multiple objects, group, or sub-objects in a viewport. Hold down **Shift** and then drag the selection. As you drag the selection, a clone is created and transformed. Now, release **Shift** and mouse button to open the **Clone Options** dialog box. Change the settings and click **OK** to create a clone.
Snapshot	You can use this feature to create an animated object over time. You can create a single clone on any frame or you can create clones on multiple frames along the animation path. The spacing between the clones is a uniform time interval.

Table 1: The list of cloning techniques	
Technique	**Description**
Array	You can use the **Array** tool to create repeating design patterns for example, legs of a round coffee table, blades of a jet engine, text on the dial of a watch, and so on. The **Array** command allows you to precisely control the transformations in 3D space.
Mirror	**Mirror** allows you to create a symmetrical copy along any combination of axes. This tool also provides an option "**No Clone**" that allows you to perform a mirror operation without creating clone.
Spacing tool	This tool distributes objects along a path defined by a spline. You can control the spacing between the objects.
Clone and Align tool	This tool allows you to distribute the source objects to a selection of destination objects. This tool is very useful when you work on an imported CAD file that contains lots of symbols. For example, you can replace the chair symbols in the CAD file with the actual chair geometry en masse.
Copy/Paste (Scene Explorer)	You can use the **Scene Explorer's Edit** menu command to copy paste nodes. The **Scene Explorer** should be in **Sort By Hierarchy** mode.

Working with the Mirror Tool

On clicking **Mirror** from the **Main** toolbar, the **Mirror** dialog box appears [see Fig. 1]. The controls in this dialog box allow you to mirror the current selection about the center of the current coordinate system. You can also create a clone while mirroring a selection. To mirror an object, make a selection in a viewport. Click **Mirror** on the **Main** toolbar or choose **Mirror** from the **Tools** menu. In the **Mirror** dialog box that appears, set the parameters and click **OK** [refer to Fig. 2]. In Fig. 2, I first selected the left leg of the robot and then used the **Mirror** dialog box to create his right leg.

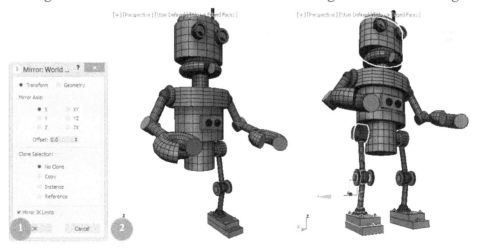

Notice in the **Mirror** dialog box, there are two options at the top: **Transform** and **Geometry**. These options control how the **Mirror** tool treats the reflected geometry. **Transform** uses the legacy mirror method. This method mirrors any word-space-modifiers [**WSM**] effect. **Geometry** applies a **Mirror** modifier to the object and does not mirror any **WSM** effect.

 Tip: Mirrored arrays
*You can create mirrored arrays using the **Mirror** and **Array** tools in succession.*

 Tip: Animating the mirror operation
*To animate the mirror operation, turn on **Auto Key** and then set a target frame for the transition to end. Now, mirror the object using the **Mirror** tool. The object will appear flatten and then will reshape itself during the transition.*

 Tip: Coordinate system
*The title bar of the **Mirror** dialog box shows the current coordinate system in use.*

Working with the Array Tool

The **Array** tool allows you to create an array of objects based on the current selection in the viewport. The **Array** button in not visible on the **Main** toolbar by default. The **Array** button is part of the **Extras** toolbar which is not visible by default.

To make it visible, RMB click on the empty gray area of **Main**  **Toolbar** and then choose **Extras** from the popup to display the **Extras** toolbar [see Fig. 3].

 Tip: Array command
*The **Array** command is also available in the **Tools** menu.*

Tip: Real-time update
*Click **Preview** in the **Array** dialog box to view the changes in the viewport as you change settings in the dialog box.*

To understand the functioning of this tool, reset 3ds Max, and create a teapot in the scene. Ensure teapot is selected in a viewport and then choose **Array** from the **Tools** menu to open the **Array** dialog box. Now, click **Preview** and set other parameters as shown in Fig. 4. Notice in Fig. 4, 3ds Max creates **4** copies of the teapot with **60** units distance between each copy.

Notice total distance is now **300** units, as shown in **Totals** section of the dialog box indicating that **5** copies of the teapot are taking up **300** units space along the X direction.

Now, if you want to distribute these teapots over a distance of say **400** units, click > on the right of the **Move** label and then set **X** to **400** [see Fig. 5], the teapots are now spread over a distance of **400** units. Similarly, you can create an array using the **Rotate** and **Scale** transformations. Settings in Figs. F6 and F7 show how you can create a 2D or a 3D array using the **Array** dialog box.

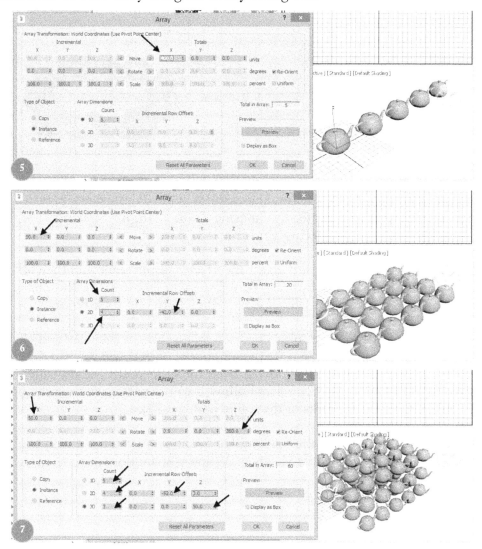

You can also create a **360** degree array using the **Array** dialog box. Reset 3ds Max and then create a **Teapot** primitive with radius **10** at the top edge of the grid [see Fig. 8]. From the **Main** toolbar > **User Center** flyout, choose **Use Transform Coordinate Center** [see Fig. 9]. Choose **Array** from the **Tools** menu to open the **Array** dialog box. Now, specify the settings, as shown in Fig. 10 to create 12 teapots in a full circle [360 degrees].

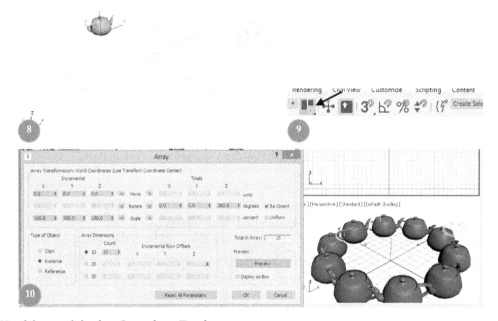

Working with the Spacing Tool

This tool allows you to distribute the selected objects along a spline or along the distance specified by two points. You can also control the spacing between two objects. This tool can be activated by choosing **Tools** > **Align** > **Spacing Tool** from the menu bar or choosing **Spacing Tool** from the **Array** flyout.

To distribute objects along a path, select the objects in the scene and then activate the **Spacing Tool** to open the **Spacing Tool** dialog box [see Fig. 11]. This dialog box provides you two methods for selecting path: **Pick Path** and **Pick Points**.

To use the **Pick Path** method, place a cursor on a spline in the view and click to select the spline as path. Now, specify the number of objects you want to distribute and then choose a distribution algorithm from the drop-down list available in the **Parameters** section [see Fig. 12]. Select **Follow**, if you want to align the pivot points of the object along the tangents of the spline [see Fig. 13].

If you click **Pick Points** from the **Spacing Tool** dialog box, you can specify the path by clicking on two places in the viewport. When you are done with the tool, 3ds Max deletes the spline.

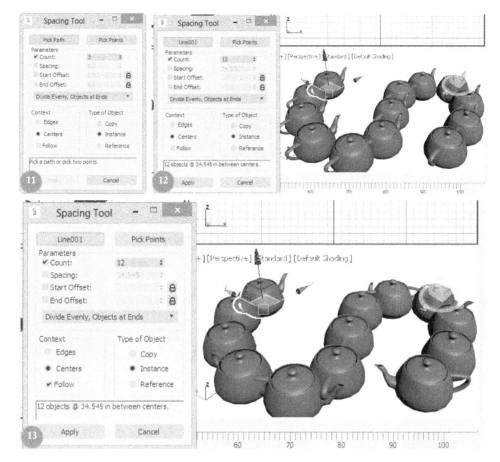

Working with Clone and Align Tool

This tool lets you distribute the source objects based on the current selection to a selection of the target objects. You can activate this tool by choosing **Align > Clone and Align** from the **Tools** menu. Alternatively, choose **Clone and Align** tool from the **Array** flyout.

To use the **Clone and Align** tool, create four teapots and a cone in the viewport [see Fig. 14]. Select cone in a viewport and then choose **Align > Clone and Align** from the **Tools** menu to open the **Clone and Align** dialog box.

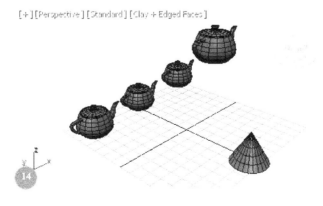

In this dialog box, click **Pick** and then click on each teapot to align the cone with the teapots [see Fig. 15]. If you want to pick multiple destination objects at once, click **Pick List** to open the **Pick Destination Objects** dialog box. In this dialog box, select the objects and then click **Pick**. This tool is very useful when you work on an CAD files. For example, you can replace the chair symbols in the CAD file with the actual chair geometry en masse using this tool.

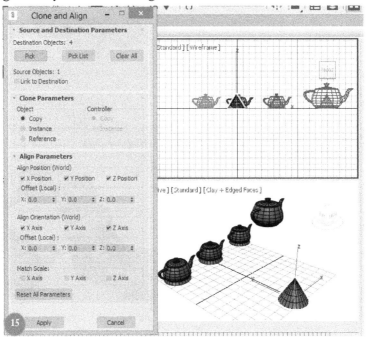

Working With the Select and Place Tool

This tool is cousin of the **AutoGrid** option found in the **Object Type** rollout. However, you can use it any time in your scene not just when you are creating an object. This tool can be activated by using one of the following four methods:

- Click the **Select and Place** icon on the **Main** toolbar.
- Choose **Placement** from the **Edit** menu.
- Press **Y** on the keyboard.
- RMB click on an object and then choose **Placement** from the **Transform** quadrant [see Fig. 16].

To place an object, you don't have to select it first. Pick the **Select and Place** tool, click-drag to place on another object [see Fig. 17].

As you drag the object, the orientation of the object changes based on the normals of the target object and object's **Up Axis** settings. The contact position of the target surface will be the object's pivot. To change the **Up Axis** settings, RMB click on the **Select and Place** tool on the **Main** toolbar to open the **Placement Settings** dialog box [see Fig. 18] and then select the axis from the **Object Up Axis** button array.

When **Rotate** is active in the **Placement Settings** dialog box, the translation of the object is prevented and object rotates around the local axis specified using the **Object Up Axis** settings. **Use Base as Pivot** is useful in those cases when the pivot is not already located in the base of the object. **Pillow Mode** is very useful when you are trying to place an object on a target whose surface is uneven. This option prevents the intersection of the objects. When **Autoparent** is active, the placed object automatically becomes the child of the other object. This is a quick way to make a parent-child relationship.

Note: Select and Rotate tool
*If you just want to rotate the object, you can use the **Select and Rotate** tool from the **Main** toolbar.*

There are some more goodies associated with this tool:

- You can clone an object while dragging it by pressing **Shift**.
- Hold **Ctrl** and then drag to position an object vertically along the **Up Axis**.
- You can prevent an object from rotating while you place it by holding **Alt**.

You can also place several objects at one go. You can either select the desired objects before picking the **Select and Place** tool or you can select additional objects using **Ctrl** when this tool is active. Each object will move according to its own pivot, unless objects are linked together.

Working With the Select and Manipulate Tool

⊞ The **Select and Manipulate** tool allows you to interactively edit the parameters of certain objects by dragging the manipulators in the viewports. The state of this tool is non-exclusive. You can manipulate objects as long as any of the select mode or one of the transform modes is active but if you want to select a manipulator helper, you must deactivate the **Select and Manipulate** tool. All those primitives with a **Radius** parameter have a built-in manipulator for the radius value. Let's see how it works:

Create a **Teapot** primitive in the scene. Pick the **Select and Manipulate** tool from the **Main** toolbar. A green ring appears beneath the teapot [see Fig. 19]. Click drag the ring to interactively change the radius of the teapot. Click on **Select and Manipulate** on the **Main** toolbar to deactivate the tool. There are three types of custom manipulators available in 3ds Max: cone angle manipulator, plane angle manipulator, and slider manipulator. The cone angle manipulator is used by a spot light's **Hotspot** and **Falloff** controls. To create a cone angle manipulator, choose **Create** panel > **Helpers** > **Manipulators** and then click **Cone Angle**. Click drag in the viewport to create the helper [see Fig. 20]. To change its parameters, go to the **Modify** panel and change the values.

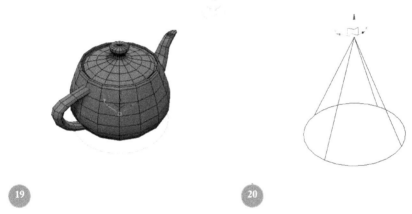

19   20

Now, let's work on a spot light to see this manipulator in action:

Create a **Teapot** primitive in the scene. Now, create a spot light and place it as shown in Fig. 21. Ensure the spot light is selected and then click **Select and Manipulate** from the **Main** toolbar. Two rings appear on the spot light [see Fig. 22].

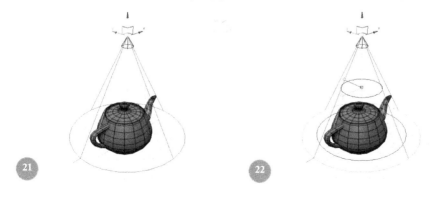

21   22

The inner ring controls **Hotspot** whereas the outer rings controls **Falloff**. Using the **Select and Manipulate** tool, click drag on the rings to interactively change these parameters. The plane angle manipulator allows you to create a lever or joystick type shape. You can use its **Angle** parameter to create a custom control. You can use this control to drive parameter of another objects.

Let's see how it works. Choose **Create** panel > **Helpers** > **Manipulators** and then click **Plane Angle**. In the **Front** viewport, click drag to create a shape [see Fig. 23]. The **Plane Angle** manipulator always created vertically along the **Y** axis of the viewport in which you are creating it. Create a teapot in the **Perspective** viewport. Ensure the **Select and Manipulate** tool is not active and manipulator is selected. Choose **Wire Parameters** > **Wire Parameters** from the **Animation** menu. In the popup that appears, choose **Object (Plane Angle Manipulator)** > **Angle** [Fig. 24]. A rubber band line appears. Click on the teapot.

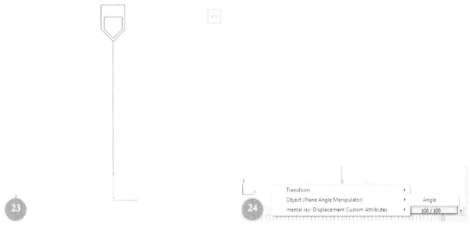

In the popup that appears, choose **Object (Teapot)** > **Radius** [see Fig. 25]. In the **Parameter Wiring** dialog box, click **One-way connection** button and then the **Connect** button [see Fig. 26] to make the connection. Now, close the dialog box. Pick the **Select and Manipulate** tool and click drag the manipulator to interactively change the radius of the teapot.

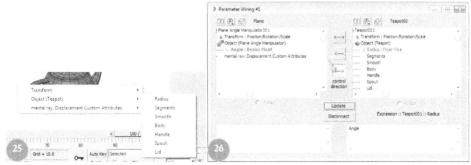

The third type of manipulator, **Slider**, which creates a graphic control in the viewport. You can wire its value to a parameter of another object within the scene. Here's how:

Create a **Slider** manipulator in the **Front** viewport. Create a teapot in the **Perspective** viewport [see Fig. 27].Wire the **Value** parameter to the **Radius** of the teapot as described above. Change the controls such as **Label**, **Minimum**, and **Maximum** values in the **Modify** panel [see Fig. 28]. Pick the **Select and Manipulate** tool and drag the manipulator's **Adjust** control to interactively change the shape of the teapot. Fig. 29 shows the components of a **Slider** control [**1.** Label, **2.** Value, **3.** Move, **4.** Show/hide, **5.** Slider bar, **6.** Adjust value, and **7.** Change width].

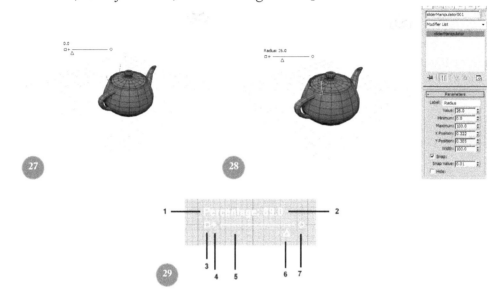

Scene Explorer

Scene Explorer [see Fig. 30] is a modeless dialog box in 3ds Max that you can use to view, sort, filter, and select objects. In addition, you can rename, delete, hide, and freeze objects. You can also modify and edit object properties en masse. Each workspace in 3ds Max comes with a different **Scene Explorer** with the same name as its workspace. **Scene Explorer** is docked to the left of the viewports.

Several explorers in 3ds Max are different versions of **Scene Explorer**. These includes: **Layer Explorer**, **Container Explorer**, **MassFX Explorer**, and **Material Explorer**. **Scene Explorer** comes with many toolbars [see Fig. 30]. Table 2 summarizes various toolbars available.

Table 2: The **Scene Explorer** toolbars	
Flag	**Toolbar**
1	Selection toolbar
4	View toolbar
5	Display toolbar

Table 2: The **Scene Explorer** toolbars	
Flag	**Toolbar**
6	Find toolbar
7	Tools toolbar

Selection Toolbar

Scene Explorer comes with two sorting modes: **Sort By Layer** mode and **Sort By Hierarchy** mode. You can use the **Sort by Hierarchy** or **Sort By Layer** button on the **Selection** toolbar [marked as 1 in Fig. 30] to use these modes. The **Sort By Layer** button [marked as 3 in Fig. 30] sets **Scene Explorer** to **Sort By Layer** mode. In this mode, you can use drag and drop feature for editing layers. Some other options are also available in this mode. The **Sort By Hierarchy** [marked as 2 in Fig. 30] button allows you to edit hierarchies using drag and drop functionality.

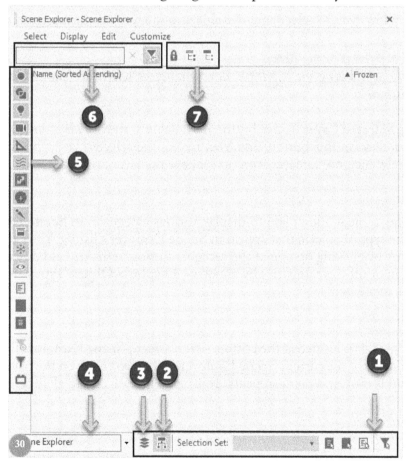

If you click on an object in **Scene Explorer**, the object is selected and the associated row in the explorer gets highlighted. To select multiple objects, click on objects with **Ctrl** held down. Press **Ctrl+A** to select all objects, **Ctrl+I** to invert the selection, and **Ctrl+D** to deselect. These commands are also available at the right of the **Selection** toolbar [marked as 1 in Figure 30]. The **Selection Set** drop-down list in the **Selection** toolbar lets you select objects using **Named Selection Sets**.

Tools Toolbar

The tools available in this toolbar [marked as 7 in Fig. 30] are dependent on whether the **Sort By Hierarchy** mode or the **Sort By Layer** mode is active. When **Lock Cell Editing** is active, you cannot change any name or settings. The **Pick Parent** button is only available in the **Sort By Hierarchy** mode. It allows you to change the parent. To make an object parent, select one or more objects and then click **Pick Parent**. Now, select the object that you want parent of the selected object.

The **Create New Layer** button is available in the **Sort By Layer** mode. When you click **Create New Layer**, a new layer is created and the selection is automatically added to this layer. The new layer you create becomes the active layer and any subsequent objects you create are added to this layer automatically. If an existing layer is selected, and you click **Create New Layer**, the new layer becomes child of the selected layer. **Add to Active Layer** is available in the **Sort By Layer** mode only. When you click on this button, all selected objects and layers are assigned to the active layer. **Select Children** allows you to select all child objects and layers of the selected items.

Tip: Selecting children
Double-clicking on a parent layer or object selects the parent and all its children.

The **Make Selected Layer Active** button is available in the **Sort By Layer** mode only. When you click on this button, 3ds Max makes the selected layer the active layer. Alternatively, click on the layer icon to make it the layer active.

Display Toolbar

The **Display** toolbar allows you to display various categories in **Scene Explorer**. It controls the type of objects that appear in **Scene Explorer's** listing. You can also solo the category by clicking on one of the category button with **Alt** held down. You can also turn on or off the categories by choosing **Display > Object Types** from **Scene Explorer's** menu bar.

View Toolbar

The **View** toolbar is located at the bottom-left corner of **Scene Explorer**. This toolbar shows the name of the current **Scene Explorer**. When you click on the black triangle located in this toolbar, a menu appears. This menu gives access to all local and global explorers.

Local and Global Scene Explorers

3ds Max comes with different **Scene Explorer** configurations. These configurations are available to every scene you create in 3ds Max. Therefore, they are referred to as **Global Scene Explorers**. On the other hand, the **Local Scene Explorers** live within a single scene and saved/loaded with the scene. The options to make a **Local** explorer **Global** are available in the menu located on the **View** toolbar [see Fig. 31].

How to delete objects?
To delete one or more objects in **Scene Explorer**, select them and then press **Delete** or RMB click on the list and then choose **Delete** from the **Quad** menu.

How to hide and show objects?
Click the light bulb icon of the layer or object to hide. The light bulb icon turns gray. Click again to reveal.

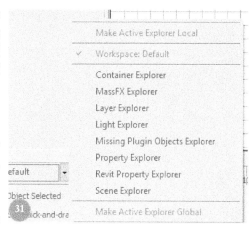

How to create hierarchies in the Sort By Hierarchy mode?
To make a parent, drag and drop the child objects' name or icon onto the object that you want to act as parent. To restore the child objects to the top level, drag them to an empty area of **Scene Explorer**. Alternatively, you can RMB click on them and then choose **Unlink** from the **Quad** menu. You can use the same techniques on the layers as well.

How to freeze objects?
To freeze objects, click on the **Frozen** column of the object. Click again to unfreeze. If you want to freeze many objects, select them and then click on the **Frozen** column of any selected objects.

How to change object properties?
To change the object properties, select one or more objects in **Scene Explorer** and then RMB. Choose **Properties** from the **Quad** menu to open the **Object Properties** dialog box. You can use this dialog box to change the properties of the selected objects.

How to rename an object?
Select the object and then RMB click. Choose **Rename** from the **Quad** menu and then type a new name for the object.

Tip: Renaming objects
Slowly double-click on the object name to rename the object if you don't want to use the **Quad** menu.

Can I add more column next to the Frozen column?
Yes, you can. RMB click on any of the column head and then choose **Configure Columns** [see Fig. 32] from the popup menu. The **Configure Column** window appears [see Fig. 33]. Click on the name of the column in this window that you

want to add. Fig. 34 shows the **Has Material** column. A tick will appear in this column if the material has been assigned to the object.

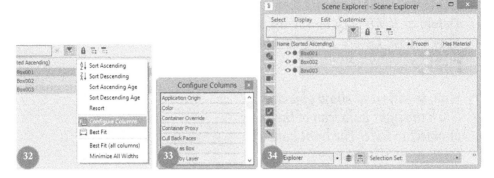

 Can I search object by names?
Yes, you can search object by using the search text box available in the **Find** toolbar. Type the search string and then press **Enter**. For example, if you have many teapots in the scene and all have default names. Entering **tea** in the search field and then pressing **Enter** will select all teapots in the scene. You can also use the wild card characters such as **?** and * to create a broader search criteria.

Working with the Precision Tools

3ds Max comes with several tools and objects that allow you to position and align objects efficiently. Two tools [**Select and Place** tool, and **Select and Manipulate** tool] I have already discussed that let you align and position objects. You have also seen the use of some helpers that are used with the **Select and Manipulate** tool.

Using Units

The units define the measurement system for the scene. The default unit system in 3ds Max is **Generic**. Besides the **Generic** units, you can also use feet and inches both decimal and fractional. The **Metric** system allows you to specify units from millimeters to kilometers. You can specify the unit system from the **Units Setup** dialog box [see Fig. 35].

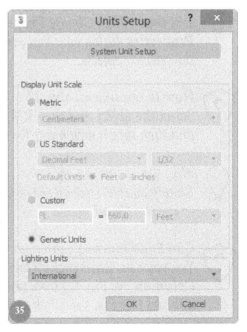

You can open this dialog box by choosing **Units Setup** from the **Customize** menu. On clicking **System Unit Setup** from this dialog box, the **System Unit Setup** dialog box appears from where you can specify the **System** units.

Q. What is the difference between the Scene and System Units?
The system units only affect how geometry appears in the viewports whereas the system units control the actual scale of the geometry.

 Caution: System units
*The system units should only be changed before you create your scene or import a **unitless** file. Do not change the system units in the current scene.*

If you change units for a scene, 3ds Max automatically changes the values for the controls. For example, if you are using **Centimeters** and value in a spinner is **30 cm**, when you change units to **Decimal Inches**; 3ds Max will change the value to **11.811** inches. Now, if you type **50cm** in the spinner and press **Enter**, 3ds Max changes value to **19.685** inches. Similarly, if you type **2'** in the spinner, the value changes to **24.0** inches.

Using Grids

Grids are two dimensional arrays that you can use to position the objects accurately. You can use grids to visualize space, scale, and distance. You can use it as construction plane to create objects as well use it for snapping objects using the snap feature. I will discuss about snap features later in this unit. 3ds Max provides two types of grids: **Home** grid and **Grid** objects.

Home Grid

The **Home** grid is defined by three intersecting planes along the world **X**, **Y**, and **Z** axes. These planes intersect at the origin defined by **0,0,0**. The **Home** grid is fixed, you cannot move or rotate it.

 Tip: Home Grid
*Press **G** to toggle the visibility of the **Home** grid.*

Grid Object

The **Grid** object [see Fig. 36] is a helper object that you can use to create a reference grid as per your needs. You can create as many **Grid** objects as you want in a scene. However, only one **Grid** object will be active at a time. When a **Grid** object is active, it replaces the **Home** grid in all viewports. You can rename and delete the **Grid** objects like any other object. The **Grid** object is available in the **Helpers** category on the **Create** panel.

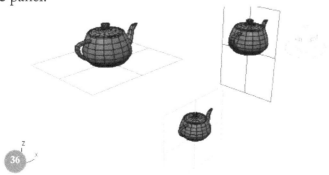

Tip: Activating the Home grid and the Grid object
*You can activate the **Home** grid by choosing **Grids and Snaps** > **Activate Home Grid** from the **Tools** menu. When you choose this command, it activates the **Home** grid in all viewports and deactivates the current active grid object. Similarly, you can activate a **Grid** object by choosing **Grids and Snaps** > **Activate Grid Object** from the **Tools** menu.*

 Tip: Aligning a Grid object to the view
*To align a **Grid** object with the current view, make sure it is selected and then choose **Grids and Snaps** > **Activate Grid Object** from the **Quad** menu. The **Grid** object is aligned and will be coplanar with the current view.*

Auto Grid

The **Auto Grid** feature lets you create objects on the surface of other objects. The **Auto Grid** option is available on the **Object Type** rollout of any category. It is also available in the **Extras** toolbar. When you activate this option and drag the cursor on the surface of an object, a construction plane is created temporarily on the surface of object.

 Tip: Select and Place tool
*The **Select and Place** tool discussed earlier provides a similar mechanism to align the objects.*

Aligning Objects

3ds Max provides six different tools for aligning the objects in a scene. These tools are available in the **Align** flyout on the **Main** toolbar.

Using with Align Tool

The **Align** tool in 3ds Max allows you to align the current selection to a target selection. You can pick the **Align** tool from the **Align** flyout on the **Main** toolbar. You can also activate this tool by choosing **Align** > **Align** from the **Tools** menu or by pressing **Alt+A**. Using this tool, you can align the position and orientation of the bounding box of a source object to the bounding box of a target object. A bounding box is the smallest box that encloses the extents (maximum dimensions) of an object. A bounding box appears when you set a viewport to non-wireframe mode. Fig. 37 shows the extents of a teapot model.

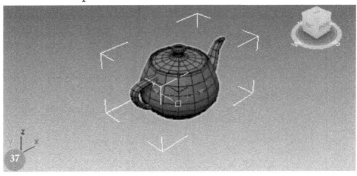

To show the bounding box, select the object and then press **J**. You can also enable the display of the bounding boxes by turning on **Selection Brackets** from the **Viewport Setting and Preference** dialog box > **Per-View Preferences** panel [see Fig. 38]. Refer to **Explore More** section of **Unit M1** for more information on **Viewport Setting and Preference** dialog box.

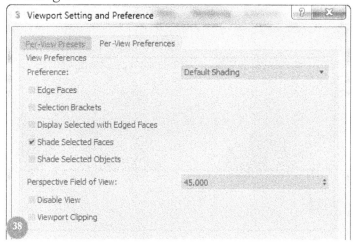

Let's dive in and align some objects. Create three boxes and assign them red, green, and blue colors [see Fig. 39]. Use the following dimensions:

Red Box: Length=52, Width=61, and Height=32
Green Box: Length=35, Width=40, and Height=12
Blue Box: Length=50, Width=40, and Height=30

RMB click on the red box and choose **Object Properties** from the **Quad** menu. In the **General** panel > **Display Properties** group, turn on **See-Through**. This will help you better see the alignment process. Now let's center align the red and blue boxes along the **X** and **Y** axes. Make sure the red box is selected and then pick the **Align** tool from the **Main** toolbar. Click the blue box. In the **Align Selection** dialog box > **Align Position (World)** group, turn on **X Position** and **Y Position**. Turn off **Z Position**. Make sure **Center** is selected in the **Current Object** and **Target Object** groups. You will see that both the objects are center aligned [see Fig. 40]. Click **OK** to accept changes.

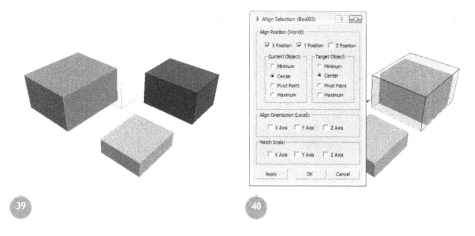

Now, let's see how to place blue box on the top of the red box.

Select the blue box and then pick the **Align** tool from the **Main** toolbar. Click red box. We have already performed alignment along the **X** and **Y** axes. Therefore, turn off **X Position** and **Y Position** and turn on **Z Position**. You will see that now the blue box is at the center of the red box. Turn on **Maximum** from the **Target Object** group. Notice the blue box's center is aligned to the center of the red box [see Fig. 41]. Now, select **Pivot Point** from the **Current Object** group. The blue box sits on the top of the red box [see Fig. 42]. Click **OK** to accept changes.

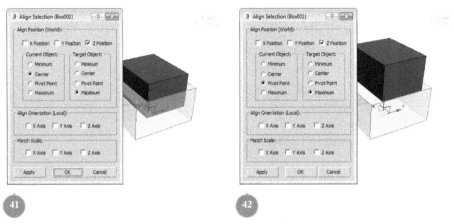

Now, let's align one corner of the green box with blue box.

Select the green box and then pick the **Align** tool from the **Main** toolbar. Click the blue box. Turn on **X Position, Y Position,** and **Z Position**. Turn on **Minimum** from the **Current Object** and **Target Object** groups [see Fig. 43]. Click **OK** to accept changes. With the green box selected, click the blue box using the **Align** tool. Now, turn on **Z Position** and turn off **X Position** and **Y Position**. Turn on **Maximum** from the **Target Object** group and click **OK**. The boxes are now stacked over each other [see Fig. 44].

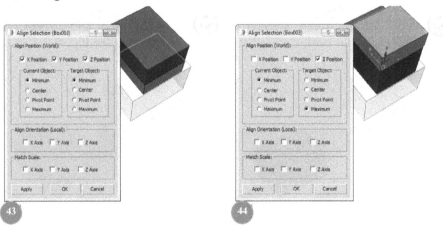

Using the Quick Align Tool

The **Quick Align** tool instantly aligns an object with the target object. The hotkeys associated with this tool are **Shift+A**. To align an object, select the source object and press **Shift+A** to activate the tool. Now, click on the target object to align two objects [see Fig. 45]. If the current selection contains a single object, this tool uses the pivot points of the two objects for alignment. If multiple objects are selected, the selection center of the source objects is aligned with the pivot of the target objects.

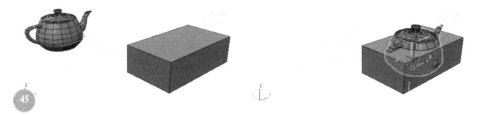

Using the Normal Align Tool

This tool allows you to align the two objects based on the directions of the normals of the selected faces. The hotkeys associated with this tool are **Alt+N**. To understand functioning of this tool, create a sphere and teapot in the scene [see Fig. 46]. Select the teapot, the source object in this case. Press **Alt+N** to activate the tool and then drag across the surface of the teapot, a blue arrow indicates the location of the current normal [see Fig. 47]. Keep dragging on the surface until you find the normal you are looking for. Now, click and drag on the surface of the sphere until you find the normal to which you want to align the source object. Release the mouse button; the teapot gets aligned with the sphere [see Fig. 48] and the **Normal Align** dialog box opens. Using the controls available in this dialog box, you can offset the position and orientation of the teapot.

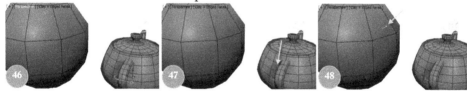

> **?** *What are normals?*
> *A normal is a vector that defines the inner and outer surfaces of a face in a mesh. The direction of the vector indicates the front [outer] surface of a face or vertex. Sometimes, normals are flipped during the modeling process. To fix this issue, you can use the **Normal** modifier to flip or unify normals. Fig. 49 shows the vertex and face normals, respectively.*

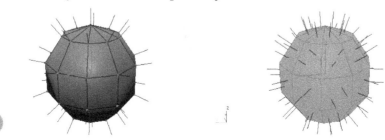

Using the Place Highlight Tool

You can use this tool to align an object or light to another object so that its highlight [reflection] can be precisely positioned. To position a light to highlight a face, make sure the viewport that you want to render is active. Choose **Place Highlight** from the **Align** flyout and drag the mouse pointer on the object to place the highlight. Now, release the mouse button when the normal indicates the face on which you want to place the highlight [see Fig. 50].

> *Note: Light type and highlights*
> *With the omni, free spot, or directional light, 3ds Max displays face normal. With a target spotlight, 3ds Max displays target of the light and base of it's cone.*

Using the Align Camera Tool

This tool lets you align the camera to a selected face normal. This tool works similar to the **Place Highlight** tool but it does not change the camera position interactively. You need to release the mouse button and then 3ds Max aligns the camera with the selected face.

Using the Align View Tool

When this tool is picked from the **Align** flyout, it opens the **Align to View** dialog box that lets you align the local axis of the selection or sub-object selection with the current viewport [see Fig. 51]. To use this tool, select the objects or sub-objects to align and then choose **Align to View** from the **Align** flyout. 3ds Max opens the **Align to View** dialog box. Choose the options from the dialog box as desired. If you want to flip the direction of alignment, turn on **Flip** on this dialog box.

Drawing Assistants

3ds Max provides several tools and utilities that help you in drawing objects with precession. Let's have a look.

Measuring Distances

The **Measure Distance** tool allows you to quickly calculate distance between two points. The calculated distance appears in **Status Bar** in Scene [display] units. To measure distance, choose **Measure Distance** from the **Tools** menu. Now, click on the point in the viewport from where you want to measure the distance. Click again in the viewport where you want to measure to. The distance between the two points is displayed in **Status Bar**.

The **Measure** utility available in the **Utilities** panel displays the measurement of a selected object or spline. To display measurement of an object, select the object and then on the **Utilities** panel, click **Measure**. The measurements are displayed in the **Measure** rollout [see Fig. 52].

There is one more utility called **Rescale World Units** that you can use to rescale the word units. You can scale entire scene or the selected objects. To rescale an object, select it and then on the **Utilities** panel click **More** to open the **Utilities** panel. Select **Rescale World Units** from the dialog box and then click **OK**. The **Rescale World Units** rollout appears in the **Utilities** panel. Click **Rescale** from this rollout to open the **Rescale World Units** dialog box [see Fig. 53].

Set **Scale Factor** in this dialog box and then turn on **Scene** or **Selection** from the **Affect** section. Click **OK** to apply the scale factor to the selected object or to entire scene. For example, you specify **Scale Factor** as **2** and turn on **Selection** from the dialog box, the selected object will be scaled to double of its current size.

Using Snaps

The Snap tools in 3ds Max allow you to precisely control the dimensions and placement of the objects when you create or transform them. You can invoke these tools using the **Snap** buttons available on the **Main** toolbar. You can also invoke these tools by choosing **Grids and Snaps** from the **Tools** menu.

2D Snap, 2.5 Snap, and 3D Snap

The hotkey for activating snap is S. The **2D Snap** tool snaps the cursor to the active construction grid including the geometry on the plane of the grid. The **Z** axis is ignored by this tool. The **2.5D Snap** tool snaps the cursor to the vertices or edges of the projection of an object onto the active grid. The **3D snap** is the default tool. It snaps the cursor directly to any geometry in the 3D space. RMB click on snap toggle button to open the **Grid and Snap Settings** dialog box [see Fig. 54]. You can specify which type of snap of you want active from the **Snaps** panel of this dialog box. For

example, if you want the cursor to snap to the pivot or vertices of the object, turn on **Pivot** and **Vertex** from this panel. To see snap in action, turn on **Pivot** and **Vertex** from the **Grid and Snap Settings** dialog box. Now, create a box and teapot in the viewport [see first image at the left of Fig. 55]. Pick the **Move** tool from the **Main** toolbar and move the teapot to one of the vertex of the box or its pivot [see middle and right image in Fig. 56].

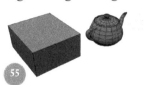 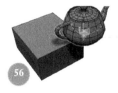

Angle Snap Toggle

You can use **Angle Snap Toggle** to rotate an object around a given axis in the increment you set. This snap toggle also works with the **Pan/Orbit** camera controls, **FOV** and **Roll** camera settings, and **Hotspot/Falloff** spotlight angles. The hotkey for invoking this toggle is **A**.

To rotate an object, click **Angle Snap Toggle** on the **Main** toolbar and then rotate the object using the **Rotate** tool. By default, the rotation takes place in five degree increments. You can change this default value by specifying a value for the **Angle** control in the **Options** panel of the **Grid and Snap Settings** dialog box.

Percent Snap Toggle

The **Percent Snap Toggle** lets you control the increments of scaling by the specified percentage. The hotkey for invoking this toggle is **Shift+Ctrl+P**. The default percentage value is **10**. You can change this default value by specifying a value for the **Percent** control in the **Options** panel of the **Grid and Snap Settings** dialog box.

Spinner Snap Toggle

This toggle allows you to set single-increment or decrement value for all the spinners in 3ds Max. The default value is **1**. To change this value, RMB click on **Spinner Snap Toggle** on the **Main** toolbar to open the **Preferences Settings** dialog box. In the **Spinners** section of the **General** panel, specify a value for the **Snap** control.

Modifiers

The modifiers in 3ds Max provide a way to edit and sculpt objects. You can change shape of an object using the modifier's properties. Fig. 57 shows the original box [first image] and the modified geometry after applying the **Bend**, **Twist**, and **Taper** modifiers, respectively.

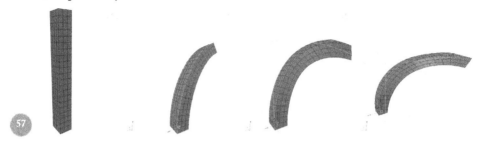

You can apply modifiers from the **Modifier** drop-down list available in the **Modify** panel of the **Command** panel [see Fig. 58]. The modifier you apply to an object are stored in a stack called modifier stack. Modifiers are described in detail in a later unit.

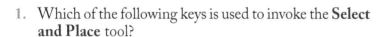

Quiz

Evaluate your skills to see how many questions you can answer correctly.

Multiple Choice
Answer the following questions, only one choice is correct.

1. Which of the following keys is used to invoke the **Select and Place** tool?

    [A] X   [B] S
    [C] Y   [D] P

2. Which of the followings is the default unit system in 3ds Max?

    [A] Generic   [B] Metric
    [C] Imperial   [D] Custom

3. Which of the following keys is used to toggle the visibility of the home grid?

    [A] H   [B] Shift+H
    [C] G   [D] Alt+G

4. Which of the following key is used to invoke the **Align** tool?

[A] Alt+T   [B] Alt+A
[C] Ctrl+T   [D] Ctrl+A

Fill in the Blanks
Fill in the blanks in each of the following statements:

1. To create clone using this command, select the object[s] that you want to clone and then choose _____ from the _____ menu or press_____.

2. _____ is used to distribute objects along a path or between two points.

3. The _____ method in the **Clone Options** dialog box allows you to create a clone dependent on the original upto the point when the object was created.

4. The _____ tool allows you to interactively edit the parameters of certain objects by dragging the manipulators in the viewports.

5. Press _____ to invoke the **Quick Align** tool.

6. A _____ is a vector that defines the inner and outer surfaces of a face in a mesh.

True of False
State whether each of the following is true or false:

1. The **Mirror** tool can be used to just create a mirror reflection.

2. The **Transform** option in the **Mirror** dialog box allows you to mirror any word-space-modifiers [WSM] effect.

3. You can not animate the mirror operation.

4. The **Clone and Align** tool lets you distribute the source objects based on the current selection to a selection of the target objects.

5. Double-clicking on a parent layer or object in **Scene Explorer** selects the parent and all its children.

6. The system units only affect how geometry appears in the viewports whereas the system units control the actual scale of the geometry.

Summary

The unit covered the following topics:

- Creating clones and duplicates
- Understanding hierarchies
- Working with the **Scene** and **Layer** Explorers
- Understanding the **Mirror, Select and Place**, and **Select and Manipulate** tools
- Working with the **Align** and **Array** tools
- Working with precision and drawing aids
- Understanding modifiers, and normals

This page is intentionally left blank

- Creating and modifying the **Standard** Primitives
- Creating and modifying the **Extended** Primitives
- Working with the **Architectural** objects
- Setting the project folder
- Using the **Align** and **Mirror** tools
- Creating clones
- Using **Scene Explorer**
- Creating a group
- Setting grid spacings
- Using the **Transform Type-In** dialog box
- Using the **Array** dialog box
- Specifying the units for the scene

Unit M3: Geometric Primitives and Architectural Objects

The 3D objects in the scene and the objects that are used to create them are known as geometries. Most of the 3D applications offer basic building blocks for creating geometries called geometric primitives. You can use these primitives and some modifiers to create basic models. In this unit, you will work with the **Standard** and **Extended** primitives as well as the **Architectural** objects.

You can edit these geometric primitives at sub-object levels to create complex models. This process is known as surface modeling that I've covered in the next unit. In this unit, I will explain **Standard** and **Extended** primitives and how you can use them to create some basic models. Geometric primitives in 3ds Max are divided into two categories: **Standard** primitives and **Extended** primitives. Let's first start exploring the **Standard** primitives.

Standard Primitives

3ds Max offers eleven standard primitives, see Fig. 1. You can combine the **Standard** primitives into more complex objects. You can then further refine them by using modifiers. You can interactively create primitives in the viewport using the mouse. Primitives can also be created by entering precise values using the keyboard. You can specify the parameters before creating the primitives and as well as modify them later from the **Parameters** rollout in the **Modify** panel. Let's take a look at different **Standard** primitives.

Box

Box is the simplest of the primitives. You can use it to create rectangular as well as cubical geometries [see Fig. 2]. To create a **Box** primitive, in the **Create** panel, click **Geometry**, and then in the **Object Type** rollout, click **Box**.

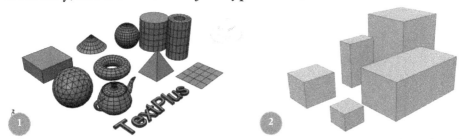

To create a box, click and drag in a viewport to specify the length and width of the box. Now, release the mouse button and drag the mouse up or down [without holding any button] to specify the height of the box and then click to complete the process.

Whenever you choose a tool from the **Object Type** rollout, the **Name and Color**, **Creation Method, Keyboard Entry**, and **Parameters** rollouts appear on **Command Panel**. You can use these rollouts to specify the initial properties of the objects.

 Tip: Navigating between the steps
If you are creating a primitive that requires two or more steps [for example
Cylinder *or* ***Torus***]*, you can pan and orbit the viewport between the steps.*
To pan the viewport, ***MMB*** *drag. To orbit, hold* ***Alt*** *and then* ***MMB*** *drag.*

Name and Color Rollout

The controls in the **Name and Color** rollout allow you to rename the objects and change their colors. Whenever you create an object, 3ds Max assigns it a default name and color. For example, if you reset the scene and create a box in the viewport, 3ds Max assigns it the name **Box001**. To change the name of the object, type a new name in the text box available in the **Name and Color** rollout. The color swatch to the right of the text box lets you change the color of the object.

On clicking the color swatch, the **Object Color** dialog box appears. You can click on one of the color swatches and then click **OK** to assign the color to the object. If you want to specify a custom color, select a color swatch associated with the **Custom Colors** control and then click **Add Custom Colors**. In the **Color Selector : Add Color** dialog box that appears, specify a color and then click **Add Color** to add the chosen color to the selected swatch in the **Object Color** dialog box. Now, click **OK** to close the dialog box and apply selected color to the object.

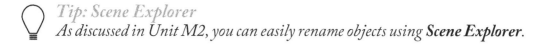

Tip: Scene Explorer
As discussed in Unit M2, you can easily rename objects using **Scene Explorer**.

Creation Method Rollout

There are two controls available in this rollout: **Cube** and **Box. Box** creates a standard box primitive with different settings for length, width, and height. **Cube** creates a cube with equal width, height, and length. Creating a cube is one step operation. Click and drag the mouse pointer in the viewport to create a cube.

Parameters Rollout

The default settings in this rollout produce a box with one segment on each side. Table 1 summarizes the controls in the **Parameters** rollout.

Table 1: The controls in the **Box's Parameters** rollout	
Control	**Description**
Length, Width, Height	The **Length**, **Width**, and **Height** controls set the length, width, and height of the box, respectively. These controls also act as readouts when you interactively create a box.
Length Segs, Width Segs, Height Segs	The **Length Segs**, **Width Segs**, and **Height Segs** controls set the number of segments [divisions] along each axis of the object. You can set these parameters before and after the creation of the box. The default value for these parameters is **1, 1, 1**.
Generate Mapping Coords	**Generate Mapping Coords** selected by default. It generates coordinates for applying material to the box.
Real-World Map Size	**Real-World Map Size** control lets you create a material and specify the actual width and height of a 2D texture map in **Material Editor**. The scaling values are controlled from the maps's [for example the **Diffuse** map] **Coordinates** rollout.

Note: Default values
Whatever values you specify for these controls become default for the current session.

Tip: Resolution
If you are planning to use the modifiers such as **Bend** *on a primitive, increase the values for the* **Length Segs**, **Width Segs**, *and* **Height Segs** *controls to get some extra resolution on the objects. Higher the resolution, smoother the bend will be.*

Keyboard Entry Rollout

You can use the controls in this rollout to define both the size of the box as well as its position in 3D space in a single operation. The method for creating objects through keyboard is generally same for all primitives; differences might occur in the type and number of controls. The **X**, **Y**, and **Z** controls define the position of the object. The default value is **0, 0, 0** which is center of the active grid.

Cone

You can use this primitive to create round upward or inverted cones [see Fig. 3]. To create a cone, click **Cone** in the **Object Type** rollout. In the viewport, drag to define the base of the cone and then release the mouse button. Now, move the mouse pointer up or down in the viewport to define the height.

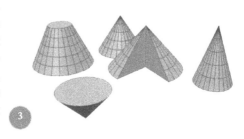

The height can be negative or positive. Click to set the height. Move the mouse pointer to define the radius of the other end of the cone. If you want to create a pointed cone, set this radius to zero.

Creation Method Rollout

Two creation methods are available for the **Cone** primitive: **Edge** and **Center**. **Edge** draws a cone from edge to edge. **Center** draws from the center out.

Parameters Rollout

The default settings in this rollout produce a smooth cone with 24 sides, one cap segment, and five height segments. Table 2 summarizes the controls in the **Parameters** rollout.

Table 2: The controls in the **Cone's Parameters** rollout	
Control	**Description**
Radius 1, Radius 2	**Radius 1** and **Radius 2** define the first and second radii of the cone. You can use these two controls to create pointed or flat-topped cones.
Height	**Height** sets the dimension of the cone along the central axis. If you set a negative value, the cone will be created below the construction plane.
Height Segments	**Height Segments** control sets the number of divisions along the major axis of the cone.
Cap Segments	**Cap Segments** sets the number of concentric divisions in the top or bottom of the cone.
Sides	**Sides** determines the number of sides around the cone.
Smooth	**Smooth** is selected by default. It blends the faces of the cone on rendering therefore producing smooth looking renders.
Slice From, Slice To	You can use the **Slice From** and **Slice To** controls to slice the cone. These two controls set the number of degrees around the local Z axis. To turn on these two controls, turn on **Slice On**.

Caution: Minimum and negative values
If you specify negative values for **Radius 1** *and* **Radius 2***, these values will be converted to* **0***. The minimum values for these controls is* **0***.*

 Note: Same value for Radius 1 and Radius 2
If you specify a same values for **Radius 1** *and* **Radius 2***, a cylinder will be created. If these two values are close in size, an object is created which resembles the effect as if a* **Taper** *modifier is applied to a cylinder.*

 Tip: Pointed cones
For improved rendering on smooth pointed cones, increase the number of height segments.

Sphere

You can use the **Sphere** primitive to create a full sphere, a hemisphere, slice of the sphere, or some part of a sphere [see Fig. 4]. To create a sphere, on the **Create** panel, click **Geometry**, and then on the **Object Type** rollout, click **Sphere**.

In the viewport, drag the mouse pointer to define the radius of the sphere, release mouse button to set the radius. To create a hemisphere, create the desired sphere of the desired radius and then set **Hemisphere** to **0.5** in the **Parameters** rollout.

Creation Method Rollout
There are two methods available for creating a sphere: **Edge** and **Center**. **Edge** draws the sphere from edge to edge. **Center** draws a sphere from center out.

Parameters Rollout
The default values in the rollout produce a smooth sphere with **32** divisions. Table 3 summarizes the controls in the **Parameters** rollout.

Table 3: The controls in the Sphere's Parameters rollout	
Control	**Description**
Radius	**Radius** specifies the radius of the sphere.
Segments	**Segments** defines the number of segments for the sphere.
Hemisphere	**Hemisphere** lets you create a hemisphere. It cuts off the sphere to create a partial sphere. You can use this control to create an animation in which the sphere will be cut off starting from its base to top.

Table 3: The controls in the **Sphere's Parameters** rollout	
Control	**Description**
Chop, Squash	**Chop** and **Squash** determine the number of vertices and faces when you create a hemisphere. **Chop** reduces the number of vertices and faces by chopping them out whereas **Squash** maintains the number of vertices and faces by squashing the geometry toward the top of the sphere. Fig. 5 shows the effect of **Chop** [left] and **Squash** [right] on a hemisphere with **16** segments.
Base To Pivot	If you turn on **Base to Pivot**, the sphere moves upward along its local Z axis and places the pivot point at its base. Fig. 6 shows the pivot at the center [left], which is default, and at the base of the sphere [right].

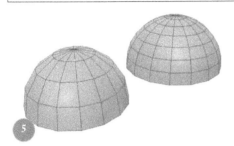

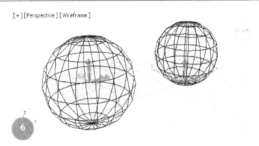
[+] [Perspective] [Wireframe]

GeoSphere

You can use the **GeoSphere** primitive to create spheres and geo-hemispheres based on three classes of polyhedrons: **Tetra, Octa,** and **Icosa** [see Fig. 7].

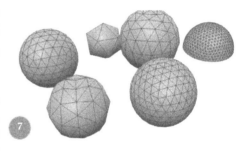

The **GeoSphere** primitive produces more regular shape than the **Sphere** primitive. Unlike the **Sphere** primitive, the geometry produced by the **GeoSphere** primitive has no poles which is an advantage is in certain modeling scenarios. Also, they appear slightly smoother than the standard sphere when rendered. To create a **GeoSphere**, on the **Create** panel, click **Geometry**, and then on the **Object Type** rollout, click **GeoSphere**. In the viewport, drag the mouse pointer to define the radius of the sphere, release mouse button to set the radius. To create a hemisphere, create the desired sphere of the desired radius and then select the **Hemisphere** check box in the **Parameters** rollout.

Creation Method rollout

There are two methods available for creating a sphere: **Diameter** and **Center**. **Diameter** draws the geosphere from edge to edge whereas **Center** draws a geosphere from the center out.

Parameters Rollout

Table 4 summarizes the controls in the **Parameters** rollout.

Table 4: The controls in the **GeoSphere's Parameters** rollout	
Control	**Description**
Radius	**Radius** sets the radius of the geosphere.
Segments	**Segments** defines the number of faces in the geosphere.
Tetra, Octa, Icosa	The controls in the **Geodesic Base Type** section let you choose one of the regular polyhedrons for geosphere geometry. **Tetra** creates a four-sided tetrahedron. The facets can vary in shape and size. The geosphere can be divided into four equal segments. **Octa** creates an eight-sided tetrahedron. The facets can vary in shape and size. The geosphere can be divided into eight equal segments. **Icosa** creates a 20-sided tetrahedron. The facets are equal in size. The geosphere can be divided into any number of equal segments.

Cylinder

Cylinder creates a cylinder that can be sliced along its major axis [see Fig. 8]. To create a cylinder, on the **Create** panel, click **Geometry**, and then on the **Object Type** rollout, click **Cylinder**. In the viewport, drag the mouse pointer to define the radius, release the mouse button to set the radius. Now, move the mouse pointer up or down to define the height, click to set it.

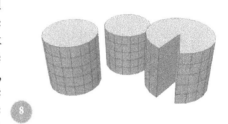

Parameters Rollout

The default controls in the **Parameters** rollout produce an **18** sided smooth cylinder with the five height segments, one cap segment, and the pivot point at its base. Table 5 summarizes the controls in the **Parameters** rollout.

Table 5: The controls in the **Cylinder's Parameters** rollout	
Control	**Description**
Radius	**Radius** sets the radius of the cylinder.
Height	**Height** defines the height of the cylinder along the cylinder's major axis.
Height Segments	**Height Segments** defines the number of divisions along the cylinder's major axis.
Sides	**Sides** sets the sides around the cylinder.
Cap Segments	**Cap Segments** sets the number of concentric divisions around top and bottom of the cylinder.

Tip: Resolution

*If you are going to use the cylinder with a modifier such as **Bend**, increase the number of height segments. If you are planning to modify the end of the cylinder, increase the number of cap segments.*

Tube

The **Tube** primitive produces a cylinder with a hole in it [see Fig. 9]. You can use this primitive to use both round and prismatic tubes. To create a **Tube**, on the **Create** panel, click **Geometry**, and then on the **Object Type** rollout, click **Tube**. In the viewport, drag the mouse pointer to define the first radius, which can be either the inner or the outer radius of the tube,

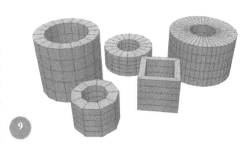

release the mouse button to set the first radius. Move the mouse pointer to create the second radius, and then click to set it. Move the pointer up or down to create the height [positive or negative] and then click to set the height of the tube.

Tip: Prismatic Tube

*To create a prismatic tube, set the number of sides to according to the type of the prismatic tube you want to create. Turn off the **Smooth** check box and create the tube.*

Parameters Rollout

Radius 1 and **Radius 2** are used to specify the inside and outside radii of the tube. The larger among the two values defines the outside radius of the tube.

Torus

You can use the **Torus** primitive to create a doughnut like shape which is ring with the circular cross section [see Fig. 10]. To create a torus, on the **Create** panel, click **Geometry**, and then on the **Object Type** rollout, click **Torus**. In the viewport, drag the mouse pointer to define a torus; the torus emerges from its center. Release the mouse button to set the radius of the torus

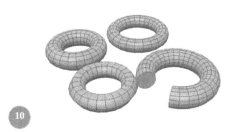

ring. Now, move the mouse pointer to define the radius of the cross section, and click to complete the creation process.

Parameters Rollout

The default values in this rollout produce a smooth torus with **12** sides and **24** segments. The pivot point of the torus is located at the center of the torus on the plane which cuts through the center of the torus. **Rotation** sets the degree of rotation.

The vertices are uniformly rotated about the circle running through the center of the torus ring. **Twist** defines the degree of twist. 3ds Max twists the cross sections about the circle running through the center of the torus.

 Caution: Twisting a close torus
*Twisting a close torus will create a constriction in the first segment. To overcome this, you can either twist the torus in the increments of **360** or turn on **Slice** and then set both **Slice From** and **Slice To** to **0**.*

The controls in the **Smooth** group control the level of smoothing. The default **All** control produces smoothing on all surfaces of the torus. **Sides** smooths the edges between the adjacent segments thus producing smooth bands which run around the torus. **None** turns off the smoothing and produces prism-like facets on the torus. **Segments** smooths each segment individually and produces ring-like segments.

Pyramid

The **Pyramid** primitive is used to create a pyramid like shape with the square or rectangle face and triangular sides [see Fig. 11]. To create a pyramid, on the **Create** panel, click **Geometry**, and then on the **Object Type** rollout, click **Pyramid**. In the viewport, drag the mouse pointer to define the base of the pyramid. Click to set it and then drag the mouse pointer up to define the height.

 Tip: Constrain the base of the pyramid to a square
*To constrain the base of the pyramid to a square, drag with the **Ctrl** key held down.*

Plane

The **Plane** primitive creates a flat plane that you can enlarge to any size [see Fig. 12]. To create a **Plane**, on the **Create** panel, click **Geometry**, and then on the **Object Type** rollout, click **Plane**. In the viewport, drag the mouse pointer to create a plane.

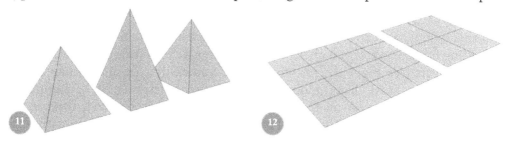

Parameters Rollout

The controls in the **Render Multipliers** group are used to set the multipliers at the render time. You can use **Scale** to specify the factor by which both length and width will be multiplied at the render time. **Density** specifies a factor by which the number of segments in both length and width are multiplied at the render time.

Teapot

The **Teapot** primitive is used to create a parametric teapot object [see Fig. 12A]. This object is comprised of a lid, body, handle, and spout. You can create the whole teapot [which is default] or combination of the parts. You can even control which parts to display after creation. To create a **Teapot**, on the **Create** panel, click **Geometry**, and then on the **Object Type** rollout, click **Teapot**. In the viewport, click and drag to define the radius. Release the mouse button to set the radius and create teapot. You can control which part of the teapot you want to create by turning on the required controls from the **Teapot Parts** group of the **Parameters** rollout.

TextPlus

The **TextPlus** primitive is used to create all-in-one text object. You can use this primitive to create an spline outline as well as solid, extruded beveled geometry. It allows you to apply different fonts and styles on a per-character basis and add animation and special effects. It is a very useful tool for producing motion graphics elements. To create the text, on the **Create** panel, click **Geometry**, and then on the **Object Type** rollout, click **TextPlus**. Click on the viewport to create the **TextPlus** object. If you want to create a region of text, click-drag in the viewport to define the region.

Layout Rollout

From this rollout, you can define the plane onto which you will type the text. The default plane is **XY** plane. Also, you can set whether you want to create a region of text or text just starting from a point [see Fig. 13].

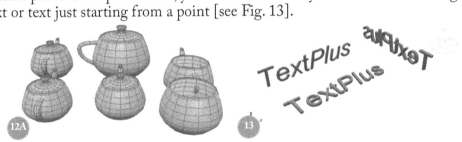

Parameters Rollout

From this rollout, you can set the font and other global parameters such as tracking and leading for the text. If you click on **Open Large Text Window**, the **Enter Text** window appears [see Fig. 14]. This window lets you easily type and format text. If you want to interactively change global parameters in the viewport, click **Manipulate Text**, some symbols appear on the text in the viewport [see Fig. 15]. You can use these symbols to manipulate the global parameters. When you are manipulating the text, you can you use the following:

- To select more than one letter, use **Ctrl+click**.
- If you click a letter with **Shift** held down, the clicked letter will be selected, all other previously selected letters will be de-selected.
- The tracking symbols only appear when you select more than one letter.
- You can change font and font type for individual characters.
- When you select letters in the **Text** field, letters are also selected in the viewport [see Fig. 16].

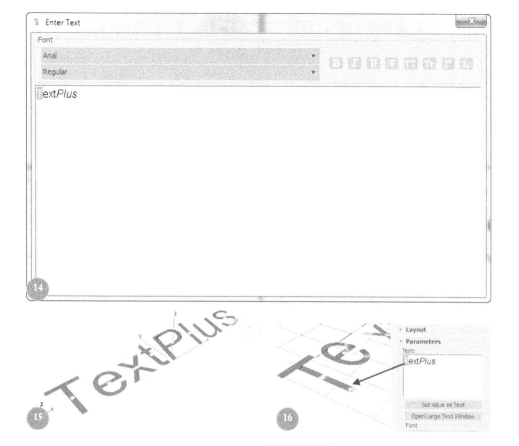

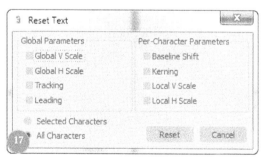

To reset the parameters, click **Reset Parameters**, the **Reset Text** dialog box appears [see Fig. 17]. Select the options that you want to reset and then click **Reset**.

Geometry Rollout

The controls in this rollout allow you to create depth using the **Extrude** and **Bevel** functions.

Values As Strings

You can also use the **TextPlus** object to display value of a object's parameter in the viewport. You can also show any value that can be returned from a script or expression. The value will dynamically update in the viewport when it changes. To see this feature in action, create a **TextPlus** object in a viewport and then type **radius:** in the **Text** field of the **Parameters** rollout. Create a sphere in a viewport. In the **Parameters** rollout of the **TextPlus** object, click **Set Value as Text** to open the **Edit Value As Text** dialog box. In this dialog box, select **Script** from the **Value Options** section [see Fig. 18] and then click **Pick Value From Scene**. Now, click on the sphere and then choose **Object (Sphere)** > **Radius** from the popup [see Fig. 19] to make the connection.

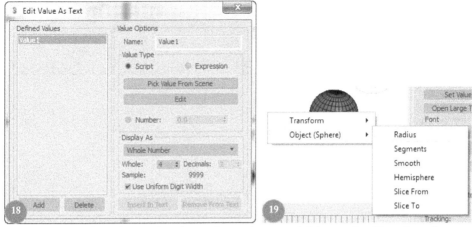

Select **Real Number** from the drop-down list available in the **Display As** section and then set **Decimals** to **2**. Now, put the cursor at the end of the text typed in the **Text** field and click **Insert In Text** from the **Edit Value As Text** dialog box. Close the dialog box. The string **%[Value1]** is appended in the **Text** field [see Fig. 20]. Now, if you change the value of **Radius** control, the value will be dynamically updated in the **TextPlus** object.

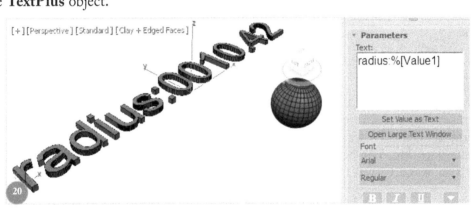

Extended Primitives

Extended primitives are little complex than the **Standard** primitives. 3ds Max offers thirteen extended primitives, see Fig. 21. You can combine **Extended** primitives with the **Standard** primitives and modifiers to create refined models. You can interactively create **Extended** primitives in the viewport using the mouse and most of the primitives can be generated

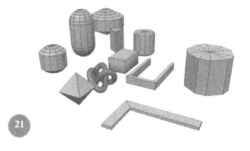

by entering precise values using the keyboard. You can specify the parameters before creating the **Extended** primitives as well as modify them later from the **Parameters** rollout in the **Modify** panel. Let's take a look at the commonly used **Extended** primitives. Experiment with the primitives that are not covered in this section. They are straight forward and you can easily understand their parameters by changing them from the **Parameters** rollout.

You can use this primitive to create different type of polyhedra objects [see Fig. 22].

Table 6 summarizes the controls in the **Parameters** rollout.

Table 6: The controls in the **Hedra's Parameters** rollout	
Control	**Description**
Family Group	The controls in this group allow you to choose the type of polyhedral you want to create. **Tetra** creates a tetrahedron. **Cube/Octa** creates a cubic or octahedral polyhedron. **Dodec/Icos** creates a dodecahedron or icosahedron. **Star 1** and **Star 2** create two different star-shaped polyhedron.
Family Parameters Group	The **P** and **Q** controls in this group change the geometry back and forth between the vertices and faces. In Fig. 23, the left polyhedron has **P** and **Q** values set to **0** each whereas the polyhedron on the right has the **P** and **Q** values set to **0.3** each. The combined value of **P** and **Q** can be equal to or less than **1**.
Axis Scaling Section	The **P**, **Q**, and **R** controls in this group allow you to push or pull the corresponding facets in or out. The polyhedron on the left in Fig. 24 is created with the default parameters. For the polyhedron on the right, I have changed **Q** and **R** values to **120** and **150**, respectively. On clicking **Reset**, the axes return to their default values.
Vertices Group	The controls in this group determine the internal geometry of each facet of the polyhedron.
Radius	Sets the radius of the polyhedron.

> *Note: Creating Extended primitives*
> *To save some space, I am not writing the process to create the **Extended** primitives. You can easily create them using the standard click–drag methods as done in the **Standard Primitives** section.*

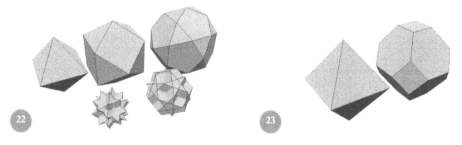

22   23

You can use this primitive to create a box with beveled or round edges [see Fig. 25]. Most of the controls in the **Parameters** rollout are similar to that of the **Box** primitive. Table 7 lists the controls that are unique to **ChamferBox**.

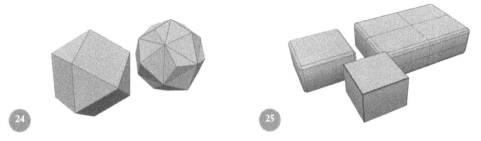

Table 7: The controls in the **ChamferBox's Parameters** rollout	
Control	**Description**
Fillet	Slices the edges of the box. Higher the value you specify, more refined fillet you will get.
Fillet Segs	Determines the number of segments in the filleted edges.
Smooth	Blends the display of faces of the box. As a result, when rendered, box appears smooth in the rendered results.

ChamferCylinder

This primitive creates a cylinder with beveled or rounded cap edges [see Fig. 26].

Most of the controls in the **Parameters** rollout are similar to that of the **Cylinder** primitive. Table 8 lists the controls that are unique to **ChamferCylinder**.

Table 8: The controls in the **Chamfer Cylinder's Parameters** rollout	
Control	**Description**
Fillet	It chamfers the top and bottom cap edges of the cylinder. Higher the value you specify, more refined fillet will be.
Fillet Segs	Determines the number of segments in the filleted edges of the cylinder.

Architectural Objects

3ds Max provides several architectural objects that you can use as a basic building blocks for architectural models such as home, offices, and so forth. Table 9 summaries the architectural objects that 3ds Max offers.

Table 9: The architectural objects	
Types	**Objects**
AEC Extended Objects	**Foliage, Railing**, and **Wall**
Stairs	**L-Type Stair, Spiral Stair, Straight Stair**, and **U-Type Stair**
Doors	**Pivot, Bifold**, and **Sliding**
Windows	**Awning, Casement, Fixed, Pivoted, Projected**, and **Sliding**

You can access all **AEC** objects from the **AEC Objects** sub-menu of the **Create** menu. You can also access these objects from the **Create** panel. Let's explore these objects.

Doors

The door objects allow you to quickly create a door. You can also set the door to be partially open even you can animate the opening. 3ds Max offers three types of doors. Table 10 summarizes these types.

Table 10: The door types	
Type	**Description**
Pivot	This door is hinged on one side only [see Fig. 27]. You can also make the door double-door, each hinged on its outer edge.
Bifold	This door is hinged in the middle as well as in the side. You can use this object to model a set of double doors [see Fig. 28].
Sliding	This type of door has a fixed half and a sliding half [see Fig. 29].

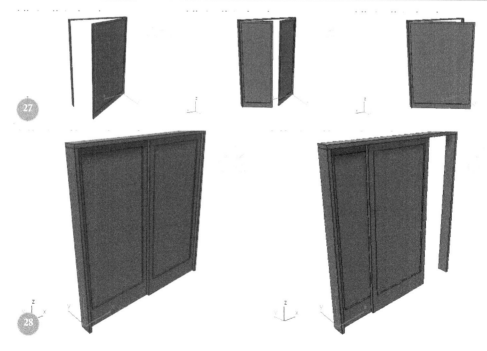

Tip: Navigating Viewport
*If while creating **AEC** objects, you need to navigate the interface between clicks, drag the **MMB** to pan the viewport, **Alt+MMB** drag to orbit the viewport, and **Alt+Ctrl+Scroll** to zoom the viewport.*

To create a door, click **Command Panel > Create** panel > **Geometry** and then choose **Doors** from the drop-down list. In the **Object Type** rollout, choose the type of the door you want to create and then set the desired create options from the rollouts. Drag the mouse in the viewport to create first two points to define the width and angle of the base of the door. Now, release the mouse button and drag to define the depth of the door and click to set. Drag the mouse to define the height of the door and then click to finish.

Assigning Material to Doors
By default, 3ds Max assigns five different IDs to the door you create. The default **Door-Template Multi-Subobject** material is found in the **Ace Templates.mat** material library. Fig. 30 shows the ID numbers and their associated parts in the door. 3ds Max does not assign a material to the door object. If you want to use the default material, you need to open the library in **Material Editor** and then assign material to your object.

Table 11 summarizes the material IDs assigned to doors.

Table 11: The material IDs	
ID	**Component**
1	Font
2	Back
3	Inner Bevel. This ID is used for glazing when you set **Panels** to **Glass** or **Beveled**.
4	Frame
5	Inner Door

Tip: The Ace Template.mat library
You can find this library at the following location:
C:\Program Files\Autodesk\3ds Max 2019\materiallibraries.

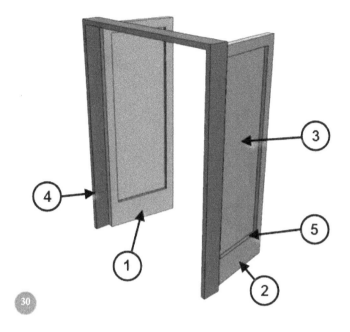

Windows

The window objects in 3ds Max allow you to create the appearance of a window. You can also set the window to be partially open even you can animate the opening. 3ds Max offers six types of windows. Table 12 summarizes the window types.

Table 12: The window types	
Type	**Description**
Casement	Two door like sashes arrangement that can swing inward or outward [see Fig. 31].
Pivoted	It pivots vertically or horizontally at the center of its sash [see Fig. 32].
Projected	It has three sashes two of which open like awning in opposite directions [see Fig. 33].
Sliding	It has two sashes one of which slides vertically or horizontally [see Fig. 34].
Fixed	It does not open [see Fig. 35].
Awning	It has a sash that is hinged at the top [see Fig. 36].

To create a window, click **Command Panel** > **Create** panel > **Geometry** and then choose **Windows** from the drop-down list. In the **Object Type** rollout, choose the type of the window you want to create and then create the window in the viewport using click-drag operations.

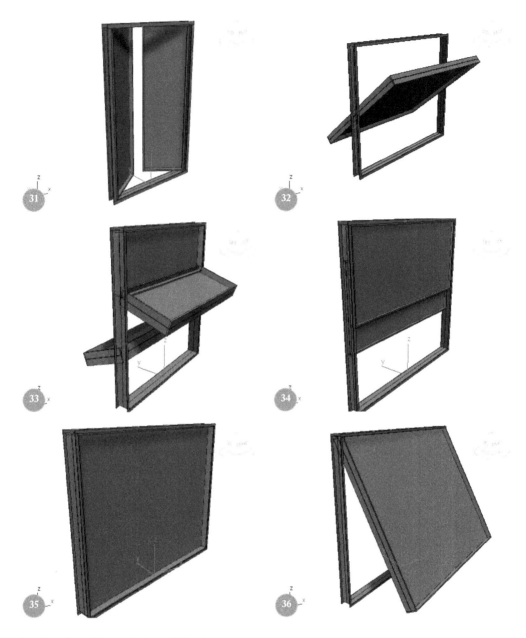

Assigning Material to Windows

By default, 3ds Max assigns five different IDs to the window you create. The default **Window-Template Multi-Subobject** material is found in the **Ace Templates.mat** material library. Fig. 37 shows the ID numbers and their associated parts in a window. 3ds Max does not assign a material to the window object. If you want to use the default material, you need to open the library in the **Material Editor** and then assign material to your object. Table 13 summarizes the material IDs assigned to windows.

Table 13: The material IDs	
ID	**Component**
1	Front Rails

Table 13: The material IDs	
ID	**Component**
2	Back Rails
3	Panels. The Opacity is set to 50%.
4	Front Frame
5	Back Frame

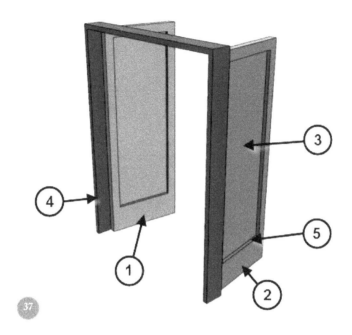

Stairs

3ds Max allows you to create four different types of stairs. The following table summarizes the types of stairs.

Table 14: The stairs types	
Type	**Description**
Spiral Stair	It allows you to create spiral staircase. You can specify radius, and number of revolutions. You can also add stringers, center pole, and more to the stairs [see Fig. 38].
Straight Stair	It allows you to create simple straight stairs [see Fig. 39].
L-Type Stair	It lets you create the L-Type stairs [see Fig. 40].
U-Type Stair	It lets you create the U-Type stairs [see Fig. 41].

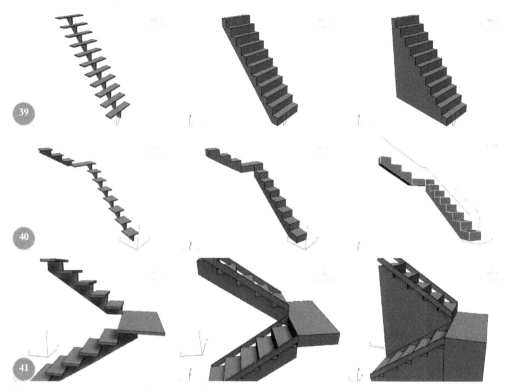

To create a stair, click **Command Panel** > **Create** panel > **Geometry** and then choose **Stairs** from the drop-down list. In the **Object Type** rollout, choose the type of the stair you want to create and then create the stair in the viewport using click-drag operations.

Assigning Material to Stairs

By default, 3ds Max assigns five different IDs to the stairs you create. The default **Stairs-Template Multi-Subobject** material is found in the **Ace Templates.mat** material library. 3ds Max does not assign a material to the stairs object. If you want to use the default material, you need to open the library in the **Material Editor** and then assign material to your object. Table 15 summarizes the material IDs assigned to stairs.

ID	Component
Table 15: The material IDs	
1	Treads of the stairs.
2	Front riser of the stairs.
3	Bottom, back, and sides of the risers of the stairs.
4	Center pole of the stairs.
5	Handrails of the stairs.
6	Carriage of the stairs.
7	Stringers of the stairs.

AEC stands for **Architecture Engineer Construction**. These objects are designed to for use in the architectural, engineering, and construction field. To create an **AEC** object, click **Command Panel > Create** panel > **Geometry** and then choose **AEC Extended** from the drop-down list. In the **Object Type** rollout, choose the type of the object you want to create and then create the object in the viewport using click-drag operations.

Railing

This tool allows you to create railings in a 3ds Max scene. The railing object includes rails, posts, and fencing [see Fig. 42]. You can create railing by specifying the orientation and height. You can also use a spline object to create railing along it. If you edit the spline, the railing object updates to follow the path. You can use railing object with the stair object to create a complete stair.

To create a railing, click **Command Panel > Create** panel > **Geometry** and then choose **AEC Extended** from the drop-down list. In the **Object Type** rollout, click **Railing** and then create the stair in the viewport using click-drag operations.

Assigning Material to Railings

By default, 3ds Max assigns five different IDs to the railings you create. The default **Rail-Template Multi-Subobject** material is found in the **Ace Templates.mat** material library. 3ds Max does not assign a material to the railing objects. If you want to use the default material, you need to open the library in the **Material Editor** and then assign material to your object. Table 16 summarizes the material IDs assigned to railings.

Table 16: The material IDs	
ID	**Component**
1	Lower rails
2	Posts of the railing
3	Solid fill of the railing
4	Top of the railing
5	Pickets of the railing

Foliage

You can use this tool to place various kinds of tree species in a scene [see Figs. F43 and F44]. This tool can produce good looking trees efficiently. You can define height, density, pruning, seed, canopy display, and level of detail for the **Foliage** object.

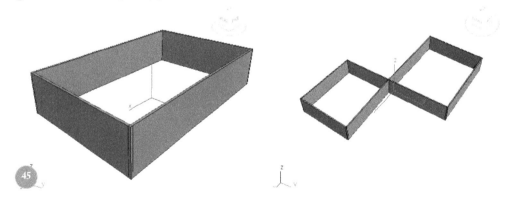

To create a tree, click **Command Panel > Create** panel > **Geometry** and then choose **AEC Extended** from the drop-down list. In the **Object Type** rollout, click **Foliage.** In the **Favorite Plants** rollout, either drag a tree to add to the scene or select the plant and then click on the viewport to place it. You can also double-click on a plant in the **Favorite Plants** rollout.

 Tip: Placing plants in the scene
You can use the **Spacing** *tool to place plants along a path.*

Wall

The **Wall** tool is used to create walls [see Fig. 45] in 3ds Max. The wall object is made up of three sub-object types: **Vertex, Segment,** and **Profile** that you can use to edit it.

You can create wall in any viewport but for vertical walls you should use a **Perspective, Camera,** or **Top** viewport. To create a wall, set the **Width** and **Height** parameters and then click in a viewport. Now, release the mouse button and then drag to specify the length, click again.

If you want to create a single wall component, RMB click, else continue clicking. To finish creating a room, click on an end segment; 3ds Max displays the **Weld Point** dialog box. You can use the options in this dialog box to either weld the two end vertices into a single vertex or you can keep the two end vertices distinct. **RMB** click to finish the wall.

Assigning Material to Walls

By default, 3ds Max assigns five different IDs to the walls you create. The default **Wall-Template Multi-Subobject** material is found in the **Ace Templates.mat** material library. 3ds Max does not assign a material to the wall object. If you want to use the default material, you need to open the library in the **Material Editor** and then assign material to your object.

Table 17 summarizes the material IDs assigned to the walls.

Table 17: The material IDs assigned to the walls	
ID	**Component**
1	Vertical ends of the wall.
2	Outside of the wall.
3	Inside of the wall.
4	Top of the wall, including any edges cut out of the wall.
5	Bottom of the wall.

Note: ID 2 and 3

The definitions of ID 2 and 3 is interchangeable because the inside and outside of the wall depend on your point-of-view and how you created the wall object.

Note: Inserting doors and windows in a wall

3ds Max automatically makes opening for doors and windows in a wall object. It also makes the linked doors and windows children of the wall object. To do this, directly create doors and windows on the wall by snapping to its faces, vertices, or edges.

Tip: Making opening using Boolean operations

*You can also make openings in a wall using the **Boolean** operations. Single wall with many doors and windows can slow down you system. To speed up, use multiple walls instead of a single wall. You can also collapse the stack to speed up the performance of your system.*

Hands-on Exercises

From the **File** menu, choose **Project > Create Default** to open the **Choose a folder** dialog box. In this dialog box, navigate to the **3dsmax2019projects** directory and then click **New Folder** and then rename the folder as **unit-m2**. Select the folder and then click **Select Folder** to create the project folder.

Exercise 1: Creating a Sofa

In this exercise, we will model a sofa using the **Box** primitive [see Fig. E1]. The following table summarizes the exercise:

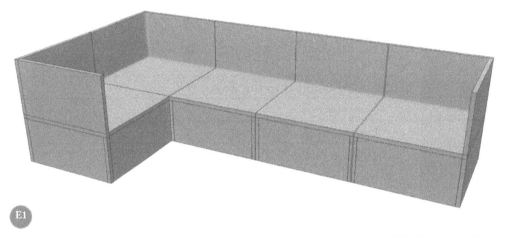

E1

Table E1	
Skill level	Beginner
Time to complete	30 Minutes
Topics in the section:	• Specifying the Units for the Exercise • Creating One Seat Section of the Sofa • Creating Corner Section of the Sofa
Project folder	**unit-m3**
Units	**US Standard – Decimal Inches**
Final exercise file	**sofa-finish.max**

Specifying the Units for the Exercise

Follow these steps:

1. From **Customize** menu choose **Units Setup**. In the **Units Setup** dialog box that appears, select **US Standard** from the **Display Unit Scale** group. Next, choose **Decimal Inches** from the drop-down list located below **US Standard** [see Fig. E2] and then click **OK** to accept the change.

What just happened?

*Here, I have set the display units for the scene. The units that you set here are used to measure geometry in the scene. You can also set the lighting units using this dialog box. Apart from the display units, you can also set the system units that 3ds Max uses for the internal mechanism. To view controls available for changing system units, click **System Unit Setup** on the **Units Setup** dialog box.*

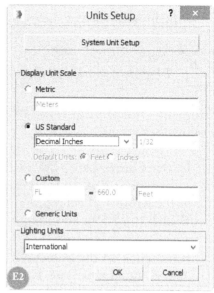

Note: Units

It is important to understand the difference between the system and display units. The scene units only affect how geometry is displayed in the viewports whereas the system units control the actual scale of the geometry.

Caution: System Units

*The system units should only be changed before you create your scene or import a **unitless** file. Do not change the system units in the current scene.*

2. RMB click on any snap toggle button in the **Main** toolbar. In the **Grid and Snap Settings** dialog box that opens, choose the **Home Grid** panel and then set **Grid Spacing** to **3**, **Major Lines every Nth Grid Line** to **4**, and **Perspective View Grid Extent** to **10**.

What Just Happened?

*The home grid provides a visual reference to the user. It helps in visualizing space, scale, and distance. Here, I have set **Grid Spacing** to **3**, the size of the smallest square of the grid. In the previous step, I have set the units to inches therefore the size of one grid space is equal to **3** inches. For example, if you create a box with width set to **24** inches, it will take **8** grid boxes.*

*The home grid displays heavier or "major" lines to mark groups of grid squares. Here, I've set the **Major Lines every Nth Grid Line** to **4**. As a result, the major grid divisions represent one feet. The **Perspective View Grid Extent** control sets the size of the home grid in the **Perspective** viewport. The **Perspective View Grid Extent** value represents the length of half the grid along an axis. Here, this means that **Grid Spacing=3** and **Perspective View Grid Extent=10**, will result in **60x60** units grid size.*

3. Close the **Grid and Snap Settings** dialog box. From the **File** menu, choose **Save** to open the **Save File As** dialog box. In the **File name** text box type **sofa-finish.max** and then click **Save** to save the file.

> *Note: Saving Files*
> *I highly recommend that you save your work regularly by pressing **Ctrl+S.***

Creating One Seat Section of the Sofa
Follow these steps:

1. In the **Create** panel **+**, click **Geometry** ⬡, and then on the **Object Type** rollout, click **Box**. In the **Perspective** viewport, drag out a box of any size. Go to the **Modify** panel 🗗, and on the **Parameters** rollout, set **Length** to **25.591**, **Width** to **25.591**, and **Height** to **1**.

2. RMB click on the **Select and Move** tool ✛ on the **Main** toolbar to open the **Move Transform Type-In** dialog box and then set **X** to **0**, **Y** to **0**, and **Z** to **11.42** in the **Absolute:World** group. Close the dialog box. Click **Zoom Extents All** 🔍 to zoom on **Box001** in all viewports [see Fig. E3].

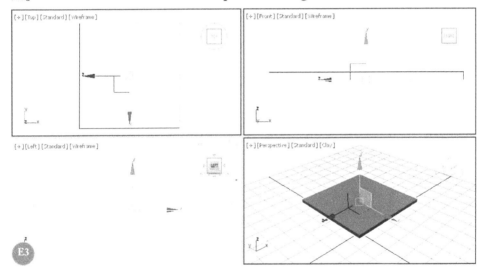

> **?** *What just happened?*
> *Here, I have set the position of the box using the **Move Transform Type-In** dialog box. This dialog box allows you to enter precise values for move, rotate, and scale transforms. To open this dialog box, RMB click on the **Select and Move** ✛, **Select and Rotate** ↻, or **Select and Scale** ▣ tool on the **Main** toolbar. You can also press **F12** while one of the aforesaid tools is active to open the dialog box.*

3. In the **Create** panel, click **Geometry**, and then in the **Object Type** rollout, click **Box**. Activate the **Top** viewport. Expand the **Keyboard Entry** rollout, and set **Length** to **25.591**, **Width** to **1**, and **Height** to **11.417**. Click **Create**. Click **Align** on the **Main** toolbar. Now, click **Box001**. In the **Align Selection** dialog box that opens, set the controls shown in Fig. E4. Click **OK** to accept the changes made [see Fig. E5].

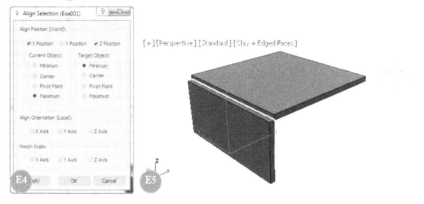

4. Align **Box001** and **Box002** using **Select and Move** [see Fig. E6]. Click **Mirror** on the **Main** toolbar to open the **Mirror** dialog box. In this dialog box, make sure **X** is selected in the **Mirror Axis** group. Select **Copy** from the **Clone Selection** group and then set **Offset** to **24.591**. Click **OK** to accept the changes made and create a mirror copy of **Box002** [see Fig. E7].

5. Activate the **Top** viewport. In the **Create** panel, click **Geometry**, and then in the **Object Type** rollout, click **Box**. Expand the **Keyboard Entry** rollout and then set **Length** to **1**, **Width** to **25.591**, and **Height** to **25.984**. Click **Create** to create a box with the name **Box004**. Make sure **Box004** is selected.

6. Activate the **Top** viewport. Click **Align** on the **Main** toolbar and then click **Box001**. In the **Align Selection** dialog box that opens, set the controls shown in Fig. E8 and click **OK** to align the objects [see Fig. E9].

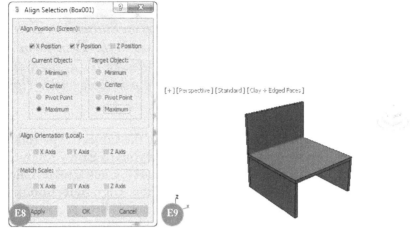

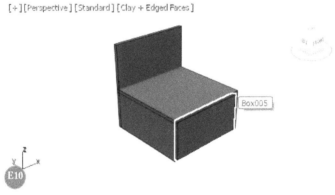

7. Activate the **Top** viewport. In the **Create** panel, click **Geometry**, and then on the **Object Type** rollout, click **Box**. Expand the **Keyboard Entry** rollout and then set **Length** to **1**, **Width** to **23.591**, and **Height** to **11.417**. Click **Create** to create a box with the name **Box005**. Next, align it as shown in Fig. E10.

8. Select **Box001** to **Box005** in **Scene Explorer**. RMB click on the selection to open a **Quad** menu. Choose **Add Selected To > New Group** from the menu. In the **Group** dialog box that opens, type the group name as **oneSeat** and click **OK**.

Creating Corner Section of the Sofa
Follow these steps:

1. Collapse **oneSeat** in the **Scene Explorer**, if no already collapsed, RMB click on it and select **Clone** from the **Quad** menu. In the **Clone Options** dialog box that opens, select **Copy** from the **Object** group. Change the **Name** to **cornerSeat** and click **OK**.

2. In the **Perspective** viewport, move the **cornerSeat** to the right of **oneSeat**. Select **cornerSeat** in **Scene Explorer**, from the **Group** menu, select **Open**. Select the right-most box. Go to the **Modify** panel, and then on the **Parameters** rollout, set **Height** to **25.984**. From the **Group** menu, select **Close**. Fig. E11 shows the **cornerSeat** and **oneSeat**. Now, make various combinations of **oneSeat** and

---

cornerSeat by making copies of them [see Fig. E12]. Press **CTRL+S** to save the file.

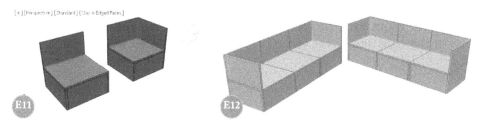

E11   E12

Exercise 2: Creating a Coffee Table

In this exercise, we will model a coffee table using the **Cylinder** and **Torus** primitives [see Fig. E1]. The following table summarizes the exercise:

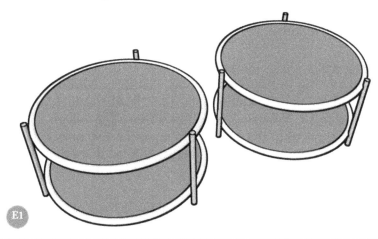

E1

Table E2	
Skill level	Beginner
Time to complete	20 Minutes
Topics in the section:	• Specifying the Units for the Exercise • Creating the Coffee Table
Project Folder	**unit-m3**
Units	**Metric - Centimeters**
Final exercise file	**coffee-table-finish.max**

Specifying the Units for the Exercise

Follow these steps:

1. Reset 3ds Max. From **Customize** menu choose **Units Setup**. In the **Units Setup** dialog box that opens, select **Metric** from the **Display Unit Scale** group. Next, select **Centimeters** from the drop-down list located below **Metric**, if already not selected. Click **OK** to accept the change. RMB click on any snap toggle button on the **Main** toolbar.

2. In the **Grid and Snap Settings** dialog box that opens, choose the **Home Grid** panel and then set **Grid Spacing** to **3**, **Major Lines every Nth Grid Line** to **4**, and **Perspective View Grid Extent** to **10**. Close the **Grid and Snap Settings** dialog box. From the **File menu**, choose **Save** to open the **Save File As** dialog box. In the **File name** text box type **coffee-table-finish.max** and click **Save** to save the file.

Creating the Coffee Table
Follow these steps:

1. In the **Create** panel, click **Geometry**, and then in the **Object Type** rollout, click **Cylinder**. Activate the **Top** viewport. Expand the **Keyboard Entry** rollout, and set **Radius** to **37.5** and **Height** to **2**. In the **Parameters** layout, set **Height Segments** to **1**, **Cap Segments** to **1**, and **Sides** to **63**. Click **Create** from the **Keyboard Entry** rollout.

2. In the **Create** panel, click **Geometry**, and then in the **Object Type** rollout, click **Torus**. Create a torus in the **Top** viewport. Go to the **Modify** panel and then in the **Parameters** rollout set **Radius 1** to **37.5**, **Radius 2** to **1.581**, **Segments** to **100**, and **Sides** to **12**. Now, click **Select and Place** tool on the **Main** toolbar and then drag torus onto the cylinder to align the two objects [see Fig. E2]. If required, use the **Move** tool to align the two objects. Place the two objects at the origin as discussed earlier.

3. Select the torus and the cylinder and then activate the **Front** viewport by MMB clicking on it. Click **Select and Move** on the **Main** toolbar and then press **Shift**, move the selection down by **30** units along the negative **Y** direction. In the **Clone Options** dialog box that appears, choose **Copy** from the **Object** group and click **OK** to create a copy of the selected objects [see Fig. E3].

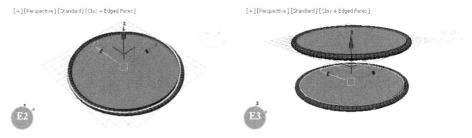

4. In the **Create** panel, click **Geometry**, and then in the **Object Type** rollout, click **Cylinder**. Create a cylinder in the **Top** viewport. Go to the **Modify** panel and then in the **Parameters** rollout set **Radius** to **1.2**, **Height** to **41**, **Height Segments** to **1**, and **Sides** to **18**.

5. Make sure that **Select and Move** tool is active and then on the **Status Bar**, enter **-40.246**, **0**, and **-35.352** in the **Transform Type-In** boxes to place the cylinder [see Fig. E4].

6. In the **Hierarchy** panel of the **Command** panel, click **Use Working Pivot** from the **Working Pivot** rollout. Choose **Array** from the **Tools** menu. Set the parameters in the **Array** dialog box, as shown in Fig. E5 and click **OK** to create two more copies of the cylinder [see Fig. E6].

7. Select all objects from the **Scene Explorer** and then choose **Group** from the **Group** menu. Name the group **coffeeTable**. Press **CTRL+S** to save the file.

Exercise 3: Creating a Foot Stool

In this exercise, we will model a foot stool using the **ChamferBox** and **OilTank** extended primitives [see Fig. E1].

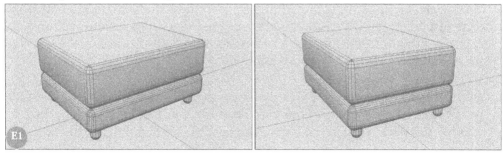

The following table summarizes the exercise:

Table E3	
Skill level	Beginner
Time to complete	20 Minutes
Topics in the section:	• Specifying the Units for the Exercise • Creating the Stool

Table E3	
Project folder	**unit-m3**
Units	**US Standard – Decimal Inches**
Final exercise file	**foot-stool-finish.max**

Specifying the Units for the Exercise

Follow these steps:

1. Reset 3ds Max. From **Customize** menu choose **Units Setup**. In the **Units Setup** dialog box that opens, select the **US standard** option from the **Display Unit Scale** group. Next, select **Decimal Inches** from the drop-down list located below the **US Standard** option, if already not selected. Click **OK** to accept the change.

2. RMB click on any snap toggle button on the **Main** toolbar. In the **Grid and Snap Settings** dialog box that opens, choose the **Home Grid** panel and then set **Grid Spacing** to **3**, **Major Lines every Nth Grid Line** to **4**, and **Perspective View Grid Extent** to **10**. Close the **Grid and Snap Settings** dialog box.

Creating the Stool

Follow these steps:

1. In the **Create** panel, click **Geometry**, and then choose **Extended Primitives** from the drop-down list located below **Geometry**. In the **Object Type** rollout, click **ChamferBox**. Create a chamfer box in the **Top** viewport.

2. Go to the **Modify** panel and then in the **Parameters** rollout set **Length** to **24.8**, **Width** to **31.5**, **Height** to **5**, **Fillet** to **1.2**, and **Fillet Segs** to **5**. Rename the chamfer box to **baseGeo**.

3. Click **Select and Move** in the **Main** toolbar and then enter **0** in all **Transform Type-In** boxes to place the box at the origin. Press **Shift+Ctrl+Z** to zoom the chamfer box to its extents. In the **Perspective** viewport, press **Shift** and drag **baseGeo** along the +**Z** axis about **5** units.

4. In the **Clone Option** dialog box that appears, make sure **Copy** is chosen from the **Object** group. Type **seatGeo** in the name text box and click **OK**. Go to the **Modify** panel and then in the **Parameters** rollout set **Height** to **8**, **Fillet** to **0.72** and **Fillet Segs** to **3**. Align the boxes [see Fig. E2].

5. In the **Create** panel, click **Geometry**, and then choose **Extended Primitives** from the drop-down list located below **Geometry**. In the **Object Type** rollout, click **OilTank**. Create an oil tank in the **Top** viewport. Go to the **Modify** panel and then in the **Parameters** rollout set **Radius** to **1.1**, **Height** to **5**, **Sides** to **25**, and **Cap Height** to **0.9**. Rename oil tank as **legGeo** and then align it [see Fig. E3]. Create three more copies of legGeo and align it viewports [see Fig. E4].

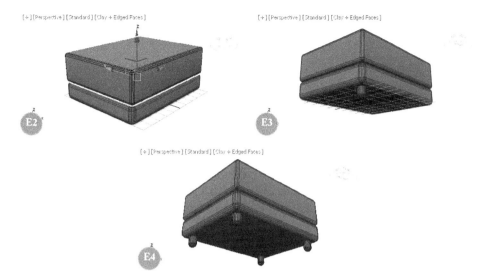

Exercise 4: Creating a Bar Table

In this exercise, we will model a bar table using the **ChamferBox** and **ChamferCyl** extended primitives [see Fig. E1].

The following table summarizes the exercise:

Table E4	
Skill level	Beginner
Time to complete	40 Minutes
Topics in the section:	• Specifying the Units for the Exercise • Creating the Bar Table
Project folder	**unit-m3**
Units	**US Standard – Decimal Inches**
Final exercise file	**bar-table-finish.max**

Specifying the Units for the Exercise
Follow these steps:

1. Reset 3ds Max. From **Customize** menu choose **Units Setup**. In the **Units Setup** dialog box that opens, select the **US standard** option from the **Display Unit Scale** group. Next, select **Decimal Inches** from the drop-down list located below the **US Standard** option, if already not selected. Click **OK** to accept the change.

2. RMB click on any snap toggle button on the **Main** toolbar. In the **Grid and Snap Settings** dialog box that opens, choose the **Home Grid** tab and then set **Grid Spacing** to **3**, **Major Lines every Nth Grid Line** to **4**, and **Perspective View Grid Extent** to **10**. Close the **Grid and Snap Settings** dialog box.

Creating the Bar Table
Follow these steps:

1. In the **Create** panel, click **Geometry**, and then choose **Extended Primitives** from the drop-down list located below **Geometry**. In the **Object Type** rollout, click **ChamferCyl**.

2. Create a cylinder in the **Top** viewport. Go to the **Modify** panel and then in the **Parameters** rollout set **Radius** to **13.78**, **Height** to **1.5**, **Fillet** to **0.15**, **Fillet Segs** to **5**, and **Sides** to **50**. Rename the cylinder as **topGeo**.

3. Click **Select and Move** in the **Main** toolbar and then enter **0** in all **Transform Type-In** boxes to place **topGeo** at the origin. Create another chamfer cylinder in the **Top** viewport and rename it as **supportGeo**.

4. Go to the **Modify** panel and then in the **Parameters** rollout set **Radius** to **1.3**, **Height** to **38**, **Fillet** to **0**, **Fillet Segs** to **1**, and **Sides** to **18**. Now, align **topGeo** and **supportGeo** in viewports [see Fig. E2].

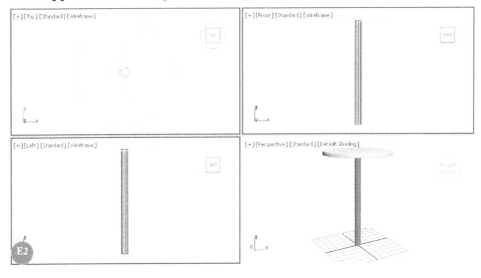

5. In the **Create** panel, click **Geometry**, and then choose **Standard Primitives** from the drop-down list located below **Geometry**. In the **Object Type** rollout, click **Tube**. Create a tube in the **Top** viewport. Place the tub, as shown in Fig. E3. Go to the **Modify** panel and then in the **Parameters** rollout set **Radius 1** to **4**, **Radius 2** to **1.3**, **Height** to **2**, and **Sides** to **50**. Rename tube as **tubeGeo** [see Fig. E3].

6. In the **Create** panel, click **Geometry**, and then choose **Extended Primitives** from the drop-down list located below **Geometry**. In the **Object Type** rollout, click **ChamferBox**. Create a box in the **Top** viewport. Go to the **Modify** panel and then in the **Parameters** rollout set **Length** to **2.1**, **Width** to **12.8**, **Height** to **1.6**, **Fillet** to **0.1** and **Fillet Segs** to **6**. Rename the box as **legGeo**.

7. From the **Object-Space Modifiers** section of the **Modifier** List, select **Taper**. In the **Parameters** layout, set **Amount** to **-0.64**. Set **Primary** to X in the **Taper Axis** area. Now, aline **legGeo** with **tubeGeo** [see Fig. E4].

8. Create another chamfer box in the **Top** viewport. Go to the **Modify** panel and then in the **Parameters** rollout set **Length** to **1.57**, **Width** to **5.6**, **Height** to **0.64**, **Fillet** to **0.07**, **Width Segs** to **32**, and **Fillet Segs** to **3**.

9. From the **Object-Space Modifiers** section of the **Modifier List**, select **Bend**. In the **Parameters** layout, set **Angle** to **213**. Select X radio button in the **Bend Axis** area [see Fig. E5].

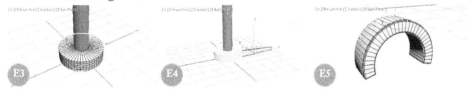

10. Create a chamfer cylinder in the **Top** viewport. Go to the **Modify** panel and then in the **Parameters** rollout set **Radius** to **1.362**, **Height** to **1.72**, **Fillet** to **0.1**, **Fillet Segs** to **5**, and **Sides** to **50**. Align the cylinder with the box and then group them with the name **grpRoller**. Align **grpRoller** with **legGeo** [see Fig. E6] and then group them as **grpLeg**.

11. Ensure **grpLeg** is selected and activate the **Top** viewport. Select **Use Transform Coordinate Center** ▦ from the **Use Center** flyout the **Main** toolbar. Choose **Array** from the **Tools** menu. Now, set the values in the **Array** dialog box, as shown in Fig. E7, and then click **OK** to create **3** more copies [see Fig. E8].

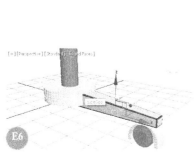

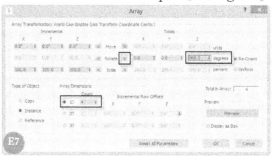

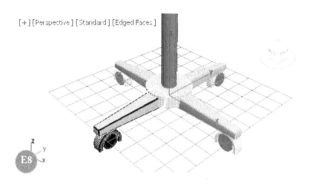

Quiz

Evaluate your skills to see how many questions you can answer correctly.

Fill in the Blanks
Fill in the blanks in each of the following statements:

1. You can use the **GeoSphere** primitive to create spheres and geo-hemispheres based on three classes of polyhedrons: _____, _____, and _____.

2. To constrain the base of the pyramid to a square, drag with the _____ key held down.

3. The default **Window-Template Multi-Subobject** material is found in the _____ material library.

True of False
State whether each of the following is true or false:

1. You can change the name of an object from the **Name and Color** rollout.

2. You can create a cube object using the **Box** tool.

3. The **GeoSphere** tool produces smooth shape than the **Sphere** tool.

Summary

The unit covered the following topics:

- Creating and modifying the **Standard** Primitives
- Creating and modifying the **Extended** Primitives
- Working with the **Architectural** objects.
- Setting the project folder
- Using the **Align** and **Mirror** tools
- Creating clones
- Using the **Scene Explorer**
- Creating a group
- Setting grid spacings
- Using **Transform Type-In** dialog box
- Using **Array** dialog box
- Specifying units for the scene

This page is intentionally left blank

- Working with the polygon modeling tools
- Using the polygon modeling techniques
- Selecting polygon sub-object
- Transforming sub-objects
- Soft selecting sub-objects

Unit M4: Polygon Modeling

In Unit M3, you have modeled objects using the parametric modeling techniques. In parametric modeling, you create primitives from the **Create** panel and modify them using the creation parameters. Then, you transform the primitives using the transformation tools to create shape of the models. **Parametric** modeling is powerful and easy but it has some limitations when it comes to creating complex models. **Surface** modeling on the other hand is more flexible and allows you to create any object that you can imagine. Once you convert an object to an editable object such as an editable poly, editable mesh, editable patch, or NURBS object; 3ds Max provides specialized toolset to create the models.

Editable Poly Object

The editable poly object is an editable object with five sub-object levels: **Vertex, Edge, Border, Polygon,** and **Element**. Sub-objects such as vertices and edges are the basic building blocks of an object. Vertices are points in 3D space. They define the structure for other sub-objects such as edges and polygons. An edge is a line connecting two vertices. The connection forms one side of the polygon. An edge cannot be shared by more than two polygons. Also, normals of the two polygons should be adjacent. When three or more edges combine together, they form a polygon. **Elements** are groups of contiguous polygons. A border can be described as the edge of a hole in the object. Fig. 1 shows various sub-object levels available for the editable poly object.

You can convert an object to an editable poly object by using one of the following methods:

1. Select an object in a viewport and then go to the **Modify** panel. Next, RMB click on the object entry in the stack display and then choose **Editable Poly** from the pop up menu displayed [see Fig. 2].
2. Select the object in a viewport and then RMB click. Choose **transform** quadrant> **Convert To:** > **Convert to Editable Poly** [see Fig. 3].
3. Apply a modifier to a parametric object that makes the object a poly object. For example, the **Turn to Poly** modifier.
4. Apply the **Edit Poly** modifier.

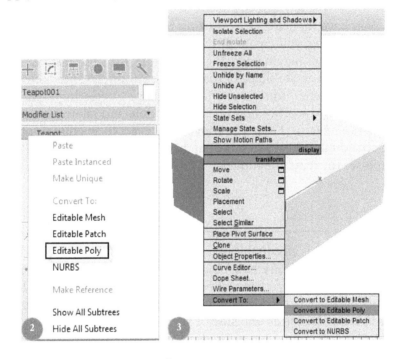

Caution: Limitations of the Edit Poly modifier
*The **Edit Poly** modifier offers most of the capabilities of the **Editable Poly** object except the **Vertex Color Information**, **Subdivision Surface** rollout, **Weight** and **Crease** settings, and **Subdivision Displacement** rollout.*

Note: Graphite Modeling Tools
*The option to convert an editable poly is also available in the **Graphite Modeling Tools**. You will learn about these tools in a later unit.*

Selecting Sub-objects

You can select sub-objects using one of the following ways:

1. Expand the object's hierarchy [by clicking the triangle] from the stack display and then choose a sub-object level [see Fig. 4]. The select sub-object will be highlighted in the stack display.
2. Click a selection button from the **Selection** rollout [see Fig. 5].
3. RMB click on an object in a viewport and then choose the sub-object level from the upper left quadrant [**tools 1**] of the **Quad** menu displayed [see Fig. 6].
4. Choose a selection or transform tool and then click on the sub-objects in a viewport using the standard selection techniques.

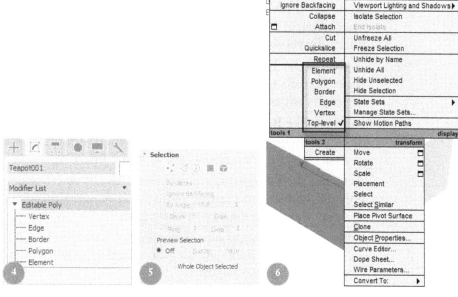

Note: Adding and removing from the selection
*To select a vertex, edge, polygon, or element, click it. To add to the sub-object selection, press and hold **Ctrl** and click. You can also drag a selection region to select a group of sub-objects. To subtract from the sub-object selection, press and hold **Alt** and click. You can also drag a selection region to deselect a group of sub-objects.*

Tip: Locking selection
Once you make the sub-object selection, you can lock the selection by pressing **Spacebar**. *Locking the selection helps in unintentionally selecting other sub-objects. To release the lock, press* **Spacebar** *again.*

Tip: Keyboard shortcuts
You can use the numeric keys from **1** *to* **5** *to activate the* **Vertex**, **Edge**, **Border**, **Polygon**, *and* **Element** *sub-object levels, respectively. Press* **6** *to return to the* **Object** *level.*

Creating and Modifying Selections

The controls available in the **Selection** and **Soft Selection** rollouts let you access different sub-object levels as well as they give you ability to create and modify selections. Let's have a look at the tools available in these two rollouts.

Selection Rollout

There are five buttons at the top of the **Selection** rollout. These buttons allow you to select the sub-object levels. Table 1 summarizes function of these buttons:

Table 1: The sub-object buttons		
Button	**Icon**	**Description**
Vertex		Activates the **Vertex** sub-object level. Allows you to select the vertex beneath the mouse pointer. Draw a region selection to select the vertices within the region.
Edge		Activates the **Edge** sub-object level. Allows you to select the edge beneath the mouse pointer. Draw a region selection to select the edges within the region.
Border		Activates the **Border** sub-object level. Allows you to select a set of edges that borders a hole in the geometry. In other words, you can select the edges that are on the border.
Polygon		Activates the **Polygon** sub-object level. Allows you to select the polygon beneath the mouse pointer. Draw a region selection to select the polygons within the region.
Element		Activates the **Element** sub-object level. Allows you to select all contiguous polygons. Draw a region selection to select multiple elements within the region.

Note: Border edges
If the concept of border edges is not clear to you, I would recommend a simple exercise. Create a **Cylinder** *primitive in the scene and then convert it to* **Editable Poly**. *Select the* **Polygon** *sub-object level and then click on the top face of the cylinder to select it. Press* **Delete** *to delete the top face. Now, activate the* **Border** *sub-object level, and click on the border to select the border element*

[see Fig. 7]. There is now only one border edge in the geometry that borders a hole in the cylinder.

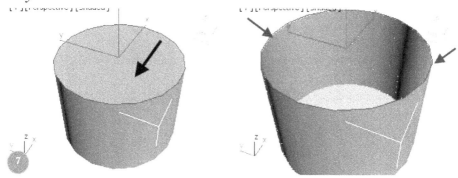

Working with Selection Sets

The **Named Selection Sets** list allows you to name a selection set [both at the object level as well as at the sub-object level] that you can recall later during the modeling process. For example, if you are modeling a face, you might want to select different sub-objects for various parts of the face. In such a case, you can create a selection set for a particular area of the face [nose, for example] and recall it later. It will save you lot of time as you do not have to recreate the selection later during the modeling process.

Caution: Selection Set Names
The selection set names are case-sensitive.

Keep the following in mind while working with the named selection sets:

- You can transfer sub-objects selection from one modifier to another. You can also transfer the sub-object selection from one level to another in the modifier stack.
- You can transfer named selection sets only between the same types of sub-objects. For example, you cannot transfer a **Vertex** selection to a **Face** selection.
- You are only allowed to transfer selection sets between the modifiers that work on the same geometry type. For example, you cannot transfer a selection set from an **Edit Spline** modifier to **Edit Poly** modifier.
- You can copy and paste selection sets between two modifiers assigned to two different objects. However, both modifiers should handle the same types of geometry.

Caution: Changing Topology
If you modify the topology of the object, you might get unpredictable results when you use the named selection set.

To create a named selection set, select the objects or sub-objects that you want part of the set and then type the name of the selection set in the **Named Selection Sets** field [see Fig. 8] of the **Main** toolbar. Press **Enter** to create the selection set.

To recall a selection, select the name from the **Named Selection Sets** list. If you want to select more than one selection set from the list, press **Ctrl** while selecting names. To remove name from the selection, press and hold **Alt** and then click the name in the list.

Once you make a sub-object selection, you can perform the following tasks:

- You can move, rotate, and scale sub-objects using the standard transformation tools.
- You can apply the object-space modifiers.
- You can bind a space warp to the selection.
- If you have made the polygon selection, you can use the **Align, Normal Align**, and **Align To View** tools from the **Align** flyout of the **Main** toolbar.

Transforming a Sub-object Selection

If you are working with an editable object such as mesh, poly, patch, or spline, you can directly manipulate the selection using the transformations tools. However, if you are using a selection modifier such as **Mesh Select** or **Spline Select**, you need to use an **XFrom Modifier** to transform the selection.

Here's how it works:

1. Create a polygon primitive such as **Box** and then convert to an **Editable Poly** object.
2. Make a sub-object selection and move it using the **Select and Move** tool. You will notice that you can easily move the selection [see Fig. 9]. Press **Ctrl+Z** to undo the last operation. Now, deselect everything. You can also press **6** on the main keyboard.
3. Apply the **Mesh Select** modifier [see Fig. 10] and then make a selection. Notice that the transformation tools are inactive on the **Main** toolbar.
4. Apply the **XFrom** modifier to the object. Expand the **XFrom** modifier in the stack display and select **Gizmo** [see Fig. 11]. Now, you can move the selection as required.

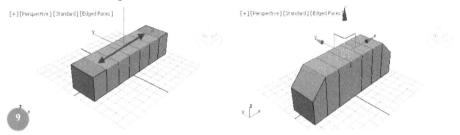

Cloning Sub-objects

When you **SHIFT+Transform** [move, scale, or rotate] a sub-object selection, the **Clone Part of Mesh** dialog box appears [see Fig. 12]. This dialog box gives you two options: **Clone to Object** and **Clone to Element**. When you select **Clone To Object**, 3ds Max creates a separate object comprises of the selected sub-objects. If you select **Clone to Element**, the selection is cloned and it becomes an element of the current object.

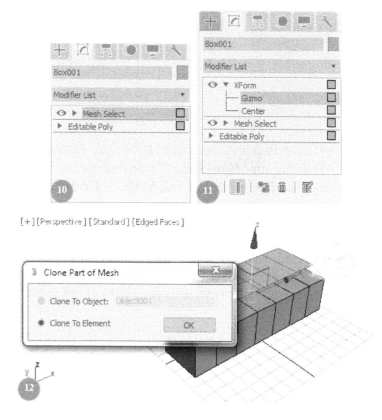

Converting Sub-Object Selections

If you make a sub-object selection, for example, a vertex selection, you can convert it to a different sub-object selection such as edge or face using the **Ctrl** and **Shift** keys:

- To convert a selection to a different sub-object selection, click on the sub-object level button in the **Selection** rollout with **Ctrl** held down [see Fig. 13].
- If you press **Ctrl+Shift** while clicking the sub-object level button, only those sub-objects will be selected whose source components were originally selected [see Fig. 14].
- If you press **Shift** while clicking the sub-object level button, only those sub-objects will be selected that border the selection [see Fig. 15].

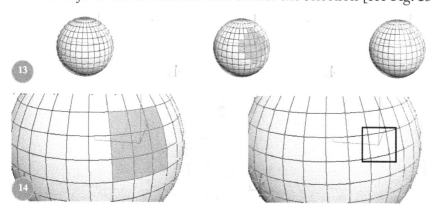

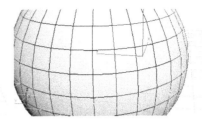

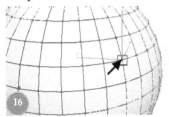

Note: Quad Menu

*The conversion commands are also available from the **Quad** menu. To convert a selection, RMB click and then choose the desired option from the upper left quadrant of the **Quad** menu with **Ctrl**, **Shift**, or **Ctrl+Shift** held down.*

Now, let's explore the other options available in the **Selection** rollout.

When **By Vertex** is selected, you can select the sub-objects that share the clicked vertex [see Fig. 16]. When **Ignore Backfacing** is selected, you can only select those sub-objects that are facing you. When off, you can select any sub-object beneath the mouse pointer.

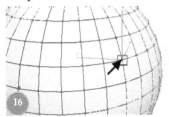

When **By Angle** is selected and you select a polygon, all neighboring polygons are also selected based on the angle value specified by the spinner on the right of **By Angle** [see Fig. 17].

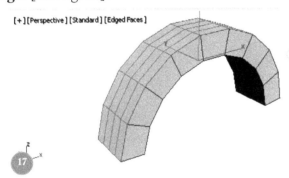

Shrink reduces the selection area by deselecting the outermost sub-objects [see Fig. 18]. On the other hand, **Grow** expands the selection in all possible directions [see Fig. 19].

Ring lets you select an edge selection by selecting all edges parallel to the selected edges. To select an edge ring, select an edge[s] and then click **Ring** to select edges parallel to the selected edges [see Fig. 20].

Tip: Quickly selecting a ring
*Select an edge and then click on another edge in the same ring with **Shift** held down.*

The spinner next to **Ring** allows you to move the selection in the either direction to other edges in the same ring. The left image in Fig. 21 shows the two edges selected. When I clicked on the up arrow of the spinner the selection moved, as shown in the right image of Fig. 21. This feature works with only the **Edge** and **Border** sub-object types.

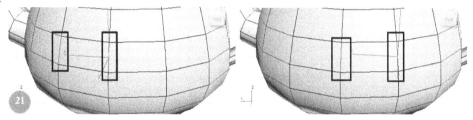

Tip: Loop
If you have selected a loop, you can use the spinner to select the neighboring loop.

Loop allows you to expand edge selection as far as possible. The selection only propagates through four-way junctions. To select a loop, select and edge and then click **Loop** [see Fig. 22].

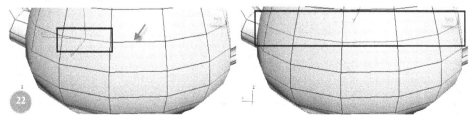

Tip: Loop selection shortcut

*You can quickly select a loop by double-clicking on an edge. At **Vertex** and **Polygon** sub-levels, you can quickly select a loop by first selecting a sub-object and then **Shift** clicking another object of same type in the same loop [see Fig. 23].*

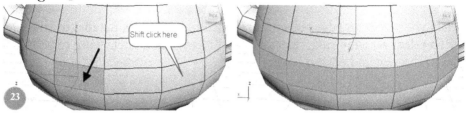

The spinner on the right of **Loop** allows you to move the selection in either direction to other edges in the same loop. If you have selected a ring, it allows you to move the ring selection. This feature works with the **Edge** and **Border** sub-objects.

The controls in the **Preview Selection** group allow you to preview a selection before actually selecting. When **Off** is selected, no preview will be available. When **SubObj** is selected, you can preview the selection at the current sub-object level. The preview appears in yellow color [see Fig. 24].

When **Multi** is selected, you can switch between various sub-object levels. For example, you can place the mouse pointer on an edge, the edge highlights, and clicking on the edge activates the **Edge** sub-object level. To select multiple sub-objects at current level, press and hold **Ctrl** and move [do not click] to add highlighted sub-objects to the preview. Now, to make the selection, click.

To remove sub-objects from the selection, move the mouse pointer over the selected sub-objects to highlight them in yellow. Now, press **Alt** and then click to deselect the sub-objects. The area below these controls displays information about the selected or highlighted polygons [see Fig. 25].

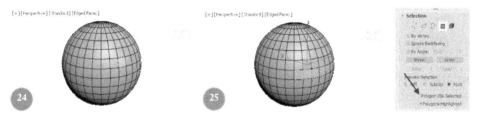

Soft Selection Rollout

The controls in the **Soft Selection** rollout let you partially select the sub-objects in the vicinity of the selected sub-objects. As you transform the sub-objects, the sub-objects in the vicinity will be transformed smoothly [see Fig. 26]. The fall off appears in the viewport as a color spectrum [**ROYGB**: red, orange, yellow, green, and blue]. The sub-objects that you explicitly select coded in red color.

When **Edge Distance** is selected, 3ds Max limits the selection to a certain number of edges specified by the spinner on right of **Edge Distance**. Fig. 27 shows the selection with **Edge Distance** value set to **1** and **7**, respectively.

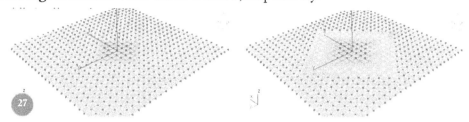

When **Affect Backfacing** is selected, those deselected faces whose normals face in the opposite direction to the average normal of the selected sub-objects are affected by the soft-selection. **Falloff** defines the distance in current units from the center to the edge of a sphere that defines the region of influence. The fall off curve appears below **Bubble**. **Pinch** affects the top point of the curve. **Bubble** lets you expand or shrink the falloff curve along the vertical axis. Experiment with these settings to get a better understanding of how these controls affect the falloff curve. **Shaded Face Toggle** displays a color gradient in the viewport [see Fig. 28].

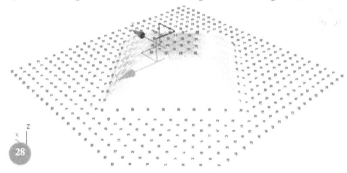

The gradient represents the weight on the faces of the geometry. This feature is only available when you are working with editable poly or patch objects. **Lock Soft Selection** locks the soft selection to prevent any changes in the procedural selection.

The controls in the **Paint Soft Selection** group, let you paint soft selection on the object using a brush. Click **Paint** and then drag the mouse pointer on the surface to paint the selection. **Blur** lets you soften the edges of the selection whereas **Revert** reverses the selection.

Object Level

When no sub-object level is active, you are at the **Object** level. The controls available at the **Object** level are also available at all sub-object levels.

Edit Geometry Rollout

The **Edit Geometry** rollout provides global controls for modifying a poly object. Let's have a look at these controls:

Repeat Last

When clicked, 3ds Max repeats the most recently used command. For example, if you apply a command such as **Bevel** to some polygons and then want to apply the same settings to other set of polygons, select them and then click **Repeat Last**. The same bevel settings will be applied to the last selected polygons.

 Caution: Which commands are repeated?
__Repeat Last__ does not repeat all commands, for example, transformations. To check which command in 3ds Max will repeat, hover the mouse pointer on __Repeat Last__. A tooltip appears indicating which command will be repeated when you click this button [see Fig. 29].

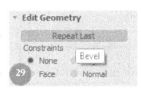

 Tip: Keyboard Shortcut
You can also use the keyboard shortcuts to repeat the last command. If you are using the __3ds Max__ mode, press semicolon (;) and if you are using the __Maya__ mode, press __G__.

Constraints

The controls in this rollout let you constrain the sub-objects transformations to edges, faces, or normals of the existing geometry. Table 2 summarizes the types of constraints.

Table 2: The **Constrains** types	
Type	**Description**
None	This is the default option. No constraints will be applied.
Edge	It constrains transformations to the edge boundaries [see Fig. 30].
Face	It constrains transformations to the face boundaries.
Normal	It allows the transformations along the normals.

Preserve UVs

When **Preserve UVs** is selected, it allows you to edit the sub-objects without affecting the UV mapping [see Fig. 31]. The image at the left of Fig. 30 is the original vertex position. I scaled the selected vertices inward to show the function of **Preserve UVs**. The middle image shows the result when **Preserve UVs** is selected. The image on at right of Fig. 31 shows the result when **Preserve UVs** is off.

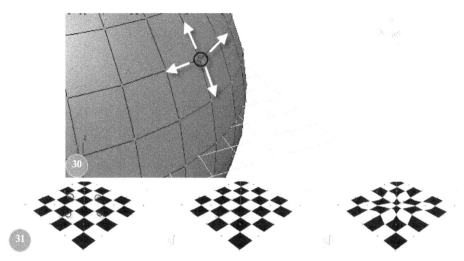

Create

Allows you to create new geometry in the scene. The result produced by **Create** depends on which sub-object level is active. Table 3 summarizes the behavior of this command.

| **Table 3:** Creating new geometry | |
Level	Description
Object, Polygon, Element	Adds polygons by clicking existing or new vertices.
Vertex	Adds vertices.
Edge, Border	Adds edges between the pairs of the non-adjacent vertices on the same polygon.

To create geometry, activate a sub-object level and then click **Create**. Now, in the active viewport click to create the geometry [see Fig. 32].

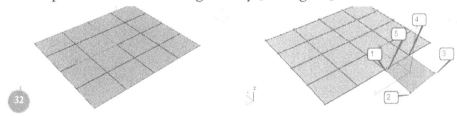

Collapse

It allows you to collapse contiguous selection of the vertices, edges, borders, or polygons by welding their vertices to a vertex. The welded vertex is placed at the center of the selection [see Figs. F33 and F34].

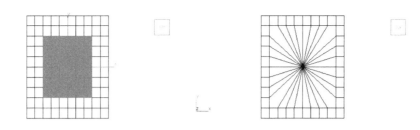

Attach

Attach allows you to attach other geometries to the selected poly object. To attach the objects, select a poly object and then click **Attach**. Now, click on the object that you want to attach; the **Attach** command remains active. If required, keep clicking on other objects to attach them to selected object. RMB click or click **Attach** again to terminate the command.

You can also attach splines, patch objects, and NURBS surfaces to a poly object. If you attach a non-mesh object it is converted to an editable format. It becomes an element of the poly object [see Fig. 35].

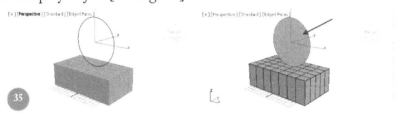

On clicking **Attach List** on the right of **Attach**, opens the **Attach List** dialog box. You can use this dialog box to attach multiple objects to the selected poly object.

Detach

Detach allows you to separate the selected sub-objects and corresponding polygons to an object or element. To detach sub-objects, select them and then click **Detach**. In the **Detach** dialog box that appears, type the name of the object in the **Detach as** field and then click **OK**.

There are two controls in the **Detach** dialog box that let you detach sub-objects as an element or a clone. These controls are **Detach To Element** and **Detach As Clone**, respectively. Select the required control and then click **OK**.

Slice Plane

This option is available at the sub-objects levels only. The controls in the group are known as knife tools. These tools subdivide along a poly plane [slice] or in a specific area [cut]. When you click **Slice Plane**, a gizmo appears in viewports. Also, **Slice** and **Reset Plane** controls become active in the rollout.

Transform the Gizmo in a viewport and then click **Slice** to create the edges where the gizmo intersects the edges [see Fig. 36]. Click **Slice Plane** to deactivate the command. Click **Reset Plane** to reset the position of the gizmo.

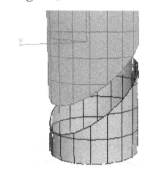

If you turn on **Split,** 3ds Max creates double sets of vertices that allows you to create hole in the geometry [see Fig. 37].

QuickSlice

QuickSlice allows you to quickly sub-divide a geometry without making adjustments to the gizmo. To slice a geometry, make a selection and then click **QuickSlice.** Now, drag the cursor in a viewport to create a slicing line. Release the mouse button to slice the selection [see Fig. 38]. You can continue slicing the geometry or RMB click to exit the command.

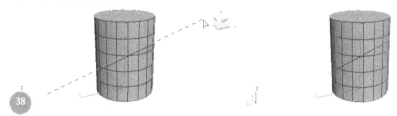

You can use **QuickSlice** in any viewport including **Perspective** and camera. 3ds Max also shows you the preview of the slice before you commit the command.

Caution: Polygons and Elements
*If you are at the **Polygon** or **Element** level, only selected sub-objects are sliced. If you want to slice entire object, use any sub-object level other than **Polygon** or **Element**.*

Cut

Cut allows you to subdivide polygons by creating edges from one polygon to another or within the polygons. It is available at the object level as well as at all sub-object levels. To create edges, click **Cut** and then click at the start point. Move the mouse pointer and then click on another point to create connected edges [see Fig. 39]. You can continue moving and clicking to create the edges. RMB click to exit the command.

Tip: Mouse pointer
The shape of the mouse pointer shows the type of sub-object it is selected. Fig. 40 shows the shape of the mouse pointer when you are cutting to a vertex, edge, or polygon, respectively.

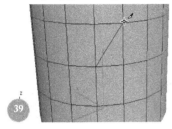

MSmooth

Applies smoothing to the selected area of the poly object [see Fig. 41]. Click **Settings** on the right of **MSmooth** to open the **MeshSmooth** caddy control [see Fig. 42] that allows you to adjust the settings used by the **MSmooth** command. Table 4 summarizes the **MeshSmooth** caddy control.

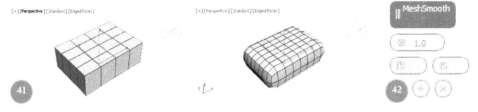

Table 4: The **MeshSmooth** caddy control	
Control	**Description**
Smoothness	Smoothness in a poly mesh is created by adding polygons to it. **Smoothness** determines how sharp the corners of the mesh are. A value of **1** adds polygons to all vertices of the mesh. If you set **Smoothness** to **0**, no polygons will be created.
Separate by Smoothing Groups	When on, the polygons are created at the edges that share atleast one smoothing group.
Separate by Materials ID	When on, the polygons are created at the edges that share the material IDs.

Tessellate

It subdivides the polygons based on the tessellate setting that can be accessed by clicking **Settings** on the right of **Tessellate**. Fig. 43 shows the **Tessellate** caddy control. Table 5 summarizes the **Tessellate** caddy control.

Table 5: The **Tessellate** caddy control	
Control	**Description**
Type	There are two tessellation types available: **Edge** and **Face**. When **Edge** is selected, 3ds Max inserts vertices at the center of each edge and then connect them. The polygons created are the number of sides of the original polygon [see Fig. 44]. On selecting the **Face** type, a vertex is created at the center of each polygon and then that vertex is connected to the original vertices. The number of polygons created are equal to the number of sides of the original polygon [see Fig. 45].
Tension	It is available for only for the **Edge** type. It determines the edge tension value. A positive value pulls the edges outward whereas a negative value pulls them inward [see Fig. 46].

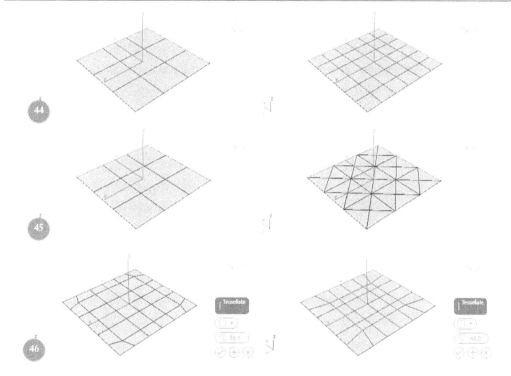

Make Planar

Makes all selected sub-objects to be coplanar. The sub-objects are forced to be coplanar along the average surface normal of the selection [see Fig. 47]. If you are at the **Object** level, all vertices of the object will be forced to be coplanar. The X, Y, and Z buttons let you to align the plane with the local coordinate system of the object. For example, if you click **Z**, the selection will be aligned according to the local **XY** axis [see Fig. 48].

View Align

It aligns all vertices of the object to the plane of the active viewport. It affects vertices only.

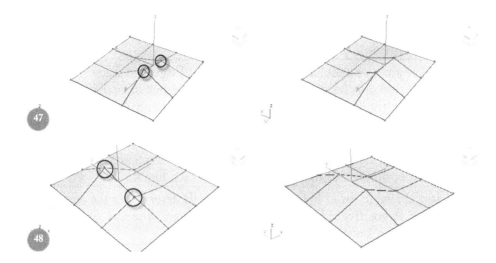

Grid Align

It aligns all vertices to the construction plane of the current view. Also, it moves them to that plane. If a **Perspective** or a camera viewport is active, this command aligns vertices to the home grid [see Fig. 49] otherwise the current construction plane is the active grid. For example, if you make the **Front** viewport active before clicking **Grid Align**, the **XZ** plane will be used for aligning process. If you are using a grid object, the current plane will be the active grid object.

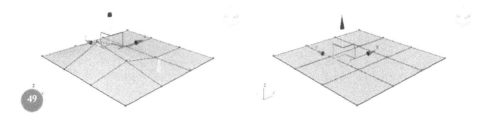

Relax

It relaxes [normalizes mesh spacing] the current selection by moving each vertex towards the average location of its neighboring vertices [see Fig. 50]. If you are at the **Object** level, 3ds Max applies smoothing to whole mesh otherwise the **Relax** function is applied to current sub-object selection.

The setting for the **Relax** command can be accessed by clicking **Settings** on the right of **Relax**. The **Relax** caddy control appears. Table 6 summarizes the **Relax** caddy control.

Table 6: The **Relax** caddy control	
Control	**Description**
Amount	Determines how far the vertex moves each iteration relax function. It defines a percentage of the distance from the original location to the average location of the neighbors.
Iterations	Determines how many times you want to repeat the **Relax** operation.
Relax Hold Boundary Points	When on [default], determines whether vertices at the edges of open meshes are moved or not.
Relax Hold Outer Points	When on, 3ds Max preserves the original position of the vertices that are farthest away from the center of the object. Fig. 51 shows a mesh when **Hold Outer Points** is off.

[+] [Perspective] [Standard] [Edged Faces]

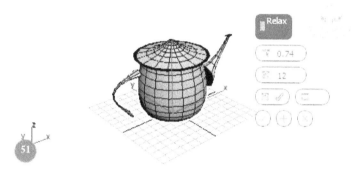

Hide Selected, Unhide All, Hide Unselected

These controls are available at the **Vertex**, **Polygon**, and **Element** sub-object levels. Table 7 summarizes the functions of these controls.

Table 7: The sub-object visibility	
Control	**Description**
Hide Selected	Hides the selected sub-objects.
Unhide All	Unhides the hidden sub-objects.
Hide Unselected	Hides unselected sub-objects.

Copy, Paste

These controls allow you to copy and paste named selection sets from one object to another. These commands use sub-object IDs, therefore, if there is some difference between the source and target meshes, on pasting, the selection may comprises of different sub-object selected. To understand the working of these two controls, create two **Teapot** primitives and then convert them to **Editable Poly**. Make the **Polygon** mode active and select some polygons on the source object. Type the name for the selection set in the **Named Selection Sets** drop-down list. Click **Copy** to open the **Copy Names Selection** dialog box, select name and then click **OK** to copy the selection set. Now, activate the **Polygon** selection level for the second teapot and click **Paste**. The polygons will be highlighted.

Delete Isolated Vertices
It is selected by default. As a result, when you delete a selection of contiguous sub-objects, the isolated vertices are deleted. If off, deleting sub-object selection leaves the vertices intact.

Full Interactivity
Allows you to toggle feedback on and off for dialogs and caddies as well as for the **Quick Slice** and **Cut** controls. When on, 3ds Max updates the viewports in real-time as you use mouse in the viewport or change values numerically using keyboard.

Vertex Level
Edges and **Polygons** make a poly object. Vertices are the basic building blocks for edges and polygons. You can manipulate vertices at the **Vertex** sub-object level. The controls available for modifying the geometry at the **Vertex** level are found in the **Edit Vertices** and **Vertex Properties** rollout.

Edit Vertices Rollout
Let's discuss the controls available in this rollout.

Remove: Remove lets you delete selected vertices. The polygons that are using these vertices are combined [see the middle image of Fig. 52]. The keyboard shortcut for the **Remove** function is **Backspace**.

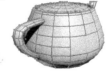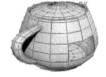

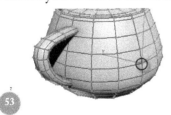 *Caution: Using Delete*
*If you use the **Delete** key instead of **Backspace**, 3ds Max can create holes in the poly mesh [see the image at the right of Fig. 52].*

Break: Creates a new vertex for each connected polygon to the original selection that allows you to move the corners of polygons [see Fig. 53].

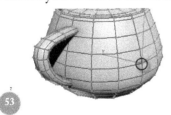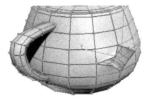

Extrude: You can use this control to extrude the vertices along a normal. 3ds Max creates new polygons that forms the sides of the extrusion [see Fig. 54]. The number of polygons in the extrusion will be equal to the number of polygons that were associated with the selected vertex. To extrude a vertex, select it and then click **Extrude**. Drag the selected vertex vertically to set the extent of the extrusion. Drag horizontally to set the size of the base. If you have selected multiple vertices, all are affected in the same way by the **Extrude** function. RMB click to end the **Extrude** operation.

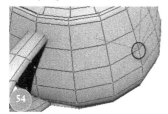 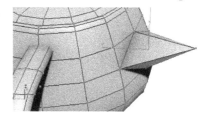

Clicking **Settings** on the right of **Extrude** opens the **Extrude** caddy control. Table 8 summarizes the **Extrude** caddy controls. Table 8 summarizes the **Extrude Vertices** caddy control.

Table 8: The **Extrude Vertices** caddy control	
Control	**Description**
Height	Determines the extent of the extrusion in scene units.
Width	Determines the size of the base of the extrusion.

Weld: This control lets you combine the contiguous selected vertices that fall within a threshold specified using the **Weld** caddy control. To weld vertices, make a selection and then click **Settings** on the right of **Weld** to open the **Weld Vertices** caddy control. Set **Weld Threshold** and then click **OK** to weld the vertices [see Fig. 55].

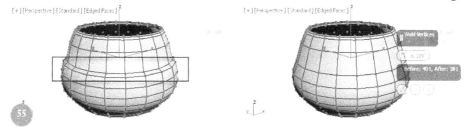

Chamfer: This control allows you to chamfer the vertices. To chamfer a vertex, select it and then click **Chamfer**. Now, drag the vertex in a viewport to apply chamfering. If you have selected multiple vertices, all vertices will be chamfered identically [see middle image in Fig. 56]. Clicking **Settings** on the right of **Chamfer** opens the **Chamfer** caddy control. Table 9 summarizes the **Chamfer** caddy control.

Table 9: The **Chamfer** caddy control	
Control	**Description**
Vertex Chamfer Amount	Determines the extent of chamfer.
Open Chamfer	When on, you can create open space around the chamfered vertices [see right image in Fig. 56]

Target Weld: It allows you to select a vertex and then weld it to a contiguous target vertex. This tool works on those vertices that are connected with a single edge. Also, this control does not allow to cross newly created edges.

To weld a vertex, select it and then click **Target Weld**. When you hover the mouse pointer over the vertex, the shape of the mouse pointer changes to a plus shape. Click and drag on the vertex, a rubber band line gets attached to the mouse pointer. Now, position the mouse pointer on the neighboring vertex and when shape of the mouse changes to a plus sign, click to weld the vertices [see Fig. 57].

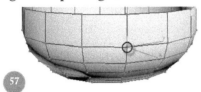 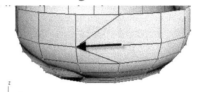

Remove Isolated Vertices: It deletes all vertices that do not belong to any polygon of the selected object.

Remove Unused Map Verts: If there are some unused map vertices that are appearing in the **Unwrap UVW** editor but cannot be used for mapping, click this control to remove them.

Weight: You can use this control to assign weight to the selected vertices. The specified weight is used by the **NURMS** subdivision function and the **MeshSmooth** modifier. The vertices with larger weights pull the smoothened result towards them.

Crease: It sets the crease value for the selected vertices. This value is used by the **OpenSubdiv** and **CreaseSet** modifiers. On increasing the crease weight, 3ds Max pulls the smoothened result towards the vertices and creates a sharp point.

Vertex Properties Rollout
The controls in this rollout are only available for the **Editable Poly** object. They are unavailable for the **Edit Poly** modifier.

Edit Vertex Colors Group: The controls in this group allow you to set the color and illumination color of the selected vertices. Click the **Color** swatch to change their color. **Illumination** allows you to change the illumination color of the vertices without changing the color of the vertices. The **Alpha** control lets you set the alpha values for the vertices. These values are used when you export the data containing full RGBA set for the color values.

Select Vertices By Group: You can turn on **Color** or **Illumination** from this group to determine whether to select vertices by using the vertex color or vertex illumination values. You can also specify a custom color for selecting vertices by using the color swatch available in this group. On clicking **Select**, 3ds Max selects the vertices depending on the selection control that you had turned on. The **Range** control allows you to specify a range for the color match.

Edge Level

Edge connects two vertices. This section covers the controls available at the **Edge** sub-object level. These controls are available in the **Edit Edges** rollout.

Insert Vertex

It allows you to subdivide the edges. To insert a vertex, click **Insert Vertex** and then click on an edge [see Fig. 58]. You can continue adding vertices as long as the command is active. RMB click to exit the command.

Remove

Removes the selected edges and combines the polygon [see Fig. 59]. The keyboard shortcut is **Backspace**. When you remove edges, the vertices remain intact [see left image in Fig. 60]. To remove the corresponding vertices, press and hold **Ctrl** when you click **Remove** [see right image in Fig. 60].

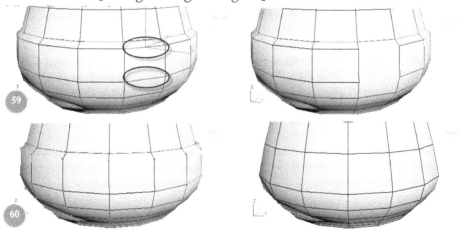

Split

It divides the mesh along the selected edges [see Fig. 61].

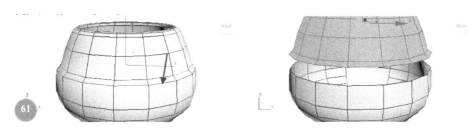

Extrude

This control allows you to extrude the edges manually or using the precise values. The precise values can be entered using the **Extrude Edges** caddy control. The controls in the **Extrude Edges** caddy control are similar to that of the **Extrude Vertices** caddy at **Vertex** level, refer to Table 8.

To extrude an edge, select it and then click **Extrude**. Drag the selected edge vertically to set the extent of the extrusion. Drag horizontally to set the size of the base [see Fig. 62]. If you have selected multiple edges, all are affected in the same way by the **Extrude** function. RMB click to end the extrude operation.

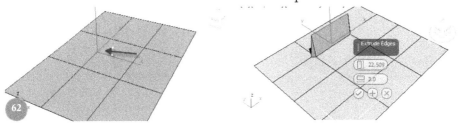

Weld, Target Weld

Refer to the **Vertex Level** section for understanding the functioning of these controls. You need to select edge instead of vertex when dealing with edge welding.

Chamfer

This control allows you to chamfer an edge creating two or more edges for each chamfered edge. 3ds Max provides two types of chamfering: **Standard Chamfer** and **Quad Chamfer**. For **Standard Chamfer**, refer to the **Vertex Level** section. The **Quad Chamfer** type is discussed next.

Quad Chamfer

When you use the **Standard Chamfer** type, 3ds Max generates quadrilaterals and triangles [see middle image in Fig. 63]. The **Quad Chamfer** type generates quadrilaterals only [see right image in Fig. 63]. The area providing support to the chamfered region might contain triangles.

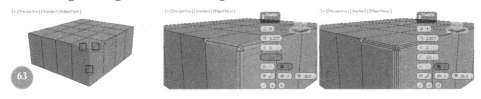

When you click on **Settings** on the right of **Chamfer**, the **Chamfer** caddy control appears. Table 10 summarizes the **Chamfer** caddy control.

Table 10: The **Chamfer** caddy control	
Control	**Description**
Edge Chamfer Amount	Determines the amount of chamfer in scene units.
Connect Edge Segments	Adds number of polygons over the region of chamfer.
Edge Tension	Determines the angle between the new polygons. At the value of **1**, all polygons will be coplanar. Fig. 64 shows the chamfered edges with **Edge Tension** set to **0, 0.5**, and **1**, respectively.
Open Chamfer	Deletes the faces created after the chamfer operation.
Invert Open	This option is available for **Quad Chamfer** only. Also, **Open Chamfer** should be on. When **Invert Open** is selected, 3ds Max deletes all faces except those created by the chamfering operation.
Smooth	When on, it applies smoothing groups after chamfering. Also, it enables the **Smooth Type** function.
Smooth Type	There are two types of smoothing methods available. **Smooth Entire Object** applies smoothing groups to entire object. **Smooth Chamfers Only** applies smoothing groups to newly created polygons.
Quad Intersections	This option defines how corners are affected when multiple edges connect to the same vertex.

Bridge

You can use the **Bridge** control to bridge the border edges to create a polygon bridge between them. Keep in mind that **Bridge** only connects the borders edges. To create bridge between the edges, select two or more border edges, and then click **Bridge**. A bridge will be created using the existing **Bridge** settings [see Fig. 65]. To set **Bridge** settings, click **Settings** on the right of **Bridge**; the **Bridge Edges** caddy control appears. Table 11 summarizes the **Bridge Edges** caddy control;.

Table 11: The **Bridge Edges** caddy control	
Control	**Description**
Segments	Specifies the number of polygons along the length of the bridge.
Smooth	Sets the maximum angle for smoothing to occur.
Bridge Adjacent	Controls the minimum angle between the adjacent edges across which bridging can occur. The edges that are at less than this angle will not be bridged.
Reverse Triangulation	When you are bridging two borders each of which contain different numbers of edges, you can use this control to define the method of triangulation. Fig. 66 shows the bridge when **Reverse Triangulation** is **On** and **Off**, respectively.
Use Edge Selection	It allows you to choose between two methods. Either you can use the existing selection or you can choose the edges using the caddy control. When you choose **Use Specific Edges**, the **Pick Edge 1**, and **Pick Edge 2** controls become available.
Pick Edge 1, Pick Edge 2	Click **Pick Edge 1** and then click a border edge in a viewport. Select the other border edge using **Pick Edge 2**, the bridge will be created between the two border edges.

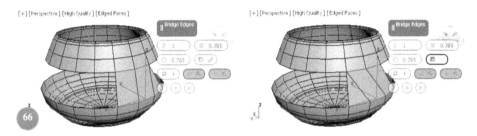

Connect

Allows you to refine selected edges by creating new edges between the selected edges. To create new edges, select the edges of the active object that you want to connect and then click **Connect** [see Fig. 67].

Caution: Connecting edges
*You can connect edges on the same polygon. The **Connect** command will stop the new edges to cross. For example, if you select all edges of a polygon face and apply this function, only neighboring edges are connected. The new edges will not cross each other [see Fig. 68].*

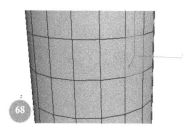
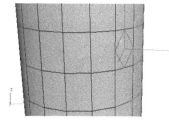

Clicking on the **Settings** on the right of **Connect** opens the **Connect Edges** caddy control that allows you to change settings for the **Connect** command and also preview the changes before committing them [see Fig. 69].

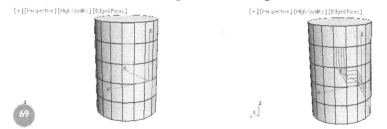

Table 12 summarizes the **Connect Edges** caddy control.

Table 12: The **Connect Edges** caddy control	
Control	**Description**
Segments	Defines the number of new edges between each adjacent pair of selected edges.
Pinch	The relative spacing between the new and connecting edges.
Slide	The relative positioning of the new edges.

Create Shape from Selection

This control allows you to create a shape (spline) from the selected edges. The pivot of the shape will be created at the geometric center of the poly object. To create a shape, select the edges of the active object and then click **Create Shape from Selection** to open the **Create Shape** dialog box. Type the new name in the **Curve Name** field and then choose **Shape Type**. Next, click **OK** to create the shape [see Fig. 70].

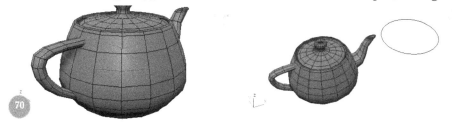

Edit Tri

This control gives you ability to modify the triangulation for the polygons. To turn on the triangulation, click **Edit Tri**. The hidden edges appear on the object [see left image in Fig. 71]. Now, to change the triangulation for a polygon, click a vertex; a rubber band line appears attached to the mouse pointer. Now, click on an adjacent vertex to create a new triangulation [see the right image in Fig. 71].

Turn

It allows you to modify polygon triangulation by clicking on the diagonals. To change triangulation, click **Turn**. The current triangulation appear on the object. Click on the diagonals to change the triangulation.

Border Level

A border can be described as the edge [boundary] of a hole. As discussed earlier, if you create a cylinder and delete its caps, the adjacent row of edges form a border. You can manipulate borders using the controls available in the **Edit Borders** rollout. Most of the controls are similar to that of the edge and vertex controls. Select border edges and experiment with these controls. One additional control appears in the **Edit Borders** rollout called **Cap**. It caps an entire border loop with a polygon. You can use it to fill holes in an object.

Polygon/Element Level

A polygon is formed by connecting three or more edges. Polygons form a surface that you can render. At the **Polygon** sub-object level, you can select polygons and then apply various polygon modeling functions to them. At the **Element** sub-object level, you can edit groups of contiguous polygons.

Tip: Highlighting polygons
When you select a polygon, it is highlighted in red color in the viewport. You can toggle this feature on and off by pressing the F2 key.

You can edit polygons and elements using the controls available in the **Edit Polygons** and **Edit Elements** rollouts, respectively.

Edit Polygons Rollout

Let's first explore the tools available in the **Edit Polygons** rollout.

Insert Vertex

Allows you to subdivide a polygon manually. It also works at the **Element** sub-object level. To subdivide the polygon, click **Insert Vertex** and then click on a polygon to subdivide it. You can continue subdividing the polygons as the command remains active until you RMB click [see Fig. 72].

Extrude

Extruding is a process in which polygons move along a normal and new polygons are created. This command lets you extrude the polygons. To extrude the polygons, select them in a viewport and then click **Extrude**. Position the mouse pointer on the polygons. The shape of the cursor changes to the **Extrude** cursor. Drag the cursor vertically to specify the extent of extrusion and horizontally to set the base [see Fig. 73]. On clicking **Settings** on the right of **Extrude**, the **Extrude Polygons** caddy control appears that allows you to specify settings for extrusion.

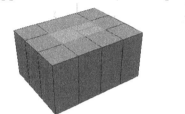 

Table 13 summarizes the **Extrude Polygons** caddy control.

Table 13: The **Extrude Polygons** caddy control	
Control	**Description**
Extrusion Type	This drop-down list provides three methods for extrusion: **Group**, **Local Normal**, and **By Polygon**. On selecting **Group**, 3ds Max extrudes polygons along the average normal of each contiguous group of polygons [see left image in Fig. 74]. When **Normal** is selected, the extrusion takes place along each normal of the selected polygon [see middle image in Fig. 74]. On selecting **By Polygon**, each 3ds Max extrudes each polygon individually [see the right image in Fig. 74].
Extrusion Height	Determines the amount of extrusion in scene units.

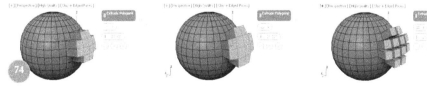

Outline

This command lets you increase or decrease the outside edge of each group of contiguous polygons. It does not scale, it just change the size of the outside edge of the selected polygons. To change the size of the outside edge of polygons, select a group of contiguous of polygons and then click **Outline**. Now, position the mouse pointer on the selected polygons and drag the pointer to outline the polygons [see Fig. 75]. Notice in Fig. 75 that the inner polygons are not affected by the **Outline** operation. If you want to manually specify the outline amount, then click **Settings** on the right of the **Outline** to open the **Outline** caddy control and specify the value using the **Amount** control.

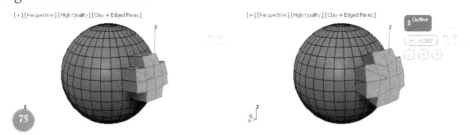

Bevel

It allows you to perform bevel function on a group of contiguous selected polygons. To bevel the polygons, select them in a viewport and then click **Bevel**. Position the mouse pointer on the polygons; the shape of the cursor changes to the **Bevel** cursor. Drag the cursor vertically to define the height and horizontally to define the outline amount [see Fig. 76].

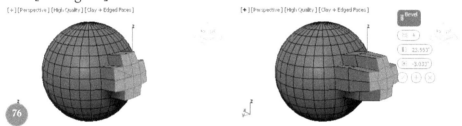

On clicking **Settings** on the right of **Bevel**, the **Bevel** caddy control appears that allows you to specify settings for extrusion. Table 14 summarizes the **Bevel** caddy control.

Control	Description
Table 14: The **Bevel** caddy control	
Bevel Type	This drop-down list provides three methods for beveling: **Group**, **Local Normal**, and **By Polygon**. On selecting **Group**, 3ds Max bevels polygons along the average normal of each contiguous group of polygons. When **Normal** is selected, the beveling takes place along each normal of the selected polygon. On selecting **By Polygon**, each 3ds Max bevels each polygon individually.
Height	Determines the amount of extrusion in scene units.
Outline	Lets you make the outer border of the selection bigger or smaller.

Inset

This command performs a bevel with no height. To inset polygons, select them and then click **Inset**, position the cursor over the polygons and the drag to define the **Inset** amount [see Fig. 77].

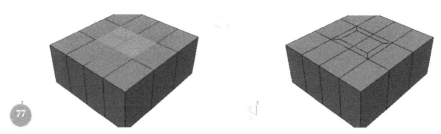

On clicking **Settings** on the right of **Inset**, the **Inset** caddy control appears that allows you to specify settings for extrusion. Table 15 summarizes the **Inset** caddy control.

Table 15: The Inset caddy control

Controls	Description
Inset Type	This drop-down list provides two methods for insetting: **Group**, and **By Polygon**. On selecting **Group**, 3ds Max insets polygons across each selection of multiple, contiguous polygons. On selecting **By Polygon**, 3ds Max insets each polygon individually.
Amount	Determines the extent of inset in scene units.

Bridge

You have seen how we have applied the **Bridge** function on the edges. It works similarly at the **Polygon** sub-object level. Here, you have to select polygons instead of edges [see Fig. 78]. Fig. 78 shows an external bridge [right] as well as internal bridge [left].

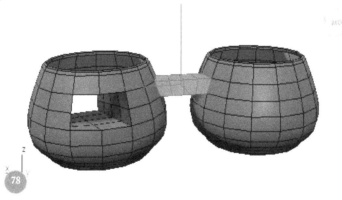

To specify settings for the **Bridge** function, click **Settings** on the right of **Bridge** to open the **Bridge Polygons** caddy control. Table 16 summarizes the **Bridge Polygons** caddy controls.

Table 16: The Bridge Polygons caddy control

Controls	Description
Segments	Determines the number of polygons along the length of the bridge.

Table 16: The **Bridge Polygons** caddy control

Controls	Description
Taper	Allows you to taper the bridge length towards its center. Negative values make bridge center smaller whereas the positive values make center bigger.
Bias	Defines the location of the maximum taper amount.
Smooth	Sets the angle for smoothing.
Twist 1, Twist 2	Allow you to twist each end of the bridge.
Use Specific Polygons, Use Polygon Selection	It allows you to choose between two methods. Either you can use the existing selection or you can choose the polygons using caddy control. When you choose **Use Specific Polygons**, the **Pick Polygon 1** and **Pick Polygon 2** controls become available.
Pick Polygon 1, Pick Polygon 2	Click **Pick Polygon 1** and then click a polygon in a viewport. Select the other polygon using **Pick Polygon 2**, the bridge will be created between the two border edges.

Flip
Allows you to reverse the direction of normals on the selected polygons.

Hinge From Edge
This command allows you to perform a hinge operation in the viewport. Make a polygon selection in a viewport and then click **Hinge From Edge**. Now, drag on an edge to hinge the selection [see Fig. 79]. On clicking **Settings** on the right of **Hinge From Edge**, the **Hinge From Edge** caddy control appears that allows you to specify settings for extrusion.

79

Table 17 summarizes the **Hinge From Edge** caddy control.

Table 17: The **Hinge From Edge** caddy control

Controls	Description
Angle	Sets the rotation angle around the hinge [see Fig. 80].
Segments	Specifies the number of polygons along the extruded side.
Pick Hinge	Click it and then click on an edge to specify the hinge edge.

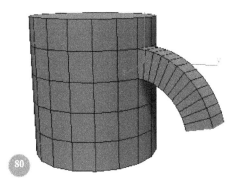

Extrude Along Spline

Allows you to extrude a selection along a spline. To extrude, create a spline and then select the polygons that you want to extrude. Click **Extrude Along Spline** and then click the spline in a viewport to extrude the polygons [see Fig. 81].

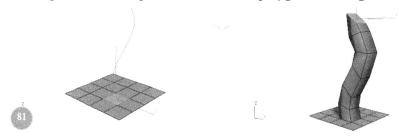

On clicking **Settings** on the right of **Extrude Along Spline**, the **Extrude Along Spline** caddy control appears that allows you to specify settings for extrusion. Table 18 summarizes the **Extrude Along Spline** caddy controls.

Table 18: The **Extrude Along Spline** caddy control	
Control	**Description**
Segments	Determines the number of polygons along the extrusion [see Fig. 82].
Taper Amount	Sets the taper amount for the extrusion.
Taper Curve	Defines the rate at which tapering occurs.
Twist	Applies a twist along the length of taper.
Extrude Along Spline Align	Aligns the extrusion along the face normal [see Fig. 83].
Rotation	Sets the rotation of extrusion.
Pick Spline	Allows you to pick a spline along which the extrusion will occur.

Edit Triangulation/Turn

Refer to the **Edge Level** section for understanding the functioning of these controls.

Retriangulate

When clicked, 3ds Max automatically performs best triangulation on the selected polygon[s].

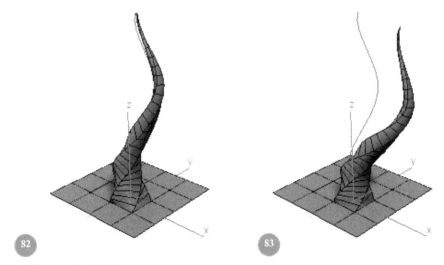

82 83

Edit Elements Rollout

Refer to **Edit Polygons** rollout for the controls available in this rollout.

Hands-on Exercises

From the **File** menu, choose **Project > Create Default** to open the **Choose a folder** dialog box. In this dialog box, navigate to the **3dsmax2019projects** directory and then click **New Folder** and then rename the folder as **unit-m4**. Select the folder and then click **Select Folder** to create the project folder.

Exercise 1: Creating a Hole

In this exercise, we will learn to create a perfect circular hole in a geometry [see Fig. E1]. Table E1 summarizes the exercise:

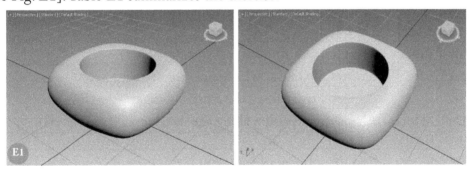

E1

Table E1:	
Skill level	Beginner
Time to complete	40 Minutes
Topics in the section:	• Specifying the Units for the Exercise • Creating the Hole
Project folder	**unit-m4**
Units	**Generic**
Final exercise file	**hole-finish.max**

Specifying the Units for the Exercise
Follow these steps:

1. From **Customize** menu choose **Units Setup**. In the **Units Setup** dialog box that appears, select **Generic Units** from the **Units Setup** dialog box. Click **OK** to accept the changes made.

2. From the **File** menu, choose **Save** to open the **Save File As** dialog box. In the **File name** text box type **hole-finish.max** and then click **Save** to save the file.

Creating the Hole
Follow these steps:

1. In the **Create** panel, click **Geometry**, and then in the **Object Type** rollout, click **Plane**. In the **Perspective** viewport, create a plane. Switch to the **Modify** panel and then in the **Parameters** rollout, change **Length** to **50**, **Width** to **50**, **Height Length Segs** to **2**, and **Width Segs** to **2**. Place the plane at the origin.

2. RMB click on the sphere and then choose **transform** quadrant > **Convert To:** > **Convert to Editable Poly**. In the **Modify** panel > **Selection** rollout, click **Vertex** to activate the vertex sub-object level.

3. Select the vertices, as shown in Fig. E2 and then in the **Modify** panel > **Edit Vertices** rollout, click **Connect** [see Fig. E3]. Similarly, connect the other vertices diagonally [see Fig. E4].

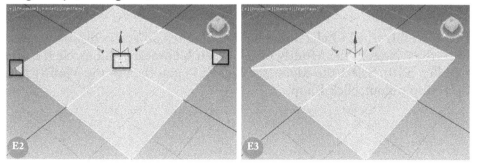

4. Select the center vertex and then in the **Modify** panel > **Edit Vertices** rollout, click **Chamfer** > **Settings** to open the **Chamfer** caddy control. Change **Vertex Chamfer Amount** to **10** and then click **OK** [see Fig. E5].

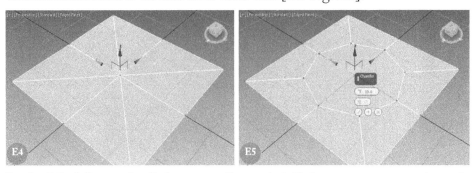

5. In the **Modify** panel > **Selection** rollout, click **Polygon** to activate the polygon sub-object level. Select the center polygon and then delete it [see Fig. E6]. In the **Modify** panel > **Selection** rollout, click **Border** to activate the border sub-object level. Select the border, as shown in Fig. E7.

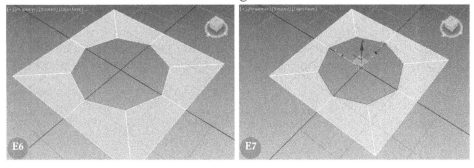

6. Invoke the **Move** tool and then drag the border along to -**Z** axis to create the extrusion [see Fig. E8]. Invoke the **Scale** tool and then scale border inwards using the **Scale** tool and the **Shift** key [see Fig. E9].

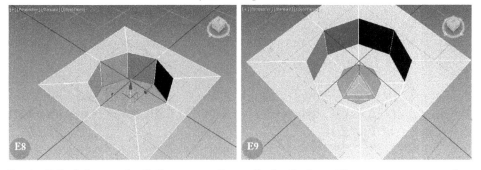

7. In the **Modify** panel > **Selection** rollout, **Ctrl+click** on **Vertex** to convert selection to vertices. Now, in the **Modify** panel > **Edit Geometry** rollout, click **Collapse** [see Fig. E10]. Select the edges [see Fig. E11] and then in the **Modify** panel > **Selection** rollout, click **Loop**.

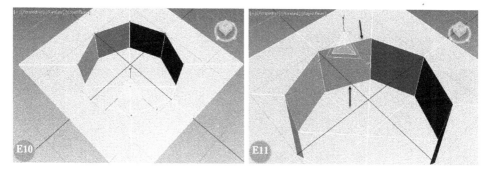

8. In the **Edit Edges** rollout, click **Chamfer > Settings** to open the **Chamfer** caddy control. Change **Edge Chamfer Amount** to **0.3** and **Connect Edge Segments** to **2**. Now, click **OK** [see Fig. E12].

9. Invoke the **Move** tool and then double-click on the outer edge to select the loop. Now, hold down **Shift** and then drag the loop along **-Z** axis to create the extrusion [see Fig. E13].

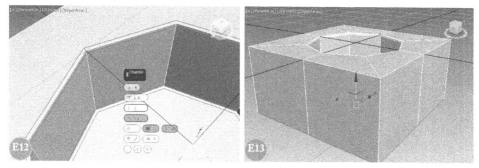

10. In the **Modify** panel > **Selection** rollout, click **Border** to activate the border sub-object level. Now, in the **Edit Borders** rollout, click **Cap** [see Fig. 14].

11. From the **Object-Space Modifiers** section of the **Modifier List**, select **MeshSmooth**. In the **Subdivision Amount** rollout, change **Iterations** to **3** [see Fig. E15].

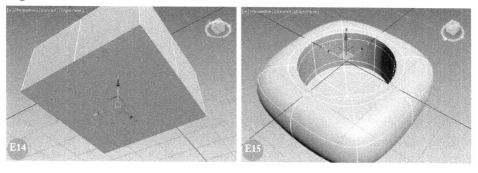

Exercise 2: Creating a Hole in a Cube

In this exercise, we will learn to create hole in a cube [see Fig. E1]. Table E2 summarizes the exercise:

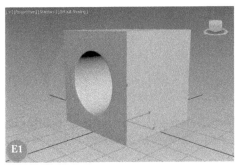

Table E2:	
Skill level	Beginner
Time to complete	40 Minutes
Topics in the section:	• Specifying the Units for the Exercise • Creating the Hole
Project folder	**unit-m4**
Units	**Generic**
Final exercise file	**hole-cube-finish.max**

Specifying the Units for the Exercise
Follow these steps:

1. From **Customize** menu choose **Units Setup**. In the **Units Setup** dialog box that appears, select **Generic Units** from the **Units Setup** dialog box. Click **OK** to accept the changes made.

2. From the **File** menu, choose **Save** to open the **Save File As** dialog box. In the **File name** text box type **hole-cube-finish.max** and then click **Save** to save the file.

Creating the Hole
Follow these steps:

1. In the **Create** panel, click **Geometry**, and then on the **Object Type** rollout, click **Box**. In the **Perspective** viewport, create a box. Switch to the **Modify** panel and on the **Parameters** rollout, change **Length** to **40**, **Width** to **40**, and **Height** to **40**. Change **Length Segs, Width Segs**, and **Height Segs** to **2** each [see Fig. E2].

2. RMB click on the sphere and then choose **transform** quadrant > **Convert To: > Convert to Editable Poly**. Now, create holes in the opposite faces of the box, as done in the previous exercise [see Fig. E3].

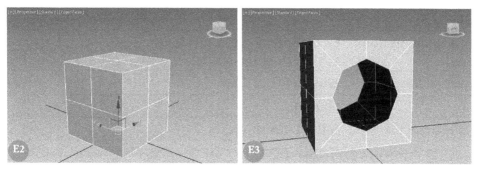

3. Select the all the border edges except the ones marked in Fig. E4. Now, in the **Edit Edges** rollout, click **Bridge** to connect the edges [see Fig. E5]. Now, bridge the remaining two edges [see Fig. E6].

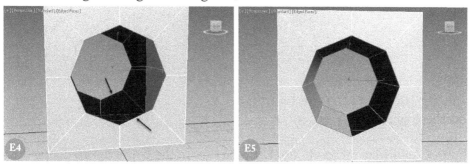

(?) *What just happened?*
Here, I have left out two edges. If we had selected all the edges, we would have not got the proper connection between the edges [refer to Fig E7].

4. Chamfer all the border edges and then apply the **MeshSmooth** modifier.

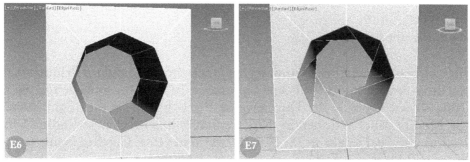

Exercise 3: Creating a Solid Model
In this exercise, we will create a solid model [see Fig. E1]. Table E3 summarizes the exercise:

Table E3:

Skill level	Beginner
Time to complete	30 Minutes

Table E3:	
Topics in the section:	• Specifying the Units for the Exercise • Creating the Model
Project folder	**unit-m4**
Units	**Generic**
Final exercise file	**solid-1-finish.max**

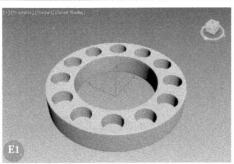

Specifying the Units for the Exercise
Follow these steps:

1. From **Customize** menu choose **Units Setup**. In the **Units Setup** dialog box that appears, select **Generic Units** from the **Units Setup** dialog box. Click **OK** to accept the changes made.

2. From the **File** menu, choose **Save** to open the **Save File As** dialog box. In the **File name** text box type **solid-1-finish.max** and then click **Save** to save the file.

Creating the Model
Follow these steps:

1. In the **Create** panel, click **Geometry**, and then choose **Standard Primitives** from the drop-down list located below **Geometry**. In the **Object Type** rollout, click **Tube**. Create a tube in the **Top** viewport. Place the tube at the origin. Switch to the **Modify** panel and then in the **Parameters** rollout, change **Radius 1** to **30**, **Radius 2** to **50**, **Height** to **15**, **Height Segments** to **1**, **Cap Segments to 2**, and **Sides** to **24** [see Fig. E2].

2. RMB click on the tube and then choose **transform** quadrant > **Convert To:** > **Convert to Editable Poly**. In the **Modify** panel > **Selection** rollout, click **Polygon** to activate the polygon sub-object level. Select the polygons, as shown in Fig. E3. Press **Ctrl+I** to invert the selection and then press **Delete** to delete the polygons [see Fig. E4].

3. In the **Modify** panel > **Selection** rollout, click **Vertex** to activate the vertex sub-object level. Select the center vertex and then in the **Modify** panel > **Edit**

Vertices rollout, click **Chamfer > Settings** to open the **Chamfer** caddy control. Change **Vertex Chamfer Amount** to **7.5** and then click **OK** [see Fig. E5].

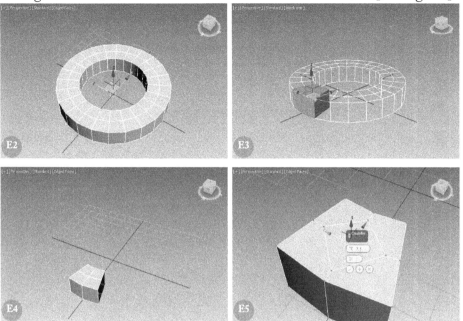

4. In the **Modify** panel > **Selection** rollout, click **Edge** to activate the edge sub-object level. Now, connect the newly created edges [see Fig. E6]. In the **Modify** panel > **Edit Geometry** rollout, click **Cut** and then create edges, as shown in Fig. E7.

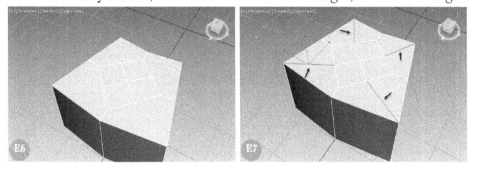

5. In the **Modify** panel > **Selection** rollout, click **Polygon** to activate the polygon sub-object level. Select the polygons, as shown in Fig. E8 and then press **Delete**. In the **Modify** panel > **Selection** rollout, click **Vertex** to activate the vertex sub-object level. Now, select the vertices as shown in Fig. E9 and then scale them using the **Scale** tool [see Fig E10].

6. Select all vertices associated with the hole and then from the **Object-Space Modifiers** section of the **Modifier** List, select **Spherify** [see Fig. E11]. RMB click on the mesh and then choose **transform** quadrant > **Convert To: > Convert to Editable Poly**. Now, create rest of the hole, as done earlier [see Fig. E12].

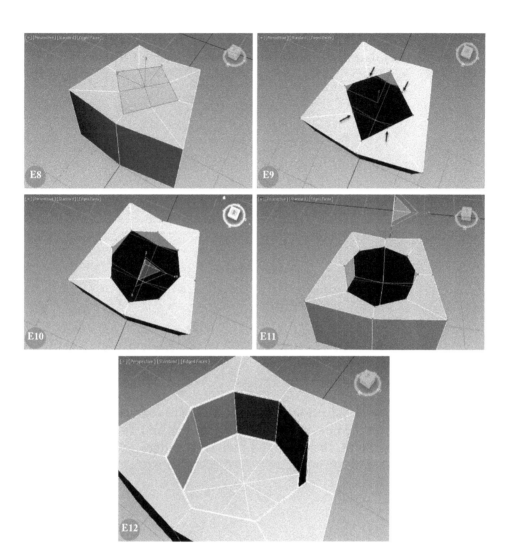

 Caution: Chamfer
Use the **Quad Chamfer** *type to avoid distortions in the mesh. It will help you to get the clean geometry when you will smooth the mesh.*

7. Make sure mesh is selected and then choose **Array** from the **Tools** menu to open the **Array** dialog box. Set the values in the dialog box, as shown in Fig. E13 and then click **OK** [see Fig. 14].

8. In the **Modify** panel > **Edit Geometry** rollout, click **Attach** > **Settings** to open the **Attach List** dialog box. Now, select all objects and click **Attach**.

9. In the **Modify** panel > **Selection** rollout, click **Vertex** to activate the vertex sub-object level. Select all boundary vertices, as shown in Fig. E15. In the **Modify** panel > **Edit Vertices** rollout, click **Weld**.

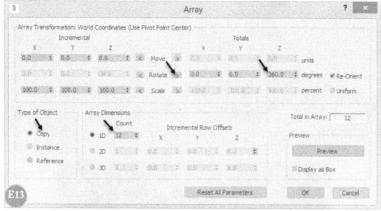

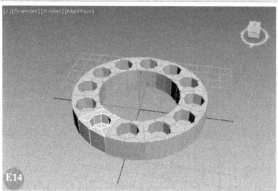

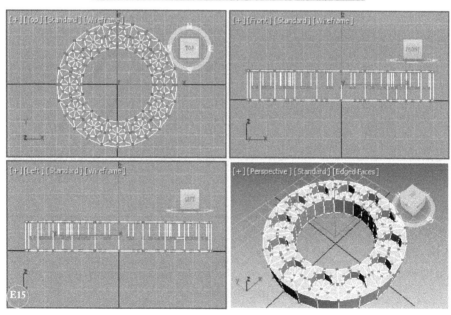

10. In the **Modify** panel > **Selection** rollout, click **Edge** to activate the edge sub-object level. Select all border edges, as shown in Fig. E16. Now, chamfer these edges [see Fig. E17]. From the **Object-Space Modifiers** section of the **Modifier List**, select **MeshSmooth**. In the **Subdivision Amount** rollout, change **Iterations** to 3 [see Fig. E18].

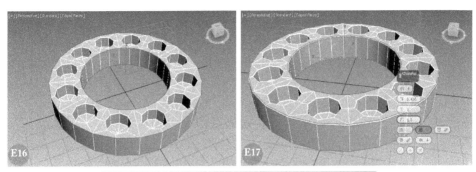

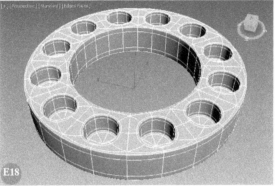

Exercise 4: Creating a Solid Model

In this exercise, we will create a solid model [see Fig. E1]. Table E4 summarizes the exercise:

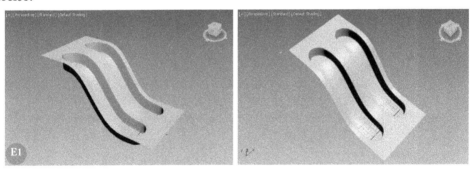

Table E4:	
Skill level	Beginner
Time to complete	30 Minutes
Topics in the section:	• Specifying the Units for the Exercise • Creating the Model
Project folder	**unit-m4**
Units	**Generic**
Final exercise file	**solid-2-finish.max**

Specifying the Units for the Exercise
Follow these steps:

1. From **Customize** menu choose **Units Setup**. In the **Units Setup** dialog box that appears, select **Generic Units** from the **Units Setup** dialog box. Click **OK** to accept the changes made.

2. From the **File** menu, choose **Save** to open the **Save File As** dialog box. In the **File name** text box type **solid-2-finish.max** and then click **Save** to save the file.

Creating the Model
Follow these steps:

1. In the **Create** panel, click **Geometry**, then click **Plane**. In the **Top** viewport, create a plane. In the **Modify** panel > **Parameters** rollout, change **Length** to **150** and **Width** to **200**. Place the plane at the origin.

2. RMB click on the sphere and then choose **transform** quadrant > **Convert To:** > **Convert to Editable Poly**. In the **Modify** panel > **Selection** rollout, click **Edge** to activate the edge sub-object level. Select the edge, as shown in Fig. E2 and then extrude the edge using **Shift** [see Fig. E3]. Again, extrude the edge, as shown in Fig. E4.

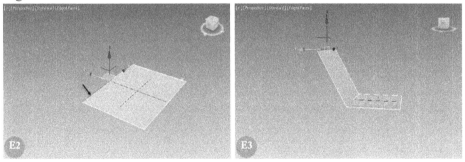

3. Select the edge ring, as shown in Fig. E5 and then in the **Modify** panel > **Edit Edges** rollout, click **Connect** > **Settings** to open the **Connect Edges** caddy control. Now, change **Segments** to **2** and **Pinch** to **80** [see Fig. E6].

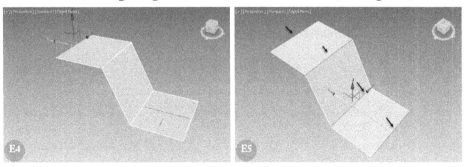

4. Select the edge ring, as shown in Fig. E7 and then in the **Modify** panel > **Edit Edges** rollout, click **Connect** > **Settings** to open the **Connect Edges** caddy control. Now, change **Segments** to **2** and **Pinch** to **-16** [see Fig. E8].

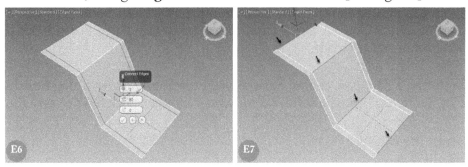

5. Select the edge rings as shown in Fig. E9 and then in the **Modify** panel > **Edit Edges** rollout, click **Connect** > **Settings** to open the **Connect Edges** caddy control. Now, change **Segments** to **1** and **Pinch** to **0** [see Fig. E10].

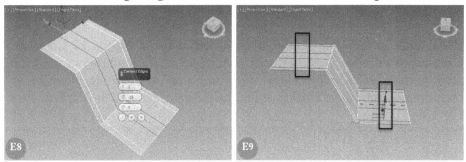

6. Select the edges, as shown in Fig. E11 and then in the **Modify** panel > **Edit Edges** rollout, click **Connect** > **Settings** to open the **Connect Edges** caddy control. Now, change **Segments** to **6** and **Pinch** to **0** [see Fig. E12].

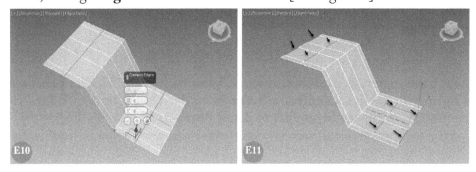

7. In the **Modify** panel > **Selection** rollout, click **Edge** to activate the edge sub-object level and then using the **Move** tool, create shape, as shown in Fig. E13. In the **Modify** panel > **Selection** rollout, click **Polygon** to activate the polygon sub-object level and then select polygons, as shown in Fig. E14.

8. In the **Modify** panel > **Edit Polygons** rollout, click **Extrude** > **Settings** to open the **Extrude Polygons** caddy control. In the caddy control, change extrusion type to **Local Normal**, and **Height** to **-35** [see Fig. E15].

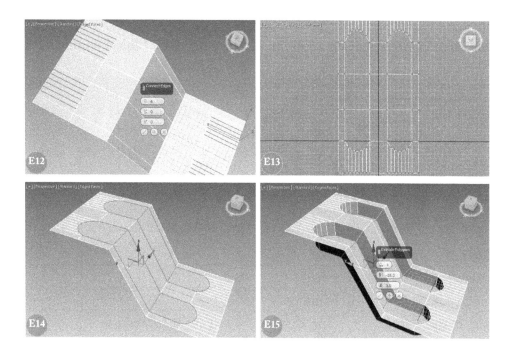

9. In the **Modify** panel > **Selection** rollout, click **Edge** to activate the edge sub-object level and then select the edges, as shown in Fig. E16. In the **Modify** panel > **Edit Edges** rollout, click **Chamfer** > **Settings** to open the **Chamfer** caddy control. In the caddy control, change **Chamfer type** to **Quad Chamfer**, **Amount** to **1.5** and then click **OK** [see Fig. E17]. From the **Object-Space Modifiers** section of the **Modifier List**, select **MeshSmooth**. In the **Subdivision Amount** rollout, change **Iterations** to **2** [see Fig. E18].

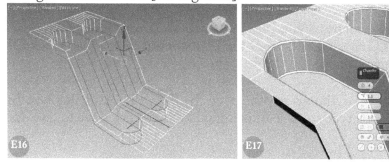

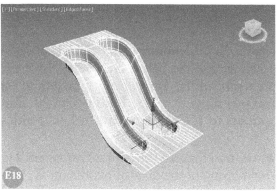

Exercise 5: Creating a Solid Model

In this exercise, we will create a solid model [see Fig. E1]. Table 5 summarizes the exercise:

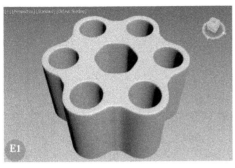 

Table E5:	
Skill level	Beginner
Time to complete	30 Minutes
Topics in the section:	• Specifying the Units for the Exercise • Creating the Model
Project folder	**unit-m4**
Units	**Generic**
Final exercise file	**solid-3-finish.max**

Specifying the Units for the Exercise
Follow these steps:

1. From **Customize** menu choose **Units Setup**. In the **Units Setup** dialog box that appears, select **Generic Units** from the **Units Setup** dialog box. Click **OK** to accept the changes made.

2. From the **File** menu, choose **Save** to open the **Save File As** dialog box. In the **File name** text box type **solid-3-finish.max** and then click **Save** to save the file.

Creating the Model
Follow these steps:

1. In the **Create** panel, click **Geometry**, and then choose **Standard Primitives** from the drop-down list located below **Geometry**. In the **Object Type** rollout, click **Tube**. Create a tube in the **Top** viewport. Switch to the **Modify** panel and then in the **Parameters** rollout, change **Radius 1** to **20**, **Radius 2** to **30**, **Height** to **0**, **Height Segments** to **1**, **Cap Segments to 1**, and **Sides** to **8**.

2. RMB click the **Move** tool to open the **Move Transform Type-In** dialog box. In the **Absolute:World** group of the dialog box, change **X, Y**, and **Z** to **0, 65**, and **0**, respectively. Choose **transform** quadrant > **Convert To:** > **Convert to Editable**

Poly. In the **Modify** panel > **Selection** rollout, click **Polygon** to activate the polygon sub-object level. Select all polygon except the top polygons [see Fig. E2] and then press **Delete** to delete selected polygons [see Fig. 3].

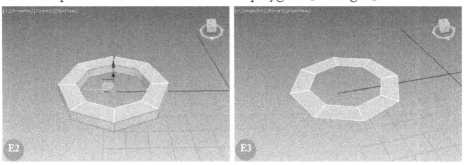

3. Press **6** to switch to the **Object** mode. Select **Use Transform Coordinate Center** from the **Use Center** flyout. Make sure mesh is selected and then choose **Array** from the **Tools** menu to open the **Array** dialog box. Set the values in the dialog box, as shown in Fig. E4 and then click **OK** [see Fig. E5]. Select **Pivot Point Center** from the **Use Center** flyout.

4. In the **Modify** panel > **Edit Geometry** rollout, click **Attach** > **Settings** to open the **Attach List** dialog box. Now, select all objects and click **Attach**.

5. Select the edges, as shown in Fig. E6 and then in the **Modify** panel > **Edit Edges** rollout, click **Bridge** to bridge the edges [see Fig. E7]. Similarly, connect all edges [see Fig. E8].

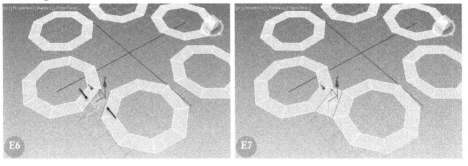

6. Select the edges, as shown in Fig. E9 and then in the **Modify** panel > **Edit Edges** rollout, click **Connect** [see Fig. E10]. Similarly, connect all edges [see Fig. E11].

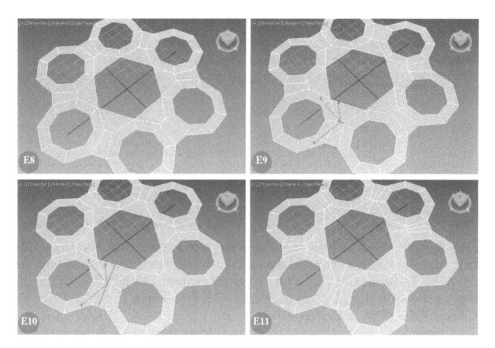

7. In the **Modify** panel > **Selection** rollout, click **Vertex** to activate the vertex sub-object level. Select the vertices, as shown in Fig. E12 and then uniformly scale them using the **Scale** tool [see Fig. E13].

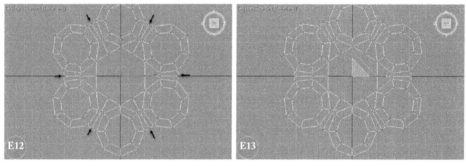

8. In the **Modify** panel > **Selection** rollout, click **Border** to activate the border sub-object level and then select the border, as shown in Fig. E14. Extrude the border using the **Scale** tool and **Shift** [see Fig. E15].

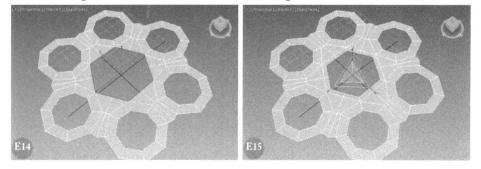

9. Select the borders, as shown in Fig. E16 and then type **Borders** in the **Named Selection Sets** drop-down list in the **Main** toolbar [see Fig. 17]. Extrude selected borders downwards using the **Move** tool and **Shift** [see Fig. E18].

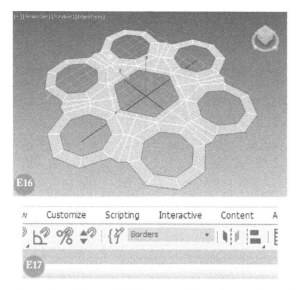

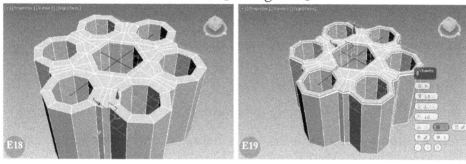

10. Select **Borders** from the **Named Selection Sets** drop-down list. In the **Modify** panel > **Edit Edges** rollout, click **Chamfer** > **Settings** to open the **Chamfer** caddy control. In the caddy control, change **Chamfer type** to **Quad Chamfer**, **Amount** to **1.5** and then click **OK** [see Fig. E19].

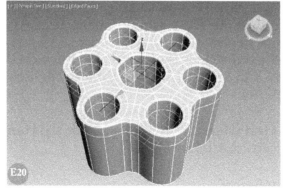

11. From the **Object-Space Modifiers** section of the **Modifier List**, select **MeshSmooth**. In the **Subdivision Amount** rollout, change **Iterations** to **3** [see Fig. E20].

In this exercise, we will create model of a bowl [see Fig. E1]. Table E6 summarizes the exercise:

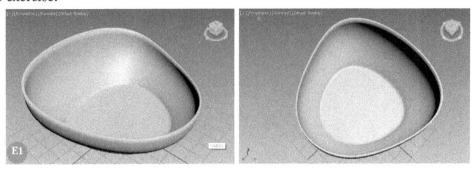

Table E6:	
Skill level	Beginner
Time to complete	20 Minutes
Topics in the section:	• Specifying the Units for the Exercise • Creating the Bowl
Project folder	**unit-m4**
Units	**Metric - Centimeters**
Final exercise file	**bowl-finish.max**

Specifying the Units for the Exercise

Follow these steps:

1. From **Customize** menu choose **Units Setup**. In the **Units Setup** dialog box that opens, turn on **Metric** from the **Display Unit Scale** group. Next, select **Centimeters** from the drop-down list located below **Metric**, if already not selected. Click OK.

2. In the **Create** panel, click **Helpers** and then on the **Object Type** rollout, click **Grid**. Create a grid on the **Top** viewport. Set the **Transform Type-In** boxes in the **Status Bar** to **0** to place the grid at the origin. Go to the **Modify** panel and then in the **Parameters** rollout, set **Length**, **Width**, and **Grid** to **60**, **60**, and **5**, respectively. Press X to open the **3ds Max Commands** list and type **Activate** in the **Search All Actions** field.

3. Select **Activate Grid Object** from the list to hide the **Home** grid and activate the grid that we just created [see Fig. E2].

What just happened?
*Here, I've created a **Grid** object that will act as a construction plane for the objects. A **Grid** object is a parametric object. You can create any number of grid objects in the scene. They are saved with the scene. When you select **Activate***

Grid Object from the **3ds Max Commands** list, the **Home** grid is deactivated and the selected **Grid** object becomes the active construction plane. Here, I have created a **60x60** *cm grid and each grid square represents size of the smallest square in the grid [5 cm].*

4. From the **File** menu, choose **Save** to open the **Save File As** dialog box. In the **File name** text box type **bowl-finish.max** and then click **Save** to save the file.

Creating the Bowl
Follow these steps:

1. In the **Create** panel, click **Geometry**, select **Standard Primitives** from the drop-down list, and then in the **Object Type** rollout, click **Cylinder**. Create a cylinder in the **Top** viewport. Go to the **Modify** panel and then in the **Parameters** rollout, set **Radius** to **25.591**, **Height** to **13**, **Sides** to **36**, and **Height Segments** to **2**. Set the **Transform Type-In** boxes in the **Status Bar** to **0** to place the cylinder at the origin [see Fig. E3]. Now, rename the cylinder as **bowlGeo**.

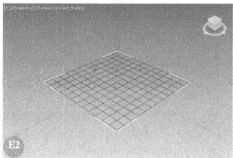

2. RMB click on **bowlGeo**. In the **transform** quadrant of the **Quad** menu that appears, choose **Convert To: Convert to Editable Poly**. Click **Polygon** in the **Modify** panel > **Selection** rollout and then select the top polygon of **bowlGeo**. Press **Delete** to remove the polygon.

3. Click **Select and Uniform Scale** on **the Main toolbar**. Select the bottom set of vertices and uniformly scale them down about **70%** [see Fig. E4]. You can use the **Scale Transform Type-In** dialog box to precisely enter the scale value.

 Tip: Percent Snap Toggle
You can activate **Percent Snap Toggle** *[Hotkey:* **Shift+Ctrl+P**] *from the* **Main** *toolbar to increment the scale values by an increment of* **10%** *[default value]. You can change the percentage value from the* **Grid and Snap Settings** *dialog box.*

4. Select the bottom polygon and then press **Delete** to delete it [see Fig. E5]. Now, select the edges, as shown in Fig. E6 and then in the **Modify** panel > **Edit Edges** rollout, click **Bridge** to bridge the edges [see Fig. E7].

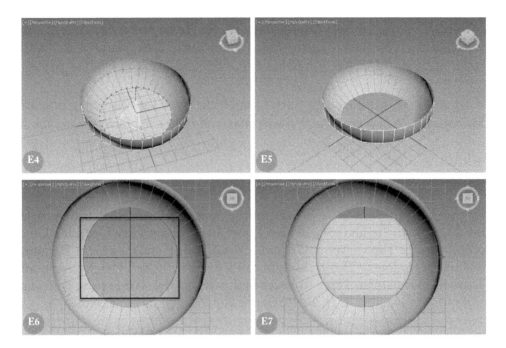

5. Select the edge ring, as shown in Fig. E8 and then in the **Modify** panel > **Edit Edges** rollout, click **Connect** > **Settings** to open the **Connect Edges** caddy control. Now, change **Segments** to **7** [see Fig. E9]. Now, bridge the edges [see Fig. E10].

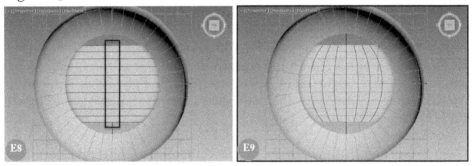

6. Press **3** to activate the border sub-object level and then select the borders [see Fig. E11]. In the **Modify** panel > **Edit Borders** rollout, click **Cap** [see Fig. E12].

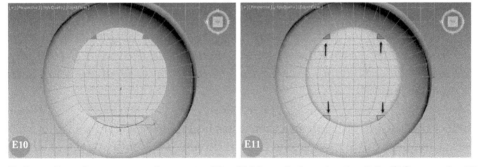

7. Select the edge ring, as shown in Fig. E13 and then in the **Modify** panel > **Edit Edges** rollout, click **Connect** > **Settings** to open the **Connect Edges** caddy

control. Now, change **Segments** to **1** [see Fig. E14]. Similarly, connect the edges on the opposite side [see Fig. E15].

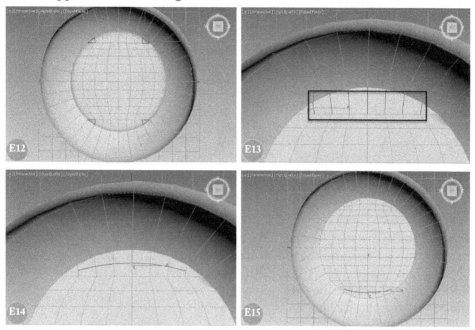

8. Select the vertices, as shown in Fig. E16 and then scale them in to maintain the topology [see Fig. E17]. Select newly created polygons and then click **Settings** on the right of **Extrude** in the **Modify** panel > **Edit Polygons** rollout. In the **Extrude's** caddy, set **Height** to **1** and click **OK** [see Fig. E18].

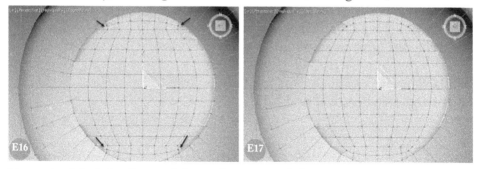

9. From the **Modifier List** > **Object-Space Modifiers** section, choose **Shell**. In the **Parameters** rollout, set **Outer Amount** to **0.5**.

10. From the **Modifier List** > **Object-Space Modifiers** section, choose **CreaseSet**. Similarly, add the **OpenSubdiv** modifier. In the **Modify** panel > **General Controls** rollout, set **Iterations** to **2**.

What just happened?
*Here, I've added the **OpenSubdiv** modifier. This modifier performs subdivision and smoothing operations on a mesh object. It can read the crease values from underlying stack entities [creases defined using the **CreaseSet** modifier] and*

*applies them to the smooth mesh. The **Iterations** attributes controls the number of times a mesh is subdivided.*

11. Expand the **CreaseSet** modifier in the modifier stack and select **Edge**. Now, select the top two loops using **Ctrl** double-clicking [see Fig. E19].

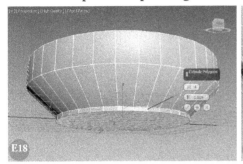
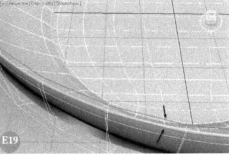

12. In the **Modify** panel > **Crease Sets** rollout, type name as **top_crease** and then click **Create Set** to create a new crease set [see Fig. E20]. Now, enter **0.5** in the spinner besides **top_crease** to round the edges [see Fig. E21].

 What just happened?
*Here, I have used the **CreaseSet** modifier to create a crease set. This modifier provides various tools to creating and managing creases in conjunction with the **OpenSubdiv** modifier. A crease set is a collection of edges and vertices having the same crease value.*

13. Similarly, create crease sets for the bottom and inner edges [see Figs. E22 and E23].

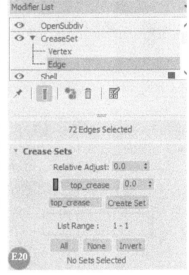

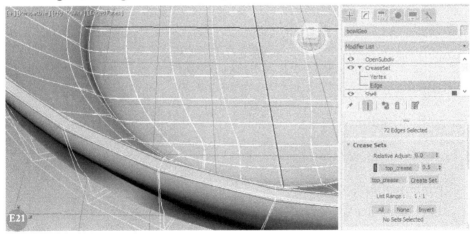

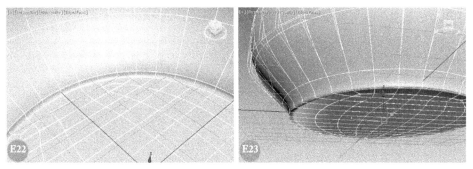

14. From the **Modifier List > Object-Space Modifiers** section, choose **Edit Poly**. From the **Modifier List > Object-Space Modifiers** section, choose **Taper**. In the modifier stack display, expand **Taper** and click on **Gizmo** sub-object. Click **Select and Uniform Scale** on the **Main** toolbar and then scale down the gizmo [see Fig. E24]. Exit **Taper's** sub-object level.

15. In the **Parameters** rollout, set **Amount** to **0.26** and **Curve** to **-0.93**. Also, set **Primary** to X and **Effect** to X [see Fig. E25].

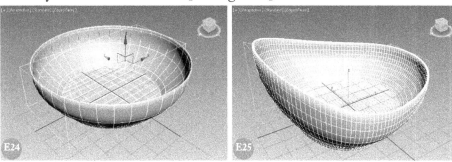

What just happened?

*I have applied the **Taper** modifier to change the shape of the bowl. This modifier produces a tapered contour by scaling the ends of the geometry. The **Taper's** gizmo allows you to manipulate the result. Amount controls the extent of scaling. The controls in the **Primary** group define the central axis for taper. **Effect** determines the direction of taper.*

Exercise 7: Creating a Kitchen Cabinet

In this exercise, we will create model of a kitchen cabinet [see Fig. E1].

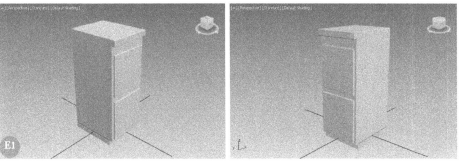

The following table summarizes the exercise:

Table E7	
Skill level	Beginner
Time to complete	20 Minutes
Topics in the section:	• Specifying the Units for the Exercise • Creating the Kitchen Cabinet
Project folder	**unit-m4**
Units	**Metric - Centimeters**
Final exercise file	**kitchen-cabinet-finish.max**

Specifying the Units for the Exercise
Follow these steps:

1. From **Customize** menu choose **Units Setup**. In the **Units Setup** dialog box that opens, select **Metric** from the **Display Unit Scale** group. Next, select **Centimeters** from the drop-down list located below **Metric**, if already not selected. Click **OK**.

2. From the **File** menu, choose **Save** to open the **Save File As** dialog box. In the **File name** text box type **kitchen-cabinet-finish.max** and then click **Save** to save the file.

Creating the Cabinet
Follow these steps:

1. In the **Create** panel, click **Geometry** and then on the **Object Type** rollout, click **Box**. Create a box in the **Top** viewport. Go to the **Modify** panel and then in the **Parameters** rollout, set **Length** to **38**, **Width** to **45**, and **Height** to **76**. Set the **Transform Type-In** boxes in the **Status Bar** to **0** to place the box at the origin [see Fig. E2].

2. Convert the **Box001** to the **Editable Poly** object. Select the top and bottom polygons of the box [see Fig. E3] and then click **Detach** from the **Modify** panel > **Edit Geometry** rollout. Click **OK** in the **Detach** dialog box to create a new object from the selected polygons with the name **Object001**.

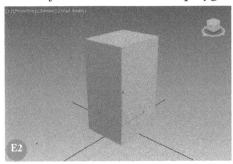
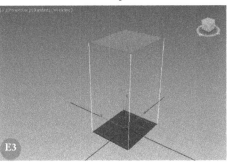

3. Select **Object001** from **Scene Explorer** and activate **Polygon** sub-object level. Now, select top and bottom polygons of **Object001**. Click **Settings** on the right of **Extrude** in the **Modify panel > Edit Polygons** rollout. In the **Extude's** caddy, set **Height** to **5** and click **OK** [see Fig. E4]. Select the polygon, as shown in Fig. E5 and then move it by **3** units in the positive X direction [see Fig. E6].

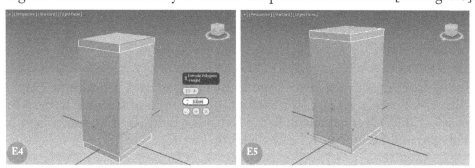

4. Select the top polygon and then click **Settings** on the right of **Extrude** in the **Modify** panel > **Edit Polygons** rollout. In the **Extude's** caddy, set **Height** to **5** and click **OK** [see Fig. E7].

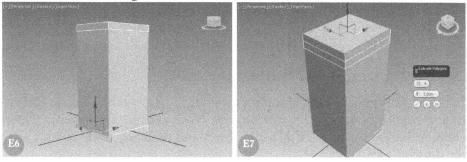

5. Similarly extrude the front polygon by **3** units [refer Fig. E8]. Select **Box001** from **Scene Explorer** and then activate the **Edge** sub-object level. Select the edges, as shown in Fig. E9.

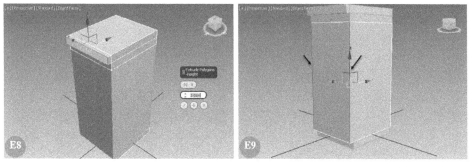

6. Click **Connect** in the **Modify** panel > **Edit Edges** rollout to connect the selected edges [see Fig. E10]. Select the polygons as shown in Fig. E11 and then click **Settings** on the right of **Inset** in the **Modify** panel > **Edit Polygons** rollout.

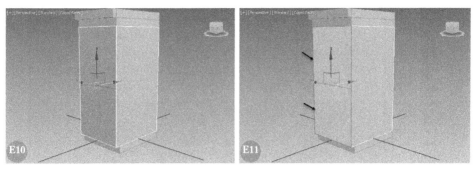

7. In the **Inset's** caddy, set **Inset Type** to **By Polygon**, and **Amount** to **2** and then click **OK** [see Fig. E12]. Click **Settings** on the right of **Extrude** in the **Modify** panel > **Edit Polygons** rollout. In the **Extrude's** caddy, set **Extrusion Type** to **By Polygon** and **Height** to **1.5** and click **OK** [see Fig. E13].

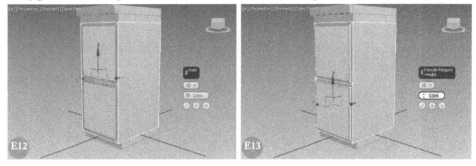

8. In the **Modify** panel > **Edit Geometry** rollout, click **Attach**. Click on **Object001** in a viewport to attach the two objects. Now, rename the resulting mesh as **cabinetGeo**. Activate the **Edge** sub-object and then select the outside edges of the drawers [see Fig. E14].

9. In the **Modify** panel > **Edit Edges** rollout, click **Chamfer** > **Settings** to open the **Chamfer** caddy control. In the caddy control, change **Chamfer type** to **Quad Chamfer**, **Amount** to **0.3** and then click **OK** [see Fig. E15].

Exercise 8: Creating a Book

In this exercise, we will create model of a book [see Fig. E1].

Table E8 summarizes the exercise:

Table E8	
Skill level	Beginner
Time to complete	20 Minutes
Topics in the section:	• Specifying the Units for the Exercise • Creating the Book
Project folder	**unit-m4**
Units	**US Standard – Decimal Inches**
Final exercise file	**book-finish.max**

Specifying the Units for the Exercise

Follow these steps:

1. From **Customize** menu choose **Units Setup**. In the **Units Setup** dialog box that opens, select **US Standard** from the **Display Unit Scale** group. Next, select **Decimal Inches** from the drop-down list located below **US Standard** and then click **OK** to accept the change.

2. From the **File** menu, choose **Save** to open the **Save File As** dialog box. In the **File name** text box type **book-finish.max** and then click **Save** to save the file.

Creating the Book

Follow these steps:

1. In the **Create** panel, click **Geometry** and then on the **Object Type** rollout, click **Box**. Create a box in the **Top** viewport. Go to the **Modify** panel, and in the **Parameters** rollout, set **Length** to **7.44**, **Width** to **9.69**, and **Height** to **2**. Set the **Transform Type-In** boxes in the **Status Bar** to **0** to place the box at the origin. Now, rename the box as **bookGeo**.

2. RMB click on **bookGeo**. In the **transform** quadrant of the **Quad** menu that appears, choose **Convert To: Convert to Editable Poly**. Click **Edge** in the **Modify** panel > **Selection** rollout and then select the edge shown in Fig. E2. Click **Ring** to select the edge ring [see Fig. E3].

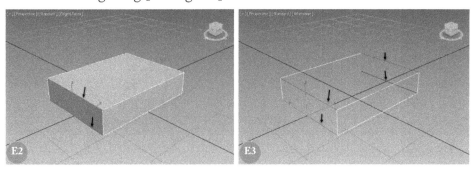

3. Click **Settings** on the right of **Connect** in the **Edit Edges** rollout. In the **Connect's** caddy, set **Slide** to **95** [see Fig. E4] and then click **OK** to connect the selected edges. Similarly, add four edge loops [**Segments: 4, Slide: 0**] to the part of the book that will make up the pages [see Fig. E5].

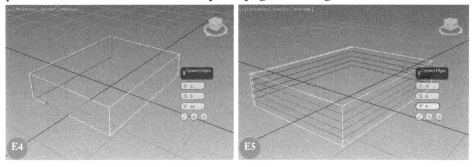

4. Click **Polygon** in the **Modify** panel > **Selection** rollout and then select the polygons shown in Fig. E6. Click **Settings** on the right of **Inset** in the **Edit Polygons** rollout. In the **Inset's** caddy, set **Amount** to **0.08** [see Fig. E7] and then click **OK** to inset the polygons.

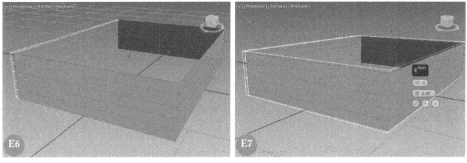

5. Click **Settings** on the right of **Extrude** in the **Edit Polygons** rollout. In the **Extrude's** caddy, set **Group** to **Local Normal** and **Height** to **-0.129** [see Fig. E8] and then click **OK** to extrude the polygons. Click **Edge** in the **Modify** panel > **Selection** rollout and then select all outer edges of the cover shown in Fig. E9.

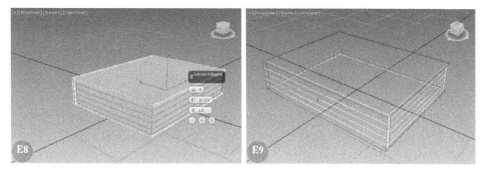

6. Click **Settings** on the right of **Chamfer** in the **Edit Edges** rollout. In the **Chamfer's** caddy, set **Chamfer Type** to **Quad Chamfer**, **Edge Chamfer Amount** to **0.01** and **Connect Edge Segments** to **2** [see Fig. E10] and then click **OK** to chamfer the edges. Click **Vertex** in the **Modify** panel > **Selection** rollout and then select the vertices in the Left viewport, as shown in Fig. E11.

7. Invoke the **Select** tool from the **Main** toolbar and then adjust the vertices in the **Left** viewport to modify the shape of the book [see Fig. E12].

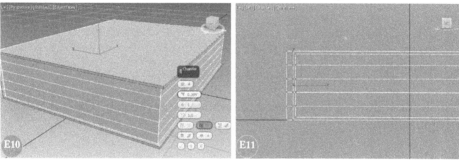

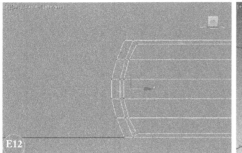 

Quiz

Evaluate your skills to see how many questions you can answer correctly.

Multiple Choice
Answer the following questions, only one choice is correct.

1. Which the following keys is used to add to the sub-object selection of a polygonal object?

    [A] Alt   [B] Ctrl
    [C] Alt+Ctrl   [D] Shift

2. Which the following keys is used to remove from the sub-object selection of a polygonal object?

    [A] Alt   [B] Ctrl
    [C] Alt+Ctrl   [D] Shift

3. Which the following keys is used to repeat the last command?

    [A] '   [B] .
    [C] >   [D] ;

4. Which of the following keys is used to enable polygon selection highlighting?

    [A] F3   [B] F2
    [C] F9   [D] F8

Fill in the Blanks

Fill in the blanks in each of the following statements:

1. The editable poly object is an editable object with five sub-object levels: _____, _____, _____, _____, and _____.

2. The editable poly object is similar to the edit mesh object with the only difference is that the edit mesh object comprises of _____ faces whereas the editable poly object comprises of polygons with any number of vertices.

3. When you convert an object to an editable poly object, you loose all of its creation parameters. If you want to retain the creation parameters, use the _____ modifier.

4. You can use the numeric keys from _____ to _____ to activate the Vertex, Edge, Border, Polygon, and Element sub-object levels, respectively. Press _____ to return to the Object level.

5. The _____ command allows you to attach other geometries to the selected poly object.

6. If a face is selected and you use the _____ key instead of _____, 3ds Max can create holes in the poly mesh.

True of False

State whether each of the following is true or false:

1. You can lock a sub-object selection by pressing **Spacebar**.

2. If you are working with an editable object such as mesh, poly, patch, or spline, you can directly manipulate the selection using the transformations tools.

3. When you **Shift**+Transform [move, scale, or rotate] a sub-object selection, the **Clone of Mesh** dialog box appears.

Summary

The unit covered the following topics:

- Working with the polygon modeling tools
- Using the polygon modeling techniques
- Selecting polygon sub-object
- Transforming sub-objects
- Soft selecting sub-objects

- Working with **Graphite Modeling Tools**
- Selecting sub-objects
- Creating models using the tools available in the **Ribbon**

Unit M5: Graphite Modeling Tools

In the previous unit, I covered everything you need to know about modeling with polygons. You created geometric primitives and converted them into editable poly objects and then used the tools and commands available in the **Command** panel to create the models. 3ds Max provides another workflow for creating and editing polygons based on the **Ribbon** interface. If you have worked with any other Autodesk product such as products from the **Revit** family, you might be aware of the **Ribbon** interface. In this unit, I describe the tools available in the **Ribbon** interface and how you can use them to improve your modeling workflow.

The Ribbon

The **Graphite Modeling** tools are available in the **Ribbon**. These tools offer vide variety of features for editing polygons. The **Ribbon** comprises all standard **Editable Poly** tools and some additional tools for creating, selecting, and editing geometries. By default, **Ribbon** sits on top of the viewports in the collapsed state [see Fig. 1].

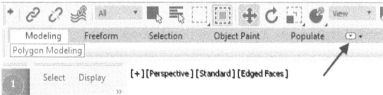

To expand **Ribbon**, either double-click on the empty gray area of the **Ribbon** or click **Show Full Ribbon** [marked with an arrow in Fig. 1]. The **Ribbon** with the **Modeling** tab appears [see Fig. 2].

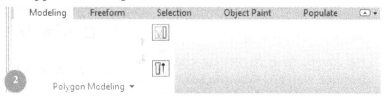

Tip: Toggling display of Ribbon
If **Ribbon** is not visible, click the **Show Ribbon** button on the **Main** toolbar or choose **Show UI** > **Show Ribbon** from the **Customize** menu.

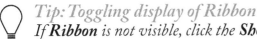 *Tip: Docking Ribbon to the right*
*You can doc the **Ribbon** on the left or right of the interface [see Fig. 3].*

Each tab in **Ribbon** comprises various panels such as the **Polygon Modeling** panel in the **Modeling** tab [marked with an arrow in Fig. 4]. The display of panel in the tab is context sensitive. To view other panels in the tab, create a primitive in a viewport and then covert it to **Editable Poly**.

When you click on the arrow on the right of the panel's name, the panel expands revealing the tools and commands available in that panel. Fig. 4 shows the expanded **Polygon Modeling** panel. Click on **Polygon Modeling** to collapse the panel [marked with an arrow in Fig. 4].

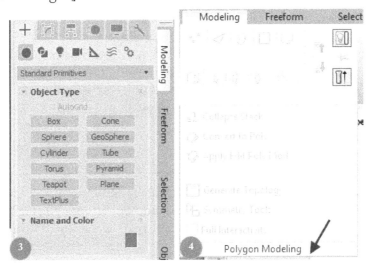

Table 1 summarizes the tabs available in the **Ribbon**.

Table 1: The tabs available in the **Ribbon**	
Tab	**Description**
Modeling	The tools in this tab are mainly used for polygon modeling. These tools are organized in different panels for easy access.
Freeform	This tab contains tools for creating and modifying geometry by painting on the surface of a geometry. You can also specify settings for paint brushes from this tab.
Selection	The special tools in this tab allow you to make sub-object selection in a unique way. For example, select sub-objects from a concave or convex area, and select sub-objects that face the viewport.

Table 1: The tabs available in the **Ribbon**	
Tab	**Description**
Object Paint	The tools available in this tab allow you to freehand paint objects anywhere in the scene.
Populate	This tab provides tools for adding animated pedestrians and idlers in the scene.

Tip: Tools help

*3ds Max provides extended tooltip for the tools available in the **Ribbon**. Position the mouse pointer on a tool; 3ds Max displays a smaller tooltip. If you place the mouse pointer on a tool for little longer, 3ds Max expands the tooltip and sometimes you will also see an illustration in the tooltip. Fig. 5 shows an expanded tooltip when mouse pointer was placed on the **Ring** tool.*

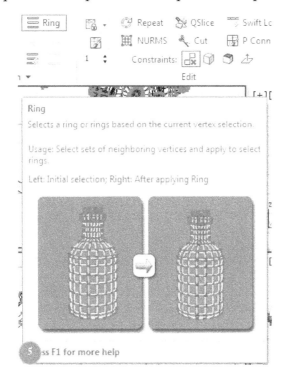

Modeling Tab

The **Modeling** tab contains the tools that you will use with the polygon models. These tools are organized in separate panels for easy access. Most of the tools in this tab are clones of the polygon editing tools found in the **Command** panel. The best way to understand these tools is to practice them. You will use these tools in the hands-on exercises of this unit.

Freeform Tab

The **Freeform** tab [see Fig. 6] provides tools for creating and modifying geometry by painting on the surface of a geometry. This tab contains three panels: **PolyDraw**, **Paint Deform**, and **Defaults**. These panels are discussed next.

PolyDraw Panel

The tools in this panel allow you to quickly sketch or edit a mesh in the main grid. You can also sketch on the surface of another object or on the object itself. This panel also provides tools for molding one object to the shape of another object. Before we explore the tools, let's understand the **Conform Options** panel which is always displayed when a conform brush tool is active.

Conform Options Panel

The options in this panel [see Fig. 7] let you specify the settings for modifying tool's effects. When any conform brush tool other than the **Conform Brush** is active, the panel is named **Transform Conform Options**. Also, an additional toggle appears with the name **Offset Relative**.

Here's the quick rundown to the options available in the **Conform Options** panel.

Full Strength: Defines the size of the center area represented by a white circle in the brush [see Fig. 8]. The **Strength %** setting [see Fig. 7] is fully applied in this area. To adjust the brush size interactively, **Shift+drag**.

Falloff: Falloff is represented by the bigger black circle [see Fig. 8]. The **Strength** in this circle decreases from full strength to zero. To adjust the brush size interactively, **Ctrl+drag**.

Conform: It defines the rate at which the **Conform** brush deforms the painted object. Higher the values you specify for this option, instant will be the conforming effect.

Mirror: When **Mirror** is active, the tool's effect is applied equally to both sides [see Fig. 9] across the mirror axis defined by the **Mirror Axis** attribute.

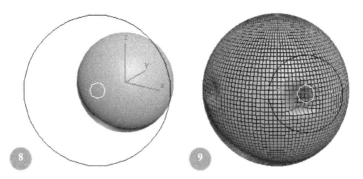

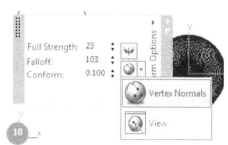

View/ Vertex Normals: These two options [see Fig. 10] control the direction in which the Conform brush moves the vertices. View pushes vertices away from the screen therefore it is dependent on the view angle of the scene. Vertex Normals pushes the vertices along their own normal toward the target.

Offset Relative: This brush is only available when you use one of the transform conform brushes. When on, it helps you in retaining the original shape of the object.

Strength %: This option defines the overall rate at which a brush deforms an object. To interactive change the value for this option, Shift+Alt+drag.

Use Selected Verts: When on, the deform tools only affect the selected vertices. When off, it affects all vertices of the object.

Ignore Backfacing: When on, the tools affects vertices facing you.

Mirror Axis X/Y/Z: Allow you to choose the axis across which the conform action will be mirrored.

Freeze Axis X/Y/Z: When any Freeze Axis button is active, the tool is prevented from moving vertices on the corresponding axis of the object. To limit the effect to a particular axis, turn on Freeze Axis for other two axes.

Freeze Selected Edges X/Y/Z: When any Freeze Selected Edges button is active, the tool is prevented from moving edges on the corresponding axis of the object. The un-selected edges move freely. These options apply to all sub-objects levels.

PolyDraw Panel - Drag and Conform Tools

The tools in this panel [see Fig. 11] produce different effects depending on which combination keys [Ctrl, Alt, and Shift] you press. Although, PolyDraw tools do not require you to select any sub-object level, however, it is recommended that you use these tools at the Vertex sub-object level for better results.

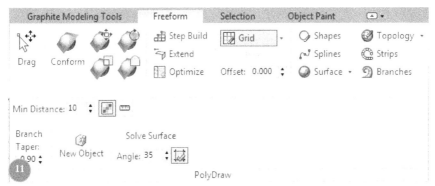

The **Min Distance** control allow you to specify a distance you need to drag the mouse before the next step in the tool is taken. There are two buttons available on the right of the **Min Distance** control: **in Pixels** and **in Units**. You can use these buttons to specify the minimum distance in pixels and world units, respectively.

The **Branch Taper** control allows you to specify the amount by which the branches taper as you draw them. On clicking the **New Object** button, 3ds Max creates a new empty editable object, activates the **Vertex** sub-object level, and keeps the current **PolyDraw** tool active. Now, you can use the **PolyDraw** tools to add geometry.

On clicking the **Solve Surface** button, 3ds Max attempts to create a workable mesh composed of mostly quads. You can use this tool to clean up the mesh after using tools such as **Draw Polygon Shapes**.

Drag: You can use the **Drag** tool to move sub-objects on a surface or grid. Table 2 summarizes the functions available with this tool.

Table 2: Functions of the **Drag** tool	
Function	**Description**
Normal	Without any modifier keys this tool move vertices by dragging them.
Shift	Moves edges.
Ctrl+Drag	Moves polygons.
Shift+Ctrl+Drag	Moves edge loops.
Shift+Ctrl+Alt+Drag	Moves elements.

You can also use this tool to move the sub-objects in screen space [perpendicular to the current view selection]. Table 3 shows these functions.

Table 3: Functions of the **Drag** tool in the screen space	
Function	**Description**
Alt+Drag	Moves vertices.
Alt+Shift+Drag	Moves edges.
Alt+Ctrl+Drag	Moves polygons.

Conform Brush: The **Conform** brushes move the conform object's vertices towards the target to mold a conform object into the shape of the target object. You can use these brushes in variety of modeling scenarios such as painting a road on a hilly terrain or painting a mask on the face of a character.

To conform an object to the target object. Select the object that you want to conform. Activate the **Vertex** sub-object level for better control. Select **Draw On: Surface** from the **Draw On** drop-down list [Surface ▾] on the **PolyDraw** panel. Click **Pick** and then click the target object in a viewport. The name of the object appears on the **Pick** [Pick] button. Click **Conform**, adjust brush size and strength and then drag the object toward the target using the **Conform** brush. The selected object takes shape of the target object. In Fig. 12, I have conformed a **Plane** primitive to a **Sphere** primitive.

12

Apart from the basic **Conform** brush that is described above, 3ds Max also provides four transformed based variants: **Move Conform Brush** , **Rotate Conform Brush** , **Scale Conform Brush** , and **Relax Conform Brush** . The **Relax Conform Brush** applies a relax effect to the vertices within a spherical volume.

PolyDraw Panel - Add Geometry and Optimize Tools

Step Build: This tool works at the **Object** level as well as the sub-objects level. You can use this tool to build a surface vertex by vertex or polygon by polygon. Table 4 summarizes the functions of this tool.

Table 4: Functions of the **Step Build** tool	
Function	**Description**
Normal	Click to place vertices on the grid or surface.
Shift+Drag	Drag over the floating vertices to fill the gaps with quad polygons.
Ctrl+Click	Click on a polygon to delete it.
Alt+Click	Click on a vertex to remove it.
Ctrl+Alt+Click	Click on an edge to remove it.
Ctrl+Shift+Click	Click to place and select vertices. You can also select the existing vertices.
Shift+Alt	Move the mouse pointer [do not drag] over the vertices to select them.
Ctrl+Shift+Alt	Drag mouse pointer to move a vertex on a grid or surface.

Caution: Vertex Ticks

*When the **Step Build** tool is active, vertex ticks are not always visible in the viewport. If you don't see the ticks at levels other than the **Vertex** level, change the display of the object to **By Object** in the object's display properties.*

Extend Tool: You can use this tool with the open edges that are on the border of the surface that have only one polygon attached. Table 5 summarizes the functions of this tool.

Table 5: Functions of the **Extend** tool	
Function	**Description**
Normal	Drag a border vertex to create a polygon.
Shift+Drag	Drag a border edge to create a polygon.
Ctrl+Shift+Drag	Drag an edge to extend its entire loop.
Ctrl+Alt+Drag	Drag between two edges to create a polygon.
Ctrl+Click	Click to delete a polygon and associated isolated vertices.
Ctrl+Shift+Alt+Drag	Drag a vertex to move it on the surface or grid.
Alt+Drag (Screen Space)	Drag a border to create a polygon.
Alt+Shift+ Drag (Screen Space)	Drag a border edge to create a polygon.

Optimize Tool: This tool is used to remove the details from the model by drawing on it. Table 6 shows the functions of this tool.

Table 6: Functions of the **Optimize** tool	
Function	**Description**
Normal	Click on the edges to collapse. It merges two vertices into one.
Shift+Drag	Drag from one vertex to another to weld them.
Ctrl+Drag	Drag between the vertices to connect them.
Alt+Click	Click to remove a vertex.
Shift+Ctrl+Click	Click to remove an edge loop.
Shift+Alt+Click	Click to remove a ring.
Ctrl+Alt+Click	Click on an edge to remove it.
Shift+Ctrl+Alt+Drag	Drag on a vertex to move it.

Draw On: The options in this drop-down list allow you to choose the entity type on which you want to draw. The **Grid** ⊞ option creates geometry on the grid of the active viewport. This option works well with the orthographic views, however, you can also use it in the **Perspective** viewport. The **Surface** ⊘ option allows you to draw on another object that you specify. The **Selection** ⊘ option lets you create geometry on the selected object.

Pick: This button lets you pick an object to draw on. To pick object, choose **Surface** from the **Draw On** drop-down list and then click **Pick**. Now, click on the object to draw on.

Offset: It specifies the distance that **PolyDraw** uses for creating the geometry.

PolyDraw Panel - Create Geometry Tools

Shapes: You can use this tool to draw polygons on a surface or grid. Click **Solve Surface** after creating the polygon to generate a workable mesh. The **Solve Surface** option will be displayed when you expand the **PolyDraw** panel [see Fig. 13].

When **Shapes** is active, you can delete a polygon by clicking on it with the **Ctrl** held down. To move a polygon, drag the mouse pointer with **Ctrl+Shift+Alt** held down.

Topology: This tool is used to create quad polygons by drawing lines in a viewport. As you draw the quads using this tool, 3ds Max fills them with a polygon. To draw the mesh, pick **Topology** and then draw lines in a viewport. When you are done with the lines, **RMB** click to complete the operation [see Fig. 14].

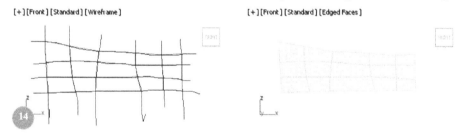

The drop-down list associated with **Topology** contains an option, **Auto Weld**. When **Auto Weld** is selected, 3ds Max automatically attaches the mesh to the selected object and weld their border vertices. If **Auto Weld** is off, **Topology** always creates a new mesh. The **Minimum Distance** control available in the expanded **PolyDraw** panel defines the resolution of the lines. The default value for this control is **10** which works well in most of the cases. When **Topology** is active, you can **Shift+Drag** to continue a line from the closest endpoint. To delete a line, click on it with **Ctrl** held down.

Splines: This tool draws a spline on a surface or grid. The splines created using this tool are renderable. Select the desired option from the **Draw On** drop-down list and then draw to create splines. All splines are combined into single [separate] object. When **Splines** is active, you can delete a spline by clicking on it with the **Ctrl** held down. You can also move a spline to the closest splines by dragging it with **Ctrl+Shift+Alt** held down.

Strips: This tool can be used to quickly layout the topology foundation for a mesh object. It paints strips of polygons that follow the mouse drag direction [see Fig. 15]. If you press **Shift** before starting the painting, 3ds Max paints from the closest existing edge. If you want to create polygon between two open edges, press **Alt** and then drag between the two open edges.

Surface: This tool paints a surface onto an object or grid. The size of the surface polygons are controlled by the **Minimum Distance** setting available in the expanded **PolyDraw** panel. The drop-down list associated with **Surface** has an option, **Quads.** When **Quads** is selected, the surface is made up of quads. When off, 3ds Max creates surface with triangles. To start the surface from an existing border edge, hold **Shift** before you start the drawing. It ensures that overlapping polygons are not created. To delete a polygon, click on it with the **Shift** held down; the associated isolated vertices are also deleted.

Branches: This tool creates multi-segmented extrusions from polygons [see Fig. 16]. This tool works only on the selected object and **Draw On** settings does not affect it. The extent of tapering of the branches is controlled by the **Branch Taper** setting available in the expanded **PolyDraw** panel. To create branches, drag the mouse pointer on the selected object, 3ds Max creates branches from the polygons closest to the mouse pointer. Press **Shift** to draw branches from all the selected polygons. If you are at the **Polygon** level, click with **Ctrl** held down to select a polygon. You can also select/de-select additional polygons with **Shilft+Alt** held down.

Paint Deform Panel

The tools in this panel [see Fig. 17] give you ability to deform mesh geometry interactively in the viewport. These tools works similarly for at the **Object** level as well at the sub-object level and are independent of any sub-object selection. To exit any tool, either click the its button or RMB click in a viewport. Let's explore various deformation tools available in 3ds Max.

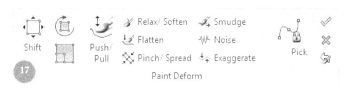

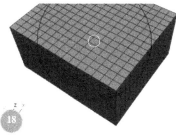 Shift/ Shift Rotate/ Shift Scale

These tools are used to move, rotate, or scale objects in the screen space [see Fig. 18]. These tools are like using the standard transformation tools with soft selection. However, with these tools no initial selection is required. You can revert to previous state by using the **Revert** tool. However, this tool only works if you have used any other deform tool such as **Push/Pull**.

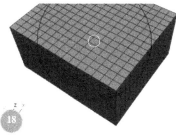 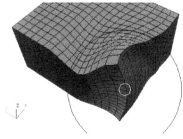

Push/Pull

This tool drags the vertices outward [see the left image in Fig. 19]. To move vertices inward, drag with the **Alt** held down [see the right image in Fig. 19]. When this tool is active you can use:

- **Ctrl** to revert to the previous saved state.
- **Shift** to relax the mesh.
- **Ctrl+Shift** to resize the brush
- **Shift+Alt** to change the strength of the brush.

Note: The Paint Options panel
*When you use any deform tool except **Shift** tools, the floating **Paint Options** panel appears [see Fig. 20]. You can use the settings from this panel to control the behavior of the deform tools.*

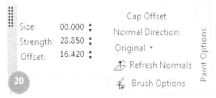

Relax/Soften

This tool allows you to soften the corners [see Fig. 21]. With other brushes, you can soften a geometry with **Shift** held down.

Smudge

The **Smudge** tool is used to move the vertices [see Fig. 22]. It is somewhat similar to the **Shift** tool however it updates the effect continuously. Also, it does not use falloff.

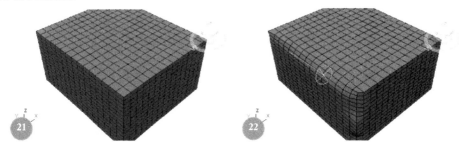

Flatten

This tool lets you flatten the concave and convex areas.

Pinch/Spread

You can use this tool to move vertices together or spread them apart. To spread, drag with the **Alt** held down.

Noise

You can use this tool to add convex noise to a surface [see Fig. 23]. To create concave noise, drag with **Alt** held down.

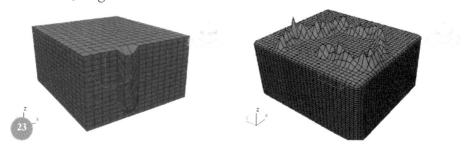

Exaggerate

This tool makes the features of the surface more pronounced by moving the convex areas outward and concave areas inward.

Constrain to Spline

Apart from the **Shift** tools, all other tools can use a spline as a path for mesh deformation. Create a spline and place it near the surface you want to deform [see left image in Fig. 24]. Click **Pick** available below **Constrain to Spline** and then click on the spline in a viewport.

Make sure **Constrain to Spline** is active then pick a deform tool such as **Noise**. Now, when you paint on the object, the deform gizmo can only be moved along the spline. Drag the mouse pointer to create the deformation [see right image in Fig. 24].

Defaults Panel

You can use this panel to save and load brush settings. The **Load All Brush Settings** option opens a dialog box that you can use to load brush settings from an existing file. The **Save All Brush Settings** option opens a dialog box that you can use to store brush settings to a file. The **Set Current Settings as Default** option saves the current brush settings as default.

Selection Tab

The **Selection** tab provides a wide array of tools that allow you to make sub-object selection such as you can select convex and concave areas, you can select the sub-object that face the camera, and so forth. Let's explore the various panels available in the **Selection** tab.

Select Panel

The tools in this panel lets you select the sub-object based on the certain topologies. Table 7 summarizes the tools available in this panel.

Table 7: The tools available in the Select panel		
Tool	**Icon**	**Description**
Tops		This tool selects the top of the extruded polygon. The selection depends on the active sub-object level. When the **Vertex, Edge**, or **Polygon** sub-object level is active, the vertices, edge outlines, or tops of the extruded polygons are selected. Fig. 25 shows the top of the extruded polygons selected.
Open		This tool selects all open sub-objects [see Fig. 26]. The final result depends on the active sub-object.
Hard		This tool is available at the **Edge** sub-object level. It selects all edges in a model whose faces do not share the same smoothing groups.
Non-Quads		This tool selects all non-quadrilateral polygons. This tool is available at **Polygon** sub-object level.

Table 7: The tools available in the **Select** panel		
Tool	**Icon**	**Description**
Patterns	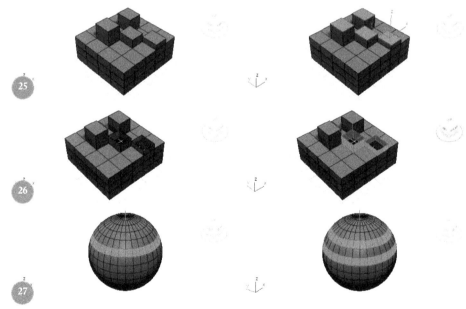 (icon)	This tool allows you to grow the current selection based on the pattern you select from the **Pattern** drop-down list. The **Pattern 1** through **8** options provide different selection patterns. Make a selection in the viewport and then experiment with various patterns. **Growlines** grows the selection with gaps of unselected lines [see Fig. 27]. **Checker** grows selection in from of a checker board pattern [see Fig. 28]. **Dots** grows the selection such that all sub-objects have gap between them [see Fig. 29]. **One Ring** grows a single polygon ring around the initial selection [see Fig. 30].
By Vertex	-	When you click a vertex using this tool, all sub-objects that use the clicked vertex are selected.
By Angle	-	When on and if you select a polygon, the neighboring polygons are also selected based on the value you set in the spinner available on the right of **By Angle**.
By Material ID	-	It opens the **Material ID** dialog box that you can use to set the material IDs. Also, you can select by ID and material name using this dialog box.
By Smoothing Group	-	It displays a dialog box that shows the current smoothing groups. To select polygon associated with a group, click the corresponding smoothing group.

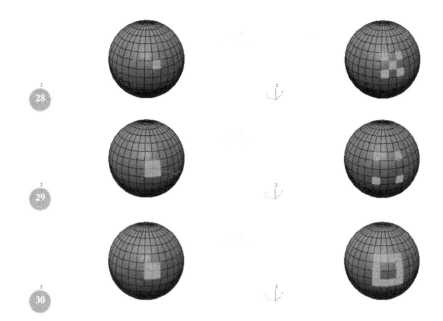

Stored Selection Panel

The options in this panel let you quickly and easily store and retrieve selections. You can also apply some basic operations between the stored selections. Table 8 summarizes the tools available in this panel.

Table 8: The tools available in the **Stored Selection** panel		
Tool	**Icon**	**Description**
Copy Store 1/ Copy Store 2		You can use these two buffers to place the current sub-object selection. When a buffer contains a selection, the associated button turns blue.
Paint Store 1/ Paint Store 2		These two tools restores the stored selection, clearing the existing selection. If you want to retain the current selection, click on these buttons with the **Shift** held down.
Add 1+2		It adds the two buffers and applies the selection at the current sub-object level.
Subtract 1-2		It selects non-overlapping area of **Store 1** and also clears both buffers.
Intersect		Selects the overlapping area of **Store 1** and **Store 2**.
Clear		Clears the stored selection.

Sets Panel

The tools in this panel gives you ability to copy and paste the named selection sets between objects. To use these tools, create named selection sets and then use the **Copy** and **Paste** tools from this panel to copy/paste selection from buffer.

By Surface Panel

The **Concave** ⬚/**Convex** ⬚ tools allow you to select sub-objects in the concave or convex area of the mesh [see Fig. 31]. The spinner located next to the drop-down list allows you to specify the degree of concavity or convexity.

By Normal Panel

The tools in this panel let you select sub-objects based on their normal directions on the world axes. To make a selection, choose an axis and then set the value for the **Angle** control. You can invert the selection by clicking **Invert**. The selection shown in Fig. 32 is created by setting **Angle** to **87** and choosing the **Z** axis.

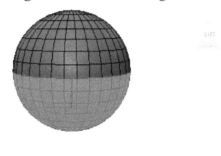

By Perspective Panel

The tools in this panel let you select sub-objects based on the extent they point toward the active view. To make a selection, define an angle using the **Angle** control and then click **Select** ⬚ [see left image in Fig. 33]. If you click **Outline** ⬚, 3ds Max selects the outermost sub-objects [see the right image in Fig. 33].

By Random Panel

The tools in this panel select sub-objects at random number or percentage. Also, you can grow or shrink the current selection randomly. To make a selection, click **Number** # or **Percent** % to enable random selection by number or percentage and then click **Select** to make the selection from the current settings. The **Select Within Current Selection** ⬚ option in the **Select** drop-down list selects random sub-objects within the current selection [see Fig. 34]. **Random Grow** ⬚ and **Random Shrink** ⬚ grows or shrinks the selection randomly.

By Half Panel

These tools let you select the half of the mesh on the specified axis based on the area or volume. To select, choose an axis and then click **Select** ⌖. To toggle the selection, click **Invert Axis** ⟳.

By Pivot Distance Panel

You can use this tool to select the sub-objects based on their distance from the pivot. The spinner in this panel defines the distance. In Fig. 35, the selection is defined by setting spinner to **99.2%**.

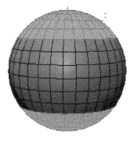

By View Panel

This feature allows you to select and grow sub-objects selection based on the current view. You can specify the distance using the **Grow From Perspective View** control.

By Symmetry Panel

You can use this feature to mirror the current sub-object selection on the specified local axis. This feature works on a symmetrical model. The center of the object is defined by the location of the pivot of the object.

By Color Panel

The options in this panel let you select vertices by color or illumination value. These options are available at only **Vertex** sub-object level. To select vertices, choose **Color** or **Illumination** from the drop-down list. Then, use the color swatch to specify a color. Next, click **Select** ⌖ to select the vertices.

By Numeric Panel

This feature allows you to select vertices by the number of connected edges or number of sides you specify. Fig. 36 shows the panel at the **Vertex** and **Polygon** levels, respectively. The

selection shown in Fig. 37 shows the selection made by specifying number of **Sides** to **4** at the **Polygon** level.

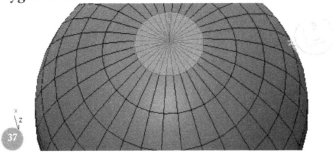

Object Paint Tab

The tools available in this tab [see Fig. 38] allow you to paint objects freehand anywhere in the scene or on the target objects. You can paint multiple objects in a specific order or randomly. The objects that you add by painting are not combined with other objects. You can use the **Fill** tool to fill an edge selection with the objects.

To understand the concept, create few primitives in the viewport and then create a teapot [see the left image in Fig. 39]. Ensure teapot is selected in a viewport and then click **Paint With Selected Object(s)** from the **Paint Objects** panel. Make sure **Scene** is selected from the **Paint On** drop-down list. Set **Spacing** to **15** and then freehand paint on the objects in the scene [see the right image in Fig. 39]. RMB click to exit the paint mode.

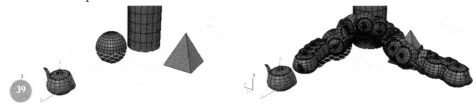

 Caution: Exiting the paint mode
You can adjust stroke after painting, therefore, do not RMB click to exit the paint mode until you are satisfied with the result.

You can use the features in the **Object Paint** tab to make creative scenes. You can also use them to populate the scenes with, for example, characters or trees. I would recommend that you practice these tools and then integrate these in your workflow to create creative artwork.

From the **File** menu, choose **Project > Create Default** to open the **Choose a folder** dialog box. In this dialog box, navigate to the **3dsmax2019projects** directory and then click **New Folder** and then rename the folder as **unit-m5**. Select the folder and then click **Select Folder** to create the project folder.

Exercise 1: Creating a Desk

In this exercise, we will model a desk [see Fig. E1].

 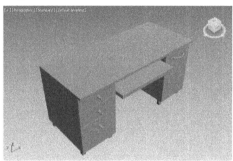

Table E1 summarizes the exercise.

Table E1	
Skill level	Intermediate
Time to complete	1 Hour
Topics in the section:	• Specifying the Units for the Exercise • Creating the Desk
Project folder	**unit-m5**
Units	**Metric - Centimeters**
Final exercise file	**desk-finish.max**

Specifying the Units for the Exercise

Follow these steps:

1. From **Customize** menu choose **Units Setup**. In the **Units Setup** dialog box that opens, select the **Metric** option from the **Display Unit Scale** group. Next, select **Centimeters** from the drop-down list located below the **Metric** option, if already not selected. Click **OK** to accept the change.

2. From the **File** menu, choose **Save** to open the **Save File As** dialog box. In the **File name** text box type **desk-finish.max** and then click **Save** to save the file.

Creating the Desk
Follow these steps:

1. In the **Create** panel, activate **Geometry**, then in the **Object Type** rollout, click **Box**. Create a box in the **Top** viewport. In the **Modify** panel > **Parameters** rollout, set **Length** to **60**, **Width** to **150**, and **Height** to **2.5**. Invoke the **Move** tool from the **Main** toolbar.

2. Set the **Transform Type-In** boxes to **0** on **Status Bar** to place the box at the origin. Create another box in the **Top** viewport. In the **Modify** panel > **Parameters** rollout, set **Length** to **60**, **Width** to **40**, and **Height** to **62**. Align the two boxes [see Fig. E2]. Create copy the box that you have just created and then align it [see Fig. E3].

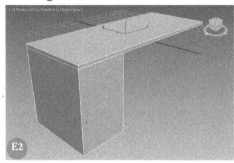 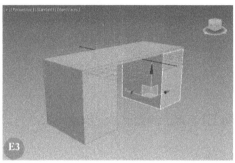

> *What next?*
> *Now, you will start using the tools and options available in the **Ribbon** to start shaping the desk. By default, the ribbon is minimized below the **Main** toolbar [see Fig. E4].*

3. Click **Show Full Ribbon** to display the full **Ribbon** [see Fig. E4]. You will notice that the tools in the **Polygon Modeling** panel are inactive because no polygon model exists in the scene [all objects are primitives at this stage]. To expand the **Polygon Modeling** panel and view all tools and options available in it, click **Polygon Modeling**. This action expands the panel and displays the tools available in it [see Fig. E5].

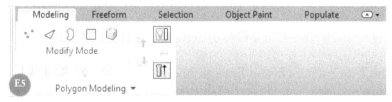

4. Select the top box. In the **Ribbon** > **Modeling** tab > **Polygon Modeling** panel, click **Convert to Poly** [refer to Fig. E6]. In the **Geometry (All)** panel, **Shift** click on **Attach**. In the **Attach List** dialog box that appears, select **Box002** and

Box003 using **Ctrl** and then click **Attach** to attach the selected boxes to the top box. Rename the unified geometry as **deskGeo**.

 Tip: Opening settings of a tool
*If you want to open settings for any tool available in **Ribbon**, **Shift** click on the tool.*

 Note: How materials of the objects are combined
*When you attach objects to a poly object, the materials of the objects are combined. If the objects being attached have no material, they inherit the material of the poly object. If the poly object that you are attaching to doesn't have a material, it inherits material of the objects being attached. In case, when both objects have materials, the resulting material is a new **Muti/Sub-object** material that includes the input materials.*

5. In the **Ribbon** > **Modeling** tab > **Polygon Modeling** panel, click **Edge**. Select the edge as shown in Fig. E7 and then in the **Ribbon** > **Modeling** tab > **Modify Selection** panel, click **Ring**. In the **Ribbon** > **Modeling** tab > **Loops** panel, click **Connect**. An edge loop appears.

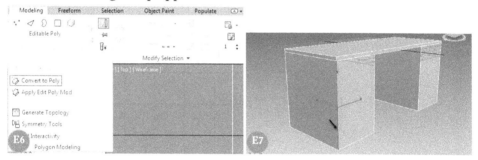

6. Select the edges shown in Fig. E8 and then connect them as done before [see Fig. E9]. Hold **Ctrl** and double-click on the edge loops that you created earlier to select them [see Fig. E10]. In the **Ribbon** > **Modeling** tab > **Edges** panel, **Shift** click on **Chamfer**. In the **Chamfer** caddy control, set **Edge Chamfer Amount** to **0.2** and then click **OK** [see Fig. E11].

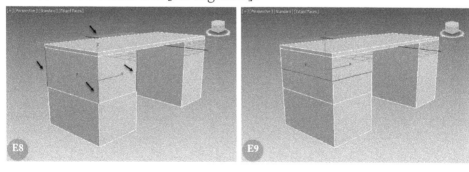

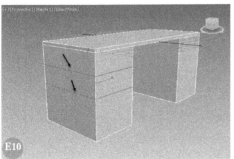
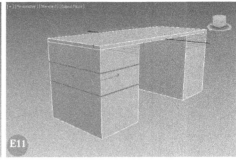

7. In the **Ribbon** > **Modeling** tab > **Polygon Modeling** panel, click **Polygon**. Select the polygons [see Fig. E12]. Invoke the **Move** tool from the **Main** toolbar. In the **Perspective** viewport, press **Shift** and then move the selected polygon slightly [about 1.2 units] outward in the negative Y direction. Release **Shift**. In the **Clone Part of Mesh** dialog box that appears, type **drawerGeo** in the text box next to **Clone To Object** and click **OK**.

8. Ensure the **drawerGeo** is selected. From the **Modifier List** > **Object-Space Modifiers** section, choose **Shell**. In the **Parameters** rollout, set **Outer Amount** to **1.5**. Align the **drawerGeo** with the **deskGeo** [see Fig. E13]. Similarly, detach the polygon shown in Fig. E14.

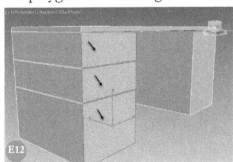
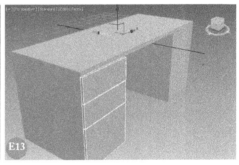

9. Name it as **drawerGeo1**, apply the **Shell** modifier and then align it with **deskGeo** [see Fig. E15]. Hide the drawer geometries from the scene using **Scene Explorer**. Now, we don't need the edges that we created earlier to create drawer therefore we will remove them to clean the model. Select those four edge loops and then press **Ctrl+Spacebar** to delete them.

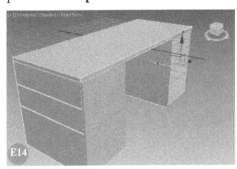
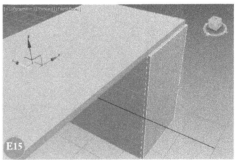

Tip: Removing Edges – Alternate Method

*In the **Ribbon** > **Modeling** tab > **Polygon Modeling** panel, click **Edge**. In the **Ribbon** > **Modeling** tab > **Edit** panel, click **Swift Loop** to make it active. Press **Ctrl+Shift** and then click on the edges on the drawers. This action will remove the edges.*

*The **SwiftLoop** tool allows you to interactively place edges. As you move the cursor over the object surface, a real-time preview is shown indicating that where the loop will be created when you click.*

Following are some different features of this tool:

■ ***Ctrl*** *click to select an edge loop and activate the **Edge** sub-object level automatically.*
■ ***Alt*** *drag a selected edge to slide the edge loop between its bounding loops. **Ctrl+Alt** drag is a same as the **Alt** drag. However, it also straighten out the edge loop, if necessary.*
■ ***Ctrl+Shift*** *click on a edge loop to remove it.*
■ ***Shift*** *click to insert a new loop and adjust it to the flow of the surrounding surface.*

10. Select **deskGeo** and activate the **Front** viewport. In the **Ribbon** > **Modeling** tab > **Polygon Modeling** panel, click **Edge**. In the **Ribbon** > **Modeling** tab > **Geometry (All)** panel, click **Slice Plane**. This action display a slice plane gizmo in the viewport and opens the **Slice Mode** panel. Adjust the position of the plane as shown in Fig. E16 and then click **Slice** on **Slice Mode** panel to subdivide the geometry [see Fig. E17].

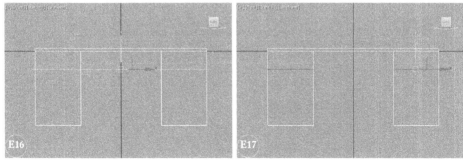

11. Similarly, add two more slices maintaining a gap of **2** units between them [see Fig. E18]. In the **Ribbon** > **Modeling** tab > **Polygon Modeling** panel, click **Polygon**. Select the polygons, refer to Fig. E19. In the **Ribbon** > **Modeling** tab > **Polygons** panel, **Shift** click **Extrude**. In the **Extrude's** caddy, set **Height** to **4** and click **OK**.

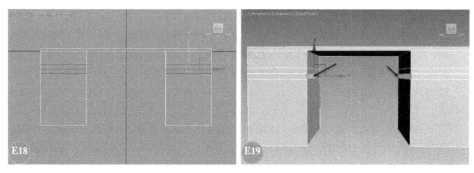

12. Select the polygons shown in Fig. E20. In the **Ribbon > Modeling** tab > **Geometry (All)** panel, click on **Detach**. In the **Detach** dialog box that appears, set **Detach as** to **sliderGeo**. Also, select the **Detach as Clone** check box and then click **OK**. Select **sliderGeo** and move it slightly toward the negative Y axis.

What just happened?
*The **Detach** tool separates the selected sub-objects and associated polygons as new object or element[s]. When you click **Detach**, the **Detach** dialog box appears. Type the name of the new object in the **Detach as** text box and click **OK** to create the new object with the specified name. The selection is removed from the original object. You can turn on **Detach To Element** to make the detached sub-object selection part of the original object but it becomes a new element. Select **Detach as Clone** to detach the selection as copy of the original selection; the selection remains intact with the original object.*

13. In the **Ribbon > Modeling** tab > **Polygon Modeling** panel, click **Polygon**. In the **Ribbon > Modeling** tab > **Polygons** panel, click **Bridge** to create a bridge between the selected polygons [see Fig. E21].

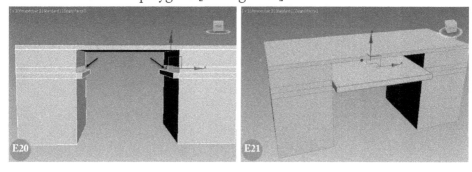

14. In the **Ribbon > Modeling** tab > **Polygon Modeling** panel, click **Border** and then select the border edges of **sliderGeo** [see Fig. E22]. In the **Ribbon > Modeling** tab > **Geometry (All)** panel, click on **Cap Poly** to cap the border edges.

15. Select **deskGeo** and then select the front polygon, refer to Fig. E23. Move it slightly toward the negative Y axis [see Fig. E23].

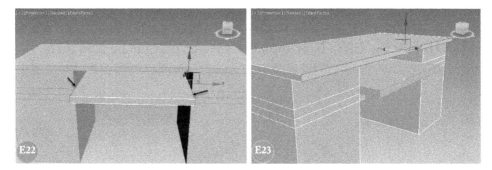

16. Ensure the **drawerGeo** and **drawerGeo1** are visible in the scene. In the **Create** panel, activate **Geometry**, then on the **Extended Primitives** > **Object Type** rollout, click **ChamferCyl**.

17. Create a cylinder in the **Top** viewport. In the **Modify** panel > **Parameters** rollout, set **Height** to **6**, **Radius** to **1.5**, and **Fillet** to **0.074**. Now, set **Height Segs** to **2**, **Fillet Segs** to **3**, and **Sides** to **18**. Align it with **drawerGeo** [see Fig. E24].

18. Select the cylinder and press **Alt+Q** to isolate it. In the **Ribbon** > **Modeling** tab > **Polygon Modeling** panel, click **Convert to Poly**. In the **Ribbon** > **Modeling** tab > **Modeling** panel, click **Edge**. Select the edge loop shown in Fig. E25.

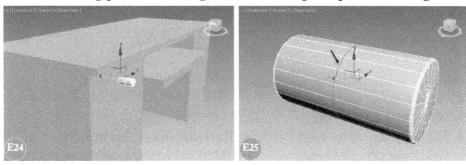

19. In the **Ribbon** > **Modeling** tab > **Edges** panel, **Shift** click on **Chamfer**. In the **Chamfer's** caddy, set **Edge Chamfer Amount** to **0.1** and click **OK** [see Fig. E26]. In the **Ribbon** > **Modeling** tab > **Polygon Modeling** panel, **Ctrl** click **Polygon**. In the **Ribbon** > **Modeling** tab > **Polygon Modeling** panel, click **Shrink** to select the polygons created using the chamfer edge operation [see Fig. E27].

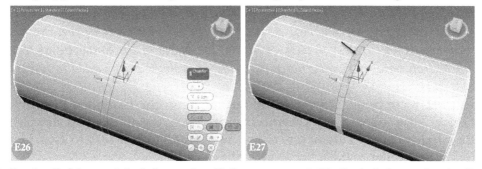

20. In the **Ribbon** > **Modeling** tab > **Polygons** panel, **Shift** click **Inset**. In the **Inset** caddy control, set **Amount** to **0.02** and click **OK** [see Fig. E28].

21. In the **Ribbon > Modeling** tab > **Polygons** panel, **Shift** click **Extrude**. In the **Extrude's** caddy, set **Extrusion Type** to **Local Normal** and **Height** to **-0.1**. Next, click **OK** [see Fig. E29]. Now, inset the selected polygon by **0.02** units.

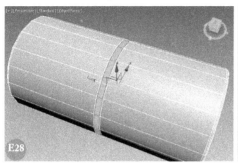
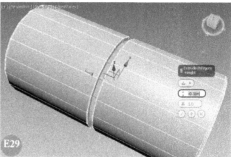

22. Now, select the edges that we created using the **Shift** and **Extrude** operations [see Fig. E30] and then scale them down by to **70%** [see Fig. E31]. In the **Ribbon > Modeling** tab > **Edit** panel, click **NURMS** to smooth the object Choose **End Isolate** from the **Tools** menu and then create two more copies of knob and align them [see Fig. E32].

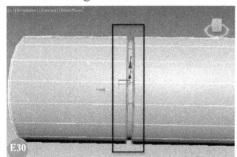
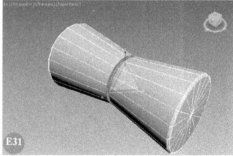

What just happened?
NURMS stands for **Non-Uniform Rational Mesh Smooth**. *This tool allows you to smooth the objects using* **NURMS** *subdivision; the same method used by the* **MeshSmooth** *and* **TurboSmooth** *modifiers. When you click* **NURMS**, *the* **NURMS** *panel appears. The* **Iterations** *spinner in this panel specifies the number of iterations used to smooth the poly object.*

Caution: Calculation Time
Specify the number of iterations carefully. It increases the number of vertices and polygons in the object. As a result, the calculation time can increase as much as four times for each iteration. The value in the **Smoothness** *spinner controls how sharp a corner must be before polygons are added to smooth it.*

23. In the **Create** panel, activate **Geometry**, then on the **Extended Primitives > Object Type** rollout, click **ChamferBox**. Create a box in the **Top** viewport. In the **Modify** panel > **Parameters** rollout, set **Length** to **2**, **Width** to **26.4**, **Height** to **1.5**, and **Fillet** to **0.05**. Set **Width Segs** to **12**.

24. From the **Modifier List** > **Object-Space Modifiers** section, choose **Bend**. In the **Parameters** rollout, set **Angle** to **152** and **Bend Axis** to X. Now, align the handle with the **drawerGeo1** [see Fig. E33].

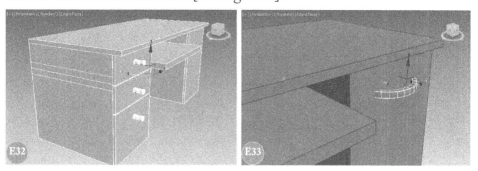

25. From the **Modifier List** > **Object-Space Modifiers** section, choose **Taper**. In the **Modify** panel > modifier stack display, expand **Taper** and click **Gizmo**. Invoke the **Scale** tool from the **Main** toolbar. Change the size of gizmo along the **x-axis** [see Fig. E34].

26. In the **Parameters** rollout, set **Amount** to **-1.1** and **Primary** to **Z**. Set **Effect** to **Y**. From the **Modifier List** > **Object-Space Modifiers** section, choose **TurboSmooth** to smooth the handle [see Fig. E35].

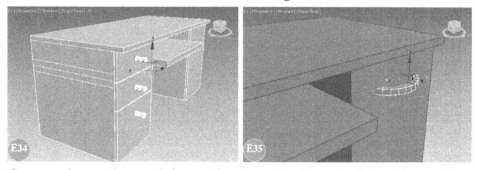

27. Convert **drawerGeo** and **drawerGeo1** to editable poly. Select **drawerGeo** and then in the **Ribbon** > **Modeling** tab > **Polygon Modeling** panel, click **Edge**. Press **Ctrl+A** to select all the edges of **drawerGeo**. In the **Ribbon** > **Modeling** tab > **Edges** panel, **Shift** click **Chamfer**.

28. In the **Chamfer Edges** caddy control, set **Chamfer Type** to **Quad Chamfer**, **Edge Chamfer Amount** to **0.07**, and click **OK**. Similarly, chamfer all edges of **drawerGeo1**, **sliderGeo**, and **deskGeo**.

29. In the **Create** panel, activate **Geometry**, then on the **Extended Primitives** > **Object Type** rollout, click **ChamferBox**. Create a box in the **Top** viewport. In the **Modify** panel > **Parameters** rollout, set **Length** to **4**, **Width** to **4**, **Height** to **8**, and **Fillet** to **0.353**. Set **Fillet Segs** to **2**. Ensure the **Length Segs**, **Width Segs**, and **Height Segs** are set to **1**.

30. Rename the box as **legGeo**. Next. align **legGeo** as shown in Fig. E36. Create seven more copies of **legGeo** and align them as shown in Fig. E37.

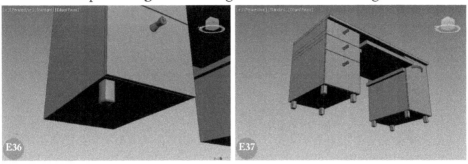

Exercise 2: Creating a USB Connector

In this exercise, we will model a USB connector [see Fig. E1].

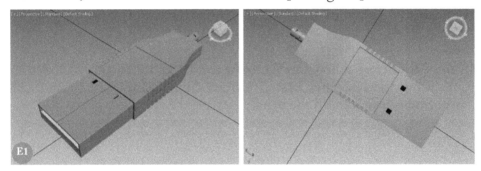

Table E2 summarizes the exercise:

Table E2	
Skill level	Intermediate
Time to complete	40 Minutes
Topics in the section:	• Specifying the Units for the Exercise • Creating the USB Connector
Project folder	**unit-m5**
Units	**Metric - Millimeters**
Final exercise file	**usbconnector-finish.max**

Specifying the Units for the Exercise

Follow these steps:

1. From **Customize** menu choose **Units Setup**. In the **Units Setup** dialog box that opens, select the **Metric** option from the **Display Unit Scale** group. Next, select **Millimeters** from the drop-down list located below the **Metric** option, if already not selected. Click **OK** to accept the change.

2. From the **File** menu, choose **Save** to open the **Save File As** dialog box. In the **File name** text box type **usbconnector-finish.max** and then click **Save** to save the file.

Creating the USB Connector
Follow these steps:

1. Create a box in the **Top** viewport. In the **Modify** panel > **Parameters** rollout, set **Length** to **15**, **Width** to **30**, **Height** to **5**, and **Width Segments** to **1**. Rename the box as **ucGeo**. Invoke the **Move** tool from the **Main** toolbar. Set the **Transform Type-In** boxes to **0** in **Status Bar** to place the box at the origin.

2. In the **Ribbon** > **Modeling** tab > **Polygon Modeling** panel, click **Convert to Poly**. Activate the **Edge** sub-object level and then in the **Ribbon** > **Modeling** tab > **Edit** panel, click **SwiftLoop**. Create two loops [refer to Fig. E2] and then slide the loops toward right using **Alt**. Deactivate **SwiftLoop**.

3. Activate **Vertex** sub-object level and then adjust the shape of the connector using the **Move** and **Scale** tools [see Fig. E3]. Activate the **Polygon** sub-object level and then select the front polygon. In the **Ribbon** > **Modeling** tab > **Polygons** panel, **Shift** click **Inset**. In the **Inset** caddy control, set **Amount** to **0.5** and then click **OK** [see Fig. E4].

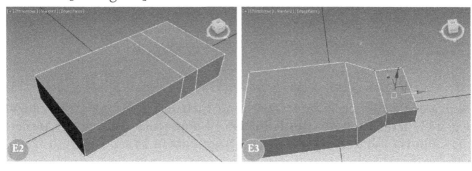

4. In the **Ribbon** > **Modeling** tab > **Polygons** panel, **Shift** click **Extrude**. In the **Extrude Polygons** caddy control, set **Amount** to **-8** and then click **OK** [see Fig. E5]. Activate **Edge** sub-object level and then select the edge shown in Fig. E6.

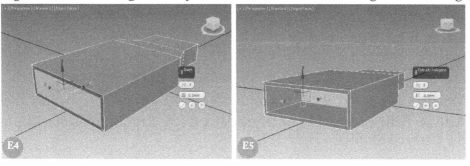

5. In the **Ribbon** > **Modeling** tab > **Modify Selection** panel, click **Ring**. In the **Ribbon** > **Modeling** tab > **Loops** panel, **Shift** click **Connect**. In the **Connect Edges** caddy control, set **Segments** to **2** and **Pinch** to **62** [see Fig. E7]. Click **OK**. Similarly, create two more edge loops [see Fig. E8].

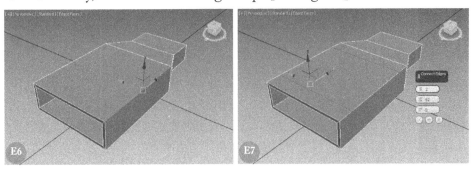

6. Activate the **Polygon** sub-object level and then select the polygon shown in Fig. E9. In the **Ribbon** > **Modeling** tab > **Polygons** panel, **Shift** click **Inset**. In the **Inset** caddy control, set **Amount** to **0.5** and then click **OK**. In the **Ribbon** > **Modeling** tab > **Polygons** panel, **Shift** click **Extrude**. In the **Extrude Polygons** caddy control, set **Amount** to **-0.3** and **then** click **OK** [see Fig. E10].

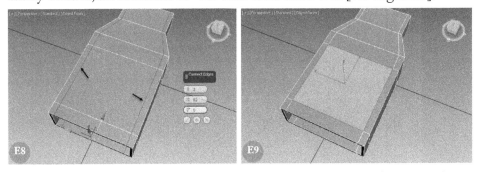

7. Activate the **Edge** sub-object level and then select the edge ring shown in Fig. E11. In the **Ribbon** > **Modeling** tab > **Loops** panel, **Shift** click **Connect**. In the **Connect Edges** caddy control, set **Segments** to **14** and **Pinch** to **-25**. Click **OK** [see Fig. E12].

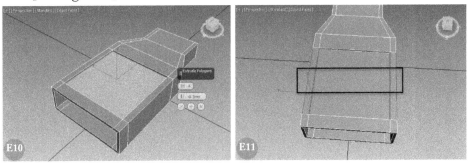

8. Activate **Polygon** sub-object level and then select every other polygon loop using the **Ctrl** and **Shift** [see Fig. E13].

9. Now, in the **Top** viewport, remove the polygons from the selection using **Alt** [see Fig. E14].

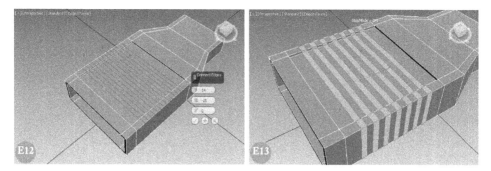

10. In the **Ribbon** > **Modeling** tab > **Polygons** panel, **Shift** click **Inset**. In the **Inset** caddy control, set **Amount** to **0.1** and then click **OK**. In the **Ribbon** > **Modeling** tab > **Polygons** panel, **Shift** click **Extrude**. In the **Extrude Polygons** caddy control, set **Extrusion Type** to **Local Normal** and **Amount** to **-0.2** and **then** click **OK** [see Fig. E15].

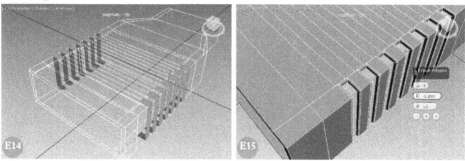

11. Activate **Edge** sub-object level and then on the **Ribbon** > **Modeling** tab > **Edit** panel, click **SwiftLoop**. Create edge loops around the sharp edges of the **ucGeo** [see Figs. E16 and E17].

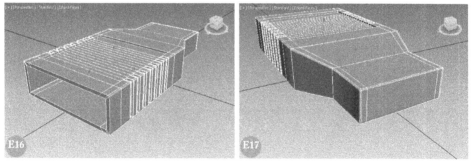

12. Now, insert an edge loop shown in Fig. E18. In the **Ribbon** > **Modeling** tab > **Edges** panel, **Shift** click **Chamfer**. In the **Chamfer** caddy, set **Edge Chamfer Amount** to **0.09** and **Connect Edge Segments** to **1**. Click **OK**.

13. Select the polygons created using the chamfer operation. In the **Ribbon** > **Modeling** tab > **Polygons** panel, **Shift** click **Extrude**. In the **Extrude Polygons** caddy, set **Amount** to **-0.04** and then click **OK** [see Fig. E19].

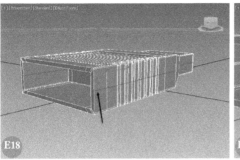
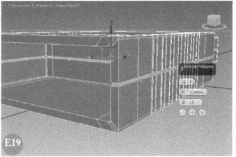

14. Create more edge loop using the **SwiftLoop** tool [see Fig. E20]. Similarly, add edge loops in the front of the connector [see Fig. 21]. From the **Object-Space Modifiers** section of the **Modifier List**, select **MeshSmooth**. In the **Subdivision Amount** rollout, change **Iterations** to **3** [see Fig. E22].

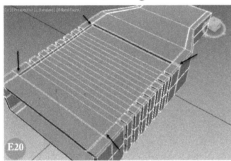
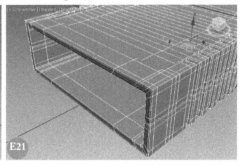

15. Create a box in the **Top** viewport. In the **Modify** panel > **Parameters** rollout, set **Length** to **14**, **Width** to **20**, **Height** to **4**, and **Width Segments** to **1**. Rename the cylinder as **cGeo**. In the **Ribbon** > **Modeling** tab > **Polygon Modeling** panel, click **Convert to Poly.**

16. Activate the **Polygon** sub-object level and then select the front polygon. In the **Ribbon** > **Modeling** tab > **Polygons** panel, **Shift** click **Inset**. In the **Inset** caddy control, set **Amount** to **0.5** and then click **OK** [see Fig. E23]. In the **Ribbon** > **Modeling** tab > **Polygons** panel, **Shift** click **Extrude**. In the **Extrude Polygons** caddy control, set **Amount** to **-6** and then click **OK** [see Fig. E24].

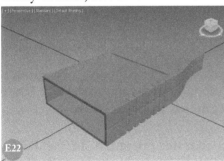
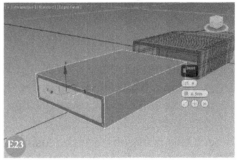

17. Activate the **Edge** sub-object level and then select the ring shown in Fig. E25. In the **Ribbon** > **Modeling** tab > **Loops** panel, **Shift** click **Connect**. In the **Connect Edges** caddy control, set **Segments** to **2** and **Pinch** to **-85**. Click **OK**.

18. Select the newly created polygons and in the **Ribbon** > **Modeling** tab > **Polygons** panel, **Shift** click **Extrude**. In the **Extrude Polygons** caddy control, set **Amount** to **-0.2**, type to **Local Normal** and then click **OK** [see Fig. E26].

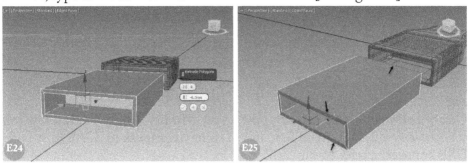

19. Activate the **Edge** sub-object level. Insert edge loops using **SwiftLoop** as shown in Fig. E27. Activate the **Polygon** sub-object level. Select the polygons shown in Fig. E28 and delete them using **Delete**.

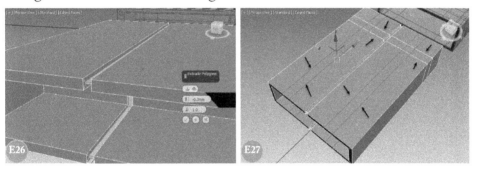

20. Activate the **Edge** sub-object level and select the outer edges shown in Fig. E29. In the **Ribbon** > **Modeling** tab > **Edges** panel, **Shift** click **Chamfer**. In the **Chamfer** caddy control, set **Chamfer Type** to **Quad Chamfer**, **Edge Chamfer Amount** to **0.06**, and **Connect Edge Segments** to **3**. Click **OK**.

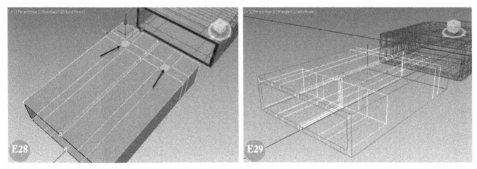

21. Select the edges that make up the holes and then on the **Ribbon** > **Modeling** tab > **Edges** panel, **Shift** click **Extrude**. In the **Extrude Edges** caddy control, set **Height** to **-0.1**, **Width** to **0**, and then click **OK**. Place the metal connector inside its case. If you find that the metal connector is large in size, you can adjust the shape by moving the vertices [see Fig. E30].

22. Now, create a new box primitive and then place inside the metal connector as shown in Fig. E31.

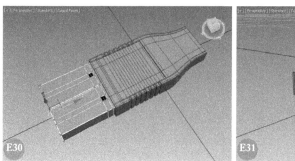 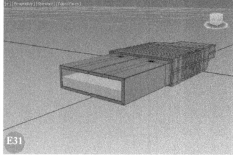

23. Create a cylinder in the **Top** viewport. In the **Modify** panel > **Parameters** rollout, set **Radius** to **2, Height** to **4.3**, and **Height Segments** to **5**. Align it with the USB connector, refer to Fig. E32.

24. In the **Ribbon** > **Modeling** tab > **Polygon Modeling** panel, click **Convert to Poly.** Activate **Polygon** sub-object level and then select the polygons shown in Fig. E33.

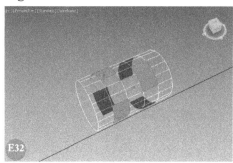 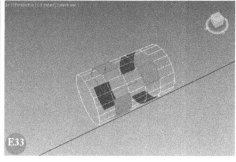

25. In the **Ribbon** > **Modeling** tab > **Polygons** panel, **Shift** click **Inset.** In the **Inset** caddy control, set **Amount** to **0.2** and then click **OK**. In the **Ribbon** > **Modeling** tab > **Polygons** panel, **Shift** click **Extrude.** In the **Extrude Polygons** caddy control, set **Amount** to **-0.5** and **then** click **OK** [see Fig. E34].

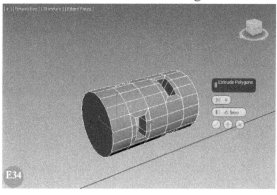

In this exercise, we will model a flash drive [see Fig. E1].

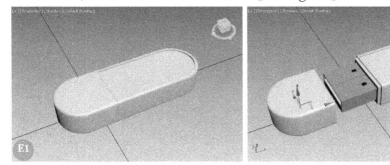

Table E3 summarizes the exercise:

Table E3		
Skill level	Intermediate	
Time to complete	1 Hour	
Topics in the section:	• Specifying the Units for the Exercise • Creating the Flash Drive	
Project folder	**unit-m5**	
Units	**Metric - Millimeters**	
Final exercise file	**flash-drive-finish.max**	

Specifying the Units for the Exercise
Follow these steps:

1. From **Customize** menu choose **Units Setup**. In the **Units Setup** dialog box that opens, select the **Metric** option from the **Display Unit Scale** group. Next, select **Millimeters** from the drop-down list located below the **Metric** option, if already not selected. Click **OK** to accept the change. RMB click on any snap toggle button on **the Main toolbar**.

2. From the **File** menu, choose **Save** to open the **Save File As** dialog box. In the **File name** text box type **flash-drive-finish.max** and then click **Save** to save the file.

Creating the Flash Drive
Follow these steps:

1. Create a cylinder in the **Top** viewport. In the **Modify** panel > **Parameters** rollout, set **Radius** to **7.5**, **Height** to **7**, **Height Segments** to **1**, and **Sides** to **32**. Rename the cylinder as **usbGeo**. Invoke the **Move** tool from the **Main** toolbar. Set the **Transform Type-In** boxes to **0** on the **Status Bar** to place the cylinder at the **origin**. In the **Ribbon** > **Modeling** tab > **Polygon Modeling** panel, click

Convert to Poly. Activate **Vertex** sub-object level and then select the vertices in the **Front** viewport [see Fig. E2].

2. In the **Top** viewport, move the selected vertices towards right along the x-axis about **25** units [see Fig. E3].

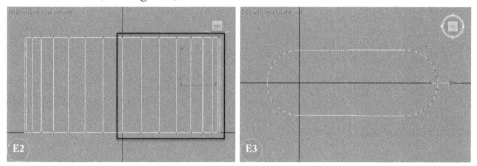

3. In the **Ribbon > Modeling** tab > **Geometry (All)** panel, click **Slice Plane**. This action will display a slice plane gizmo in the viewport and opens the **Slice Mode** panel. Adjust the position of the plane as shown in Fig. E4 and then click **Slice** on **Slice Mode** panel to subdivide the geometry. In the **Ribbon > Modeling** tab > **Geometry (All)** panel, click **Slice Plane** to deactivate the slice plane feature.

4. Activate **Edge** sub-object level and then in the **Front** viewport, drag a selection window to select the edges [see Fig. E5].

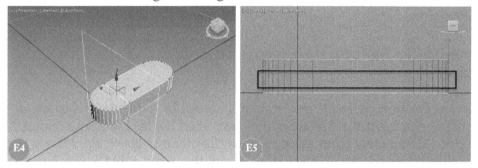

5. Press **Ctrl+I** to invert the selection. **Remove** the edges from the selection that you created using **Slice Plane**. In the **Ribbon > Modeling** tab > **Edges** panel, **Shift** click **Chamfer**. In the **Chamfer** caddy control, set **Edge Chamfer Amount** to **0.8** and **Connect Edge Segments** to **7** [see Fig. E6]. Click **OK**. Activate **Polygon** sub-object level and then select polygons [see Fig. E7].

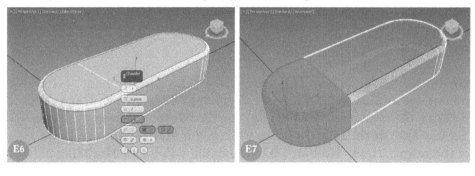

6. In the **Ribbon > Modeling** tab > **Geometry (All)** panel, click **Detach**. In the **Detach** dialog box that appears, type **capGeo** in the **Detach as** text box and then click **OK**. Move the cap slightly towards left and then apply a **Shell** modifier to it. In the **Parameters** rollout, set **Inner Amount** to **0.4** and **Outer Amount** to **0**.

7. Activate the **Border** sub-object level for **usbGeo** and then make the border selection [see Fig. E8]. In the **Ribbon > Modeling** tab > **Geometry (All)** panel, click **Cap Poly** to create a polygon.

8. Activate the **Polygon** sub-object level and then select the newly created polygon. In the **Ribbon > Modeling** tab > **Polygons** panel, click **Shift** click **Inset**. In the **Inset** caddy control, set **Amount** to **0.5** and then click **OK**. In the **Ribbon > Modeling** tab > **Polygons** panel, **Shift** click **Extrude**. In the **Extrude Polygons** caddy control, set **Amount** to **0.8** and then click **OK** [see Fig. E9].

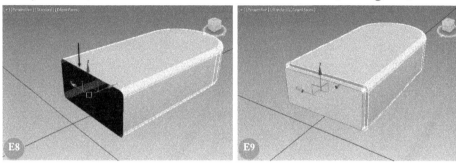

9. Activate the **Edge** sub-object level and then select the edge loops shown in Fig. E10. In the **Ribbon > Modeling** tab > **Edges** panel, **Shift** click **Chamfer**. In the **Chamfer** caddy control, set **Edge Chamfer Amount** to **0.1** and **Connect Edge Segments** to **4**. Click **OK** [see Fig. E11].

10. Activate the **Polygon** sub-object level and then select the top polygon of the **usbGeo** [see Fig. E12]. In the **Ribbon > Modeling** tab > **Polygons** panel, **Shift** click **Inset**. In the **Inset** caddy control, set **Amount** to **0.3** and **then** click **OK** [see Fig. E13].

11. In the **Ribbon > Modeling** tab > **Polygons** panel, **Shift** click **Extrude**. In the **Extrude Polygons** caddy control, set **Amount** to **-0.4** and **then** click **OK** [see Fig. E14].

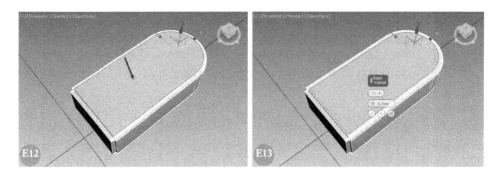

12. Activate the **Edge** sub-object level and then select the loop shown in Fig. E15. In the **Ribbon** > **Modeling** tab > **Edges** panel, **Shift** click **Chamfer**. In the **Chamfer** caddy control, set **Edge Chamfer Amount** to **0.4** and **Connect Edge Segments** to **3**. Click **OK** [see Fig. E16]. Now, create the USB connector as done in the previous exercise [see Fig. E17].

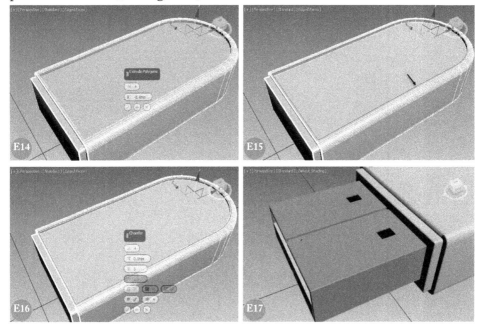

Quiz

Evaluate your skills to see how many questions you can answer correctly.

Multiple Choice
Answer the following questions, only one choice is correct.

1. Which the following panels is used to quickly sketch or edit a mesh on the grid or a surface?

   [A] PolyDraw   [B] SketchDraw
   [C] ObjectPaint   [D] None of the above

2. Which of the following keys is used to interactively change the conform brush's strength?

[A] Ctrl+drag   [B] Alt+Drag
[C] Shift+drag   [D] Ctrl+Shift+Drag

3. Which of the following tools is used to quickly layout the topology foundation for a mesh object?

[A] Splines   [B] Stripes
[C] Surface   [D] Branches

Fill in the Blanks
Fill in the blanks in each of the following statements:

1. The Graphite Modeling tools are available in the _____.

2. This _____ tool is used to remove the details from the model by drawing on it.

True of False
State whether each of the following is true or false:

1. When the **Step Build** tool is active, vertex ticks are not always visible in the viewport.

2. The options in the **Stored Selection Panel** let you quickly and easily store and retrieve selections.

Summary
The unit covered the following topics:

- Working with the **Graphite Modeling Tools**
- Selecting sub-objects
- Creating models using the tools available in the **Ribbon**

- Generate planar and 3d surfaces
- Paths and shapes for the loft components
- Generate extrusions
- Generate revolved surfaces
- Define motion path for animations

Unit M6: Spine Modeling

A shape in 3ds Max is an object consists of one or more lines. These lines which can be 2D or 3D, are used to create components for other objects. 3ds Max provides two types of shape objects: **Splines** and **NURBS** curves. Most of the default shapes in 3ds Max are splines.

3ds Max provides thirteen basic spline objects, five extended spline objects, and two types of NURBS curves. You can use these objects in the following ways:

- Generate planar and 3d surfaces
- Paths and shapes for the loft components
- Generate extrusions
- Generate revolved surfaces
- Define motion path for animations

Apart from what mentioned above, you can also render the shape as is. When rendering is enabled for shapes, 3ds Max renders them using a circular or rectangular cross-section.

You can convert a basic spline or an extended spline to an editable spline object. This object offers a variety of controls to create less regular and complex shapes. It allows you to edit the shape at the sub-object level. However, when you convert a spline to an **Editable Spline** object, you loose the parametric nature of the spline and cannot adjust the creation parameters. The **Editable Spline** object will be discussed later in this unit. You can use the **Edit Spline** modifier to retain the parametric nature of a primitive spline. This modifier matches all the capabilities of the **Editable Spline** object with some exceptions given next:

- The **Rendering** and **Interpolation** rollouts are not available when you are use the **Edit Spline** modifier.
- The direct vertex animation capabilities are not available.

It is recommended that you use the base **Editable Spline** object to edit the splines rather than store the changes in an **Edit Spline** modifier. The **Editable Spline** object is more reliable and efficient than the **Edit Spline** modifier.

Spline and Extended Splines Primitives

You can access the shape creation tools from the **Create** ➕ panel. Go to the **Create** panel and then click **Shapes** 🔲.

A drop-down list appears below the **Shapes** button with the entries: **Splines, NURBS Curves, Compound Shape, CFD, Max Creation Graph,** and **Extended Splines** [see Fig. 1]. Table 1 summarizes the available tools.

You can also access these tools from the **Create** menu. If you are using the enhanced menu system, you can access shapes from the **Objects** menu.

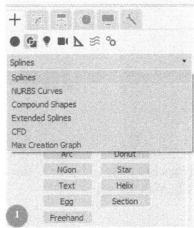

Table 1: The shapes tools available in 3ds Max	
Splines	**Line, Rectangle, Circle, Ellipse, Arc, Donut, NGon, Star, Text, Helix, Egg, Section,** and **Freehand**
NURBS Curves	**Point Curve** and **CV Curve**
Extended Splines	**WRectangle, Channel, Angle, Tee,** and **Wide Flange**

Spline Primitives
In this section, I will explain the basic spline primitives. Let's start with the **Line** spline.

Line Spline
A **Line** spline is a free-form spline that is made up of multiple segments. To create a line, go to the **Create** panel, click **Shapes**, and then click **Line** on the **Object Type** rollout. Notice that various rollouts appear in the **Create** panel. Choose the creation method from the **Creation Method** rollout. Click or drag in the viewport to create the first vertex [If you click, a **Corner** vertex is created otherwise a **Bezier** vertex will be created]. Now, click or drag to create additional points. To finish the creation method, do one of the following: either RMB click to create an open spline [see Fig. 2] or click on the first vertex and then choose **Yes** from the **Spline** message box that appears [see Fig. 3].

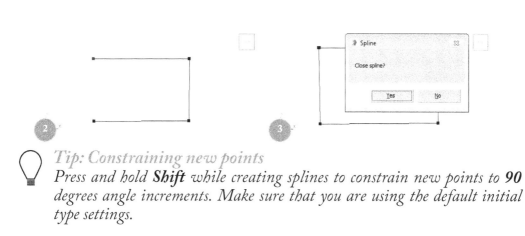

Tip: Constraining new points

Press and hold **Shift** while creating splines to constrain new points to **90** degrees angle increments. Make sure that you are using the default initial type settings.

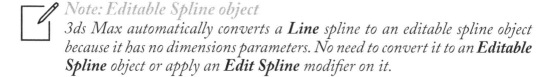

Tip: Constraining new points to a custom angle increment

You can also constrain new points to a custom angle increment value. Select **Grids And Snaps** > **Grid And Snap Settings** from the **Tools** menu. In the **Grid and Snap Settings** dialog box that appears, choose the **Options** panel and then set a value for the **Angle** spinner. Close the dialog box. Now, click **Angle Snap Toggle** on the **Main** toolbar. Press and hold **Ctrl** while creating new points to constrain them to the value you specified for the **Angle** spinner.

Tip: Panning and orbiting while creating splines

If a spline requires two or more steps for its creation [such as **Line** or **Donut**], you can pan and orbit the viewport between the creation steps.

Note: Editable Spline object

3ds Max automatically converts a **Line** spline to an editable spline object because it has no dimensions parameters. No need to convert it to an **Editable Spline** object or apply an **Edit Spline** modifier on it.

Now, let's take a look at the various aspects/parameters associated with the **Line** spline. Many of them are common to most of the spline objects.

Combining Shapes While Creating Them

3ds Max allows you to combine shapes to create compound shapes. You can use this feature to create complex shapes. To create a compound shape, on the **Create** panel, clear the check box preceding the **Start New Shape** button and then begin creating shapes. Each spline that you create, added to the compound spline.

You can check whether all splines are part of a compound shape or not. Go to the **Modify** panel and then click **Editable Spline** in the modifier stack. You will notice that all splines are selected in the viewport [see Fig. 4].

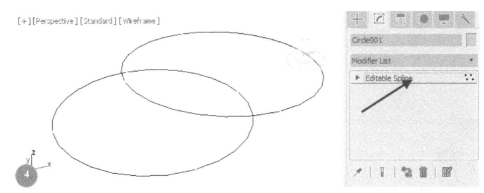

Caution: Parametric nature of splines

You cannot change creation parameters of a compound shape. For example, if you first create a circle, and then add a rectangle to create a compound shape, you cannot switch back and change the creation parameters of the circle.

Creation Method Rollout

The controls in this rollout allow you to specify what type of vertex that will be created when you click or drag vertices in the viewport. The creation method options for the **Line** spline are different from other spline primitives.

Table 2 summarizes the controls available in the **Creation Method** rollout.

Table 2: Controls in the **Creation Method** rollout of the **Line** spline	
[Group]/Control	**Description**
[Initial Type Group]	The controls in this group set the type of vertex created when you click [not drag] a vertex location.
Corner	**Corner** creates sharp points and spline created is linear to either side of the point.
Smooth	**Smooth** creates a smooth curve through the vertex that you can adjust manually. The curvature of the spline segment is controlled by the spacing of the vertices. Fig. 5 shows the splines created using the **Corner** [left image] and **Smooth** [right image] initial type options.
[Drag Type Group]	The controls in this group define the type of vertex created when you drag a vertex location.
Corner, Smooth	The **Corner** and **Smooth** controls work as discussed above.
Bezier	The **Bezier** control produces a smooth adjustable curve. The amount of curvature and direction of the curve are controlled by dragging the mouse at each vertex. You can manually change the smoothness or curvature by manipulating the vertex handles [refer third image in Fig. 6].

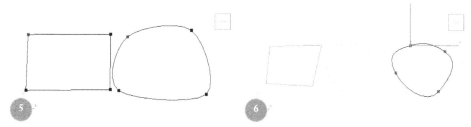

Keyboard Entry Rollout

You can use the **Keyboard Entry** rollout to precisely place vertices of a spline. To add a vertex, enter its coordinates in the **X**, **Y**, and **Z** spinners and then click **Add Point** to add a new point.

The subsequent points you insert will be added to the existing line until you click **Close** or **Finish**. **Close** closes the shape whereas **Finish** completes the line without closing it.

Rendering Rollout

The options in this rollout let you toggle the shape renderability in the viewports as well as in the rendered output. You can also use the options to generate the mapping coordinates and convert the mesh to an editable mesh or editable poly object.

Table 3 summarizes the controls available in the **Rendering** rollout.

Table 3: Controls in the **Rendering** rollout of the **Line** spline	
Control	**Description**
Enable In Renderer	Select the **Enable In Renderer** check box to render the shape as 3D mesh using the **Radial** or **Rectangular** parameters set for the renderer. When selected, **Renderer** gets selected in this rollout. Now, you have two options for controlling the size of the mesh: **Radial** and **Rectangular**. **Radial** renders the shape with a circular cross section whereas **Rectangular** displays the mesh of the spline as a rectangle. Fig. 7 shows the spline shape with the circular cross section on rendering [**Thickness=2, Sides=12**]. Fig. 8 shows the mesh with the rectangular cross section [**Length=6, Width=2**].
Enable In Viewport, Use Viewport Settings	Select the **Enable In Viewport** check box to display the shape in the viewport as a 3D mesh with the circular or rectangular cross section [see Figs. 9 and 10]. Select **Use Viewport Settings** to display the mesh using the **Viewport** settings. When on, **Viewport** is activated and then you can use the **Viewport** settings to control the appearance of mesh of the spline in the viewport.

Table 3: Controls in the **Rendering** rollout of the **Line** spline	
Control	**Description**
Generate Mapping Coords	Select **Generate Mapping Coords** to apply mapping coordinates to the spline mesh. 3ds Max generates coordinates in **U** and **V** directions. The **U** coordinate wraps around the spline whereas the **V** coordinate is mapped along the length of the spline.
Real-World Map Size	The **Real-World Map Size** check box will only be available if you turn on **Generate Mapping Coords**. This control allows you to specify the actual width and height of a 2D texture map in **Material Editor**.
Auto Smooth	**Auto Smooth** is turned on by default. The spline is automatically smoothed using the threshold value defined by the **Threshold** spinner available below **Auto Smooth**. This value is an angle measured in degrees.

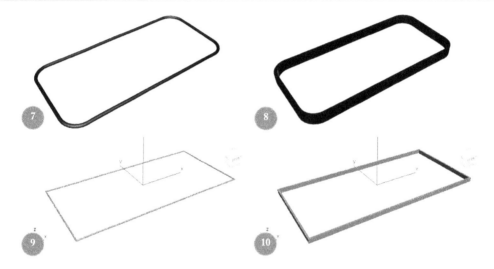

Radial and Rectangular Options: Now, let's have a look at the various controls available for the radial and rectangular cross sections. Table 4 summarizes these controls.

Table 4: Various controls available for radial and rectangular cross sections	
Control	**Description**
Thickness	Controls the diameter of the rendered spline mesh. Fig. 11 shows the splines rendered with the **Thickness** value set to **0.5** and **1**, respectively.
Sides	Controls the number of sides [or facets] of the mesh. Fig. 12 shows the splines rendered with the **Sides** value set to **4** and **62**, respectively.
Angle	It controls the orientation of the rendered cross section. Fig. 13 shows the splines rendered with the **Angle** value set to **0** and **60**, respectively.

Table 4: Various controls available for radial and rectangular cross sections

Control	Description
Length	Controls the size of the cross section along the local Y-axis.
Width	Controls the size of the cross section along the local X-axis.
Aspect	It controls the aspect ratio of width to length. If the **Lock** button next to the spinner is active, adjusting length or width automatically adjusts the other to maintain the aspect ratio.

Interpolation Rollout

The controls on this rollout allow you to adjust the smoothness of a curve. Each spline segment is made up of divisions called steps. Higher the number of steps, smoother the curve will be. By default, **Optimize** is turned on. When on, 3ds Max removes the steps that are not necessary. For example, 3ds Max will not add steps on the straight lines when **Optimize** is selected. When **Adaptive** is selected, the **Steps** control becomes inactive. It sets the number of steps for each spline to produce smooth looking result. Fig. 14 shows the wireframe view of the spline mesh created using the **Optimize** and **Adaptive** options.

Note: Adaptive
*When **Adaptive** is selected, the straight segments get zero steps.*

Creation Method Rollout

Many spline shapes in 3ds Max allow you to use a creation method. You know the **Line** spline's creation methods. The **Text** and **Star** splines do not have a **Creation Method** rollout. Most of the spline primitives have the **Edge** and **Center** creation methods. If the **Edge** method is selected, the first click defines a point on the side or at a corner of the shape and then you drag a diameter or drag to a diagonal point. In the **Center** method, the first click defines the center of the shape and then you drag a corner point or radius.

Rectangle Spline

It creates square or rectangular splines [see Fig. 15]. If you want to create a square spline, press and hold **Ctrl** while dragging in a viewport. To create a rectangular spline, first select a creation method and then drag the mouse pointer in a viewport to create a rectangle.

Table 5 summarizes the controls available in the **Parameters** rollout of the **Rectangular** spline:

Table 5: Controls in the **Parameters** rollout of the **Rectangular** spline	
Control	**Description**
Length, Width	The **Length** and **Width** controls specify the size of the rectangle along the Y and X axes, respectively.
Corner Radius	The **Corner Radius** control allows you to create rounded corners. See right-most image in Fig. 15.

Circle Spline

It allows you to create close circular splines made up of four vertices [see Fig. 16]. To create a circular spline, first select the creation method and then drag the mouse pointer in a viewport to draw a circle. Table 6 summarizes the controls available in the **Parameters** rollout of the **Circle** spline:

Table 6: Controls in the **Parameters** rollout of the **Circle** spline	
Control	**Description**
Radius	The **Radius** control specifies the center to edge distance of the circle.

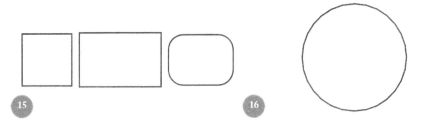

Ellipse Spline

You can use it to create circular or elliptical splines [see Fig. 17]. If you want to create a circular spline, press and hold **Ctrl** while dragging in the viewport. To create an elliptical spline, first select the creation method and then drag the mouse pointer in the viewport to draw the ellipse.

Table 7 summarizes the controls available in the **Parameters** rollout of the **Ellipse** spline:

Table 7: Controls in the **Parameters** rollout of the **Ellipse** spline	
Control	**Description**
Length, Width	The **Length** and **Width** controls specify the size of the ellipse along the local Y and Z axes, respectively.
Outline, Thickness	The **Outline** control lets you create an elliptical outline, see middle image in Fig. 17. The **Thickness** control lets you specify the thickness of the ellipse.

Arc Spline

You can use the **Arc** spline to create open and closed partial circles made up of four vertices [see Fig. 18].

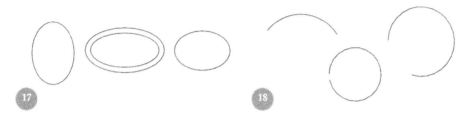

17   18

Creation Method Rollout

The **Arc** spline provides two methods for creating arcs: **End-End-Middle** and **Center-End-End**. To create an arc using the **End-End-Middle** method, make sure **End-End-Middle** is selected in the **Creation Method** rollout and then drag in the viewport to define the two ends of the arc. Now, release the mouse button. Move the mouse pointer up or down to specify the third point between the two end points.

To create an arc using the **Center-End-End** method, make sure **Center-End-End** is selected in the **Creation Method** rollout and then click to set the radial center of the arc. Drag the mouse pointer and click to specify the start point of the arc. Now, move the mouse and click to specify the other end of the arc. Table 8 summarizes the controls available in the **Parameters** rollout of the **Arc** spline:

Table 8: Controls in the **Parameters** rollout of the **Arc** spline	
Control	**Description**
Radius	**Radius** specifies the radius of the arc.
From, To	**From** specifies the location of the start point which is measured as angle from the local positive Y-axis. **To** specifies the location of the end point which is measured as angle from the local positive X-axis.
Pie Slice	When **Pie Slice** is on, it creates straight segments from the endpoints to the radial center which results in closed spline [see Fig. 19].
Reverse	When **Reverse** is on, the direction of the **Arc** spline is reversed.

Donut Spline

It creates the donut like shape of two concentric circles [see Fig. 20]. To create a **Donut** spline, first select a creation method. Drag the mouse pointer and then release the mouse button to define the first circle of the donut. Move the mouse pointer and then click to define the second concentric donut circle.

Table 9 summarizes the controls available in the **Parameters** rollout of the **Donut** spline:

Table 9: Controls in the **Parameters** rollout of the **Donut** spline	
Controls	**Description**
Radius 1, Radius 2	The **Radius 1** and **Radius 2** controls specify the radius of the first and second circle, respectively.

NGon Spline

It creates flat sided splines with N number of sides and vertices [see Fig. 21]. To create an **NGon** spline, select a creation method and then drag the mouse pointer in a viewport. Release the mouse button to create the spline.

Table 10 summarizes the controls available in the **Parameters** rollout of the **NGon** spline:

Table 10: Controls in the **Parameters** rollout of the **NGon** spline	
Control	**Description**
Radius, Inscribed, Circumscribed	The **Radius** control specifies the distance from the radial center to the edge of the NGon. If **Inscribed** is on [default], the distance is measured from the radial center to the corners. If **Circumscribed** is on, the distance is from the radial center to the side centers.
Sides	**Sides** specifies the number of sides which ranges from **3** to **100**.
Corner Radius	**Corner Radius** controls rounding applied to the corners of the NGon.
Circular	When **Circular** is on, 3ds Max creates a circular NGon which is equivalent to a circular spline but it may contain more than four vertices. The **Circle** spline creates a circular spline object with four control vertices.

Star Spline

It creates closed star-shaped splines with any number of points [see Fig. 22]. To create a **Star** spline, drag the mouse pointer and then release the mouse button to define the first radius. Move the mouse pointer and then click to define the second radius. The second radius can be less, equal, or greater than the first radius depending on how you moved the mouse pointer.

Table 11 summarizes the controls available in the **Parameters** rollout of the **Star** spline:

Table 11: Controls in the **Parameters** rollout of the **Star** spline	
Control	**Description**
Radius 1, Radius 2	The **Radius 1** and **Radius 2** controls specify the first set of vertices [created with the first drag] and second set of vertices, respectively.
Points	**Points** controls the number of points on the star. **Distortion** allows you to produce a sawtooth effect. This effect is generated by rotating **Radius 2** vertices about the center of the star.
Fillet Radius 1, Fillet Radius 2	**Fillet Radius 1** and **Fillet Radius 2** let you smooth the first and second set of vertices, respectively. The rounding is created by producing two **Bezier** vertices per point.

Text Spline

It creates splines in the shape of the text [see Fig. 23]. The text can be created using any **Windows** font [both **TrueType** and **OpenType**] installed on your system as well using the **Type 1 PostScript** font installed in the **Fonts** folder of the 3ds Max installation folder.

To create text, enter the text in the **Text** text box and then either click in a viewport to place the text or drag the mouse pointer to place the text in a viewport and then release the mouse button.

Table 12 summarizes the controls available in the **Parameters** rollout of the **Text** spline:

Table 12: Controls in the **Parameters** rollout of the **Text** spline	
Control	**Description**
Text Controls	From this rollout, you can choose the font, font size, text alignment, kerning [distance between letters], and leading [distance between lines] for the text that you enter in the **Text** text box. The **Text** text box does not support word-wrap however you can paste multiple lines from the clipboard.

Helix Spline

It creates spiral like shapes [see Fig. 24]. To create a **Helix** spline, click and drag the mouse pointer to set the starting point as well as its starting radius [**Center Creation** method] or diameter [**Edge Creation** method]. Now, move the mouse pointer vertically and then click to define the height. Move the mouse pointer and then click to define the end radius.

Table 13 summarizes the controls available in the **Parameters** rollout of the **Helix** spline:

Table 13: Controls in the **Parameters** rollout of the **Helix** spline	
Control	**Description**
Radius 1, Radius 2	The **Radius 1** and **Radius 2** controls specify the radius of helix start and end, respectively. **Height** controls the height of the helix.
Turns	**Turns** specifies the number of turns in the helix.
Bias	**Bias** forces the turns in the helix to accumulate at the one end of the helix. Fig. 25 shows the rendered helix with **Bias** set to **-1, 0.2**, and **1**, respectively.
CC and CCW	**CC** and **CCW** specify whether helix should turn clockwise or counterclockwise.

Egg Spline

It creates an egg shaped spline [see Fig. 26]. To create an **Egg** spline, drag the mouse pointer vertically to define the initial dimension of the egg. Now, drag horizontally to change the orientation [angle] of the egg. Release the mouse button to compete the creation process.

Table 14 summarizes the controls available in the **Parameters** rollout of the **Egg** spline:

Table 14: Controls in the **Parameters** rollout of the **Egg** spline	
Controls	**Description**
Length, Width	The **Length** and **Width** controls specify the length and width of the egg along its long and short axes, respectively.
Outline, Thickness	When **Outline** is on, **Thickness** sets the distance between the main shape of the egg and its outline.
Angle	**Angle** specifies the angle of rotation around shape's local Z axis. When **Angle** is equal to **0**, the narrow end of the egg is at the top.

Section Spline

The **Section** spline is a special type of spline that lets you generate splines based on a cross-sectional slice through a geometry. To create a **Section** shape, click **Section** from the **Object Type** rollout and then drag a section plane in the viewport. Now, place and orient the plane in the viewport using transformation tools [see Fig. 27]. Notice a yellow line is displayed where the section intersects the mesh. Now, on the **Section Parameters** rollout, click **Create Shape**. In the **Name Section Shape** dialog box that appears, type the name for the spline and then click **OK**. Now, select the shape in **Scene Explorer** and then move it away using the **Move** tool [see Fig. 28].

Table 15 summarizes the controls available in the **Section Parameters** rollout of the **Section** spline.

Table 15: Controls in the **Section Parameters** rollout of the **Section** spline

[Group]/Control	Description
Create Shape	When you click this button, a shape is created based on the currently displayed intersection lines. The shape generated is an editable spline.
[Update]	The controls in this group specify when the intersection line is updated.
When Section Moves	It updates the intersection line when you move or resize the section shape.
When Section Selected	It updates the intersection line when you select the section shape. Click **Update Section** to update the intersection.
Manually	It updates the intersection line only when you click **Update Section**.
[Section Events]	These controls let you specify the extents of the cross section.
Infinite	When on, the selected plane is infinite in all directions [see Fig. 29].
Section Boundary	When on, the cross section is generated only for objects that are within or touched by the boundary of the section shape [see Fig. 30].
Off	No cross section is displayed or generated.
Color Swatch	You can use it to change the display color of the intersection.

Section Size Rollout

The **Length** and **Width** controls in the **Section Size** rollout control the size of the section rectangle.

Freehand Spline

You can use the **Freehand** spline to create hand-drawn splines directly in the viewport. You can use mouse or any other pointing device to draw the spline. You can also draw it on the selected objects in the viewport; it will automatically follow the contours.

Table 16 summarizes the controls available in the **Freehand Spline** rollout of the **Freehand** spline.

Table 16: Controls in the **Freehand Spline** rollout of the **Freehand** spline

[Group]/Control	Description
Show Knots	When on, the knots are displayed on the spline [see the right image in Fig. 31].
[Create Group]	
Granularity	Defines the number of cursor position samples taken before a knot is created.
Threshold	Defines how far the cursor must move before a knot is created. Higher the value you specify, more the distance between the knots will be.
Constrain	When on, you can constrain the spline to the selected objects. To constrain the spline, select the objects in the viewport and then turn on **Constrain**. Selected objects will appear in the list box. You can pick additional objects using the **Pick Object** button. To clear the list, click **Clear**. Now, drag on the selected objects to constrain the spline [see Fig. 32].
[Options Group]	
Curved, Straight	You can use these settings to define whether the segments between the knots are curved or straight.
Closed	Select this check box to close the spline.
Normals	When on, 3ds Max shows the resulting normals of the constrained spline in the viewport [see right image in Fig. 32].
Offset	You can use **Offset** to control the distance between the spline and the surface of the constraining object.
[Statistics Group]	
Number of Splines	Displays the number of splines in the shape.
Original Knots	Displays the number of knots automatically created while drawing the spline.
New Knots	Displays the new number of knots.

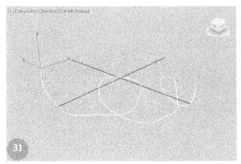 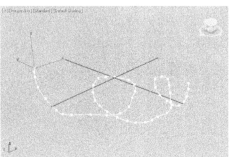

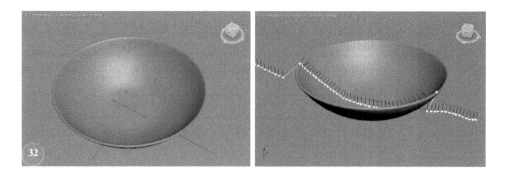

Extended Spline Primitives

In this section, I will explain the extended spline primitives. Let's start with the **WRectangle** spline.

WRectangle Spline

The **WRectangle** spline [walled rectangle] lets you create a closed shape from two concentric rectangles. Each rectangle is made up of four vertices [see Fig. 33]. To create a **WRectangle** spline, drag the mouse pointer in a viewport and then release the mouse button to define the outer rectangle. Move the mouse pointer and then click to define the inner rectangle.

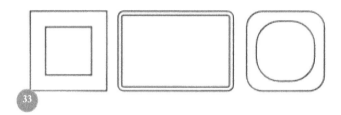

Table 17 summarizes the controls available in the **Parameters** rollout of the **WRectangle** spline.

Table 17: Controls in the **Parameters** rollout of the **WRectangle** spline	
Control	**Description**
Length, Width	These controls define the length and width of the **WRectangle** section.
Thickness	Controls the thickness of the **WRectangle** section.
Sync Corner Fillets	When on, the value specified for **Corner Radius 1** is used for both the interior and exterior corners.
Corner Radius 1	When **Sync Corner Fillets** is off, it controls the radius of the exterior corners.
Corner Radius 2	This control is only available when **Sync Corner Fillets** is off. It controls the radius of the interior corners.

Channel Spline

It creates a closed C shaped spline [see Fig. 34]. To create a **Channel** spline, drag the mouse pointer in a viewport and then release the mouse button to define the outer perimeter. Move the mouse pointer and then click to define the thickness of the walls of the channel.

Table 18 summarizes the controls available in the **Parameters** rollout of the **Channel** spline.

Table 18: Controls in the **Parameters** rollout of the **Channel** spline	
Control	**Description**
Length, Width	These controls define the length and width of the channel section.
Thickness	Controls the thickness of the channel section.
Sync Corner Fillets	When on, the value specified for **Corner Radius 1** is used for both the interior and exterior corners.
Corner Radius 1	When **Sync Corner Fillets** is off, it controls the radius of the exterior corners.
Corner Radius 2	This control is only available when **Sync Corner Fillets** is off. It controls the radius of the interior corners.

Angle Spline

It creates a closed L shaped spline [see Fig. 35]. To create an **Angle** spline, drag the mouse pointer in a viewport and then release the mouse button to define the initial size of the angle. Move the mouse pointer and then click to define the thickness of the walls of the angle. Table 19 summarizes the controls available in the **Parameters** rollout of the **WRectangle** spline.

Table 19: Controls in the **Parameters** rollout of the **Angle** spline	
Control	**Description**
Length, Width	These controls define the height and width of the vertical leg and horizontal legs, respectively.
Thickness	Controls the thickness of the legs of the angle.
Sync Corner Fillets	When on, the value specified for **Corner Radius 1** controls the radius for both the vertical and horizontal legs.

Table 19: Controls in the **Parameters** rollout of the **Angle** spline

Control	Description
Corner Radius 1	When **Sync Corner Fillets** is off, it controls the exterior radius between the vertical and horizontal legs of the spline.
Corner Radius 2	This control is only available when **Sync Corner Fillets** is off. It controls the interior radius between the vertical and horizontal legs of the spline.
Edge Radii	Controls the interior radius at the outermost edges of the vertical and horizontal legs.

Tee Spline

It creates a closed T shaped spline [see Fig. 36]. To create a **Tee** spline, drag the mouse pointer in a viewport and then release the mouse button to define the initial size of the tee. Move the mouse pointer and then click to define the thickness of the walls of the tee.

Table 20 summarizes the controls available in the **Parameters** rollout of the **Tee** spline.

Table 20: Controls in the **Parameters** rollout of the **Tee** spline

Control	Description
Length, Width	These controls define the height and width of the vertical web and flange crossing, respectively.
Thickness	Controls the thickness of the web and flange.
Corner Radius	Controls the radius of the two interior corners between the vertical web and horizontal flange.

Wide Flange Spline

It creates a closed I shaped spline [see Fig. 37]. To create a **Wide Flange** spline, drag the mouse pointer in a viewport and then release the mouse button to define the initial size of the wide flange. Move the mouse pointer and then click to define the thickness of the walls of the wide flange.

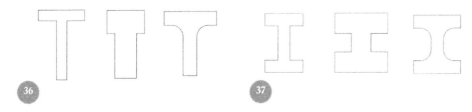

36   37

Table 21 summarizes the controls available in the **Parameters** rollout of the **Wide Flange** spline.

Table 21: Controls in the **Parameters** rollout of the **Wide Flange** spline

Controls	Description
Length, Width	These controls define the height and width of the vertical web and horizontal flange crossing, respectively.
Thickness	Controls the thickness of the wide flenges.
Corner Radius	Controls the radius of the two interior corners between the vertical web and horizontal flanges.

Editing Splines

You can convert a spline object to an editable spline object. The editable spline object allows you to create complex shapes using the three sub-object levels that this object provides: **Vertex, Spline,** and **Segment**.

The vertices define points and curve tangents. The segments connects vertices. The splines are made up of one or more connected segments.

You can convert a spline object into an **Editable Spline** object by using one of the following methods:

1. Select a spline in a viewport and then go to the **Modify** panel. Next, RMB click on the spline entry in the stack display and then choose **Editable Spline** from the pop up menu displayed [see Fig. 38].
2. Select a spline in a viewport and then RMB click. Choose **Transform** [in lower right quadrant] > **Convert To:** > **Convert to Editable Spline** [see Fig. 39].
3. Select a spline in a viewport and then apply the **Edit Spline** modifier to it.
4. Import a **.shp** file to the scene.
5. Merge a shape from a 3ds Max file.

Note: Edit Spline modifier
*You can use the **Edit Spline** modifier to convert a spline to the editable spline object. However, when you convert a spline to an **Editable Spline** object, you lose the creation parameters of the spline.*

Note: Line spline
*By default, the **Line** spline to an editable spline object because it has no dimensions parameters. Therefore, you don't need to convert a **Line** spline to the editable spline object.*

Note: Compound shapes
A compound shape made up of two or more splines is automatically an editable spline object.

Selecting Sub-objects

You can select sub-objects using one of the following ways:

1. Expand the spline object's hierarchy from the stack display and then choose a sub-object level [see Fig. 40].
2. Click a selection button from the **Selection** rollout [see Fig. 40].
3. RMB click on a spline object in a viewport and then choose the sub-object level from the upper left quadrant of the **Quad** menu displayed [see Fig. 41].
4. Choose a selection or transform tool and then click on the sub-objects in a viewport using the standard selection techniques.

> *Note: Cloning sub-objects*
> *You can clone the sub-objects by first selecting them and then press and hold* **Shift** *while transforming them.*

> *Note: Adding and removing from the selection*
> *To select a segment, vertex, or spline, click it. To add to the sub-object selection, press and hold* **Ctrl** *and click. You can also drag a selection region to select a group of sub-objects. To subtract from the sub-object selection, press and hold* **Alt** *and click. You can also drag a selection region to deselect a group of sub-objects.*

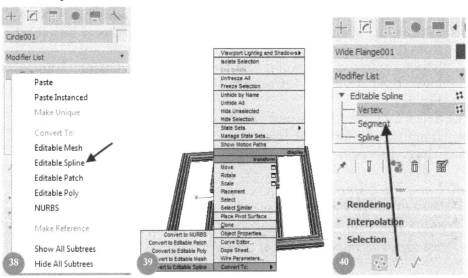

Vertex Level

Vertices define points and curve tangents for a spline object. To select a vertex type, select vertex or vertices and then RMB click. Now, choose the required level from the upper left quadrant of the **Quad** menu [see Fig. 42].

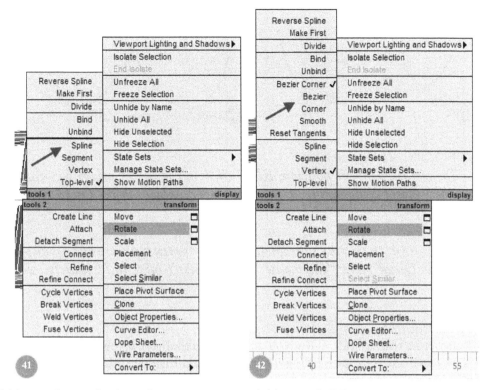

Table 22 shows the list of vertex types available in 3ds Max.

Table 22: The vertex types	
Type	**Description**
Corner	Creates non-adjustable vertices that generates sharp corners [see Fig. 43].
Bezier	Creates adjustable vertices with locked continuous tangent handles that produces a smooth curve. The curvature is determined by the direction and magnitude of the tangent handles [see Fig. 44]. You can adjust the tangent handles using the **Move** and **Rotate** tools.
Bezier Corner	Creates adjustable vertices with discontinuous tangent handles that produces a sharp corner [see Fig. 45]. The curvature is determined by the direction and magnitude of the tangent handles. You can adjust the tangent handles using the **Move** and **Rotate** tools.
Smooth	Creates non-adjustable vertices that generates smooth continuous curves. The curvature is determined by the spacing between the adjacent vertices [see Fig. 46].

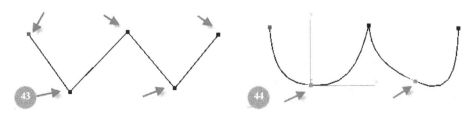

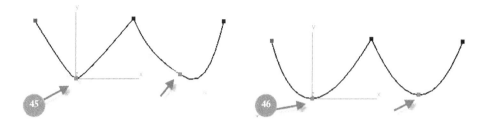

Selection Rollout

The controls in this rollout allow you to select sub-object levels of a spline, work with named selection sets and tangent handles, and display settings. Also, you can see information about the selected entities in this rollout.

At the top of the rollout, there are three buttons: **Vertex**, **Segment**, and **Spline**. These buttons let you select sub-object levels of a spline. The **Copy** and **Paste** controls in the **Named Selections** rollout allow you to place selection into the copy buffer and paste selection from the copy buffer, respectively.

Generally, you can transform bezier handles of a single vertex in the viewport even if multiple vertices are selected. If you want to simultaneously transform bezier handles of multiple vertices, select the **Lock Handles** check box. When **Alike** is on, as you drag handle of an incoming or outgoing vector, all incoming and outgoing handles move simultaneously [except the broken tangents]. If you select the **All** control, any handle you move will affect all other handles regardless of whether they are broken.

When the **Area Selection** check box is selected, you can define a radius in the associated spinner. When you click a vertex, all vertices that fall with in the specified radius of the clicked vertex will be selected. When the **Segment End** check box is selected, you can select a vertex by clicking on a point on the segment close to the vertex. You can add to the selection using **Ctrl**. The **Select By** control allows you to select vertices on the selected spline or segment. You need to first select a spline or segment using the **Spline** or **Segment** sub-object level and then you need to switch to the **Vertex** sub-object level. Click **Select By** to open the **Select By** dialog box. Now, click the desired button on the dialog box to select the vertices.

The **Show Vertex Numbers** check box toggles the display of vertex numbers in the viewport. The numbers are displayed next to the selected spline's vertices. If you turn on **Selected Only**, the vertex number only appears for the selected vertices.

Geometry Rollout
Now, let's explore the options available for editing the editable spline object at sub-object levels. These options are listed in the **Geometry** rollout.

New Vertex Type Group
The controls in this group let you choose the type of tangency for vertices that are created when you clone segments or splines using the **Shift** key.

Caution: Scope
*These controls have no effect on the tangency of the vertices created using tools such as **Create Line**, **Refine**, and so on. **Linear** sets linear tangency for the new vertices. **Smooth** sets smooth tangency. When on, the new overlapping vertices will be welded together. **Bezier Corner** sets the **Bezier** corner tangency.*

Note: Editable spline - object level
*The following controls are also available at the editable spline object level: **New Vertex Type** group, **Create Line**, **Attach**, **Attach Mult.**, **Cross Section**, **Automatic Welding**, and **Insert**. This level is the one that is active when no sub-object level is selected.*

To use the **Connect Copy** feature, create a **Circle** spline and then convert it to editable spline. Activate the **Segment** sub-object level and then select the segments, as shown in the left image of Fig. 45. Select the **Connect** check box in the **Connect Copy** section. Now, invoke the **Scale** tool and then scale the segments outward with **Shift** held down. Max connects the newly created vertices with the original vertices [see right image in Fig. 47].

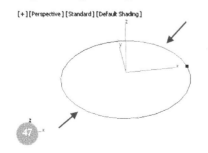
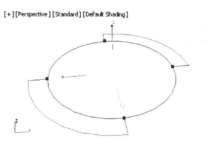

Create Line

Create Line adds more lines to the existing selected spline. The lines are separate splines but are part of the selected spline. To add another spline to the selected spline, select the existing spline and then create the new spline in the same way as you create the line spline.

Break

Break allows you to split a spline at the selected vertex or vertices. To split a spline, select on or more vertices and then click **Break**. Two overlapping vertices will be created at the break point. Use the **Move** tool to separate the vertices [see Fig. 48].

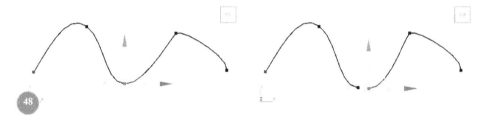

Attach

Attach attaches another spline object from the scene to the selected spline to create a compound shape. To attach a spline, select the spline and then click **Attach**. Now, hover the mouse pointer on the target spline. When the shape of the mouse pointer changes, click on the target spline to attach it to the selected spline.

When you attach shapes, the materials assigned to the two objects are combined. Here's how:

- If the target object does not have a material assigned, it inherits the material from the selected object.
- If the selected object does not have a material assigned, it inherits the material from the target object.
- If both objects have materials, the **Attach Options** dialog box appears [see Fig. 49]. Select the desired options from the dialog box and then click **OK**. The resulting material will be a **Multi-Subobject** material.

> *Caution: Target shape's creation parameters*
> *The target shape loses all its creation parameters. If there is any modifier stack attached to the target shape, it will be collapsed.*

Attach Multiple

Attach Multiple lets you attach multiple shapes to a selected spline in a single operation. To understand this feature, select a spline object and then click **Attach Multiple**. Now, select the shapes in the **Attach Multiple** dialog box that appears [see Fig. 50] and click **OK** to attach the selected shapes.

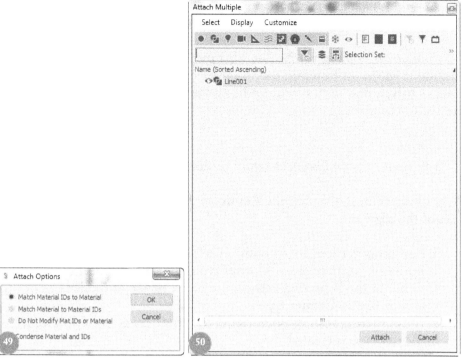

Note: *Reorienting attached splines*

*When **Reorient** is on, the attached splines are reoriented so that the local coordinate system of the attached splines is aligned with the selected spline.*

Cross Section

Cross Section allows you to create a spline cage out of cross sectional shapes. To create spline cage, make sure that all splines are attached. Click **Cross Section** and then click on the first spline, then second, and so on. RMB click to complete the process and create a cage [see Fig. 51].

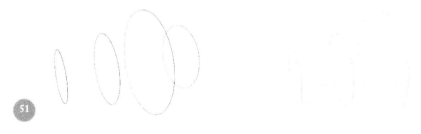

Tip: *Keeping vertices together*

*If you want to edit the spline cage, turn on **Area Selection** in the **Selection** rollout before selecting the vertices otherwise you would not be able to keep their position together.*

Refine

Refine adds vertices to the spline object without changing the curvature of the spline. To add vertices, click **Refine** and then hover the mouse pointer on the segments in a viewport. The shape of the mouse pointer changes on the eligible segments. Now, click to add a vertex. When you are done, click **Refine** again or press RMB.

If you click on an existing vertex, 3ds Max displays the **Refine & Connect** dialog box asking if you want to refine the vertex or connect to the vertex. If you choose **Connect Only**, a new vertex will not be created instead the clicked vertex will be connected to the existing vertex.

 Caution: Connecting vertices
*You must turn on **Connect** before clicking **Refine**.*

The type of vertex created during the **Refine** operation is dependent on the bordering vertices of the segment:

- If bordering vertices are smooth, a vertex of **Smooth** type is created.
- If bordering vertices are of **Corner** type, a vertex of **Corner** type is created.
- If either of the bordering vertices are of a **Corner** or **Bezier Corner** type, a vertex of **Bezier Corner** type is created.
- If the bordering vertices do not fit in the above mentioned criterion, a vertex of **Bezier** type is created.

Connect: It creates a new spline sub-object by connecting the two vertices.

To understand functioning of **Connect**, create two straight lines in a viewport and attach them [see Fig. 52]. Select the **Vertex** sub-object level. Select **Connect**. Notice that there are some options that get activated in the **Refine** group. Now, click **Refine** and then click on the first segment. Now, click on the second segment [see Fig. 53], RMB click to create to connect two vertices [see Fig. 54].

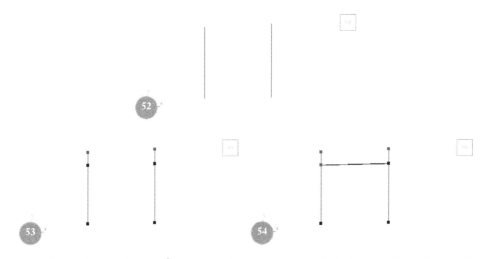

When **Linear** is on, the **Refine** operation creates straight lines using the vertices of the **Corner** type. When off, the created vertices are of **Smooth** type. **Closed** allows you to create closed splines by connecting the first and last vertices [see Fig. 55, numbers show clicking order].

When **Bind first** is on, it sets the first vertex created to be bound to the center of the selected segment [see Fig. 56]. **Bind last** sets the last vertex created to be bound to the center of the selected segment.

Note: Bound vertices

*Binding vertices helps in connecting splines when building a spline network for use with the **Surface** modifier. To distinguish the bound vertices from the standard vertices, 3ds Max makes them black. You cannot transform a bound vertex directly. However, you can move it by shifting the connected vertices. You can also change the type of the bound vertices from the upper left quadrant of the **Quad** menu.*

Automatic Welding

When on, the end vertex is welded automatically, if you move or place the vertex and the vertex fall within a distance specified using **Threshold**.

Note: Automatic welding

This feature is available at the object as well as at all the sub-object levels.

Weld

Weld welds two end vertices or two adjacent vertices into a single vertex. To weld vertices, move the vertices close to each other and click **Weld**. If the vertices fall within a threshold defined by the control next to **Weld**, the selected vertices are welded to a single vertex [see Fig. 57].

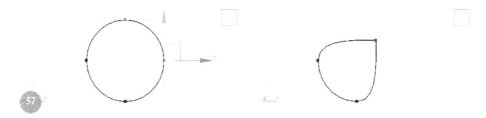

Connect

Connect connects two end vertices. To connect the vertices, click **Connect** and then drag the mouse pointer from one end vertex to another end vertex. It creates a linear segment by ignoring the tangent values of the end vertices. To connect the end points, click **Connect** and hover the cursor over one of the end vertex. When shape of the cursor changes, drag mouse pointer to the other end vertex to make the connection.

Insert

Insert lets you add one or more vertices creating additional segments in a spline. Click **Insert** and then click on the spline to attach the mouse pointer to the spline. Now, click to place the vertex; the spline gets attached with the mouse pointer. Now, continue clicking to create more vertices. RMB click to complete the operation. You are still in the insert mode, you can continue adding vertices on another segment or you can RMB click to exit. A single click create a corner vertex whereas dragging the mouse pointer creates a bezier vertex.

Make First

It allows you to define which vertex in a spline is the first vertex. The first vertex in a spline is indicated by a small box around it. To make a vertex first vertex, select the vertex and then click **Make First**. If you are editing an open spline, the first vertex should be end point that is already not a first vertex. On closed spline, you can make any vertex first vertex. The first vertex has special significance in many operations in 3ds Max. Table 23 summarizes the importance of first vertex:

Table 23: First vertex use	
Use	**Description**
Loft Path	Indicates the start of the path [Level 0].
Loft Shape	Controls the initial skin alignment.
Path Constraint	Indicates the start of the path [indicates 0% on the location of the path].
Trajectory	Indicates the first position key.

Fuse

Fuse lets you move all selected vertices to their averaged center. To fuse the vertices, select them [first attach all splines] and then click **Fuse** to move the vertices to same location [see Fig. 58]. Note that the **Fuse** operation does not weld the vertices, it simply moves them to the same location.

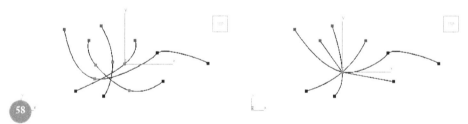

Cycle

Cycle allows you to select a specific vertex from the group of coincident vertices [vertices that shares the same location]. To select a specific vertex, select one or more vertices that share the same location, and then click **Cycle** repeatedly until you select the vertex you are looking for. Fuse two or three splines and then use **Cycle** to select the coincident vertices. Check the info about the selected vertex at the bottom of the **Selection** rollout.

CrossInsert

CrossInsert adds vertices at the intersection of two splines that are part of the same spline object. To add vertex, click **CrossInsert** and then click at the intersection of the two splines. If the distance between the splines is within the threshold defined by the control next to **CrossInsert**, the vertices are added [they are not welded] to both splines [see Fig. 59].

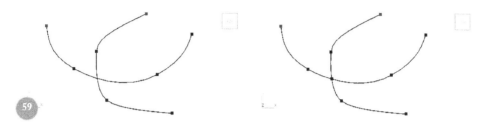

59

Fillet

Fillet lets you create the rounded corners by adding new control vertices. You can create rounded corners by dragging the mouse pointer in a viewport or by entering precise values in the control on the right of **Fillet**. To fillet the vertices, click **Fillet** and then drag the vertices in a viewport to add rounded corners. As you drag with **Fillet**, the control on its right shows the fillet amount [see Fig. 60]. You can continue dragging to add fillet to other vertices. To finish the operation, RMB click.

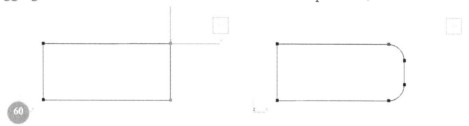

60

Chamfer

Chamfer chops off the selected vertices by creating segments connecting new vertices [see Fig. 61]. Like **Fillet** you can chamfer edges interactively or by entering precise values.

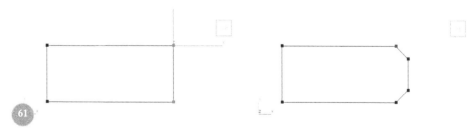

61

> *Note: Fillet/Chamfer functions*
> *Unlike the **Fillet/Chamfer** modifiers, you can apply these functions to any type of vertex. These modifiers only work with the **Corner** and **Bezier Corner** vertices.*

Tangent

The controls available in this group let you copy paste vertex handles from one vertex to another. To copy tangent, select a vertex and then click **Copy**. Click on the tangent to copy tangent to the clipboard. Now, select another vertex, click **Paste**, and then click on the tangent of the vertex to paste the tangent [see Fig. 62]. When **Paste Length** is on, the length of the handle is also copied.

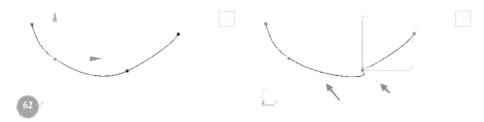

Hide

It allows you to hide the selected vertices and connected segments.

Unhide All

Unhide All allows you to unhide all hidden objects.

Bind/Unbind

Bind lets you create bound vertices. To create a bound vertex, click **Bind** and then drag from any end vertex to any segment expect the one connected to the vertex, a dashed line connects the vertex and the current mouse position. When the mouse is over an eligible segment, the pointer changes to a **Connect** symbol. When you release the mouse button, the vertex jumps to the center of the segment and bound to it. **Unbind** lets you disconnect the bind vertices.

Delete

Allows you to delete the selected vertices as well as one attached segment per deleted vertex.

Show selected segs

Lets you display the selected segments in red color at the **Vertex** sub-object level [see Fig. 63]. When off, the segments displayed in red only at **Segment** sub-object level.

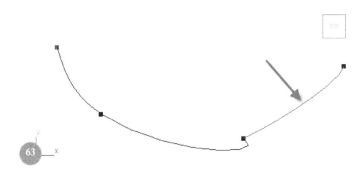

A segment is a part of spline between two vertices of the spline. You can select one or more segments by activating the **Segment** sub-object level. Once selected, you can transform them using the transformation tools.

Most of the controls available for segments are similar to those discussed in the **Vertex Level** section. The other controls available at the segment sub-object level are discussed next.

Geometry Rollout

Divide

Divide subdivides the selected segment(s) by adding a number of vertices that are specified by using the control available on the right of this spinner. To subdivide a segment, select segment or segments of the spline. Now, specify the number of vertices and then click **Divide** [see Fig. 64]. The distance between the vertices is dependent on the curvature of the segment.

Delete

Deletes the selected segments from the spline [see Fig. 65].

Detach

It lets you detach/copy selected segments from the spline. To detach segment or segments, select them and then click **Detach**. In the **Detach** dialog box that appears, type name in the **Detach as** text box and then click **OK**. The segment will be detached from the spline and new shape will be created [see Fig. 66].

There are some other controls that can be used with the detach operation. Table 24 summarizes these options.

Table 24: The **Detach** options	
Control	**Description**
Same Shp	When on, **Reorient** gets deactivated. The detached segment remains part of the same spline. If **Copy** is also on, the detached segment is copied at the same location.
Reorient	When on, the detached segment copies the transformation values of the spline's creation local coordinate system.
Copy	Copies the selected segment without detaching it from the spline.

Surface Properties Rollout
The controls in this layout allow you to apply different material IDs to spline segments. The material appears on the renderable shapes. To assign material ID to a segment or segments, select them and then enter the **ID** in the **Set ID** spinner. **Select ID** lets you select the segments corresponding to the material ID set in the spinner on the right of **Select ID**. The drop-down list below **Select ID** shows the name of the sub-materials, if you have applied **Multi-Subobject** material to the object. If you have applied a material other than the **Multi-Subobject** material, this drop-down list will be inactive.

When **Clear Selection** is on, selecting a new ID or material name deselects the previously selected segments or splines.

Changing Segment Properties
You can switch between the **Curve** or **Line** type for the selected segments. To change the type, select segments and then RMB click. Now, choose **Line** or **Curve** from the upper left quadrant of the **Quad** menu [see Fig. 67]. Fig. 68 shows a segment converted from the **Curve** type to the **Line** type.

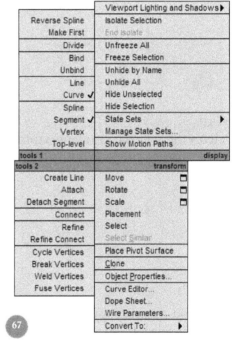

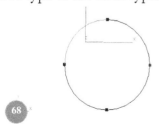

The **Spline** sub-object level allows you to select single spline or multiple splines in a single object. Once selected, you can transform them using the transformation tools. Most of the controls available for segments are similar to those discussed in the **Vertex Level** and **Segment Level** sections. The other controls available at the **Segment** sub-object level are discussed next.

Geometry Rollout
Connect Copy Group

Connect Copy works when you make a clone of the spline using **Shift**. You must turn on **Connect** before the cloning operation. When on, 3ds Max creates a new spline sub-object that connects the vertices of the original and cloned objects [see Fig. 69]. **Threshold** defines the distance that the soft selection uses during the **Connect Copy** operation.

Outline

Outline makes a copy of the spline. The copy offsets in all directions specified by the spinner on the right of **Outline**. You can also create an outline interactively by using the mouse. To create an outline, select one or more splines and then click **Outline**. Now, drag a spline to create outline [see Fig. 70]. When **Center** is on, the original spline and its outline moves away from an invisible center line by the distance specified by dragging operation or by the value specified for the spinner on the right of **Outline**.

Caution: Selecting splines
If there is one spline is in the scene, it is automatically selected for the outlining process. However, if you are using spinner to add outline, you must select it first.

Note: Open spline
If you are outlining an open spline, the outlining process creates a single closed spline [see Fig. 71].

71

Boolean

Boolean combines two splines. It alters the first spline you select and deletes the other one. There are three types of **Boolean** operations available. Table 25 summarizes those operations:

Table 25: The boolean operations	
Operation	**Description**
Union	Combines two overlapping splines into a single spline. The overlapping portion is removed.
Subtraction	Subtracts the overlapping portion of the second spline from the first spline.
Intersection	Leaves the overlapping portions of the two splines.

To boolean splines, make sure both splines are part of a single spline object [use **Attach** to attach them]. Select a spline and then click **Union, Subtraction**, or **Intersection**. Now, click **Boolean**. Hover the mouse pointer on the second spline and then click when shape of the cursor changes to complete the operation [see Fig. 72].

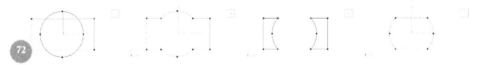

72

Mirror

Mirror allows you to mirror splines horizontally, vertically, and diagonally. To mirror a spline, ensure it is selected and then click **Mirror Horizontally, Mirror Vertically,** or **Mirror Both**. Next, click **Mirror** to complete the operation [see Fig. 73].

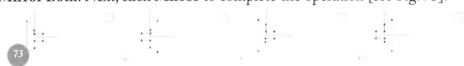

73

If **Copy** is on, 3ds Max creates a mirror copy of the spline [see Fig. 74].

74

When **About Pivot** is on, 3ds Max mirrors the spline along its geometric center otherwise mirrors along the spline object's pivot point [see Fig. 75].

75

Trim

Trim allows you to clear the overlapping segments in a shape. The two splines must overlap each other and they should be part of the same spline object. To trim a spline, select the spline that will be used to trim the target spline. Click **Trim** and hover the cursor over the spline that you want to trim and then click when the shape of the cursor changes [see Fig. 76].

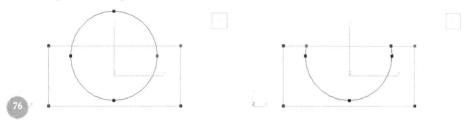

76

Extend

Extend allows you to extend an open spline. To extend spline, you need a segment that can extend to an intersecting segment of the spline. **Extend** does not work if intersection is not possible. To understand the **Extend** feature, create a circle and a line [see the left image in Fig. 77]. Convert the circle to an editable spline object and then attach is with the line. Select the **Spline** sub-object mode, click **Extend**. Now, click on the each end of the line to extend it to the circle [see the right image in Fig. 77]. When the **Infinite Bounds** check box is selected, 3ds Max treats open splines as infinite in length.

77

Explode

Explode breaks the segment of the selected spline and convert segments into separate splines or objects. There are two options available for the explode operation: **Splines** and **Objects**. If you choose **Objects**, the **Explode** dialog box appears. Type a name in the **Object Name** text box and click **OK**. Each successive object will use a name appended with an incremental three-digit number. For example, if you type name as **myShape** and click **OK**. The name of other objects will be: **myShape001**, **myShape002**, **myShape003**, and so on.

> ✎ *Note: Explode and Detach*
> **Explode** *is* **Detach** *on steroids.*

Changing the Spline Type

You can change the spline type from **Curve** to **Line** and visa-versa. To change type, select the spline and RMB click. Choose **Line** or **Curve** from the upper left quadrant of the **Quad** menu. Right image in Fig. 78 shows the spline object converted from **Curve** type into **Line** type.

78

> ✎ *Note: Checking self-intersecting splines*
> *You can use the **Shape Check** utility to check self-intersecting splines and NURBS curves. The self-intersecting shapes may produce unpredictable results when used in the loft, extrude, or lathed operations. To check intersection point, go to the **Utilities** panel and then click on **More** to open **Utilities** dialog box. Select **Shape Check** from the **Utilities** list and click **OK**. The **Shape Check** rollout appears in the **Utilities** panel. Click **Pick Object** and then click the spline or NURBS curve in a viewport. The red squares appear on the intersection points [see Fig. 79].*

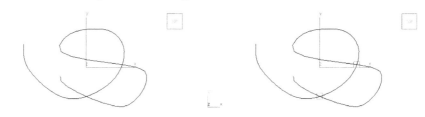

79

Hands-on Exercises

From the **File** menu, choose **Project** > **Create Default** to open the **Choose a folder** dialog box. In this dialog box, navigate to the **3dsmax2019projects** directory and then click **New Folder** and then rename the folder as **unit-m2**. Select the folder and then click **Select Folder** to create the project folder.

Exercise 1: Creating the Apple Logo

In this exercise, you will create 3D Apple logo [see Fig. E1].

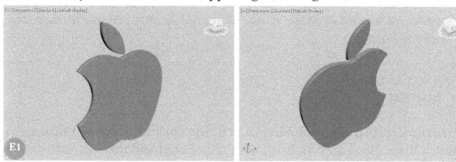

The following table summarizes the exercise:

Table E1	
Skill level	Basic
Time to complete	30 Minutes
Topics in the section	• Getting Started • Creating the Logo
Project Folder	**unit-m6**
Units	**Generic**
Final exercise file	**logo-finish.max**

Getting Started

Follow these steps:

1. Go to the **Create** panel, click **Geometry**, and then click **Plane**. In the **Front** viewport, create a plane. In the **Modify** panel > **Parameters** rollout, set **Length** to **180** and **Width** to **150**. Set **Length Segs** and **Width Segs** to **2** each. Also, clear the **Real-World Map Size** check box.

2. Click **Material Editor** from the **Main** toolbar. Create a **Standard** material using the **Material Editor** and apply it to the plane. Use the **apple-logo.jpg** for the **Diffuse** map. You need to turn on the **Show Shaded Material in Viewport** check box for the material to display the image on the plane in the viewport.

3. Ensure in the **Coordinates** rollout, **Use Real-World Scale** is off and **U Tiling** and **V Tiling** are set to **1**. Make sure the **Front** viewport is active and then press **G** to turn off the grid. Also, set the shading to **Default Shading** in the **Front** viewport. RMB click on the plane and then choose **Object Properties** from the **Quad** menu to open the **Object Properties** dialog box. In the **Interactivity** section of the dialog box, turn on the **Freeze** check box and in the **Display Properties** section, clear the **Show Frozen in Gray** check box [see Fig. E2].

 What just happened?
Here, I've froze the object. Once you freeze the object, you won't be able to accidentally select or move it and it would be easy for you to trace the logo using splines.

Creating the Logo
Follow these steps:

1. Go to the **Create** panel, click **Shapes**, and then click **Line**. In the **Front** viewport, create a shape [see Fig. E3]. Ensure line is selected and then activate the **Vertex** mode from the **Modify** panel. Now, adjust the shape of the line according to the background image [see Fig. E4]. Make sure the X position of the two end vertices is same.

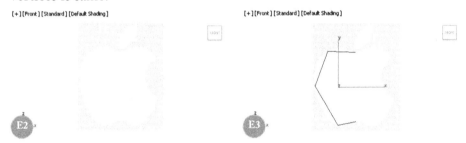

2. Activate the **Spline** level and select the spline in the viewport. Now, in the **Modify** panel > **Geometry** rollout, turn on the **Copy** check box and then click **Mirror**. Press **S** to turn on the **Snap** toggle and then snap the copied spline with the original spline [see Fig. E5].

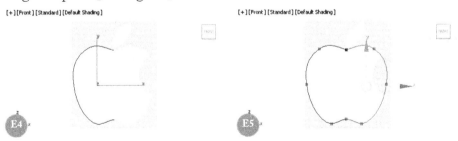

3. Weld the end vertices that you just snapped [see Fig. E6]. Go to the **Create** panel, click **Shapes**, and then click **Circle**. Select **Edge** from the **Creation Method** rollout. Create a circle [see Fig. E7].

 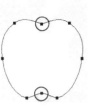 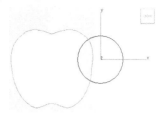

4. Select the profile curve of the logo and then in the **Create** panel, select **Shapes > Compound Shapes > ShpBoolean**. In the **Boolean Parameters** rollout, click **Add Operands** and then select the **Circle** in the viewport. In the **Operands Parameters** rollout, click **Subtract** to subtract circle from the profile curve [see Fig. E8]. Create two circles for the upper part of the logo [see Fig. E9].

5. Create a **ShpBoolean** object and connect the two circles with it. In the **Operands Parameters** rollout, click **Intersect** to create the shape of the leaf [see Fig. E10].

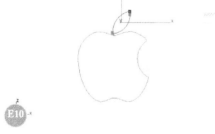

6. Convert the curves to editable spline and then attach them. Now, to make the unified spline smooth, on the **Modify** panel > **Interpolation** rollout, set **Steps** to **32**. Hide the plane object using **Scene Explorer**.

7. From the **Modifier List > Object-Space Modifiers** section, choose **Bevel**. In the **Bevel Values** rollout, select the **Level 2** and **Level 3** checkboxes. Now, set **Start Outline** to **-0.5**, **Level 1 Height** to **0.5**, **Level 1 Outline** to **0.5**, **Level 2 Height** to **5**, **Level 2 Outline** to **0**, **Level 3 Height** to **0.5**, and **Level 3 Outline** to **-0.5**.

Exercise 2: Creating Bowling Pin and Ball

In this exercise, you will create model of the bowling pin and ball [see Fig. E1]. Table E2 summarizes the exercise:

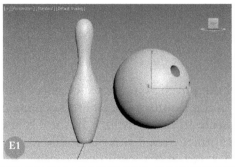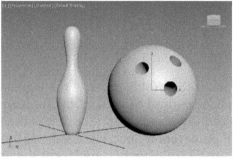

Table E2:	
Skill level	Beginner
Time to complete	20 Minutes
Topics in the section:	• Specifying the Units for the Exercise • Creating the Bowling Pin • Creating the Ball
Project folder	**unit-m6**
Units	**Generic**
Final exercise file	**pin-finish.max**

Specifying the Units for the Exercise
Follow these steps:

1. From **Customize** menu choose **Units Setup**. In the **Units Setup** dialog box that appears, select **Generic Units** from the **Units Setup** dialog box. Click **OK** to accept the changes made.

2. From the **File** menu, choose **Save** to open the **Save File As** dialog box. In the **File name** text box type **pin-ball-finish.max** and then click **Save** to save the file.

Setting the Blueprint
Follow these steps:

1. Switch to the **Create** panel, click **Geometry**, then click **Plane**. In the **Front** viewport, create a plane. In the **Modify** panel > **Parameters** rollout, change **Length** to **100** and **Width** to **75**. Align the plane, as shown in Fig. E2. Also, clear the **Real-World Map Size** check box.

2. Click **Material Editor** from the **Main** toolbar. Create a **Standard** material using **Material Editor** and apply it to the plane. Use the **pin-reference.jpeg** for the **Diffuse** map. You need to turn on the **Show Shaded Material in the Viewport**

check box for the material to display the image on the plane in the viewport. In the **Coordinates** rollout, **Use Real-World Scale** is off and **U Tiling** and **V Tiling** are set to **1**. Change **V Offset** to **-0.043**. Also, Change **Opacity** of the material to **50**.

3. In the **Front** viewport, change display mode to **Default Shading** [see Fig. E3]. RMB click on the plane and then choose **Object Properties** from the **Quad** menu. Select the **Freeze** check box from the **Interactivity** area and clear the **Show Frozen in Gray** check box from the **Display Properties** area.

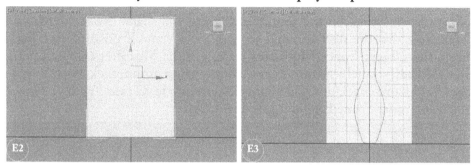

Creating the Bowling Pin
Follow these steps:

1. In the **Create** panel, click **Shapes**, and then click **Line**. Using the **Line** tool, create a half profile of the pin and then move the line to the right [see Fig. E4]. In the **Modify** panel > **Selection** rollout, click **Vertex** to activate the vertex sub-object level.

2. Select all vertices except the first and last vertex and then RMB click; choose **Smooth** from the **Quad** menu > **tools 1** quadrant [see Fig. E5].

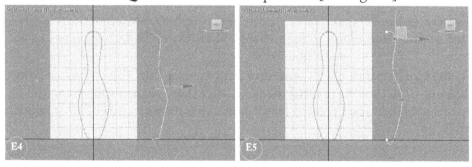

3. In the **Modify** panel > **Selection** rollout, click **Segment** to activate the segment sub-object level. Select the segment, as shown in Fig. E6. RMB click; choose **Line** from the **Quad** menu > **tools 1** quadrant. Now, align the bottom two points [see Fig. E7].

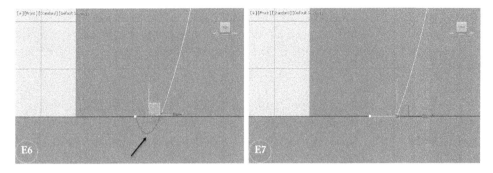

4. Move the line back on the profile and adjust the shape using the **Move** tool. Make sure that the start and end vertices are at same X position [see Fig. E8]. From the **Object-Space Modifiers** section of the **Modifier List**, select **Lathe**. In the **Modify** panel > **Parameters** rollout > **Align** group, click **Min**. Now, select the **Weld Core** check box and change **Segments** to **32** [see Fig. E9]. Now, hide the plane using Scene Explorer [see Fig. E10].

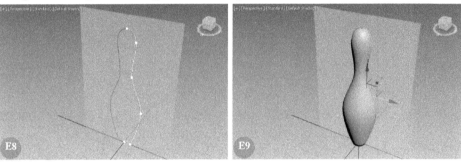

Creating the Ball
Follow these steps:

1. In the **Create** panel, click **Geometry**, and then on the **Object Type** rollout, click **Sphere**. In the **Perspective** viewport, create a sphere. Switch to the **Modify** panel and on the **Parameters** rollout, change **Radius** to **35** and **Segments** to **45**.

2. In the **Create** panel, click **Geometry**, and then on the **Object Type** rollout, click **Sphere**. Select the **AutoGrid** check box and then create **3** spheres on the surface of the sphere we just created [see Fig. E11]. Change radius of all small spheres to **5**.

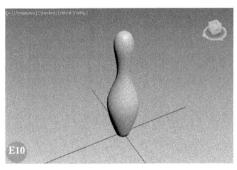
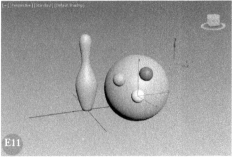

3. Change coordinate system to **Local** and then invoke the **Scale** tool. Now, scale the spheres along the **Z** axis about **350** units [see Fig. 12].

4. Select the bigger sphere. In the **Create** panel, click **Geometry,** and then choose **Compound Objects** from the drop-down list located below **Geometry.** Click **ProBoolean** and then make sure that **Subtraction** is selected in the **Parameters** rollout. Click **Start Picking** and then click on small sphere one-be-one to create holes [see Fig. 13]. Click the **Start Picking** button again to finish the operation.

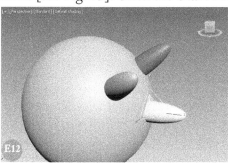 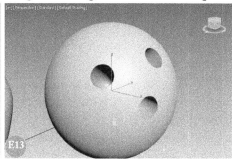

Exercise 3: Creating a Corkscrew

In this exercise, you will model a corkscrew using the **Helix** Spline and the **Loft** compound object [see Fig. E1].

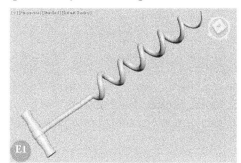 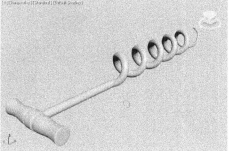

Table E3 summarizes the exercise:

Table E3	
Skill level	Beginner
Time to complete	15 Minutes
Topics in the section:	• Specifying the Units for the Exercise • Creating the Corkscrew
Project folder	**unit-m6**
Units	**Generic Units**
Final exercise file	**corkscrew-finish.max**

Specifying the Units for the Exercise

From **Customize** menu choose **Units Setup**. In the **Units Setup** dialog box that opens, select the **Generic Units** option from the **Display Unit Scale** group.

Creating the Corkscrew

Follow these steps:

1. Go to the **Create** panel, click **Shapes**, then click **Helix**. In the **Top** viewport, create a shape. In the **Modify** panel > **Parameters** rollout, set **Radius 1** to **8**, **Radius 2** to **8**, **Height** to **120**, and **Turns** to **5.5**. In the **Front** viewport, rotate it by **90** degrees around Y-axis [see Fig. E2].

2. RMB click on the helix and then choose **Convert To: > Convert to Editable Spline** from the **transform** quadrant of the **Quad** menu. In the **Modify** panel > **Selection** rollout, click **Vertex** and then move the **first yellow** vertex toward left about **60** units in the **Front** viewport [see Fig. E3].

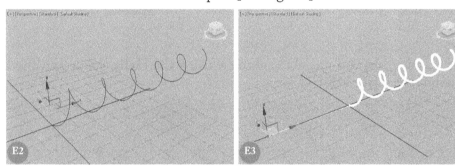

E2   E3

3. Apply the **Normalize Spline** modifier to the helix. In the **Modify** panel > **Parameters** rollout, set **Seg Length** to **5**. RMB click on the helix and then choose **Convert To: > Convert to Editable Spline** from the **transform** quadrant of the **Quad** menu.

What just happened?
You might have noticed that there were lots of vertices on the helix when I converted it into an editable spline. To reduce the number of vertices, I have applied the Normalize Spline modifier to the helix spline. This modifier add new control points at regular intervals.

4. Go to the **Create** panel, click **Shapes**, then click **Circle**. In the **Left** viewport, create a circle. In the **Modify** panel > **Parameters** rollout, set **Radius** to **2.5**. Select helix in a viewport. Go to the **Create** panel, click **Geometry > Compound Objects**, then click **Loft**. In the **Creation Method** rollout, click **Get Shape** and then click circle in a viewport to loft the circle along the helix [see Fig. E4].

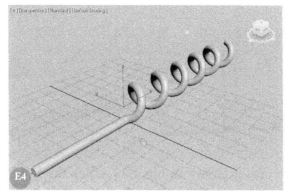

5. In the **Modify** panel > **Skin Parameters** rollout > **Options** group, set **Shape Steps** to **1** and **Path Steps** to **2**. In the **Modify** panel > **Deformations** rollout, click **Scale**. In the **Scale Deformation** dialog box that opens, click **Insert Corner Point** and then add a point below the **80** mark [see Fig. E5]. Now, click **Move Control Point** and move the end point downward [see Fig. E6] to scale the end area of the corkscrew [see Fig. E7].

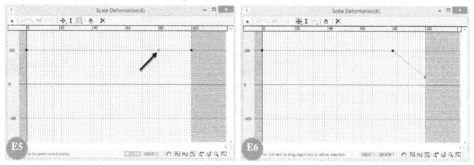

6. Go to the **Create** panel, click **Geometry** > **Standard Primitives**, then click the **Cylinder** button. In the **Front** viewport, create a cylinder. In the **Modify** panel > **Parameters** rollout, set **Radius** to **4.857**, **Height** to **43.771**, **Height Segments** to **6**, and **Sides** to **18**. Now, align the cylinder with the corkscrew [see Fig. E8].

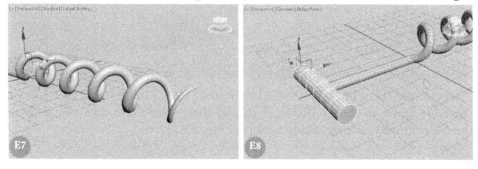

7. Convert cylinder into an editable poly object and then activate the **Edge** mode. Select the edges, as shown in Fig. E9. In the **Modify** panel > **Edit Edges** rollout, click the **Connect** > **Settings** button to open the **Connect Edges** caddy. Set **Segments** to **2**, **Pinch** to **-18**, and then click **OK** to connect the edges [see Fig. E10].

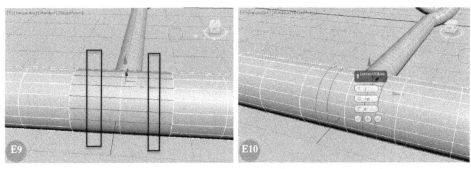

8. Select polygon loops, as shown in Fig. E11. Click the **Inset Settings** button to open the **Inset** caddy. Set **Type** to **Group, Amount** to **0.31**, and then click **OK** [see Fig. E12].

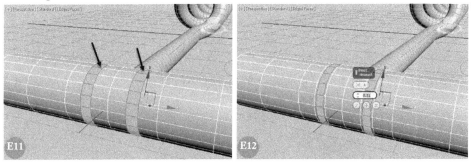

9. Click the **Extrude Settings** button to open the **Extrude Polygons** caddy. Set **Type** to **Local Normals, Height** to **-0.1**, and then click **Apply and Continue**. Now, set **Amount** to **-0.2** and then click **OK** [see Fig. E13]. Now, select the polygon loops, as shown in Fig. E14.

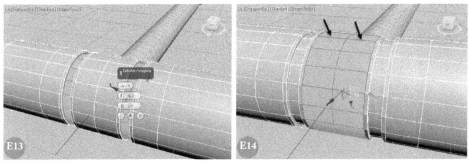

10. First extrude them by **0.4** units and then inset by **0.3** units [see Fig. E15]. Select the edge loops, as shown in Fig. E16 and then scale them down by **25%** using the **Select and Uniform Scale** tool [see Fig. E17].

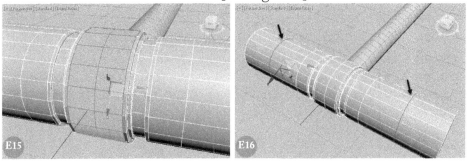

11. Now, select the border edges at both ends of the cylinder and then chamfer them [see Fig. E18]. Now, apply the **TurboSmooth** modifier to the cylinder.

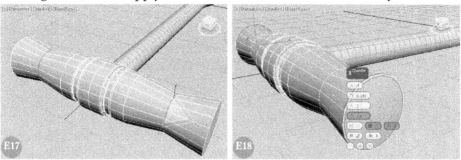

Exercise 4: Creating a Model of a Glass and Liquid

In this exercise, you will model a glass and liquid [see Fig. E1].

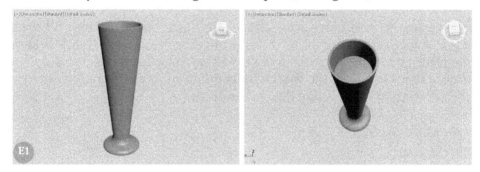

Table E4 summarizes the exercise:

Table E4	
Skill level	Intermediate
Time to complete	1 Hour
Topics in the section:	• Specifying the Units for the Exercise • Setting the Blueprint • Creating the Glass • Creating the Liquid
Project folder	**unit-m6**
Units	**Generic Units**
Final exercise file	**glass-liquid-finish.max**

Specifying the Units for the Exercise

From **Customize** menu choose **Units Setup**. In the **Units Setup** dialog box that opens, select the **Generic Units** option from the **Display Unit Scale** group.

Setting the Blueprint

Follow these steps:

1. Go to the **Create** panel, click **Geometry**, then click **Plane**. In the **Front** viewport, create a plane. In the **Modify** panel > **Parameters** rollout, set **Length** to **100** and **Width** to **75**. Also, clear the **Real-World Map Size** check box.

2. Click **Material Editor** from the **Main** toolbar. Create a standard material using **Material Editor** and apply it to the plane.

3. Use the **glassRef.png** for the **Diffuse** map. You need to turn on the **Show Shaded Material in the Viewport** check box for the material to display the image on the plane in the viewport. Ensure in the **Coordinates** rollout, make sure **Use Real-World Scale** is off and **U Tiling** and **V Tiling** are set to **1**.

4. Make sure the **Front** viewport is active and then press **G** to turn off the grid. Also, change display mode to **Default Shading** [see Fig. E2]. RMB click on the plane and then choose **Object Properties** from the **Quad** menu. Select the **Freeze** check box from the **Interactivity** group and clear **Show Frozen in Gray** check box from the **Display Properties** area.

Creating The Glass

Follow these steps:

1. Go to the **Create** panel, click **Shapes**, then click **Line**. In the **Front** viewport, create a shape [see Fig. E3].

2. In the **Modify** panel > **Selection** rollout, click **Vertex**. In the **Modify** panel > **Geometry** rollout, click **Fillet**. Click and drag over the vertices to get the shape [see Fig. E4]. Make sure the X coordinate value for the selected vertices, shown in Fig. E5, is same.

3. Make sure the profile of the curve is selected and then apply the **Lathe** modifier to it. In the **Modify** panel > **Parameters** rollout, click **Min** in the **Align** group. Set **Segments** to **32**. Now, turn on **Weld Core** and then click **Y** from the **Direction** group [see Fig. E6]. Hide the plane and then rename the geometry as **glassGeo**.

Creating The Liquid

Follow these steps:

1. Select **glassGeo** and then on the **Ribbon > Polygon Modeling** panel, click **Convert to Poly**. Activate **Edge** sub-object level and then on the **Ribbon > Edit** panel, click **SwiftLoop**. Insert an edge loop as shown in Fig. E7. Click **SwiftLoop** again to deactivate it. Activate **Polygon** sub-object level and then select the inner polygons shown in Fig. E8.

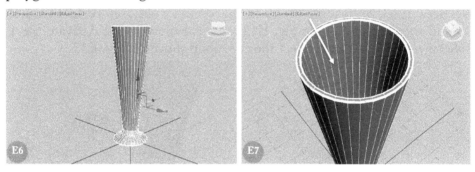

2. **Shift** drag the selected polygons to the right. In the **Clone Part of Mesh** dialog box that opens, select **Clone to Object** and then type **liquidGeo** as the name of the clone, and then click **OK** [see Fig. E9]. Make sure all polygons of **liquidGeo** are selected and then click **Flip** on the **Modify** panel > **Edit Polygons** rollout to flip the normals.

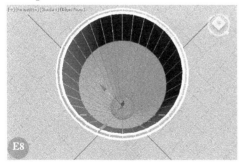
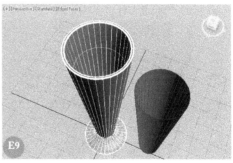

> **?** *What just happened?*
> *When we created **liquidGeo** using the **Shift** drag method, you would have noticed that the outer area of the geometry is appearing dark. It happens because of the wrong orientation of the surface normals. By flipping the polygons, normals are properly oriented now.*

3. Select **liquidGeo** and then activate **Border** sub-object level. Now, select the border [see Fig. E10].

4. In the **Ribbon > Geometry (All)** panel, click **CapPoly**. Now, activate **Polygon** sub-object level and then select the cap polygon. In the **Ribbon > Polygons** panel, **Shift** click **Inset**. In the **Inset** caddy control, set **Amount** to **5** and then click **OK** [see Fig. E11].

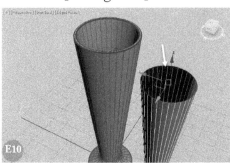
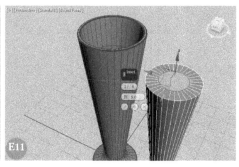

5. In the **Ribbon > Polygon Modeling** panel, **Ctrl** click **Vertex**. In the **Ribbon > Vertices** panel, **Shift** click **Weld**. In the **Weld's** caddy, set **Weld Threshold** to **15** and then click **OK** [see Fig. E12] to weld the vertices. Activate the **Edge** sub-object level and then select the edge loop shown in Fig. E13.

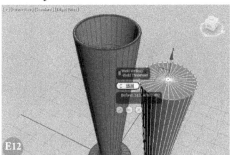
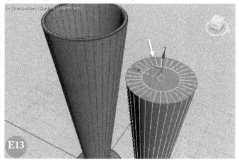

6. In the **Ribbon > Edges** panel, **Shift** click **Chamfer**. In the **Chamfer** caddy control, set **Edge Chamfer Amount** to **0.09** and **Connect Edge Segments** to **2** [see Fig. E14]. Click **OK**. Align the **glassGeo** and **liquidGeo** using the **Align** tool [see Fig. E15].

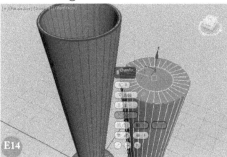
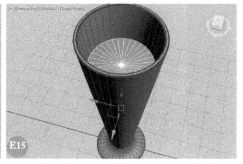

In this exercise, we are going to create model of a jug using spline and polygon modeling techniques [see Fig. E1].

The following table summarizes the exercise.

Table E5	
Skill Level	Intermediate
Time to Complete	30 Minutes
Topics in this section:	• Getting Ready • Creating Shape of the Jug Using Line and NGon Spline Primitive • Creating the Handle of the Jug Using Extrude Along Spline Feature • Refining the Model
Project Folder	**unit-m6**
Final Exercise File	**jug-finish.max**

Getting Ready

From **Customize** menu choose **Units Setup**. In the **Units Setup** dialog box that opens, select the **Generic Units** option from the **Display Unit Scale** group.

Creating Shape of the Jug Using Line and NGon Spline Primitive

Follow these steps:

1. Activate the **Front** viewport. Go to the **Create** panel, click **Shapes**, and then ensure that **Splines** is selected in the drop-down list below the **Shapes** button. In the **Object Type** rollout, click **Line**. Expand the **Keyboard Entry** rollout, and then click **Add Point** to add a point at the origin. Now, set **Y** to **30** and then click **Add Point**. This action creates a line in the **Front** viewport [see Fig. E2]. This line will serve as path for the **Loft** tool. Click **Select Object** on the **Main** toolbar to deactivate the line tool.

2. In the **Object Type** rollout, click **NGon** and then create an **NGon** in the **Front** viewport. In the **Modify** panel > **Parameters** rollout, set **Radius** to **7**, and **Sides**

to **26**. Select the **Circular** check box. Create four more copies of the **NGon**. The total number of **NGons** will be **5** [see Fig. E3]. Change the radius of the three right-most **NGons** to **4** [see Fig. E4].

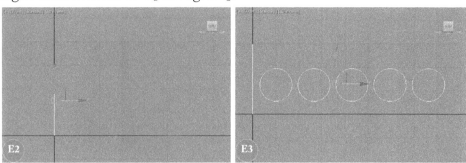

Why NGon is used instead of Circle?

*You can also use the **Circle** primitive to create the shapes for the jug but by default a **Circle** spline object just has four vertices. The **NGon** primitive we have used has 26 sides. As a result, a smooth surface will be created when you will loft the shapes along the path.*

3. The last **NGon** will be the spout of the jug. Select it and then covert into the **Editable Spline** object. Activate the **Vertex** sub-object level and then select the top four vertices as shown in Fig. E5.

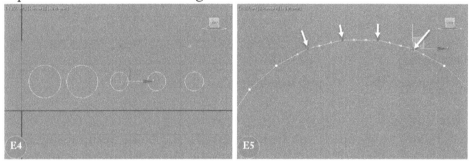

4. RMB click on the vertices and then choose **Corner** from the **tool1** quadrant of the **Quad** menu. Now, select the middle two vertices and move them using the **Select and Move** tool [see Fig. E6]. Ensure the vertices are still selected and them RMB click. In the **tool1** quadrant of the **Quad** menu, choose **Smooth** to make the shape of the spout [see Fig. E7]. If you want, you can fillet the other two corner vertices to create a smooth curve. Deactivate the **Vertex** sub-object level.

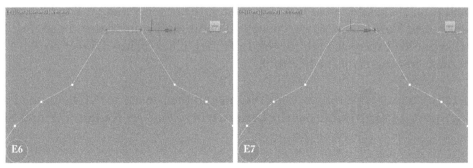

5. Select the **Line** in the **Front** viewport. Go to the **Create** panel, click **Geometry**, and then ensure that **Compound Objects** is selected in the drop-down list below the **Geometry** button. In the **Object Type** rollout, click **Loft**. In the **Path Parameters** rollout, ensure **Path** to set to **0** and click **Get Shape** button on the **Creation Method** rollout. Now, click on the first **NGon** that you have created. Set **Path** to **1** and then click **Get Shape**. Now, click on the second **NGon** in the **Front** viewport.

6. Similarly, pick the other three **NGons** with **Path** value set to **82, 85**, and **100**, respectively. This action creates the shape of the jug in the viewport [see Fig. E8].

7. In the **Modify** panel, clear **Cap End** check box from the **Skin Parameters > Capping** group. In the **Options** group, set **Shape Steps** to **0** and **Path Steps** to **3**. Select the **Linear Interpolation** check box. Now, delete all spline objects from the scene.

8. Add a **Shell** modifier to the stack and then set **Outer Amount** to **0.559** in the **Modify** panel > **Parameters** rollout [see Fig. E9].

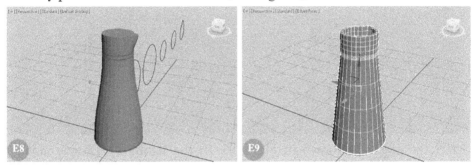

Creating the Handle of the Jug Using Extrude Along Spline Feature

Follow these steps:

1. Convert model to an **Editable Poly** object. Select all polygons and then in the **Modify** panel > **Polygon : Smoothing Groups** rollout, click **Auto Smooth**. Now, select the edges as shown in Fig. E10. In the **Ribbon > Loops** panel, click **Connect** with the **Shift** held down, the **Connect Edges** caddy appears in the viewport. Set **Segments** to **4** [see Fig. E11] and click **OK**.

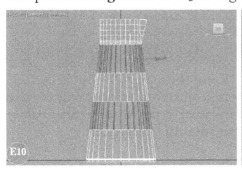
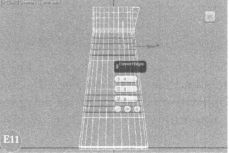

2. In the **Left** viewport, create a shape as shown in Fig. E12. Now, select the vertices shown Fig. E13 and then click **Connect** from the **Modify** panel > **Edit Vertices** rollout to connect the vertices. Similarly, connect the other vertices diagonally [see Fig. 14].

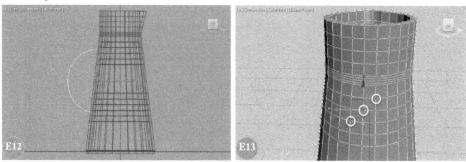

3. Select the center vertex and click **Chamfer** > **Settings** button on the **Modify** panel > **Edit Vertices** rollout. In the **Chamfer** caddy control, set **Amount** to **1.059** and click **OK** [see Fig. E15].

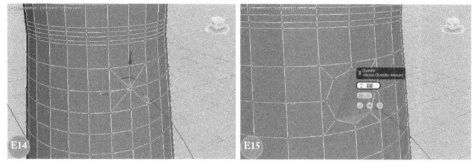

4. Select the edges, as shown in Fig. E16. In the **Ribbon** > **Loops** panel, click **Connect** with the **Shift** held down, the **Connect Edges** caddy appears in the viewport. Set **Segments** to **3** [see Fig. E17] and click **OK**. Similarly, connect other edges [see Fig. E18].

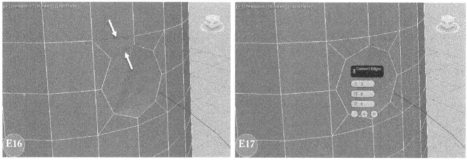

5. Select the vertices, as shown in Fig. E19 and then apply the **Spherify** modifier to round the shape [see Fig. 20]. Convert geometry to editable poly to bake the **Spherify** modifier. Select all polygons and then in the **Modify** panel > **Polygon : Smoothing Groups** rollout, click **Auto Smooth** [see Fig. 21].

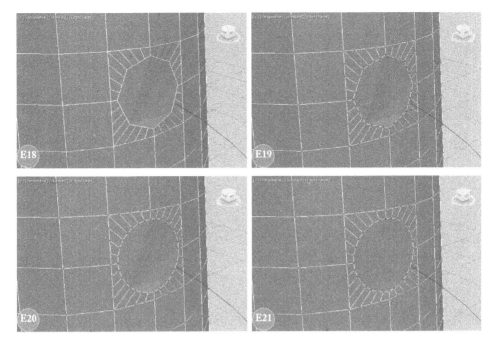

6. Convert geometry to editable poly. Similarly, create the round shape for the other part of the handle [see Fig. E22]. Convert geometry to editable poly. Select the polygon, as shown in Fig. E23 and then on the **Ribbon > Polygon** panel, click **Extrude on Spline** with the **Shift** held down, the **Extrude Along Spline** caddy control appears.

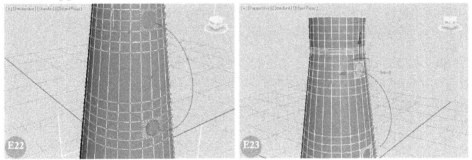

7. Click **Pick Spline** and then click on the curve in a viewport to extrude the selected polygon along the spline. In the **Extrude Along Spline** caddy, set the values as shown in Fig. E24 and then click **OK**.

8. Select the polygon shown in Fig. E25 and then bridge them [see Fig. E26]. In the **Ribbon > Edit** panel, click NURMS to display smooth model in the viewport. [see Fig. 27].

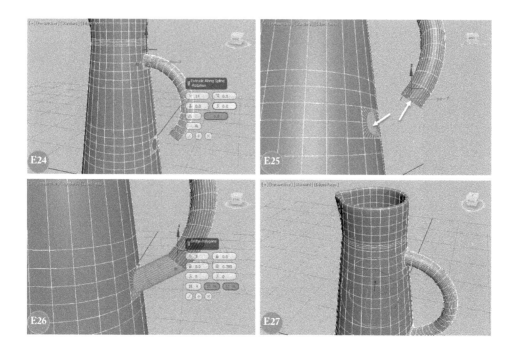

Quiz

Evaluate your skills to see how many questions you can answer correctly.

Multiple Choice
Answer the following questions, only one choice is correct.

1. Which of the following keys is used to constrain new points to 90 degrees angle increments while creating splines?

   [A] Shift   [B] Alt
   [C] Ctrl   [D] Shift+Alt

2. Which of the following is used to create splines in the shape of the text?

   [A] Text Object   [B] Text spline
   [C] Text   [D] All of the above

3. Which of the following keys is used to break a tangent and move its handles independently?

   [A] Alt   [B] Shift
   [C] Ctrl   [D] Shift+Alt

Fill in the Blanks

Fill in the blanks in each of the following statements:

1. 3ds Max provides two types of shape objects _____ and _____ curves.

2. You can use the _____ modifier to retain the parametric nature of a primitive spline.

3. The _____ and _____ rollouts are not available when you are use the **Edit Spline** modifier.

4. A _____ spline is a free-form spline that is made up of multiple segments.

5. The _____ spline is used to create spiral like shapes.

6. The _____ spline is a special type of spline that lets you generate splines based on a cross-sectional slice through a geometry objects.

7. To reset the tangent position, RMB click on the vertex or vertices and then choose _____ from the upper left quadrant of the **Quad** menu.

True of False

State whether each of the following is true or false:

1. 3ds Max allows you to combine shapes to create compound shapes.

2. You cannot change creation parameters of a compound shape.

3. You cannot clone the sub-objects by first selecting them and then press and hold **Shift** while transforming them.

4. The **Fuse** tool lets you move all selected vertices to their averaged center.

5. The **Fillet** tool lets you create the linear corners by adding new control vertices.

Summary

The unit covered the following topics:

- Generate planar and 3d surfaces
- Paths and shapes for the loft components
- Generate extrusions
- Generate revolved surfaces
- Define motion path for animations

- Using modifiers
- Stack display
- Object-Space modifiers vs World-Space modifiers
- How transform affects modifiers

Unit M7: Modifiers

Modifiers in 3ds Max allow to sculpt or edit the objects without changing its base structure. For example, if you apply a **Taper** modifier to a cylinder, you will still be able to change its parametric properties such as **Radius** and **Height**. Modifiers can change the geometry of the objects as well as their properties. In other words, modifiers add more parameters to the objects.

Following are some points that you should remember about modifiers:

- When you apply modifiers to the objects, they are stored in a stack and displayed as a stack in the **Modify** panel. You can change the order of the modifiers in the stack to change the effect of the modifier. You can also collapse the stack to make the changes permanent.
- You can apply any number of modifiers to an object.
- When you delete a modifier, its effect on the object also vanishes.
- You can copy modifiers from one object to another.
- The order of the modifier in the stack determines the final effect. Each modifier in the stack affects the modifiers that are applied after it.
- You can apply modifiers to sub-object levels.
- You can toggle the effect of the modifiers from the stack display.

Object Space Modifiers Vs World Space Modifiers

Some modifiers that 3ds Max offers operate in the world-space. These modifiers use the world-space coordinates and are applied to the object after all object-space modifiers and transforms have been applied. You can apply the world-space modifiers like any other object-space modifier. A world-space modifier is indicated by either an asterisk of the text **WSM**.

On the other hand, the object-space modifiers affect the geometry of the object in local space. They use object's local coordinate system. The local coordinate system relates specifically to the selected object. Each object has its own local center and coordinate system. The local center and the coordinate system define the object's local space. Unlike the world coordinate system, the directions of the object's axes [X, Y, and Z] depends on the current transform of the object.

Transform

Transform [move, rotate, and scale] are the most basic manipulations of the 3d objects. Unlike most of the modifiers, transforms are independent of internal structure of an object. The transformation values are stored in a matrix called **Transformation Matrix**. This matrix is applied to the entire object. The matrix is applied after all object-space modifiers have been applied but before the word-space modifiers.

Data Flow

Once you create an object and apply a modifier to it, 3ds Max evaluates the flow as per the table given below:

Order	Category	Modifiers/Transform/Properties	Illustration
Table 1: The data flow			
1	Creation Parameters	Cylinder	
2	Object Modifiers	Bend, Taper	
3	Transforms	Rotate, Position, and Scale	
4	Space Warps	Ripple	
5	Object Properties	Checker Material	

You can access modifiers from the **Modifiers** menu, the **Modifier** list from the **Modify** panel, and from the applicable **Modifier Set** menu. To keep all modifiers organized, they are grouped in the **Modifier** menu. The following table summarizes the options available in the **Modifier** menu.

Table 2: The **Modifier** menu overview	
Menu Item	**Sub-menu Items**
Selection Modifier	FFD Select, Mesh Select, Patch Select, Poly Select, Select By Channel, Spline Select, and Volume Select.
Patch/Spline Editing	Cross Section, Delete Patch, Delete Spline, Edit Patch, Edit Spline, Fillet/Chamfer, Lathe, Normalize Spline, Renderable Spline Modifier, Surface, Sweep, Trim/Extend, Optimize Spline, Spline Mirror, and Spline Relax.
Mesh Editing	Cap Holes, Chamfer, Delete Mesh, Edit Mesh, Edit Normals, Edit Poly, Extrude, Face Extrude, MultiRes, Normal Modifier, Optimize, ProOptimizer, Quadify Mesh, Smooth, STL Check, Symmetry, Tessellate, Vertex Paint, and Vertex Weld.
Conversion	Turn to Mesh, Turn to Patch, and Turn to Poly.
Animation	Attribute Holder, Flex, Linked XForm, Melt, Morpher, Patch Deform, Patch Deform (WSM), Path Deform, Spline Influence, Spline Morph, Spline Overlap, Path Deform (WSM), Skin, Skin Morph, Skin Wrap, Skin Wrap Patch, SpineIk Control, Surf Deform, and Surf Deform (WSM).
Cloth	Cloth, Garment Maker, and Welder.
Hair and Fur	Hair and Fur (WSM)
UV Coordinates	Camera Map, Camera Map (WSM), MapScaler (WSM), Projection, Unwrap UVW, UVW Map, UVW Mapping Add, UVW Mapping Clear, UVW and UVW XForm.
Cache Tools	Point Cache and Point Cache (WSM).
Subdivision Surfaces	Crease, CreaseSet, HSDS Modifier, MeshSmooth, OpenSubdiv, and TurboSmooth.
Free Form Deformers	FFD 2x2x2, FFD 3x3x3, FFD 4x4x4, FFD Box, and FFD Cylinder.
Parametric Deformers	Affect Region, Bend, Data Channel, Displace, Lattice, Mirror, Noise, Physique, Push, Preserve, Relax, Ripple, Shell, Slice, Skew, Stretch, Spherify, Squeeze, Twist, Taper, Substitute, XForm, and Wave.
Surface	Disp Approx, Displace Mesh (WSM), Material, and Material By Element.

Table 2: The **Modifier** menu overview	
Menu Item	**Sub-menu Items**
NURBS Editing	Displace Approx, Surf Deform, and Surface Select.
Radiosity	Subdivide and Subdivide (WSM).
Cameras	Camera Correction.

Using the Modify Panel

To apply a modifier to an object, select the object in the scene and then go to the **Modify** panel. The name of the selected object appears on the top of the **Modify** panel. Apply a modifier to the object by using one of the following methods:

- Choose a modifier from the **Modifier** list available in the **Modify** panel. You can either use mouse to click on the **Modifier** or use the keyboard. For example, if you are looking for the **Mirror** modifier, type **mi**, the modifiers whose name start with **mi** [in this case the **Mirror** modifier only] appear in the **Modifier** list. Now, you can click on the **Modifier** or press **Enter** to apply it.
- Choose a modifier from the **Modifiers** menu.
- If the **Modifier** buttons are available in the on the **Modify** panel, click one of the buttons.

Tip: Dragging a modifier to an object
*To drag a modifier form one object to another object in the scene, select an object that already has a modifier. To copy a modifier without instancing it, drag the modifier name from the stack display to the target object in the scene. If you want to create an instance, **Ctrl+drag** the modifier's name.*

Tip: Modifier Instances
*When you create an instance of a modifier, its name appears in italics in the **Modify** panel indicating that the modifier is instanced.*

Using the Configure Modifier Sets Dialog box

When you click on the **Configure Modifier Sets** button in the **Modify** panel [below modifier stack], a menu is displayed. Choose **Show Buttons** from the menu to display the modifier buttons below the **Modifier** list. The buttons associated with the currently selected set will be displayed in the **Modify** panel. You can select various sets from the menu. Fig. 1 shows the buttons associated with the **Selection Modifiers** set.

When you choose the **Configure Modifier Sets** option from the menu, the **Configure Modifier Sets** dialog box appears [see Fig. 2]. This dialog box lets you create custom modifier and button sets for the **Modify** panel. To create a new set, specify the number of desired buttons using the **Total Buttons** option and then drag a modifier from the modifier list to a button.

You can also add a modifier by first highlighting the button and then double-clicking a modifier in the **Modifier List**. When you assign a modifier by double-clicking on its name, the highlight moves to the next button in the **Modifiers** group. Now, enter the name of the new set in the **Sets** edit field and then click **Save** to save the set. Click **OK** from the **Configure Modifier Sets** dialog box to exit it. Similarly, you can modify an existing set.

Using the Modifier Stack

The modifier stack [also referred to as just stack] is a list of modifiers that you apply to an object. The stack is evaluated from bottom to top. The first entry in the stack [from bottom] is always the object. The object-space modifiers appear above the object type. The world-space modifiers and space warps bound to the object are placed at the top.

You can use the stack in one of the following ways:

- Find a particular object and adjust its parameters using rollouts.
- Change the order of modifiers.
- Deactivate the effect of modifier in the stack, viewport, or both.
- Select components [such as **Gizmo** or **Center**] of a modifier.
- Delete modifiers.

The buttons at the bottom of the stack allow you to manage the stack. Table 3 summarizes the functioning of the buttons.

Table 3: The buttons found below the modifier stack

Name	Icon	Description
Pin Stack		It locks the stack and all controls in the **Modify** panel to the selected object stack.
Show end result on/off toggle		When active, it shows the effect of the entire stack on the selected object. When inactive, shows the result up to the currently highlighted modifier.
Make unique		It makes an instanced object unique.
Remove modifier from the stack		It deletes the current modifier from the stack.
Configure Modifier Sets		When this button is clicked, a menu is displayed that lets you configure the modifier button sets.

Tip: Copying and pasting modifiers
*You can copy and paste modifiers between the object. RMB click on a modifier, a popup menu appears. You can use the **Cut**, **Copy**, **Paste**, and **Paste Instanced** options from the menu to edit the stack.*

Caution: World-space modifiers
*While copy pasting the modifiers, ensure that you select the world-space and object-space modifiers separately. The **Cut**, **Copy**, and **Paste** options are disabled in the menu if you select both types of modifiers.*

Caution: Word-space modifiers
If you paste a word-space modifier in a section of object-space modifiers, the paste occurs at the top of the world-space section.

Collapsing the Stack

You can collapse the modifier stack of an editable object to merge the cumulative effect of the collapsed modifiers. You can collapse the modifier stack in one of the following situations:

- You have finished the model and you want to keep it as is.
- You want to discard animation tracks.
- You want to save the memory by simplifying the model.

In most of the cases, collapsing the entire modifier stack or part of the stack saves memory. However, some modifiers such as **Bevel** when collapsed increases the file size as well as the memory used.

Caution: Parametric nature of the objects
Once you collapse the modifier stack, you lose access to the parametric creation parameters of the object.

Tip: Preserving the original copy
*Before you collapse a stack, choose **Save As > Save Selected** from the **File** menu to preserve a copy of the original parametric object.*

3ds Max provides two options to collapse the stack: **Collapse To** and **Collapse All**. You can access these options by RMB clicking on the stack. The **Collapse To** option collapses the stack up to and including the chosen modifier to an editable object. You can still adjust the modifiers above the chosen modifier. The resultant object type depends on the uppermost modifier and the type of geometry it outputs. For example, if the uppermost modifier is **Edit Poly**, the resultant object will be an **Editable Poly** object. If no such modifier exists in the stack, the resultant object is an editable mesh. The **Collapse All** option collapses the entire stack. It does not affect any world-space bindings.

Exploring Modifiers

As already discussed, 3ds Max offers two types of modifiers: word-space modifiers and object-space modifiers. Let's explore these modifiers.

Word-Space Modifiers

The word-space modifiers act as object-specific space warps. They use world-space rather than object-space. When you apply a world-space modifier to the an object, it appears at the top of the modifier stack. The world-space modifiers are discussed next:

Hair and Fur (World Space)

This modifier is the engine of the **Hair and Fur** feature in 3ds Max. You can apply this modifier to either a mesh object or a spline object. If you apply it to splines, the hair grows between the splines. When you select an object on which you have applied this modifier, hair is displayed in the viewport. You cannot select the fur itself in the viewport. However, you can select hair guides using the **Guides** sub-object level.

Note: Hair in the viewports
*The hair only renders in the **Perspective** or **Camera** viewport. If you try to render an orthographic viewport, 3ds Max presents a warning that says that the hair will not appear in the render.*

Camera Map (World Space)

This modifier is similar to the **Camera Map** modifier. It is used to apply the **UVW** mapping coordinates to the object based on a specified camera. It causes the object to blend with the background if you apply same map to the object as you apply to the scene environment. To apply a **Camera Map** modifier, create a scene with a camera and one or more objects. Ensure that the object that you want to map is visible to the camera in the scene. Apply the **Camera Map** modifier and then click **Pick Camera** from the **Camera Mapping** rollout and click on the camera in a viewport. Now, you need to apply a map to the background.

Press **8** to open the **Environment & Effects** dialog box. Assign a map using the **Environment Map** button. Now, open **Material Editor** and drag the map from the **Environment and Effects** dialog box to **Material Editor**, choose **Instance** from the dialog box that appears and then click **OK**. Set the tiling in the **Coordinates** rollout, if required.

Apply a material to the object in the scene and then assign the map you just created to the **Diffuse** component of the material [see Fig. 3]. To create the render shown in Fig. 3, I have applied a **Checker** map to both the environment and the object. Notice that the **Checker** map on the object matches the background but the shading effect of the material makes the object visible. To blend the object completely in the background, set the **Specular Level** and **Glossiness** of the material to **0**. Also, turn off the **Self Illumination** color and set the **Self Illumination** to **100**. Now, take a render using the camera that you have assigned to the modifier [see Fig. 4].

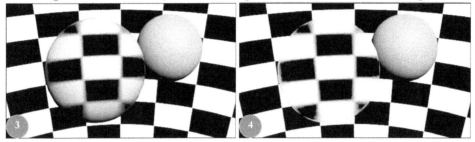

Displace Mesh (World Space)
This modifier allows you to see the effect of the **Displacement** mapping on editable mesh objects in the viewports. Also, you can see the effect of the **Displacement** mapping if you have applied a **Disp Approx** modifier to an object. This is useful when you want to visualize the effect of **Displacement** mapping in the viewports especially when you have animated the **Displacement** map or when you want to create an editable mesh from the displace geometry in the scene.

To understand the functioning of this modifier, create a **Plane** primitive with **Length**, **Width**, **Length Segs**, and **Width Segs** values set to **150, 150, 50,** and **50**, respectively. Apply the **Disp Approx** modifier to the plane. Open **Material Editor** and apply the **Standard** material to the plane. Connect the **Noise** map to the **Displacement** slot of the material. Adjust the properties of the **Noise** map, if required. Now, add the **Displace Mesh (WSM)** modifier to the stack. The effect of the **Displacement** map appears in the viewport [see Fig. 5].

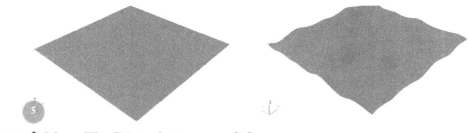

⑤

> ✎ *Note: The Disp Approx modifier*
> *If you are applying displacement to an editable mesh object, you don't need to apply this modifier in order to see the displacement effect in the viewport.*

If you have changed parameters of the map [the **Noise** map in this case], click **Update Mesh** on the **Displacement Approx** rollout to update the mesh in the viewports. When **Subdivision Displacement** is on, this modifier uses the settings that you specify on the **Subdivision Method** group of the rollout. You can also use the presets available in the **Subdivision Presets** group of the rollout. If **Subdivision Displacement** is off, this modifier applies the map by moving the vertices just as the **Displace** modifier does.

MapScalar (Word Space)

This modifier is used to maintain the scale of a map that is applied to the object. In other words, it lets you resize the geometry without changing the scale of the map. Create a box and set its **Length**, **Width**, and **Height** to **70** each. Create a **Standard** material with a **Checker** map connected to its **Diffuse** slot. Apply the material to the box. Add the **MapScalar** modifier to the stack. In the **Parameters** rollout of the modifier, set scale and offset values using the **Scale**, **U Offset**, and **V Offset** controls. Now, resize the box using the **Scale** tool. You will notice that the scale of the map does not change regardless of how the geometry is scaled [see Fig. 6].

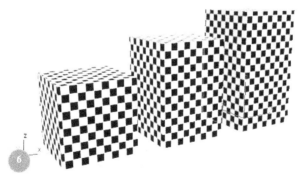

Patch Deform (World Space)

This modifier allows you to deform an object based on the contours of a patch object.

Point Cache (World Space)

This modifier allows you to store the modifier and sub-object animation to a disk file in your HDD. This file records changes in the vertex positions. When animation is played back, this file is used instead of the modifier keyframes. This modifier is useful when computation for vertex animation slows down the system and playback. This modifier is also useful in cloth animations.

Subdivide (World Space)

This modifier is similar to the object-space **Subdivide** modifier. However, in the world-space version, the size limit is on for the mesh after it is transformed into world space coordinates.

Surface Mapper (World Space)

This modifier takes a map assigned to the **NURBS** surface and then projects it onto the modified objects. It is useful in applying a single map to a group of surface sub-objects within the same **NURBS** model.

Create a **Point Surf** NURBS object and a teapot in the scene [see the left image in Fig. 7]. Create a **Standard** material and connect a **Checker** map to the **Diffuse** component of the material. Apply the material to both the **NURBS** object and teapot. Select the **Teapot** in a viewport and then add the **Surface Mapper** modifier to the stack of the **Teapot**. In the **Parameters** rollout of the **Modify** panel, click **Pick NURBS Surface** and then click on the **NURBS** object in a viewport. The **NURBS** object projects the map onto the **Teapot** [see the right image in Fig. 7].

SurfDeform (World Space)

The functioning of this modifier is same as of the **PathDeform (WSM)** modifier, except that it uses a **NURBS Point** or **CV** surface instead of a curve.

PathDeform (World Space)

The **PathDeform** modifier deforms an object based on a shape, spline, or NURBS curve. This modifier works the same as the object-space **PathDeform** modifier. Create a line and a cone in the scene [see Fig. 8]. Apply the **PathDeform (WSM)** modifier to the cone. In the **Modify** panel > **Parameters** rollout, click on the **Pick Path** button and then click the line in the viewport. Now, click **Move to Path** button to snap the cone to the line [see Fig. 9].

Adjust the **Stretch** spinner to stretch the cone along the line [see Fig. 10]. Adjust the **Height Segments** spinner of the cone object to smooth the stretch. You can also use the radius controls to adjust the shape [see Fig. 11]. Now, if you want to create a growing vine like animation, you can animate the **Stretch** control.

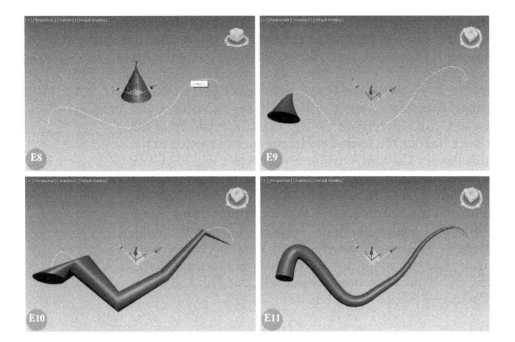

Object-Space Modifiers

The object-space modifiers affect the geometry in the local space. These modifiers are discussed next:

Affect Region

This modifier is a surface modeling tool. It work well with at the **Vertex** sub-object level. You can use it to create a bubble or indentation in the surface. When you add this modifier to stack, it assigns an arrow like gizmo to the object that you can use in the viewport to alter the geometry. The controls in the **Parameters** rollout allow you to numerically control the shape of the deformation [see Fig. 12].

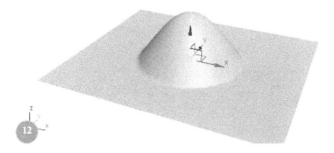

Attribute Holder

This modifier allows you to hold custom attributes for the objects in the **Modify** panel. It is an empty modifier to which you can add the custom attributes. It is a stripped down version of the **Parameter Collector** dialog box that can collect only the custom attributes and appears on the **Modify** panel instead of a floating dialog box. Create a **Cylinder** primitive in the scene with the **Radius** and **Height** parameters set to **10** and **100**, respectively. Add the **Bend** modifier to the stack followed by the

Attribute Holder modifier. Ensure that the **Attribute Holder** modifier is highlighted in the stack. Choose **Parameter Editor** from the **Animation** menu to open the **Parameter Editor** dialog box. Alternatively, you can press **Alt+1**.

In this dialog box, set **Add to Type** to **Selected Object's Current Modifier, Parameter Type** to **Float, UI Type** to **Slider,** and **Name** to **Cylinder Height** [see Fig. 13]. Click **Add** from the **Attribute** Rollout, the **Cylinder Height** control appears in the **Modify Panel > Custom Attributes** rollout [see Fig. 14]. Click **Add** on the **Attribute** rollout of the **Parameter Editor** dialog box. Set **Add to Type** to **Selected Object's Current Modifier, Parameter Type** to **Integer, UI Type** to **Spinner,** and **Name** to **Cylinder H Segments.** In the **Integer UI Options** rollout, set **Range > From** and **Range > To** to **1** and **60,** respectively. Similarly, add two more float spinners with the name **Bend Angle,** and **Bend Direction,** respectively [see Fig. 15]. Close the **Parameter Editor** dialog box.

Press **Alt+5** to open the **Parameter Wiring** dialog box. In the left pane of the dialog box, choose **Objects > Cylinder001 > Modified Object > Cylinder (Object) > Height.** In the right pane, choose **Objects > Cylinder001 > Modified Object > Attribute Holder > Custom_Attributes > Cylinder Height.** Now, click **Two-way connection** followed by **Connect** to create a connection between the selected attributes [see Fig. 16]. The label on the **Connect** button changes to **Update.** Similarly, connect the **Cylinder (Object) > Height Segments, Bend > Angle,** and **Bend > Direction** controls from the left pane to **Cylinder H Segs, Bend Angle,** and **Bend Direction,** respectively, controls of the right pane [see Fig. 17]. Close the **Parameter** Wiring dialog box.

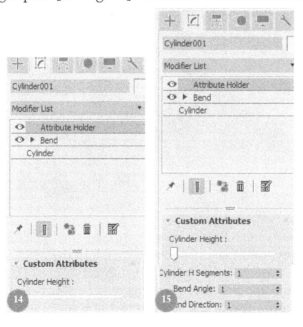

Now, experiment with the controls available in the **Modify** panel > **Custom Attributes** rollout of the **Attribute Holder** modifier [see Fig. 18].

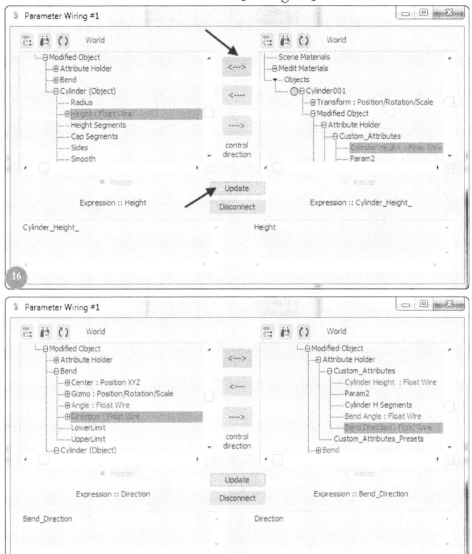

Bend

You can use this modifier to create a uniform 360 degree bend on a geometry about a single axis. You can limit bend to a section of the geometry as well as you can control the bend angle and direction.

To bend an object, add the **Bend** modifier to the stack. In the **Parameters** rollout of the modifier, set **Angle** and **Direction** in the **Bend** group to specify the angle to bend from the vertical plane and direction of the bend relative to the horizontal plane, respectively. Specify the axis to be bent from the **Bend Axis** group. To limit the bend effect to a particular area of the object, select the **Limit Effect** check box and then specify the limit using the **Upper Limit** and **Lower Limit** controls [see Fig. 19].

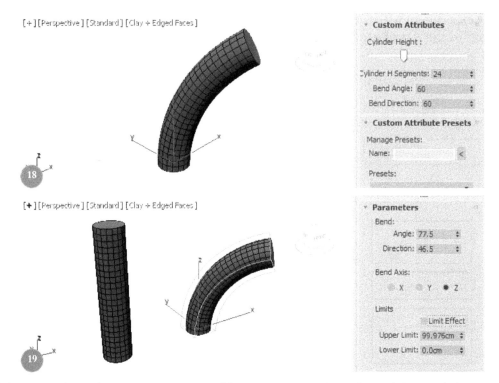

This modifier offers two sub-objects. You can change the effect of the modifier using the **Gizmo** sub-object by transforming or animating it [see Fig. 20]. You can translate or animate the **Center** sub-object to change the shape of the **Gizmo** resulting in the change of the bend effect [see Fig. 21].

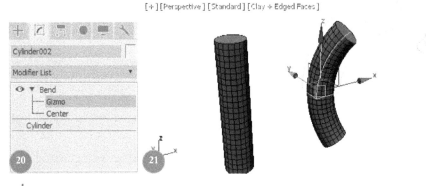

Bevel

This modifier allows you to extrude spline shapes into 3D objects and then applies a flat or round bevel on the edges. You can control the beveling from the **Bevel Values** rollout of the modifier. Create a **Text** spline and then add a **Bevel** modifier to the stack. Adjust the parameters in the **Parameters** and **Bevel Values** rollouts of the modifier [see Fig. 22].

Keep Lines From Crossing
Separation: 2.54cm

▸ **Bevel Values**

Start Outline: 0.0cm

Level 1:
Height: 25.4cm
Outline: -0.508cm

☑ Level 2:
Height: 15.24cm
Outline: 0.508cm

Level 3:

22

Bevel Profile

This modifier is another version of the **Bevel** modifier but it extrudes a shape using a path or profile [beveling profile]. Create a shape and profile curve and then apply the **Bevel Profile** modifier to the shape's stack.

Create a **Text** object and a **Helix** object. Select the **Text** object and add **Bevel Profile** to the stack. In the **Modify** panel > **Parameters** rollout > **Bevel Profile** group, click **Pick Profile** and then click the **Helix** object in a viewport to create bevel [see Fig. 23].

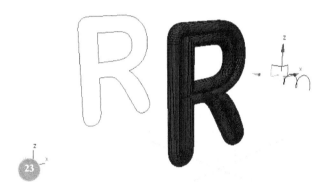

23

Camera Map

This modifier is the object-space version of the **Camera Map (WSM)** modifier. It assigns the planar mapping coordinates based on the current frame and a specified camera. This behavior is different from the **Camera Map (WSM)** modifier which updates the coordinates at every frame.

Cap Holes

This modifier build faces on the holes in a mesh. This modifier works well with the planar holes, however, it does a reasonable job when applied to non-planar holes [see Fig. 24].

Cross Section

This modifier creates a skin across multiple various shaped splines by connecting the vertices of the 3D splines. The result is another spline object to which you can apply the **Surface** modifier to create a patch surface. These two modifiers sometimes also referred to as **Surface Tools**.

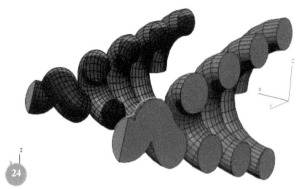

Create an **Arc** object in the scene and convert it to **Editable** spline. Now, create three more copies of the **Arc** object and change their shape using the **Scale** tool [see the left image in Fig. 25]. Attach all splines to form a single spline object. Add the **Cross Section** modifier to form a combined spline [see the middle image in Fig. 25]. Now, add the **Surface** modifier to the stack to create skin [see the right image in Fig. 25].

To change the shape, edit the combined spline at sub-objects level. The output of the **Surface** modifier is a patch surface. Therefore, you can add the **Edit Patch** modifier to the stack and edit the surface using the patch edit controls.

Data Channel

The **Data Channel** modifier is used to automate complex modeling operations. You can feed mesh data through a series of controls to create variety of effects that dynamically update in the viewport.

Delete Mesh

This modifier allows you to parametrically delete sub-object selection based on faces, vertices, edges, and objects. Create a **Teapot** object and then add the **Poly Select** modifier to the stack. Select the polygons as shown in the left image of Fig. 26. Add a **Delete Mesh** modifier to delete the selected faces [see the right image in Fig. 26].

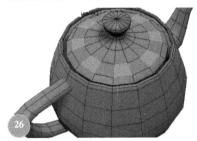
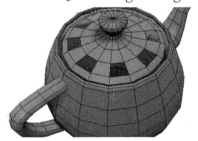

Delete Patch

It provides parametric deletion based on the patch sub-object selection. The possible choices are vertices, edges, patches, and elements.

Delete Spline

It provides parametric deletion based on the **Spline** sub-object selection. The possible choices are vertices, segments, and splines. Create a **Line** object. Add the **Spline Select** modifier to the stack and then select a segment. Now, add the **Delete Spline** modifier to the stack to delete the selected segment [see Fig. 27].

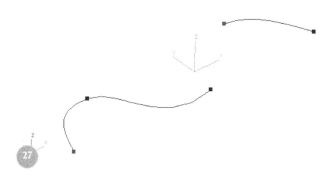

Displace Approx

See the **Displace Mesh Modifier (World Space)**.

Displace

This modifier pushes the object's geometry to reshape it using a map or bitmap texture. This modifier allows you to apply the effect using two methods:

- Apply the effect directly onto the object using the **Strength** and **Decay** values.
- Apply the effect using the grayscale values of a bitmap image.

You can use this modifier to simulate magnetic push like effect by animating its gizmos. The four gizmos provided by this modifier are: **Planar, Cylindrical, Spherical**, and **Shrink Wrap**. These gizmos are used to distribute the force specified by the **Strength** and **Decay** values.

Create a **Plane** primitive with **30** length and width segments. Add a **Displace** modifier to the stack and then set **Strength** to **-100** and **Decay** to **-0.66** in the **Parameters** rollout of the modifier. Choose **Spherical** from the **Map** group of the rollout and then select **Gizmo** sub-object from the stack. Now, use the **Move** tool to see the effect of this modifier [see the left image in Fig. 24]. You can also use a bitmap or map to produce this effect. Click **None** associated with the **Map** control in the **Image** group to open **Material/Map Browser**. Double-click on **Noise** to select this map. Select **Planar** from the **Map** group, the effect of the modifier is displayed in the viewport [see the right image in Fig. 28].

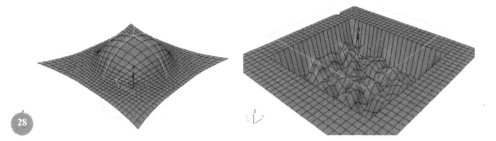

To change the parameters of the **Noise** map, drag the **Map** button to **Material Editor**. Choose **Instance** from the dialog box displayed. Now, double-click on the map node to view its properties. Change the properties as per your requirement.

Edit Mesh
The **Edit Mesh** modifier has all the capabilities of the **Editable Mesh** object except that you cannot animate sub-objects.

Edit Normals
You can use this modifier to procedurally and interactively change the vertex normals of an object. This modifier is specifically used when you intend to output the meshes for the game and 3D rendering engines that support specified normals. The orientation of the vertex normals affects how light is reflected by the neighboring surfaces. By default in 3ds Max, rules of real-world physics are followed in which the angle of reflection is equal to the angle of incidence. However, using this modifier, you can set the angle of reflection as required.

Edit Patch
The **Edit Patch** modifier has all the capabilities of the **Editable Patch** object except that you cannot animate sub-objects.

Edit Poly
The **Edit Poly** modifier has all the capabilities of the **Editable Poly** object except **Vertex Color** information, **Subdivision Surface** rollout, **Weight** and **Crease** settings, and **Subdivision Displacement** rollout. This modifier lets you animate sub-object transforms and parameters.

Edit Spline
The **Edit Spline** modifier has all the capabilities of the **Editable Spline** object. The **Rendering** and **Interpolation** rollouts are not available for this modifier. Also, you cannot create direct vertex animation using this modifier.

Extrude
This modifier allows you to add depth to a shape object. It also makes the shape object parametric. Create a **Rectangle** shape object and covert it to editable spline. Create an outline and apply **Extrude** modifier to the spline object. In the **Parameters** rollout, specify a value for the **Amount** control to set the depth of extrusion [see Fig. 29]. Specify a value for the **Segments** control to set the segments that will be created for the extruded object.

You can use the **Cap Start** and **Cap End** controls to generate a flat surface over the start and end of the extruded object [see Fig. 29]. The controls in the **Output** group let you choose the output mesh type when stack is collapsed. The available options are **Patch**, **Mesh**, and **NURBS**.

Face Extrude

This modifier extrudes the faces along their normals [see Fig. 30]. There are many differences between the **Face Extrude** function and the **Face Extrude** modifier. The one big difference is that all parameters of this modifier are animatable.

FFD

FFD stands for **Free-Form** deformation. You can use these modifiers in a variety of ways. You can use it to create bulge in a mesh, animate dancing cars, and so on. When you apply a **FFD** modifier such as **FFD 2x2x2**, **FFD 3x3x3**, or **FFD 4x4x4**, it surrounds the selected geometry with a lattice. You can transform the lattice and use its control points to adjust the shape of the geometry [see Fig. 31].

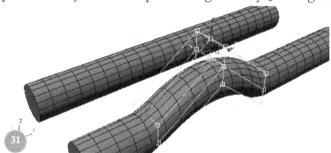

Each modifier provides a different lattice resolution [**2x2x2**, **3x3x3**, and **4x4x4**]. For example, a **4x4x4** resolution produces a lattice with four control points across each of its dimensions resulting in **12** points in each side of the lattice.

There are three sub-objects available with this modifier. At the **Control Points** sub-object level, you can select the control points of the lattice and then change the shape of the underlying geometry by transforming them. At the **Lattice** sub-object level, you can transform the lattice box separately from the geometry. At **Set Volume** level, the color of the lattice control points turns green. You can select and manipulate the points without affecting the underlying geometry. You should use this level to set the initial state of the lattice.

Note: The FFD(box) and FFD(cyl) modifiers
*You can use the **FFD(box)** and **FFD(cyl)** modifiers to create box-shaped or cylinder-shaped FFD lattices. These modifiers are also available as space warps.*

Fillet/Chamfer

This modifier lets you fillet or chamfer corner vertices between linear segments of the shape objects. This modifier rounds corners where the segments meet by adding new control vertices. It also bevels the corners. This modifier works on the splines at the sub-object level. It does not work between two independent shape objects.

Create a **Star** shape object in the scene and add the **Fillet/Chamfer** modifier to the stack. Now, at the **Vertex** sub-object level of the modifier, select the vertices that you want to affect and then specify the desired settings in the **Edit Vertex** rollout to generate different shapes [see Fig. 32].

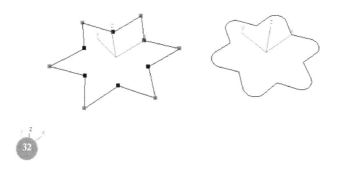

Flex

This modifier creates virtual springs between vertices of an object thus simulating a soft body dynamics behavior. You can control the stiffness and stretching of the springs. You can also control the sway of the springs that is how much the spring angle changes in relation with the movement of the springs. This modifier works with NURBS, patches, polygon and mesh objects, shapes, FFD space warps, and any plug-in-based object types that can be deformed.

HSDS

HSDS stands for **Hierarchical SubDivision Surfaces**. This modifier implements the Hierarchical SubDivision Surfaces. You can use this modifier to as a finishing tool for subdivision surfaces.

Lathe

You can use the **Lathe** modifier to rotate a shape or NURBS curve about a specified axis. Create a **Shape** object [see the left image in Fig. 33] and add the **Lathe** modifier to the stack. In the **Parameters** rollout of the modifier, ensure that **Degrees** is set to **360** to create a full 360 degrees lathe. Specify the segments for the lathe object using the **Segments** control. Click **Y** in the direction group to set the **Y** axis as the axis of revolution relative to the pivot point of the object. Click **Min** from the **Align** group to align the axis of revolution to the minimum extent of the shape. The right image in Fig. 29 shows the full lathe object.

You can select the **Weld Core** check box to weld vertices that lie on the axis of revolution. This modifiers also presents the **Axis** sub-object. At this level, you can transform and animate the axis of revolution.

Lattice

This modifier allows you to create renderable structure from a geometry. It can be thought of an alternative method to create wireframe effect. It gives you options to create joints, struts, or both. Fig. 34 shows a sphere with joints, struts, and both join and struts, respectively.

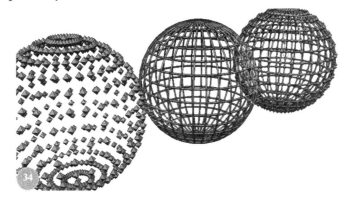

Linked XForm

This modifier links the transform of any object or sub-object selection to another object. The other object is called the control object. The transforms of the control object are passed onto the object or sub-object selection.

Create a **Sphere** and a **Cone** primitive in the scene. **Cone** will be the control object. Now, select sphere and add **Linked XForm** modifier to the stack. In the **Parameters** rollout, click **Pick Control Object** and then click on cone in a viewport. Now, when you transform the cone, the sphere will also receive the transforms.

Delete the modifier from the stack and convert sphere to **Editable Poly**. At **Vertex** sub-object level, select some vertices [see left image in Fig. 35]. Link **Cone** to vertices as discussed above. Now, when you move the cone, the selected vertices will also receive the transform.

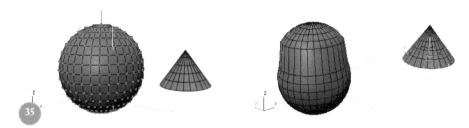

MapScalar
See the **MapScalar Modifier (Word Space)** modifier.

Material
This modifier allows you to animate, or change the assignment of the existing material IDs on an object.

MaterialByElement
This modifier allows you to apply different material IDs to objects containing multiple elements. You can apply IDs at random or you can use a formula. Select **Random Distribution** from the **Parameters** rollout to assign the material IDs to different elements at random. The **ID Count** control lets you assign the minimum number of materials IDs to be assigned. Select **List Frequency** to define a percentage of each [up to eight] of the material IDs.

Melt
This modifier allows you to create realistic melting effect on all types of objects, including editable patches and NURBS objects. It also works on the sub-object selections passed up the stack. Create a cylinder with enough sub-divisions and then apply the **Melt** modifier to it. In the **Melt** group of the **Parameters** rollout, specify the strength of the melt using the **Amount** control. The **% of Melt** control in the **Spread** group lets you specify the spread of the melt [see Fig. 36]. The controls in the **Solidity** group determine the center of the melted object. There are several presets available in this group that you can use to specify the solidity of the object. If you want to specify a custom solidity, select **Custom** from this group.

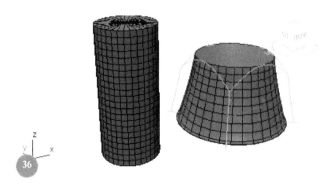

This modifier has two sub-objects, **Gizmo** and **Center**. You can transform and animate these two sub-objects to change the effect of the melt.

Mesh Select

This modifier provides a superset of the selection functions available in the **Edit Mesh** modifier. It allows you to pass the sub-object selection up the stack to other subsequent modifier.

MeshSmooth

This modifier allows you to smooth the geometry by subdividing it. You can use this modifier to produce a **Non-Uniform Rational MeshSmooth** object, **NURMS** in short. A **NURMS** objects is similar to the **NURBS** object in which you set different weights for vertices [see Fig. 37]. You can farther alter the geometry by modifying the edge weight.

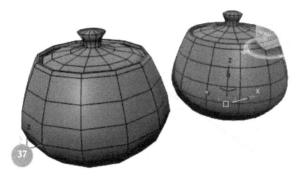

You can choose the desired method from the **Subdivision Method** drop-down list of the **Subdivision Method** rollout. The available methods are: **NURMS**, **Classic**, and **Quad** Output. The **Iteration** control in the **Subdivision Amount** rollout lets you specify the number of times you want to subdivide the mesh.

Mirror

This modifier allows you to parametrically mirror an object or a sub-object selection [see Fig. 38]. Apply this modifier to the stack and then select the axis or axis pair from the **Mirror Axis** group of the **Parameters** rollout. If you want to create a copy of the object, select the **Copy** check box and then specify the offset distance using the **Offset** control.

Tip: Modeling a character
When you have created one side of a character and you want to mirror the other side, use the **Symmetry** *modifier instead of the* **Mirror** *modifier as the* **Symmetry** *modifier allows you to weld the seam which results in a better looking model.*

Morpher

You can use this modifier to change the shape of the mesh, patch, or **NURBS** model. Morphing is generally used for lip-sync and facial expressions. This modifier also allows you to morph splines and world-space **FFDs**. Also, you can morph from one shape to another using this modifier.

MultiRes

This modifier reduces the number of polygons in a mesh to improve the rendering time [see Fig. 39]. You can also reduce the number of vertices and polygons using the **Optimize** modifier. However, this modifier has certain advantages over the **Optimize** modifier such as it is faster and lets you specify exact percentage for reduction. You can also specify the vertex count for reductions.

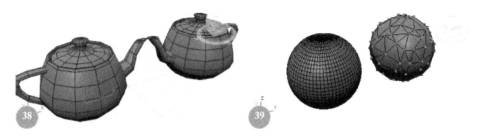

To reduce the polygons, apply this modifier to the stack. In the **Generation Parameters** group of the **MultiRes Parameters** rollout, click **Generate** to initialize the modifier. In the **Resolution** group, specify a value for the **Vert Percent** or **Vert Count** to reduce the polygons.

Noise

This modifier alters the position of the vertices of an object along any combination of three axes [see Fig. 40]. You can use it to create random variations in the shape of the object. You can also animate the change in shape of the mesh. Add the modifier to the stack and then in the **Strength** group of the **Parameters** rollout, set the strength using the **X, Y,** and **Z** controls. Select the **Fractal** check box from the **Noise** group to produce a fractal like effect [see Fig. 41]. When you select this check box, the **Roughness** and **Iterations** controls appear in the rollout. You can use these controls to determine the extent of the fractal variation and number of iteration used by the modifier, respectively.

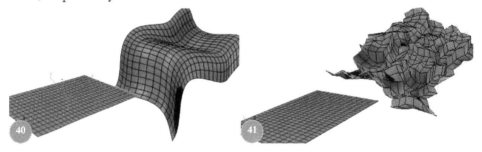

Normal

This modifier allows you to unify or flip the normals of an object without first converting it to an **Edit Mesh** modifier. Select the **Unify Normals** check box in the **Parameters** rollout to unify the normals so that they all point in the same direction, usually outward. Select the **Flip Normals** check box to reverse the direction of all surface normals.

Normalize Spline

You can use this modifier to add new control points at regular interval in a spline [see Fig. 42]. This is useful in normalizing the spline that you will use with the motion paths. The **Set Length** control in the **Parameters** rollout lets you set the length of the spline segments. 3ds Max uses this control to set the vertices at the regular intervals.

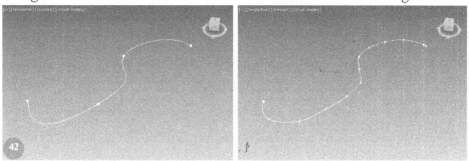

Optimize

See the **MultiRes Modifier**.

Patch Select

This modifier provides a superset of selection functions available in the **Edit Patch** modifier.

Patch Deform

See the **PatchDeform Modifier (World Space)** modifier.

PathDeform

See the **PathDeform Modifier (World Space)** modifier.

Point Cache

See the **Point Cache Modifier (World Space)** modifier.

Poly Select

This modifier provides a superset of selection functions available in the **Edit Poly** modifier.

Preserve

When you push and pull vertices to model a surface, the edges of the mesh get stretched that results in an irregular geometry. This modifier allows you to retain [as much as possible] the original length of the edge thus producing a cleaner mesh.

Projection

This modifier is generally used for producing normal bumps maps. Apply this modifier to the low-resolution object and then pick a high resolution object as the source of the projected normals.

Projection Holder

This modifier appears when the **Project Mapping** feature of the **Projection** modifier is used. It contains data generated by the **Project Mapping** feature such as the **UVW** mapping data.

ProOptimizer

This modifier allows you to interactively reduce the number of vertices in a model while preserving the original appearance/features of the model such as material, mapping, and vertex color information. When this modifier is used, the memory requirement for a model are reduced. You can optimize a model using one of the following two methods:

- You can use the **ProOptimizer** modifier to interactively optimize the model.
- You can use the **Batch ProOptimizer** utility to optimize multiple scenes at one go. When you use this utility, you can optimize the meshes before you import them to save the time.

Push

This modifier allows you to push the selected vertices inward or outward along the average vertex normals to create an inflation like effect [see Fig. 43].

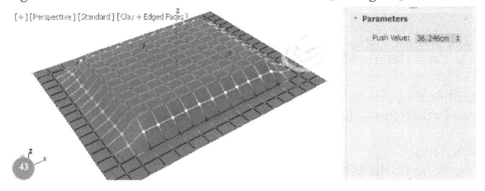

Quadify Mesh

You can use this modifier to convert object structure to quadrilateral polygons using the relative size that you specify. This modifier helps you to create mesh with rounded model with help of the **Smooth** modifier.

Relax

This modifier allows you to reduce the surface tension by moving the vertices closer to or away from their neighbors. This results in smooth object, however, the model appears little smaller than the un-relaxed model.

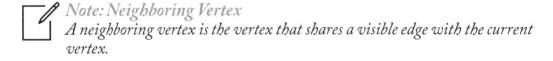

Note: Neighboring Vertex
A neighboring vertex is the vertex that shares a visible edge with the current vertex.

Renderable Spline

This modifier makes a spline object renderable without needing to convert it to an **Editable Spline** object. It also allows you to apply same rending properties to multiple splines. This modifier is useful when you link an AutoCAD drawing.

Ripple

You can use this modifier to create a ripple effect on the geometry [see Fig. 44]. You can use its **Gizmo** sub-object to change the ripple effect.

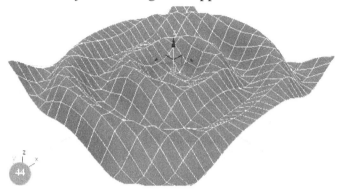

Note: The Ripple space warp

*The **Ripple** space warp has the same features as the **Ripple** modifier, however, you can apply the **Ripple** space warp to a large number of objects.*

Select By Channel

This modifier is used with the **Channel Info** utility. When you save a vertex selection into a sub-component using the **Channel Info** utility, you can use this modifier to quickly access the selection.

Shell

This modifier allows you to give thickness to an object by creating extra set of faces on the opposite direction of the existing faces [see Fig. 45]. You can specify the offset distances using the **Inner Amount** and **Outer Amount** controls available in the **Parameters** rollout.

Skew

This modifier can be used to create a uniform offset in an object's geometry [see Fig. 46]. You can control and direction of the skew on any of three axes. You can also limit the skew effect by selecting the **Limit Effect** check box and then using the **Upper Limit** and **Lower Limit** controls.

Skin Modifier
This modifier is a skeleton deformation tool that allows you to deform one object with another object. You can deform the **Mesh, Patch,** and **NURBS** objects using the bones, splines, and other objects.

Skin Morph
This modifier allows you to use a bone's rotation to drive the deformation of the mesh object. This modifier is used with other modifiers such as **Skin** and **Physique**.

Skin Wrap
You can use this modifier to deform an object with another object. Although, you can use this modifier in a variety of ways but its primary use is to animate a high-resolution object mesh with help of a low-resolution mesh.

Skin Wrap Patch
This modifier allows you to deform a mesh object with help of a patch object. Each point on the patch object influences a surrounding volume of points on the mesh object.

Slice
You can use this modifier to slice though selected objects or sub-objects using a cutting plane. Its functioning is similar to the **Slice** function of the **Editable Mesh** object. However, it does not require to be an **Editable Poly** or **Editable Mesh** object. You can also animate the position and rotation of the slicing plane.

Smooth
You can smooth a faceted geometry using this modifier. It eliminates the faceting by grouping the faces into smoothing groups. It smoothens the faces based on the angle of adjacent faces.

Spherify
This modifier distorts an object into a spherical shape [see Fig. 47]. The end result is dependent on the topology of the object.

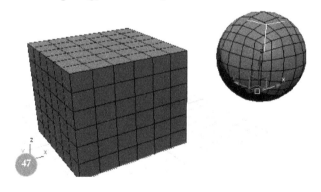

Spline IK Control

The basic use of this modifier is to prepare a spline or **NURBS** curve for use with the **Spline IK Solver**. When this modifier is applied to a spline object, you can transform its vertices without needing to access the **Vertex** sub-object level. It places knots [control points] at each vertex and then you can manipulate the knots to change the shape of the spline.

Spline Influence Modifier

This modifier creates a soft selection of the spline knots. The selection is shown in the viewport as a color gradient ranging from red to blue. The red color represents completely selected knots whereas the blue color represents the un-selected knots.

Spline Mirror Modifier

Similar to the Symmetry modifier, this modifier duplicates a spline along a specified axis. Available normals are also duplicated.

Spline Morph Modifier

You can use this modifier to morph between splines using either a progressive or blended method.

Spline Overlap Modifier

This modifier allows you to detect self-overlapping splines and adjusts the displacement of the intersection elements.

Spline Relax Modifier

This modifier relaxes knot positions and/or handles resulting in the smooth out splines.

Spline Select

This modifier is a superset of the selection functions found in the **Edit Spline** modifier. It passes a sub-object selection up the stack to other modifiers.

Squeeze

The modifier lets you create a squeezing [create bulge] effect on the objects [see Fig. 48]. The vertices closest to the object's pivot point move inward. The squeeze operation is applied around the **Squeeze** gizmo's local Z axis.

STL Check

This modifier checks if the object is correct for exporting to an **STL** file format. **STL** [**stereolithography**] files are used by the specialized machines to create prototype models based on the supplied **STL** file. The **STL** file must have a complete and closed surface.

Stretch

The **Stretch Modifier** allows you to create traditional squash and stretch effects that are used in animations [see Fig. 49]. This modifier applies a scale effect along a specified axis and opposite scale along the two remaining minor axes.

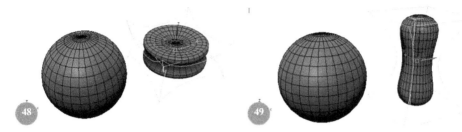

Subdivide Modifier

See the **Subdivide Modifier (World Space)** modifier.

Substitute

This modifier allows you to replace one or more objects with other objects in a viewport or at render time. The substitute object can be instanced in the current scene or can be referenced from an external file. This modifier is useful for the designers who use 2D shapes in their AutoCAD drawings. When they link the AutoCAD drawing to 3ds Max, they want to see how the object will look like in their design. This modifier allows them to achieve that objective.

Surface

See the **Cross Section** modifier.

Surface Select

This modifier allows you to add a **NURBS** sub-object selection in the stack. Then, you can modify the selected sub-objects. It can select any kind of NURBS sub-objects except imports.

SurfDeform

See the **SurfDeform Modifier (World Space)** modifier.

Sweep

You can use this modifier to extrude a cross section along an underlying spline or **NURBS** curve path. It provides a number of pre-made cross sections such as angles, channels, wide flenges, and so on [see Fig. 50]. You can also use a custom spline or NURBS curve as custom sections.

Symmetry

See the **Mirror** modifier.

Taper

This modifier creates tapered contours by scaling both ends of an object's geometry [see Fig. 51]. It scales up one end and scales down the other end. You can also limit the taper effect.

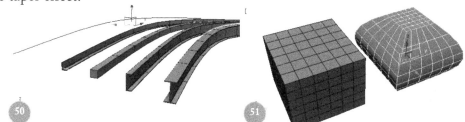

Tessellate

This modifier is used to subdivide the faces of a mesh [see Fig. 52]. It is useful in smoothing the curved surface and creating additional geometry for other modifiers to act on. The **Tension** control in the **Parameters** rollout allows you to add convexity or concavity to the subdivided surface.

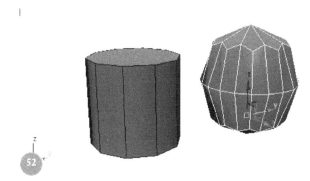

Trim/Extend

This modifier is used to clean up the overlapping or open splines in a multi-spline shape. To trim you need the intersecting splines. If the section intersects at both ends, the entire section will be deleted by this modifier up to the two intersections. To extend, you need an open spline.

TurboSmooth

This modifier is like the **MeshSmooth** modifier with the following differences:

- **TurboSmooth** is faster and memory efficient than the **MeshSmooth** modifier.
- **TurboSmooth** uses a single subdivision method, NURMS. It has no sub-object levels and outputs a triangle-mesh object.

Turn To Mesh Modifier/ Turn To Patch Modifier/ Turn To Poly Modifier

These modifiers allow you to apply the object conversions in the modifier stack. When you apply general purpose modifiers, these modifiers give you ability to explicitly control the output type of the object before hand.

Twist

This modifier creates a twisting effect on the surface of an object [see Fig. 53]. You can control the angle of twist as well as you limit the effect of the **Twist** modifier. When you add this modifier to the stack, its gizmo is placed at the pivot point of the object and the gizmo lines up with the local axis of the object.

53

UVW Mapping Modifiers

These modifiers are used to control the texture mapping. You can use them to manage UV coordinates and to apply materials to the objects.

UVW Map

Use this modifier to control how mapped and procedural materials appear on the surface of the object. The mapping coordinates defines how bitmaps are projected onto an object.

UVW Mapping Add

This modifier is added to the object's modifier stack when you add a channel in the **Channel Info** utility.

UVW Mapping Clear

This modifier is added to the object's modifier stack when you clear a channel with the **Channel Info** utility.

UVW Mapping Paste

This modifier is added to the object's modifier stack when you paste a channel with the **Channel Info** utility.

UVW XForm

You can use this modifier to adjust the tiling and offset in existing UVW coordinates. If you have an object with complex UVW coordinates already applied, you can apply this modifier to adjust those coordinates further.

Vertex Weld

This modifier works similar to the **Weld** feature in an **Editable Poly** and similar objects. You can use this modifier to combine the vertices that lies within a specified distance from each other.

VertexPaint

This modifier allows you to paint vertex colors onto an object. The amount of color that 3ds Max applies to the vertex depends on the distance of the vertex from the position of the cursor on the face. You can also paint vertex alpha and illumination values as well.

Volume Select

This modifier lets you make a sub-object selection of vertices or faces. You can use a cylinder-shaped or sphere shaped gizmo, or an object in the scene to define the volume of the selection area to which you can then apply other modifiers.

Wave

This modifiers creates a wave like effect [see Fig. 54]. You can use the standard **Gizmo** and **Center** sub-objects to change the wave effect. This modifier is similar to the **Wave** space warp which is useful when you want to create a wave effect on the large number of objects.

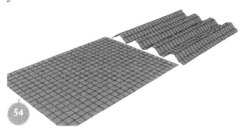

XForm

This modifier is used to apply transformations to the objects. You can use it to animate the transformations of a sub-object selection. Also, you can transform an object at any point in the stack.

Hands-on Exercises

From the **File** menu, choose **Project > Create Default** to open the **Choose a folder** dialog box. In this dialog box, navigate to the **3dsmax2019projects** directory and then click **New Folder** and then rename the folder as **unit-m7**. Select the folder and then click **Select Folder** to create the project folder.

Exercise 1: Creating a Microphone

In this exercise, we will create a microphone [see Fig. E1]. Table E1 summarizes the exercise:

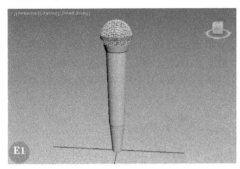 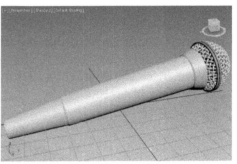

Table E1:	
Skill level	Intermediate
Time to complete	40 Minutes
Topics in the section:	• Specifying the Units for the Exercise • Creating the Microphone
Project folder	**unit-m7**
Units	**Generic**
Final exercise file	**microphone-finish.max**

Specifying the Units for the Exercise

Follow these steps:

1. From **Customize** menu choose **Units Setup**. In the **Units Setup** dialog box that appears, select **Generic Units** from the **Units Setup** dialog box. Click **OK** to accept the changes made.

2. From the **File** menu, choose **Save** to open the **Save File As** dialog box. In the **File name** text box type **microphone-finish.max** and then click **Save** to save the file.

Creating the Microphone

Follow these steps:

1. In the **Create** panel, click **Geometry**, and then in the **Object Type** rollout, click **Plane**. In the **Perspective** viewport, create a plane. Switch to the **Modify** panel and then in the **Parameters** rollout, change **Length** to **50**, **Width** to **50**, **Length Segs** to **30**, and **Width Segs** to **30**.

2. RMB click on the plane and then choose **transform** quadrant > **Convert To:** > **Convert to Editable Poly**. In the **Modify** panel > **Selection** rollout, click **Edge** to activate the edge sub-object level.

3. Select the edge, as shown in Fig. E2 and then in the **Modify** panel > **Selection** rollout, click **Ring** followed by **Loop** to make the selection [see Fig. E3].

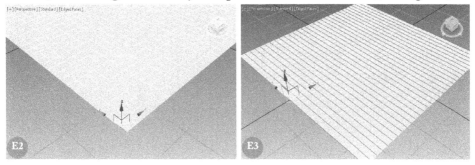

 What next?
Now, we will create a shape from the selected edges. Next, we will use different modifiers to create metal grid pattern for the mic.

4. In the **Edit Edges** rollout, click **Create Shape From Selection** to create the shape [see Fig. E4]. Delete **Plane**.

5. In the **Modify** panel > **Selection** rollout, click **Vertex** to activate the vertex sub-object level. Now, select every alternative row of vertices in the **Left** viewport, as shown in Fig. E5. Move the selected vertices by **0.4** unit in the **+Y** direction [see Fig. E6]. Invert the selection by pressing **Ctrl+I** and then move the vertices by **0.4** unit in the **-Y** direction [see Fig. E7].

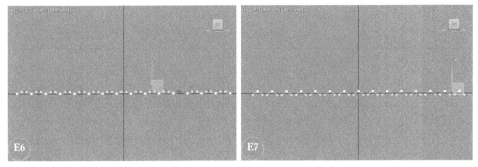

6. In the **Modify** panel > **Selection** rollout, click **Spline** to activate the spline sub-object level. Select alternate splines, as shown in Fig. E8. From the **Object-Space Modifiers** section of the **Modifier** list, select **Mirror**. In the **Parameters** layout, change **Mirror Axis** to **Z** [see Fig. E9]. Now, convert spline to **Editable Spline**.

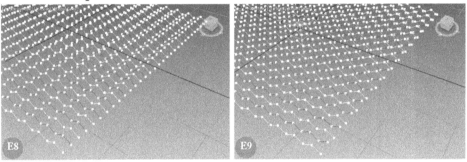

7. Create a copy of the shape using **Shift** and the **Rotate** tool by rotating it **90** degrees. Make sure the newly created spline is selected and then from the **Object-Space Modifiers** section of the **Modifier** list, select **Mirror**. In the **Parameters** layout, change **Mirror Axis** to **Z** [see Fig. E10]. Convert shape to **Editable Spline**.

 What next?
Now, we will create a sphere and then conform the splines to the sphere.

8. In the **Create** panel, click **Geometry**, and then in the **Object Type** rollout, click **Sphere**. In the **Perspective** viewport, create a sphere. Switch to the **Modify** panel and then in the **Parameters** rollout, change **Radius** to **12**, **Segments** to **60**, and **Hemisphere** to **0.5**. Also, select the **Squash** check box.

9. Convert sphere to editable poly and delete the bottom faces [see Fig. E11]. From the **Object-Space Modifiers** section of the **Modifier** List, select **XForm**. Now, using the **Scale** tool, scale down the **Sphere** using the **XForm** gizmo [see Fig. E12]. Make sure you are at the **Object** level before scaling the sphere.

10. Attach the two spline objects using the **Attach** function and then select the new spline. From the **Object-Space Modifiers** section of the **Modifier** list, select **Skin Wrap**. In the **Parameters** rollout, click **Add** and then click on the **Sphere** the viewport. Now, turn off the **XForm** modifier.

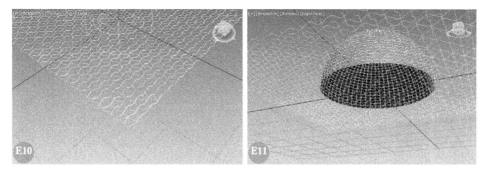

11. Select **Spline** and then select **Skin Wrap** modifier in the **Modify** panel. In the **Parameters** rollout, select the **Weight All Points** check box. Change **Fallloff** to **2**, **Distance Infl** to **10**, and **Face Limit** to **30**. Select the **Blend To Base Mesh** check box and then change **Bend Distance** to **200** [see Fig. E13].

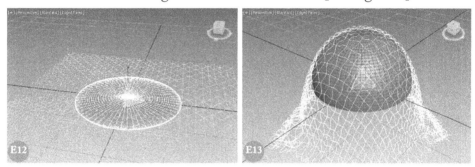

12. From the **Object-Space Modifiers** section of the **Modifier** list, select **Renderable Spline**. In the **Parameters** rollout, select the **Enable In Renderer** and **Enable In Viewport** checkboxes. Change **Thickness** to **1**, **Sides** to **6**, and **Threshold** to **180** [see Fig. E14].

13. From the **Object-Space Modifiers** section of the **Modifier** List, select **Symmetry**. In the **Parameters** rollout, change **Mirror Axis** to **Z** [see Fig. E15].

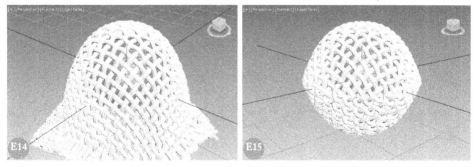

14. In the **Create** panel, click **Geometry**, and then in the **Object Type** rollout, click **Tube**. In the **Parameters** rollout, change **Radius 1** to **14.7**, **Radius** to **13.86**, **Height** to **1.208**, and **Sides** to **42**. Now, align the tube, as shown in Fig. E16. From the **Object-Space Modifiers** section of the **Modifier** list, select **Mirror**. In the **Parameters** rollout, change **Mirror Axis** to **Z** and **Offset** to **-0.31**. Also, select the **Copy** check box [see Fig. E17].

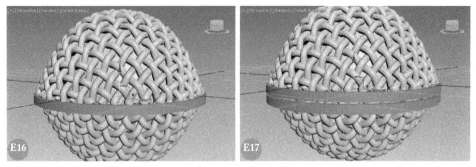

15. From the **Object-Space Modifiers** section of the **Modifier** list, select **Chamfer**. In the **Parameters** rollout, change **Amount** to **0.06** [see Fig. E18].

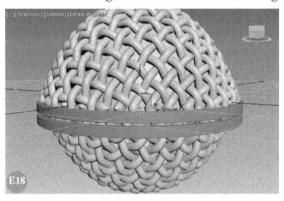

16. Select **Sphere** and then from the **Object-Space Modifiers** section of the **Modifier** list, select **Taper**. In the **Parameters** rollout, change **Amount** to **0.01** and **Curve** to **0.3**.

17. Using the **Line** tool, create a shape, as shown in Fig. E19. Now, smooth the vertices of the line using the **Fillet** function. From the **Object-Space Modifiers** section of the **Modifier** list, select **Lathe**. In the **Modify** panel > **Parameters** rollout > **Align** group, click **Min**. Now, select the **Weld Core** check box and change **Segments** to **32** [see Fig. E20].

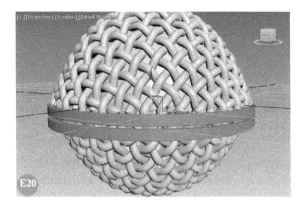

Exercise 2: Creating a Model of a Building

In this exercise, we will model a building using various modifiers [see Figs. E1 through E4].

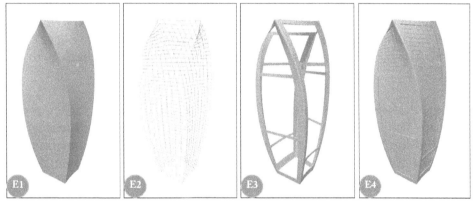

Table E2 summarizes the exercise:

Table E2	
Skill level	Intermediate
Time to complete	45 Minutes
Topics in the section:	• Specifying the Units for the Exercise • Creating the Tower • Creating the Mullions • Creating the Outer Shell
Project folder	**unit-m7**
Units	**Metric - Meters**
Final exercise file	**building-finish.max**

Specifying the Units for the Exercise

Follow these steps:

1. From **Customize** menu choose **Units Setup**. In the **Units Setup** dialog box that opens, select the **Metric** option from the **Display Unit Scale** group. Next, select **Meters** from the drop-down list located below the **Metric** option, if already not selected. Click **OK** to accept the change.

2. From the **File** menu, choose **Save** to open the **Save File As** dialog box. In the **File name** text box type **building-finish.max** and then click **Save** to save the file.

Creating the Tower

Follow these steps:

1. In the **Create** panel, click **Geometry**, and then on the **Object Type** rollout, click **Box**. In the **Perspective** viewport, drag out a box of any size. Go to the **Modify** panel, and in the **Parameters** rollout, set **Length** to **80**, **Width** to **80**, and **Height** to **400**. Also, set **Length Segs** to **8**, **Width Segs** to **8**, and **Height Segs** to **50** [see Fig. E5].

2. Change the name of the object to **Tower**. Now, you will apply various modifiers to create distinct building shape. From the **Object-Space Modifiers** section of the **Modifier** list, select **Taper**. In the **Taper** group of the **Parameters** rollout, set **Amount** to **0.35** and curve to **2.04**. The building bulges out [see Fig. E6].

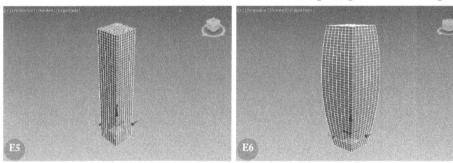

3. From the **Object-Space Modifiers** section of the **Modifier** list, select **Bend**. In the **Bend** group of the **Parameters** rollout, set **Angle** to **27.5** and **Bend Axis** to **Y**. The building bends along the Y axis [see Fig. E7]. From the **Object-Space Modifiers** section of the **Modifier** list, select **Twist**. In the **Twist** group of the **Parameters** rollout, set **Angle** to **45.5** and **Bias** to **93.5**. The building twists along the Z axis [see Fig. E8].

Creating the Mullions

Follow these steps:

1. Select **Tower** in **Scene Explorer** and then RMB click on it. From the **Quad** menu that opens, choose **Clone** to open the **Clone Options** dialog box. Select

Reference from the **Object** group. Next, type **Mullions** in the **Name** text box and the click **OK**.

2. In **Scene Explorer**, click **Tower's** bulb icon to hide it. Go to the **Modify** panel and from the **Object-Space Modifiers** section of the **Modifier** list, select **Edit Poly**. In the **Selection** rollout, click **Polygon** and then select the center polygons [see Fig. E9]. Click **Grow** thrice to select all top polygons of the building [see Fig. E10].

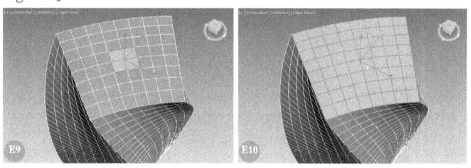

3. Delete the selected polygons by pressing **Delete**. Similarly, delete the bottom polygons. From the **Object-Space Modifiers** section of the **Modifier** list, select **Lattice**. In the **Struts** group of the **Parameters** rollout, set **Radius** to **0.5**, and **Sides** to **5**. Also, turn on **Smooth**.

Creating the Outer Shell
Follow these steps:

1. In **Scene Explorer**, click the **Mullions's** bulb icon to hide it. Select **Tower** and create a clone with the name **Shell**. Make sure to select **Reference** from the **Object group** in the **Clone Options** dialog box.

2. Make sure **Tower** and **Mullions** are not visible in the scene and **Shell** is visible in the scene. Select the top and bottom polygons of **Shell** and delete them as done earlier. Also, turn off the **Twist**, **Bend**, and **Taper** modifiers.

3. In the **Selection** rollout, make sure the **Ignore Backfacing** check box is clear. In the **Front** viewport, select polygons [see Fig. E11]. Press **Delete** to remove the selected polygons. Similarly, remove polygons from the other remaining two sides. Use a different pattern for these sides [see Fig. E12].

4. In the **Selection** rollout, click **Edge** and then select the four corner edges [see Fig. E13]. Now, click **Loop** to select the loops. In the **Edit Edges** rollout, click **Chamfer's** settings box to open the **Chamfer** caddy controls. Set **Amount** to **1.636** and **Segments** to **5** [see Fig. E14].

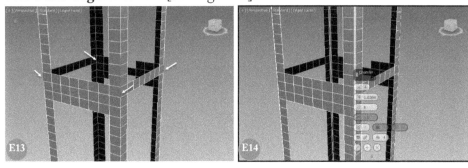

5. Click **OK**. From the **Object-Space Modifiers** section of the **Modifier** list, select **Shell**. In the **Parameters** rollout, set **Outer Amount** to **2.0** [see Fig. E15]. Now turn on the **Twist, Taper**, and **Bend** Modifiers. Turn on the **Tower** and **Mullions** from **Scene Explorer**. Assign colors of your choice to **Tower, Shell**, and **Mullions** [see Fig. E16]. Now, create different version of the building [see Fig. E17].

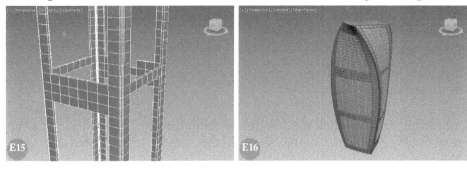

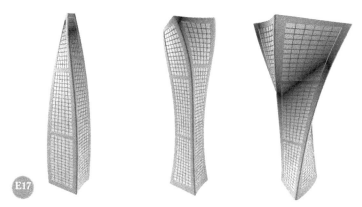

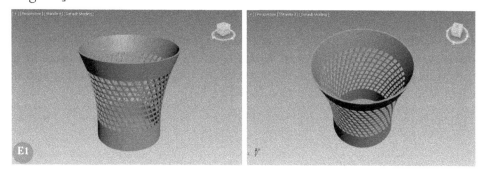

Exercise 3: Creating a Model of a Paper Basket

In this exercise, you will model a melted waste paper basket using various modifiers [see Fig. E1].

Table E3 summarizes the exercise:

Table E3	
Skill level	Beginner
Time to complete	35 Minutes
Topics in the section:	• Specifying the Units for the Exercise • Creating the Basket
Project folder	**unit-m7**
Units	**Metric - Centimeters**
Final exercise file	**basket-finish.max**

Specifying the Units for the Exercise

Follow these steps:

1. From **Customize** menu choose **Units Setup**. In the **Units Setup** dialog box that opens, select the **Metric** option from the **Display Unit Scale** group. Next, select **Centimeters** from the drop-down list located below the **Metric** option, if already not selected. Click **OK** to accept the change.

2. From the **File** menu, choose **Save** to open the **Save File As** dialog box. In the **File name** text box type **basket-finish.max** and then click **Save** to save the file.

Creating the Basket
Follow these steps:

1. In the **Create** panel, click **Geometry**, and then on the **Object Type** rollout, click **Cylinder**. In the **Perspective** viewport, drag out a cylinder of any size. Go to the **Modify** panel, and on the **Parameters** rollout, set **Radius** to **14.5** and **Height** to **30**. Also, set **Height Segments** to **12** and **Sides** to **40** [see Fig. E2].

2. From the **Object-Space Modifiers** section of the **Modifier List**, select **Edit Poly**. In the **Selection** rollout, click **Vertex** and then select top row of vertices of the cylinder in the **Front** viewport. RMB click on the **Select and Move** button on the **Main** toolbar.

3. In the **Offset:Screen** group of the **Move Transform Type-In** dialog box that opens, set **Y** to **5** and then press **Enter** to move the vertices by **5** units in the **Y** direction [see Fig. E3].Select all the vertices except the bottom row and move them by **6** units in the **Y** direction [see Fig. E4].

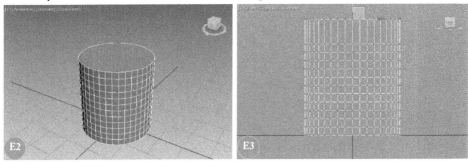

4. In the **Selection** rollout, click **Polygon** and then select all the middle polygons [see Fig. E5]. In the **Edit Polygons** rollout, click **Inset Settings** button. In the **Inset** caddy control, select **By Polygon** from **Group**. Now, set amount to **0.3** and click **OK** to inset the selected polygons [see Fig. E6]. Delete the polygons.

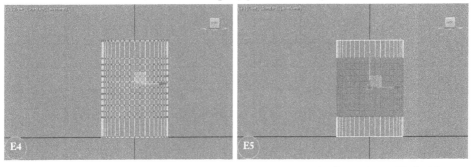

5. Select the top cap polygon and delete it as well [see Fig. E7]. From the **Object-Space Modifiers** section of the **Modifier List**, select **Shell**. In the **Parameters** layout, set **Outer Amount** to **0.5**.

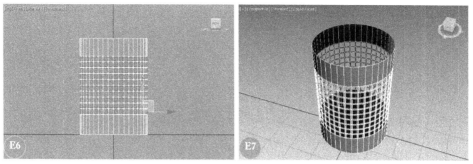

6. From the **Object-Space Modifiers** section of the **Modifier List**, select **Taper**. In the **Parameters** layout, set **Amount** to **0.44** and **Curve** to **-0.7**. From the **Object-Space Modifiers** section of the **Modifier List**, select **Twist**. In the **Parameters** layout, set **Angle** to **66.5**.

Exercise 4: Creating a Rope

In this exercise, we will create a rope [see Fig. E1].

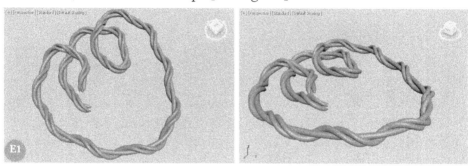

Table E4 summarizes the exercise:

Table E4	
Skill level	Beginner
Time to complete	40 Minutes
Topics in the section:	• Specifying the Units for the Exercise • Creating the Rope
Project folder	**unit-m7**
Units	**Generic**
Final exercise file	**rope-finish.max**

Specifying the Units for the Exercise

Follow these steps:

1. From **Customize** menu choose **Units Setup**. In the **Units Setup** dialog box that appears, select **Generic Units** from the **Units Setup** dialog box. Click **OK** to accept the changes made.

2. From the **File** menu, choose **Save** to open the **Save File As** dialog box. In the **File name** text box type **rope-finish.max** and then click **Save** to save the file.

Creating the Rope
Follow these steps:

1. In the **Create** panel, click **Shapes,** and then click **Freehand.** Using the **Freehand** tool, create a spline [see Fig. E2]. You can also open the **rope-curve-start.max** file, if you want to follow along.

2. From the **Object-Space Modifiers** section of the **Modifier List,** select **Spline Relax.** In the **Modify** panel > **Relax** rollout, change **Amount** to **1** and **Iterations** to **7** [see Fig. E3].

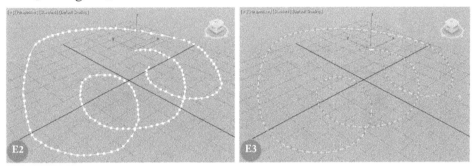

3. From the **Object-Space Modifiers** section of the **Modifier List,** select **Optimize Spline.** In the **Modify** panel > **Optimize Spline** rollout > **Reduce Knots** group, change **By %** to **10** [see Fig. E4].

4. From the **Object-Space Modifiers** section of the **Modifier List,** select **Renderable Spline.** In the **Modify** panel > **Parameters** rollout, select **Enable in Renderer** and **Enable in Viewport** check boxes, if not already selected. Now, change **Thickness** to **2** [see Fig. E5].

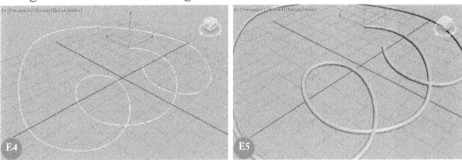

What next?
Notice in Fig. E5 the segments are going through each other instead of overlapping. Next, we will fix it.

5. From the **Object-Space Modifiers** section of the **Modifier List,** select **Spline Overlap.** In the **Modify** panel > **Overlap** rollout, change to **1.584** [see Fig. E6].

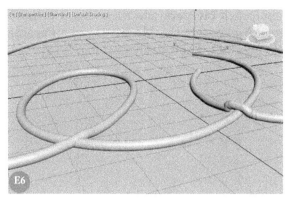

What next?
Notice in Fig. E6, the overlapping of segments is not clean because of the irregular distribution of the knots. Let's fix that.

6. Add the **Normalize Spline** modifier above the **Renderable Spline** in the stack [see Fig. E7]. In the **Modify** panel > **Parameter** rollout > **Normalize By** group, change **Seg Length** to **4.683** [see Fig. E8].

7. Select the **Renderable Spline** modifier in the stack and then in the **Parameters** rollout > **Capping Options** group, change **Segments** to **5** and **Sphere** to **1** [see Fig. E9]. Also, ensure that the **Twist Correction** check box is selected.

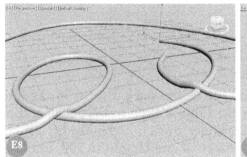
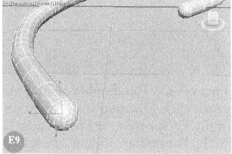

8. In the modifier stack, turn off the **Renderable Spline** modifier. From the **Object-Space Modifiers** section of the **Modifier List**, select **Noise**. In the **Modify** panel > **Parameters** rollout > **Noise** group, change **Scale** to **10**. In the **Strength** group, change **Z** to **50** [see Fig. 10].

What just happened?
Here, the **Noise** modifier modulating the position of the knots and as you can see in Fig. E10, the **Noise** modifier is affecting whole spline. If you want to affect a part of the spline, you need to use the influencers.

9. In the **Create** panel, click **Helpers**, and then click **Influence**. Click-drag in the viewport to create the gizmo. In the **Modify** panel > **Parameters** rollout, change **Near** and **Far** to **31** and **42**, respectively [see Fig. E11].

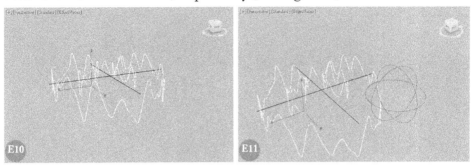

10. Select the spline. From the **Object-Space Modifiers** section of the **Modifier List**, select **Spline Influence**. In the **Modify** panel > **Influence Parameters** rollout, click **Pick** and then click on the gizmo in the viewport. Also, change **Falloff Type** to **Smooth**.

11. Move the **Noise** modifier at the top of the stack. If you now move the influencer in the viewport, you will notice the knots are being affected only inside the area of the influencer [see Fig. E12]. Turn on the **Renderable Spline** modifier in the stack display [see Fig. E13].

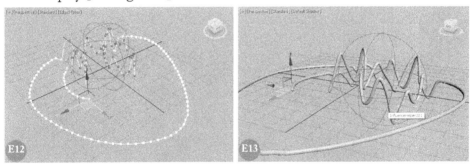

12. Turn off the **Renderable Spline** modifier in the stack display. In the **Create** panel, click **Geometry**, and then on the **Object Type** rollout, click **Cylinder**. In the **Perspective** viewport, create a cylinder. Switch to the **Modify** panel and on the **Parameters** rollout, change **Radius** to **2** and **Height** to **500**, and **Height Segments** to **35** [see Fig. E14]. Create two more copies of the cylinder and then align them as shown in Fig. E15.

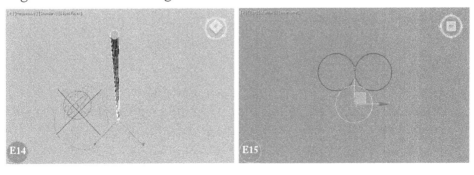

13. Convert one of the cylinders to editable poly and then attach the remaining two cylinders using the **Attach** function.

14. From the **Object-Space Modifiers** section of the **Modifier List**, select **Path Deform**. In the **Modify** panel > **PathDeform** rollout, click **None** and then click the spline in the viewport. Change **Stretch** to **1.827** and then in the **Rotation** group, change **Twist** to **3000** [see Fig. E16]. Turn off **Noise** from the spline's modifier stack. Now, change the **Stretch** value according to the length spline.

15. From the **Object-Space Modifiers** section of the **Modifier List**, select **TurboSmooth**. Place the **TurboSmooth** modifier below the **Path Deform** modifier. In the **TurboSmooth** rollout, change **Iterations** to **2** [see Fig. E17].

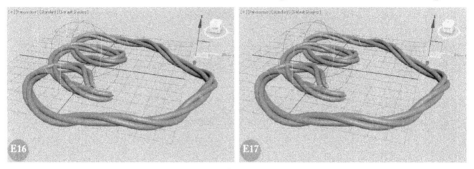

16. Select spline and then select the **Spline Overlap** modifier in the stack display. In the **Overlap** rollout, adjust the **Thickness** value as per your requirement [see Fig. E18].

17. In the **Modify** panel > **Path Deform** modifier > **Path Deform** rollout > **Rotation** group, change **Twist** to **5569** [see Fig. E19].

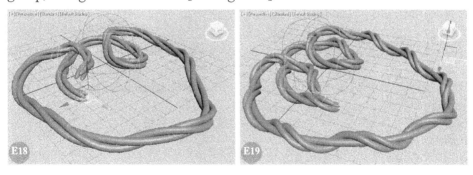

Quiz

Evaluate your skills to see how many questions you can answer correctly.

Multiple Choice
Answer the following questions, only one choice is correct.

1. Which of the following keys is used to create an instance of a modifier?

    [A] Shift   [B] Alt
    [C] Ctrl   [D] Shift+Alt

2. Which of the following modifiers is used to add depth to a shape object?

    [A] Edit Spline   [B] Extrude
    [C] Chamfer   [D] All of the above

Fill in the Blanks
Fill in the blanks in each of the following statements:

1. OSM and WSM stand for _____ and _____.

2. The transformation values are stored in a matrix called _____.

3. The hair only renders in the _____ or _____ viewports.

True of False
State whether each of the following is true or false:

1. You can copy and paste modifiers between the object.

2. The **Fillet/Chamfer** modifier lets you fillet or chamfer corner vertices between linear segments of the shape objects.

Summary
The unit covered the following topics:

  • Using modifiers
  • Stack display
  • Object-Space modifiers vs World-Space modifiers
  • How transform affects modifiers

Unit MB - Bonus Hands-on Exercises [Modeling]

From the **File** menu, choose **Project > Create Default** to open the **Choose a folder** dialog box. In this dialog box, navigate to the **3dsmax2019projects** directory and then click **New Folder** and then rename the folder as **unit-mb**. Select the folder and then click **Select Folder** to create the project folder.

Exercises - Modeling

Exercise 1: Creating a Serving Bowl

In this exercise, you will create model of a bowl [see Fig. E1]. Table E1 summarizes the exercise:

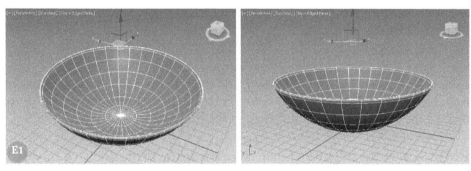

Table E1:	
Skill level	Beginner
Time to complete	20 Minutes
Topics in the section:	• Specifying the Units for the Exercise • Creating the Bowl
Project folder	**unit-mb**
Units	**Metric - Centimeters**
Final exercise file	**bowl-finish.max**

Specifying the Units for the Exercise
Follow these steps:

1. From **Customize** menu choose **Units Setup**. In the **Units Setup** dialog box that appears, select **Metric** from the **Display Unit Scale** group. Next, choose **Centimeters** from the drop-down list located below **Metric**. Click **System Unit Setup** to open the **System Unit Setup** dialog box and then make sure **1 Unit** is equal to the **1 Centimeters** [see Fig. E2]. Click **OK** and then click **OK** in the **Units Setup** dialog box.

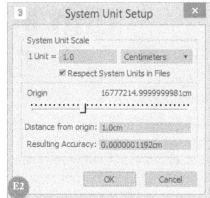

2. RMB click on any snap toggle button in the **Main** toolbar. In the **Grid and Snap Settings** dialog box that opens, choose the **Home Grid** panel and then set **Grid Spacing** to **3**, **Major Lines every Nth Grid Line** to **4**, and **Perspective View Grid Extent** to **10**. Close the **Grid and Snap Settings** dialog box. From the **File** menu, choose **Save** to open the **Save File As** dialog box. In the **File name** text box type **bowl-finish.max** and then click **Save** to save the file.

Creating the Bowl
Follow these steps:

1. In the **Create** panel, click **Geometry**, and then on the **Object Type** rollout, click **Sphere**. In the **Perspective** viewport, create a sphere. Switch to **Modify** panel and on the **Parameters** rollout, change **Radius** to **26**.

2. RMB click on the sphere and then choose **transform** quadrant > **Convert To:** > **Convert to Editable Poly**. In the **Modify** panel > **Selection** rollout, click **Polygon** to activate the polygon sub-object level.

3. In the **Front** viewport, select the polygons, as shown in Fig. E3 and then press **Delete** to delete the selected polygons [see Fig. E4]. In the **Modify** panel > **Selection** rollout, click **Vertex** to activate the vertex sub-object level and then select the vertices, as shown in Fig. E5.

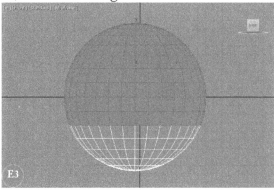

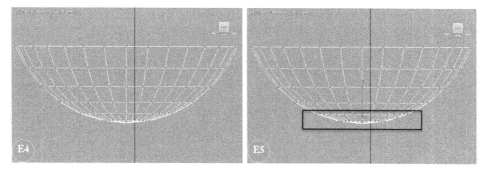

4. In the **Modify** panel > **Edit Geometry** rollout, click **Z** button corresponding to the **Make Planer** control to make the selected vertices coplanar [see Fig. E6]. Press **Ctrl+A** to select all vertices and then slightly scale them down along the negative **Y** axis using the **Scale** tool [see Fig. E7]. Press **6** to switch to the **Object** mode and then place the bowl at the origin. Fig. E8 shows the bowl at the origin.

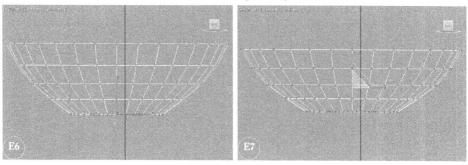

 What next?
*If you look at Fig. E8, the surface of the bowl is paper thin. To give it some volume, we will use the **Shell** modifier.*

5. From the **Object-Space Modifiers** section of the **Modifier List**, select **Shell**. In the **Parameters** layout, change **Outer Amount** to **0.7** and **Segments** to **2** [see Fig. E9]. From the **Object-Space Modifiers** section of the **Modifier List**, select **Edit Poly**.

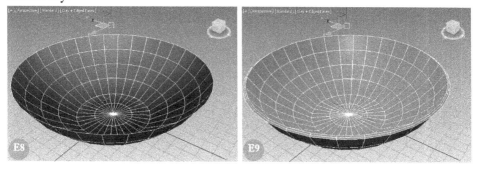

6. In the **Modify** panel > **Selection** rollout, click **Edge** to activate the edge sub-object level and then select the newly added segment [see Fig. E10]. Move it slightly up using the **Move** tool.

7. Select the outer edge loops, as shown in Fig. E11. In the **Modify** panel > **Edit Edges** rollout, click **Chamfer** > **Settings** to open the **Chamfer** caddy control. In the caddy control, change **Amount** to **0.13** and then click **OK** [see Fig. E12].

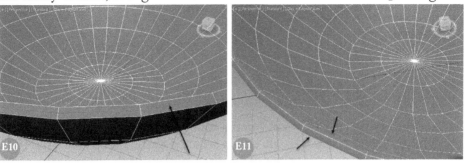

8. From the **Object-Space Modifiers** section of the **Modifier List**, select MeshSmooth [see Fig. E13].

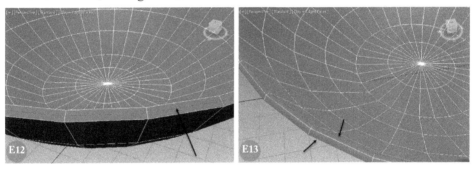

Exercise 2: Creating a Plate

In this exercise, you will create model of a plate [see Fig. E1]. Table E2 summarizes the exercise:

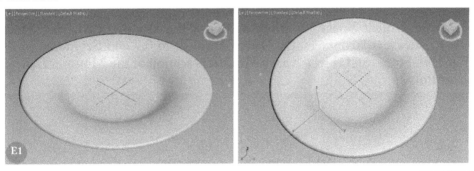

Table E2:	
Skill level	Beginner
Time to complete	20 Minutes
Topics in the section:	• Specifying the Units for the Exercise • Creating the Plate
Project folder	**unit-mb**
Units	**Generic**
Final exercise file	**plate-finish.max**

Specifying the Units for the Exercise

Follow these steps:

1. From **Customize** menu choose **Units Setup**. In the **Units Setup** dialog box that appears, select **Generic Units** from the **Units Setup** dialog box. Click **OK** to accept the changes made.

2. From the **File** menu, choose **Save** to open the **Save File As** dialog box. In the **File name** text box type **plate-finish.max** and then click **Save** to save the file.

Creating the Plate

Follow these steps:

1. Enable 2D snapping from the **Main** toolbar. In the **Create** panel, click **Shapes,** and then click **Line**. In the **Front** viewport, create a shape [see Fig. E2].

2. From the **Object-Space Modifiers** section of the **Modifier List**, select **Lathe**. In the **Modify** panel > **Parameters** rollout > **Align** group, click **Min** [see Fig. E3]. Now, select the **Weld Core** check box and change **Segments** to **32** [see Fig. E4].

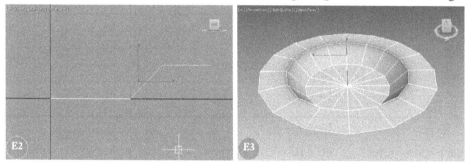

3. From the **Object-Space Modifiers** section of the **Modifier List**, select **Shell**. In the **Parameters** layout, change **Outer Amount** to **2**. From the **Object-Space Modifiers** section of the **Modifier List**, select **Edit Poly**.

4. In the **Modify** panel > **Selection** rollout, click **Edge** to activate the edge sub-object level. Now, select the edge loop, as shown in Fig. E5. In the **Modify** panel > **Edit Edges** rollout, click **Chamfer** > **Settings** to open the **Chamfer** caddy control. In the caddy control, change **Amount** to **4.5** and then click **OK** [see Fig. E6].

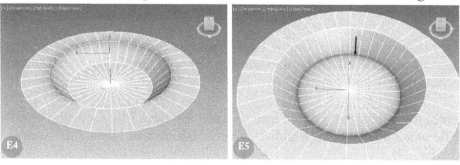

5. Press **6** to switch to the **Object** level. From the **Object-Space Modifiers** section of the **Modifier List**, select **MeshSmooth** [see Fig. E7].

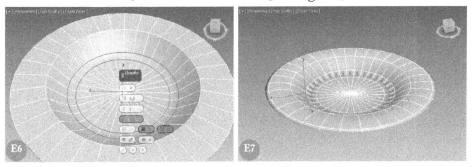

Exercise 3: Creating a Braided Cable

In this exercise, we will create a braided cable [see Fig. E1]. Table E3 summarizes the exercise:

Table E3:	
Skill level	Intermediate
Time to complete	40 Minutes
Topics in the section:	• Specifying the Units for the Exercise • Creating the Cable
Project folder	**unit-mb**
Units	**Generic**
Final exercise file	**braided-cable-finish.max**

Specifying the Units for the Exercise

Follow these steps:

1. From **Customize** menu choose **Units Setup**. In the **Units Setup** dialog box that appears, select **Generic Units** from the **Units Setup** dialog box. Click **OK** to accept the changes made.

2. From the **File** menu, choose **Save** to open the **Save File As** dialog box. In the **File name** text box type **braided-cable-finish.max** and then click **Save** to save the file.

Creating the Cable

Follow these steps:

1. In the **Create** panel, click **Shapes, and** then click **Rectangle**. In the **Front** viewport, create a rectangle and then place it at the origin. In the **Modify** panel > **Parameters** rollout, change **Length** to **30** and **Width** to **30**. Now, align the rectange, as shown in Fig. E2.

2. RMB click on the rectangle and then choose **transform** quadrant > **Convert To:** > **Convert to Editable Spline**. Create a copy of the rectangle using Shift and snap the end vertices [see Fig. E3].

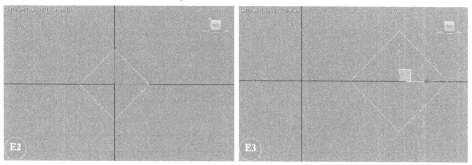

3. Select one of the rectangles and then in the **Modify** panel > **Geometry** rollout, click **Attach** and then click on the other rectangle to attach the rectangles. In the **Modify** panel > **Selection** rollout, click **Segment** to activate the segment sub-object level. Now, select and delete segments, refer to Fig. E4.

4. Select the segments, refer to Fig. E5 and then in the **Modify** panel > **Geometry** rollout, click **Detach** to open the **Detach** dialog. In this dialog, type **RightShape** in the **Detach as** text box and then click **OK**. Now, rename the remaining shape as **LeftShape**.

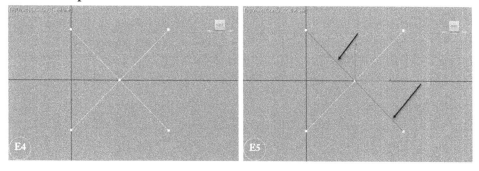

5. Select **LeftShape**, in the **Modify** panel > **Selection** rollout, click **Vertex** to activate the vertex sub-object level. Select the center vertices and then in the **Modify** panel > **Geometry** rollout, click **Weld** to weld the vertices. Repeat the process for **RightShape**. Place the shape at the origin [see Fig. E6].

6. In the Prespective viewport, move the spline by **63** units along the **+Y** axis and then select **Use Transform Coordinate Center** from the **Use Center** flyout [see

Fig. E7]. Choose **Array** from the **Tools** menu to open the **Array** dialog box. Set the values as shown in Fig. E8, Fig. E9 shows the result.

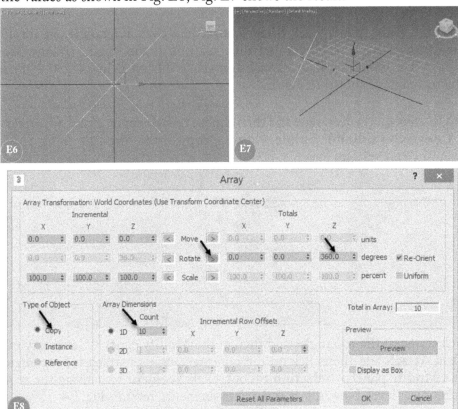

7. Select **LeftShape** and then in the **Modify** panel > **Geometry** rollout, click **Attach Mult** to open the **Attach Multiple** dialog box. Select all left shapes and then click **Attach**. Similarly, repeat the process for the right shapes.

8. Select **LeftShape** and then in the **Modify** panel > **Selection** rollout, click **Vertex** to activate the vertex sub-object level. Select **Use Transform Coordinate Center** from the **Use Center** flyout. Select the center vertices [see Fig. E9] and then scale them by **94%** [see Fig. E10]. Now, press **Ctrl+I** to invert the selection and then scale them by **104%**.

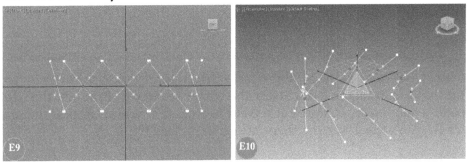

9. Select **RightShape**. Scale the center vertices by **104%** and rest of the vertices by **94%** [see Fig. E11]. Now, attach **LeftShape** and **RightShape** as done earlier. Now, weld the top and bottom vertices [see Fig. E12].

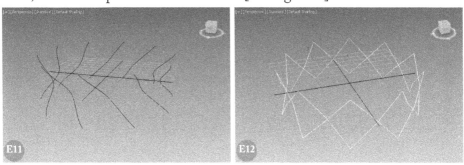

10. In the **Front** viewport create **30** copies of the spline using **Shift** and then attach them [see Fig. E13].

11. From the **Object-Space Modifiers** section of the **Modifier** List, select **Sweep**. In the **Modify** panel > **Selection Type** rollout, change **Built-In Section** to **Pipe**. In the **Parameters** section, change **Radius** to **5.229** and **Thickness** to **0.21** [see Fig. E14].

12. Move the pivot point at the bottom of the cable [see Fig. E15].

13. Create a line using the **Line** tool and rename it as **Path** [see Fig. E16]. Select the cable and then from the **World-Space Modifiers** section of the **Modifier** list, select **Path Deform**.

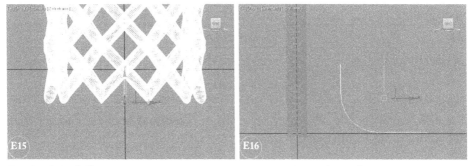

14. In the **Modify** panel > **Parameters** rollout, click **Pick Path** and then click **Path** in the viewport. Now, in the **Path Deform Axis** group, change axis to **Y**. In the **Path Deform** section, change **Percent** to **-38.5** [see Fig. E17].

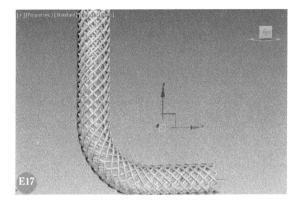

E17

Exercise 4: Creating a Chair

In this exercises, you will create model of a chair, as shown in Fig. E1.

E1

The following table summarizes the exercise:

Table E4	
Skill level	Intermediate
Time to complete	40 Minutes
Topics in the section	• Getting Started • Creating the Frame of the Chair • Creating Seats of the Chair
Project Folder	**unit-mb**
Units	**Decimal Inches**
Final exercise file	**chair-finish.max**

Getting Ready

Start a new scene in 3ds Max and set units to **Decimal Inches**. Ensure that the project folder is set to **unit-mb**.

Follow these steps:

1. Go to the **Create** panel, click **Shapes** and then click **Line**. Expand the **Keyboard Entry** rollout and then set **X**, **Y**, and **Z** to **9.886**, **-10.75**, and **0.086**, respectively. Click **Add Point** to create the 1st point. Similarly create other points using the values given in Table EM1.1. After entering the values shown in the table, click **Finish**; the line appears in the viewports [see Fig. E2].

Table EM1.1 - Coordinates for creating points			
Point	X	Y	Z
1st	9.886"	-10.75"	0.086"
2nd	-9.836"	-10.75"	0.086"
3rd	-9.836"	-10.75"	14.834"
4th	6.285"	-10.75"	14.834"
5th	9.886"	-10.75"	27.011"

2. In the **Modify** panel > **Rendering** rollout, turn on the **Enable In Renderer** and **Enable In Viewport** checkboxes. Now, set **Thickness** to **0.9** and **Sides** to **14**. Make sure **Line001** is selected and then create a copy of the line by **Shift** dragging it about **21** units along the **Y** axis [see Fig. E3].

[+][Perspective][Standard][Default Shading]   [+][Perspective][Standard][Default Shading]

E2   E3

3. Select **Line001** and then in the **Modify** panel > **Geometry** rollout, click **Attach**. Now, click **Line002** in the viewport to attach the two lines. Turn on **Vertex** snapping from the **Main** toolbar. Activate the **Vertex** sub-object level and then click **Create Line** from the **Geometry** rollout.

4. Drag from one vertex to another to create a line [see Fig. E4]. Click **Yes** when prompted to weld the vertices. Click on **Create Line** to deactivate it. Disable snapping. Select all vertices and then RMB click. Choose **Bezier Corner** from the **tool1** quadrant of the **Quad** menu.

5. Select the vertices [see Fig. E5] and then click **Weld** from the **Geometry** rollout to weld the vertices. Now, select the vertices shown in Fig. E6. In the **Geometry** rollout, type **1.5** in the field located next to **Fillet** control and then press **Enter** to fillet the vertices [see Fig. E7].

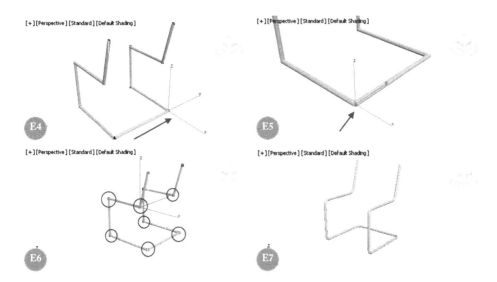

6. In the **Create** panel, click **Geometry** and then on the **Object Type** rollout, click **Tube**. Create a tube in the viewport. Go to the **Modify** panel and then in the **Parameters** rollout, set **Radius 1** to **0.641**, **Radius 2** to **0.429**, and **Height** to **2.133**. Also, set **Sides** to **32**. Align the tube with the frame [see Fig. E8]. Create a copy of the tube and then align it with the other side of the frame.

Creating Seats of the Chair

Follow these steps:

1. In the **Create** panel, click **Geometry** and then in the **Object Type** rollout, click **Box**. Create a box in the **Top** viewport. Go to the **Modify** panel and then on the **Parameters** rollout, set **Length** to **24.283**, **Width** to **14.152**, and **Height** to **2.988**. Set **Length Segs**, **Width Segs**, and **Height Segs** to **4, 4,** and **3**, respectively. Align the box, as shown in Fig. E9. From the **Modifier List > Object-Space Modifiers** section, choose **Turbosmooth**. In the **Parameters** rollout, set **Iterations** to **2**.

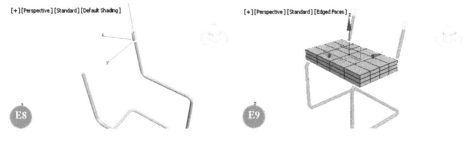

2. Now, we'll create piping for the seat. Convert the object to editable poly. Activate the **Edge** mode and select the edge loops [see Fig. E10]. In the **Modify** panel > **Edit Edges** rollout, click **Create Shape From Selection** to open the **Create Shape** dialog box. Click **OK** to close the dialog box and create the shape.

3. Select **Shape001** and then in **Modify** panel > **Rendering** rollout, set **Thickness** to **0.2** [see Fig. E11]. Select **Box001** and then in **Modify** panel > **Edit Geometry** rollout, click **Attach**. Click on **Shape001** to combine the two objects.

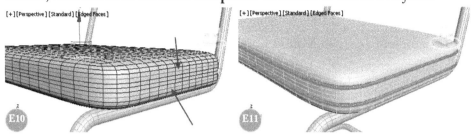

4. From the **Modifier List** > **Object-Space Modifiers** section, choose **FFD 3x3x3**. Activate the **Control Points** sub-object level and select the middle control points. Move the points downwards to create a bend in the seat [see Fig. E12]. Convert the stack to the editable poly. Now, create a copy of the seat and then rotate/scale to create the back support [see Fig. E13].

💡 *Tip: Aligning back seat*
*To easily align [rotate] the back support with the frame, move the pivot point at the bottom of the back support. Also, use the **Local** coordinate system.*

Exercise 5: Creating a Lamp

In this exercise, you will create a model of a lamp [see Fig. E1].

The following table summarizes the exercise:

Table E5:	
Skill level	Intermediate
Time to complete	40 Minutes
Topics in the section	• Getting Started • Creating the Lamp
Project Folder	**unit-mb**
Units	**Generic**
Final exercise file	**lamp-finish.max**

Getting Ready

Start a new scene in 3ds Max and set units to **Generic**. Ensure that the project folder is set to **unit-mb**.

Creating the Lamp

Follow these steps:

1. In the **Create** panel, click **Geometry** and then on the **Extended Primitives** > **Object Type** rollout, click **Hedra**. Create a hydra in the viewport. Go to the **Modify** panel and then on the **Parameters** rollout > **Family** group, select **Dodec/Icos**. In the **Family Parameters** group, set **P** and **Q** to **0.32** and **0.35**, respectively. Set **Radius** to **40** [see Fig. E2]. Convert hedra to editable poly. Activate the **Polygon** mode and select the polygon shown in Fig. E3.

2. In the **Ribbon** > **Modeling** tab > **Modify Selection** panel, click **Similar** [see Fig. E4] to select the polygon similar to the selected polygon [see Fig. E5]. Press **Delete** to delete the selected polygons. Press **Ctrl+A** to select all polygons.

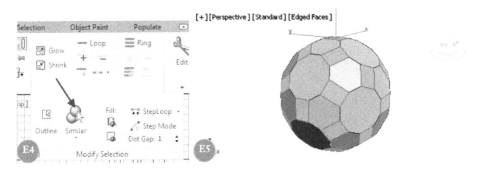

3. Click **Settings** on the right of **Extrude** in the **Modify** panel > **Edit Polygons** rollout. In the **Extrude Polygon** caddy control, set extrude **Type** to **Local Normal** and **Height** to **10** and click **Apply and Continue**. Now, click **OK** [see Fig. E6]. In the **Modify** panel > **Selection** rollout, click **Grow**. Press **Ctrl+I** to invert the selection and then press **Delete** to delete the polygons. Select all polygons and then in the **Modify** panel > **Polygon: Smoothing Groups** rollout, click **Select By SG** to smooth the polygon [see Fig. E7].

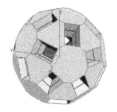

4. Activate the **Edge** mode and then select the edges, as shown in Fig. E8. In the **Ribbon** > **Modeling** tab > **Modify Selection** panel, click **Similar**. Click **Settings** on the right of **Chamfer** in the **Modify** panel > **Edit Edges** rollout. In the **Chamfer's** caddy, set **Chamfer Type** to **Quad Chamfer**, **Edge Chamfer Amount** to **0.294**, and **Connect Edge Segments** to **1**. Click **OK**.

5. Select the **Element** mode and click on the hedra in the viewport. In the **Ribbon** > **Modeling** tab > **Subdivision** panel, click **Tessellate** [see Fig. E9]. Activate the **Edge** mode and then select the edges shown in Fig. E10. In the **Ribbon** > **Modeling** tab > **Modify Selection** panel, click **Similar**. In the **Modify** panel > **Edit Edges** rollout, click **Create Shape From Selection** to open the **Create Shape** dialog box. Click **OK** to create the shape [see Fig. E11].

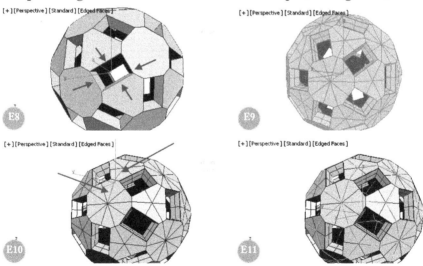

6. Select **Shape001**. In the **Modify** panel > **Rendering** rollout, turn on the **Enable In Renderer** and **Enable In Viewport** checkboxes. Now, set **Thickness** to **0.9** and **Sides** to **14**. Select **Hedra001** and then on the **Modifier List** > **Object-Space Modifiers** section, choose **Turbosmooth**. In the **Parameters** rollout, set **Itera-**

tions to **2** [see Fig. E12]. Select **Shape001** and **Hedra001**. Group them with the name **Lamp**.

[+] [Perspective] [Standard] [Default Shading]

E12

7. Now, create the stand for the lamp and align it with the stand.

Exercise 6: Creating a Waste Bin

In this exercise, you will create a model of a waste bin [see Fig. E1].

E1

The following table summarizes the exercise:

Table E6	
Skill level	Intermediate
Time to complete	50 Minutes
Topics in the section	• Getting Started • Creating the Waste Bin
Project Folder	**unit-mb**
Units	**Decimal Inches**
Final exercise file	**bin-finish.max**

Getting Ready

Start a new scene in 3ds Max and set units to **Decimal Inches**. Ensure that the project folder is set to **unit-mb**.

Creating the Waste Bin
Follow these steps:

1. In the **Create** panel, click **Geometry** and then in the **Object Type** rollout, click **Cylinder**. Create a cylinder in the **Top** viewport. Go to the **Modify** panel and then on the **Parameters** rollout, set **Radius** to **15**, **Height** to **45**, **Sides** to **50**, and **Height Segments** to **30**. Convert cylinder to editable poly. Activate the **Polygon** mode, select the top polygon and then delete it [see Fig. E2].

2. Select the top and bottom polygon loops [see Fig. E3] and then click **Settings** on the right of **Extrude** in the **Modify** panel > **Edit Polygons** rollout. In the **Extrude Polygons** caddy control, set **Extrude Type** to **Local Normal** and **Height** to **1.2** and click **OK**.

3. Ensure the newly created polygons are still selected and then click **Settings** on the right of **Bevel** in the **Modify** panel > **Edit Polygons** rollout. In the **Bevel** caddy control, set **Bevel Type** to **Local Normal**, **Height** to **0.6**, **Outline** to **-0.9333**. Click **OK** [see Fig. E4].

4. Select every alternate column of polygons using **Shift**, see Fig. E5. Now, using the **Alt** key, remove polygons form the selection [see Fig. E6]. Click **Settings** on the right of **Extrude** in the **Modify** panel > **Edit Polygons** rollout. In the **Extrude Polygons** caddy control, set **Extrude Type** to **Local Normal** and **Height** to **-0.5** and click **OK**.

5. From the **Modifier List** > **Object-Space Modifiers** section, choose **Shell**. In the **Modify** panel > **Parameters** rollout, set **Outer Amount** to **0.15** [see Fig. E7]. Now, apply a **TurboSmooth** modifier to the cylinder. Now, we'll create lid for the waste bin.

6. In the **Create** panel, click **Geometry** and then in the **Object Type** rollout, click **Cylinder**. Create a cylinder in the **Top** viewport. Go to the **Modify** panel and then in the **Parameters** rollout, set **Radius** to **17**, **Height** to **2**, **Sides** to **50**, and **Height Segments** to **1**.

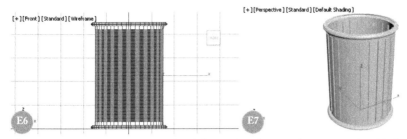

7. Convert cylinder to the editable poly object. Activate the **Polygon** mode and select the bottom polygon [see Fig. E8], and then click **Settings** on the right of **Inset** in the **Modify** panel > **Edit Polygons** rollout. In the **Inset Polygons** caddy control, set **Amount** to **1** and click **OK** [see Fig. E9].

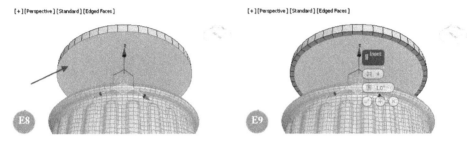

8. Click **Settings** on the right of **Extrude** in the **Modify** panel > **Edit Polygons** rollout. In the **Extrude Polygons** caddy control, set **Extrude Type** to **Local Normal** and **Height** to **-1** and click **OK** [see Fig. E10]. Now, align the lid with the bin.

9. Select the outer edges [refer to Fig. E11] of lid and then chamfer them. Refer to Fig. E12 for chamfer settings. Select the top polygon of the lid and then click **Settings** on the right of **Inset** in the **Modify** panel > **Edit Polygons** rollout. In the **Inset** caddy control, set **Amount** to **9** and click **OK**. Make sure the polygon is still selected and then move it slightly upwards [see Fig. E13]. Let's now create handle for the lid.

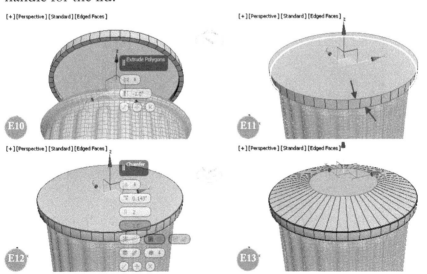

10. In the **Create** panel, click **Geometry** and then on the **Object Type** rollout, click **Torus**. Create a torus in the **Top** viewport. Go to the **Modify** panel and then on the **Parameters** rollout, set **Radius 1** to **4.64**, **Radius 2** to **0.84**, **Segments** to **50**, and **Sides** to **18**. Also, select the **Slice On** check box and then set **Slice From** and **Slice To** to **90**, and **270**, respectively. Now, align the torus at the center of the lid [see Fig. E14].

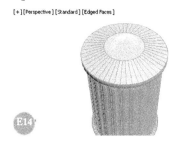

Exercise 7: Creating a Bottle

In this exercise, you will create a bottle using the **Loft** compound object [see Fig. E1].

The following table summarizes the exercise:

Table E7	
Skill level	Intermediate
Time to complete	45 Minutes
Topics in the section	• Getting Started • Creating the Bottle
Project Folder	**unit-mb**
Units	**Generic**
Final exercise file	**bottle-finish.max**

Getting Ready

Follow these steps:

1. Go to the **Create** panel, click **Geometry**, and then click **Plane**. In the **Front** viewport, create a plane. In the **Modify** panel > **Parameters** rollout, set **Length** to **180**, **Width** to **150**, **Length Segs** to **2**, and **Width Segs** to **2**. Also, clear the **Real-World Map Size** check box.

2. Click **Material Editor** from the **Main** toolbar. Create a standard material using the **Material Editor** and apply it to the plane. Use the **whiskey.jpg** for the **Diffuse** map. You need to turn on the **Show Shaded Material in Viewport** check box for the material to display the image on the plane in the viewport.

3. Ensure in the **Coordinates** rollout, **Use Real-World Scale** is off and **U Tiling** and **V Tiling** are set to **1** each. Make sure the **Front** viewport is active and then press **G** to turn off the grid. Also, set the shading to **Default Shading** in the **Front** viewport.

4. RMB click on the plane and then choose **Object Properties** from the **Quad** menu to open the **Object Properties** dialog box. In the **Interactivity** section of the dialog box, turn on the **Freeze** check box and on the **Display Properties** section, clear the **Show Frozen in Gray** check box [see Fig. E2].

Creating the Bottle
Follow these steps:

1. Go to the **Create** panel, click **Shapes**, and then click **Line**. In the **Front** viewport, create a shape [see Fig. E3] that is aligned with the vertical center of the bottle [create the first point at the bottom of the bottle]. You can create line anywhere in the scene but placing it at the center of the bottle will help you in the modeling process.

2. Go to the **Create** panel, click **Geometry**, and then click **Rectangle**. Create a rectangle in the top viewport. In the **Modify** panel > **Parameters** rollout, set **Length** to **40**, **Width** to **40**, and **Corner Radius** to **8**. Go to the **Create** panel, click **Geometry**, and then click **Circle**. Create a circle in the top viewport. In the **Modify** panel > **Parameters** rollout, set **Radius** to **7.5** [see Fig. E4].

3. Ensure the line is selected in and then click **Loft** on **Create** panel > **Geometry** > **Compound Objects** > **Object Type** rollout. Click **Get Shape** on the **Creation Method** rollout and then click the rectangle in the viewport to create the lofted object. In the **Path Parameters** rollout, set **Path** to **100**. Click **Get Shape** on the **Creation Method** rollout and then click the circle in the viewport to create the basic shape of the bottle [see Fig. E5].

E4   E5

4. **RMB** click on the lofted objects and choose **Object Properties** from the **Quad** menu to open the **Object Properties** dialog box. In the **Display Properties** group of the dialog box, select the **See-Through** check box. Click **OK** to close the dialog box.

What just happened?
Notice in Fig. E5, the image is obscured by the lofted object. Here, I have enabled the x-ray mode for the object so that we can see through it.

5. Enable the **Shape** sub-object level of the **Loft** object from the **Modify** panel and then select the rectangle shape on the loft object. Create a copy of the shape using **Shift+Drag** operation. Now, uniformly scale the copied rectangle so that it fits in the profile of the bottle [see Fig. E6]. Repeat the process until you get a rough shape using the copies of rectangle and circle [see Fig. E7].

E6   E7

6. Now, hide the plane geometry and turn off the x-ray mode [see Fig. E8] from the **Object Properties** dialog box. Make sure bottle is selected and then in **Modify** panel > **Skin Parameters** rollout, clear the **Cap End** check box. From the **Modifier List > Object-Space Modifiers** section, choose **Shell**. In the **Parameters** rollout, set **Outer Amount** to 0 and **Inner Amount** to 1.

E8

7. If you render the geometry, you would see that facets are appearing on the bottle. Let's fix it. From the **Modifier List > Object-Space Modifiers** section, choose

Smooth. In the **Parameters** rollout, turn on the **Auto Smooth** check box to smooth the geometry.

What just happened?

*Here, I've applied the **Smooth** modifier to eliminate the facets on geometry by grouping faces into smoothing groups. Faces in the same smoothing group appear as a smooth surface when you render the geometry.*

Exercise 8: Creating a Chair

In this exercise, you will create a chair using the spline and polygon modeling techniques [see Fig. E1].

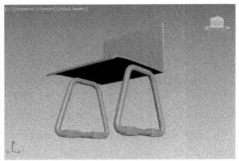

The following table summarizes the exercise:

Table E8	
Skill level	Intermediate
Time to complete	45 Minutes
Topics in the section	• Getting Started • Creating the Chair
Project Folder	**unit-mb**
Units	**Decimal Inches**
Final exercise file	**chair1-finish.max**

Getting Ready

We'll first create a box that will work like a template that will help us in the modeling process. Follow these steps:

1. In the **Create** panel, click **Geometry** and then on the **Object Type** rollout, click **Box**. Create a box in the **Top** viewport.

2. Go to the **Modify** panel and then in the **Parameters** rollout, set **Length** to **20**, **Width** to **20**, and **Height** to **30**. Set **Length Segs**, **Width Segs**, and **Height Segs** to **1**, **4**, and **2**, respectively. Set the **Transform Type-In** boxes in the **Status Bar** to **0** to place the box at the origin [see Fig. E2].

Creating the Chair
Follow these steps:

1. Activate the **Front** viewport and enable snapping [**Vertex**] by pressing S. Go to the **Create** panel, click **Shapes**, and then click **Rectangle**. In the **Front** viewport, create a shape [see Fig. E3]. Convert rectangle to editable spline. Activate the **Vertex** level and then press **Ctrl+A** to select all vertices. RMB click and then choose **Corner** from **Quad** menu > **tool1** quadrant. Now, move the top vertices as shown in Fig. E4.

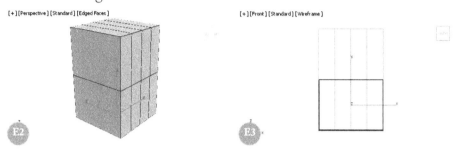

2. Press **Ctrl+A** to select all vertices and then on the **Modify** panel > **Geometry** rollout, enter **2** [type 2 and then press **Enter**] in the **Fillet** field to fillet all the vertices [see Fig. E5]. In the **Modify** panel > **Rendering** rollout, select the **Enable In Renderer** and **Enable In Viewport** checkboxes. Now, set **Thickness** to **1.5**. Turn off snapping.

3. In the **Create** panel, click **Geometry** and then in the **Extended Primitives** > **Object Type** rollout, click **ChamferBox**. Create a box in the **Top** viewport. Go to the **Modify** panel and then on the **Parameters** rollout, set **Length** to **1.9**, **Width** to **4.02**, **Height** to **1.9**, and **Fillet** to **0.045**. Set **Length Segs**, **Width Segs**, **Height Segs** and **Fillet Segs** to **1**, **1**, **1**, and **3**, respectively. Align it with the base of the chair [see Fig. E6]. Create a copy of the box and then align, as shown in Fig. E7.

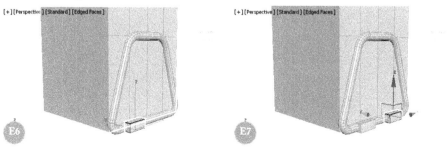

4. Select the line and the two chamfer boxes. Click **Mirror** on the **Main** toolbar. In the **Mirror** dialog box that appears, set the values shown in Fig. E8 and click **OK** to accept the value and create copy of the selected geometry [see Fig. E9]. Hide **Box001**.

5. In the **Create** panel, click **Geometry** and then on the **Object Type** rollout, click **Plane**. Create a plane in the **Top** viewport. In the **Modify** panel > **Parameters** rollout, set **Length, Width, Length Segs**, and **Width Segs** to **23, 20, 1**, and **1**, respectively. Align it with the base [see Fig. E10]. Convert the plane to editable poly.

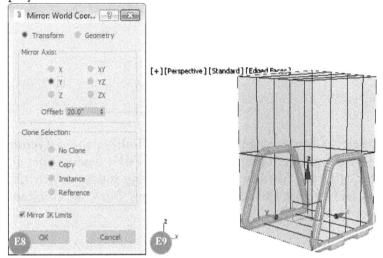

6. Active the **Edge** mode and select the back edge [refer to Fig. E11]. Now, extrude the edge upward by **15** units [see Fig. E12] using **Shift+drag**. Similarly, extrude the front edge [see Fig. E13]. Now, select the middle edge. Click **Settings** on the right of **Chamfer** in the **Modify** panel > **Edit Edges** rollout.

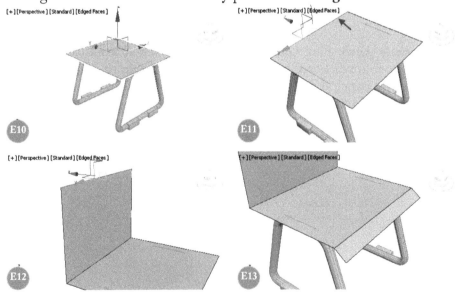

7. In the **Chamfer** caddy control, set **Chamfer Type** to **Standard Chamfer**, **Edge Chamfer Amount** to **1.5**, and **Connect Edge Segments** to **4**. Click **OK** [see Fig. E14]. Now, create edges as shown in Fig. E15 using the **Swift Loop** tool.

8. From the **Modifier List > Object-Space Modifiers** section, choose **Shell**. In the **Modify** panel > **Parameters** group, set **Outer Amount** to **0.53**. From the **Modifier List > Object-Space Modifiers** section, choose **Turbosmooth**. In the **Modify** panel > **Parameters** group, set **Iterations** to **2**.

Exercise 9: Creating a Flask

In this exercise, you will create a flask using the spline and polygon modeling techniques [see Fig. E1].

The following table summarizes the exercise:

Table E9	
Skill level	Intermediate
Time to complete	60 Minutes
Topics in the section	• Getting Started • Creating the Flask
Project Folder	**unit-mb**
Units	**Generic**
Final exercise file	**flask-finish.max**

Getting Ready

Start a new scene in 3ds Max and set units to **Generic**. Ensure that the project folder is set to **unit-mb**.

Creating the Flask
Follow these steps:

1. First, create the main body of the flask using the **Loft** compound object, as done in a previous exercise. Set the **Radius** of the top-most circle to **12** and bottom-most circle to **18** units [see Fig. E2]. In the **Create** panel, click **Geometry** and then in the **Object Type** rollout, click **Tube**.

2. Create a tube in the viewport. Go to the **Modify** panel and then in the **Parameters** rollout, set **Radius 1** to **13, Radius 2** to **12**, and **Height** to **12**. Also, set **Sides** to **24**. Align the tube with the rest of the flask [see Fig. E3].

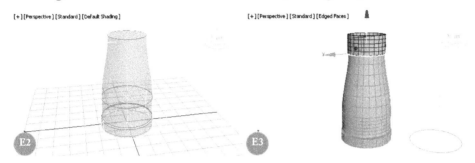

3. Make sure tube is selected and then RMB click on it. From the **Quad** menu > **display** quadrant, choose **Isolate Selection**. Convert tube to editable poly and activate the **Vertex** mode.

4. In the **Top** viewport select the vertices [see Fig. E4] and then in **Front** viewport, remove the bottom vertices from the selection [see Fig. E5]. We don't want to move the bottom vertices in order to seamlessly align the spout and the main body.

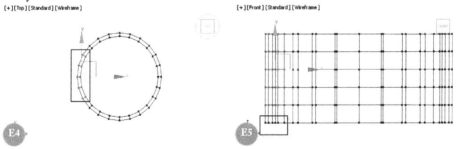

5. Move the vertices in the **Top** viewport towards left [see Fig. E6]. Remove the second row of vertices [from bottom] from the selection and move rest of the vertices in the **Top** viewport.

6. Repeat the process row by row [see Fig. E7]. Select the vertices shown in Fig. E8 and then scale them in using the **Select and Uniform Scale** tool to tighten the spacing [see Fig. E9]. You can further refine the shape by moving vertices and polygons.

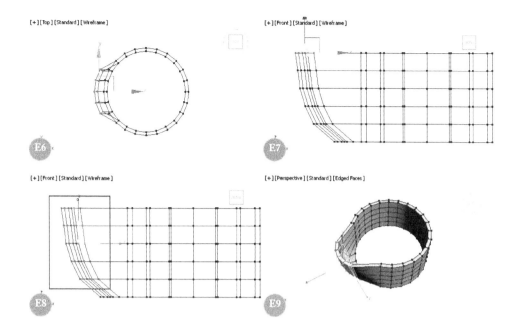

7. Create a hole [as done in **Exercise 1** of **Unit-M1**] in the tube for handle [refer to Figs. E10 and E11.

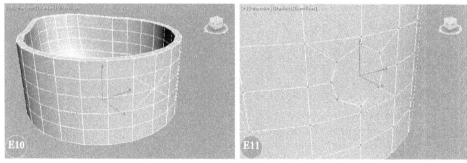

8. Select the newly created border and then extrude edges using the **Scale** tool [see Fig. E12]. Select the polygons, as shown in Fig. E13 and then extrude them by **8** units [see Fig. E14].

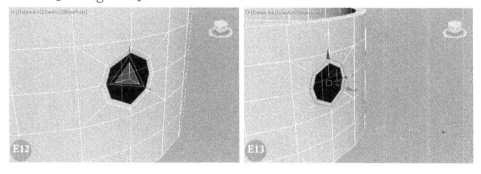

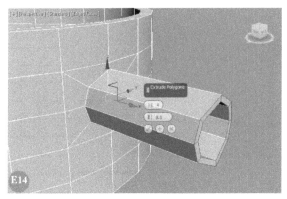

9. From the **Modifier List > Object-Space Modifiers** section, choose **CreaseSet**. Similarly, add the **OpenSubdiv** modifier. In the **Modify** panel > **General Controls** rollout, set **Iterations** to **2**. Expand the **CreaseSet** modifier in the modifier stack and select **Edge**. Now, select the top and bottom loops using **Ctrl** double-clicking [see Fig. E15].

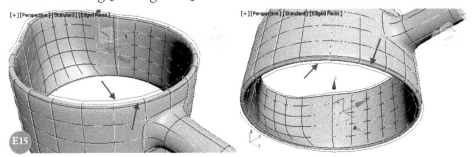

10. In the **Modify** panel > **Crease Sets** rollout, type name as **spout_crease** and then click **Create Set** to create a new crease set. Now, enter **0.9** in the spinner besides **spout_crease** to round the edges [see Fig. E16].

11. Similarly, add crease at the end of the handle [see Fig. E17]. Make sure tube is selected and then RMB click on it. From the **Quad** menu > **display** quadrant, choose **End Isolate** [see Fig. E18]. Create a cylinder and align it [see Fig. E20].

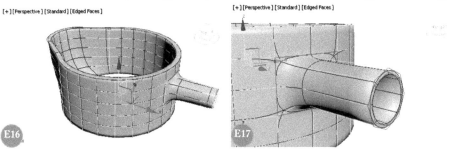

12. Create a tube and apply the **Taper** and **Bend** modifiers to it [see Fig. E20]. Now, create a cap using the **Geosphere** [see Fig. E21].

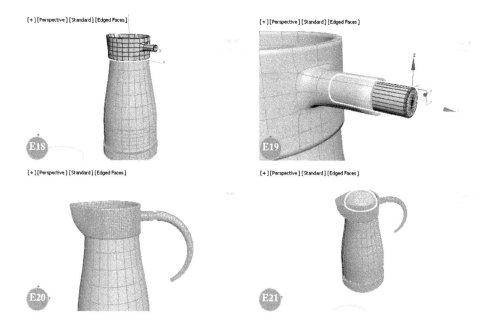

Exercise 10: Creating an Exterior Scene

In this exercise, you will model an exterior scene using various modeling techniques [see Fig. E1.

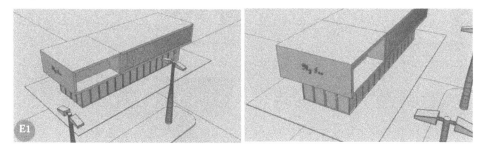

The following table summarizes the exercise:

Table E10 - Creating an Exterior Scene	
Skill level	Intermediate
Time to complete	60 Minutes
Topics in the section	• Getting Started • Creating the Scene
Project Folder	**unit-mb**
Units	**Meters**
Final exercise file	**ext-finish.max**

Getting Ready

Start a new scene in 3ds Max and set units to **Meters**. Ensure that the project folder is set to **unit-mb**.

Creating the Scene
Follow these steps:

1. In the **Create** panel, click **Geometry** and then in the **Object Type** rollout, click **Box**. Create a box in the viewport. Go to the **Modify** panel and then in the **Parameters** rollout, set **Length** to **20**, **Width** to **60**, and **Height** to **8**. Create another box and then set its **Length** to **14**, **Width** to **52**, and **Height** to **8**. Also, set **Length Segs**, **Width Segs**, and **Height Segs** to **4, 14,** and **1**, respectively. Now, align the boxes [see Fig. E2].

2. Select the **Box001** in a viewport and then convert it to **Editable Poly**. Activate the **Edge** mode and then connect the edges [see Fig. E3]. Activate the **Polygon** mode and then inset the front two faces [see Fig. E4]. Now, extrude the faces by -5 units [see Fig. E5].

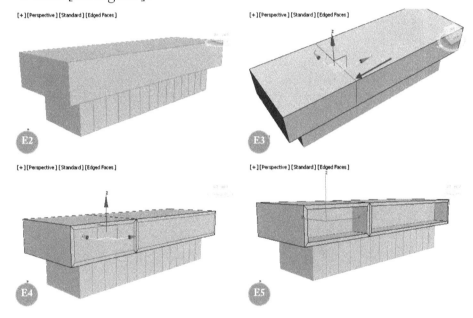

3. Create a box and then set its **Length** to **4.61**, **Width** to **0.602**, and **Height** to **6.827**. Also, set **Length Segs**, **Width Segs**, and **Height Segs** to **1, 1,** and **1**, respectively. Now, align the box [see Fig. E6]. You might need to adjust the height of the cube as per the inset amount you have specified. Create instances of the box using **Shift** dragging [see Fig. E7].

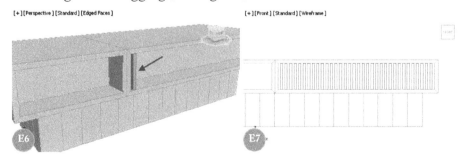

4. Select **Box002** and convert it to **Editable Poly**. Select the polygon shown in Fig. E8. Now, inset the polygons by **0.22** units [see Fig. E9]. Now, extrude the polygons by **-0.25** units. Make sure the polygons are still selected and then enter **glassSelection** in the **Named Selection Sets** field on the **Main** toolbar.

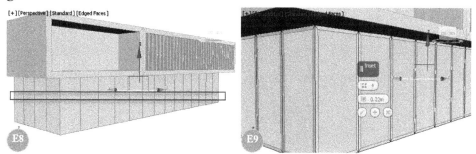

5. Create a **Plane** primitive and then set its **Length** and **Width** to **600**, and **800**, respectively. Align the plane as shown in Fig. E10. Create a box with **Length** to **36**, **Width** to **71**, and **Height** to **0.2**. Also, set **Length Segs**, **Width Segs**, and **Height Segs** to **1**, **1**, and **1**, respectively. Align it as shown in Fig. E11. Also, align the plane below it.

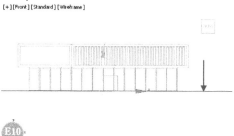

6. Create a **Rectangle** spline in the viewport and then set its **Length**, **Width**, and **Corner Radius** to **12**, **48**, and **4**, respectively. Apply the **Extrude** modifier to it and then set **Amount** to **0.4**. Align the rectangle, as shown in Fig. E12.

7. Now, create a light pole using the spline and polygon modeling techniques. Create an instance of the pole and align [see Fig. E13]. Create doors for the building [see Fig. E14]. Now, create a logo using the **TextPlus** primitive [see Fig. E15].

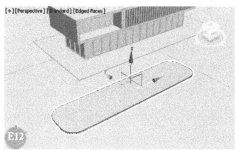
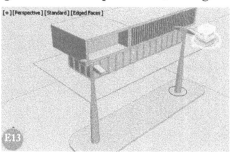

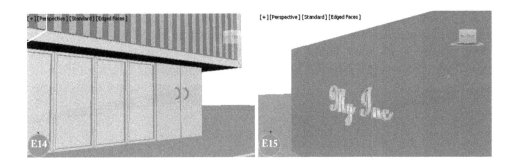

Unit MP: Practice Activities [Modeling]

Practice Activities

Activity 1: Creating a Road Side Sign

Create a road side sign, as shown in Fig. A1, using the **Box**, **Pyramid**, and **Box** primitives.

Activity 2: Creating a Robo Model

Create a robot model, as shown in Fig. A2, using the **Standard** primitives.

 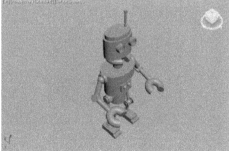

Hints:

- *The primitives used in the model shown in Fig. A2 are:* **Box**, **Sphere**, **Cylinder**, **Pyramid**, **Cone**, **Torus**, *and* **Pipe***.*
- *The fingers are created using* **Torus** *primitives. Select* **Slice On** *in the* **Parameters** *rollout of torus to create opening in the torus.*

- Use **Auto Grid** and **Select and Place** features of 3ds Max to align and place body parts.
- Create one leg and then use the **Mirror** tool to create a copy on the other side. Apply same concept on eyes and hands. Create a group before applying the **Mirror** tool.
- Create layers for different parts in **Layer Explorer**. For example, keep all geometries that make hand in the hands layer, and so on.
- Try to use various features of **Scene Explorer**.

Activity 3: Creating a Coffee Table

Create the coffee table model [see Fig. A3] using the **Box** primitive.

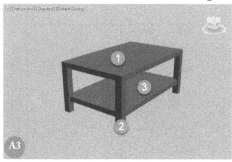 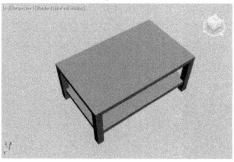

Dimensions:
1: Length=35.433", Width=21.654", Height=1.5"
2: Length=34.037", Width=20.8", Height=1.5"
3: Length=2", Width=2", Height=13.78"

Activity 4: Creating a 8-Drawer Dresser

Create the 8-drawer model [see Fig. A4] using the **Box** primitive. Create the knobs using the **Sphere** and **Cylinder** primitives.

Dimensions:
1: Length=65", Width=21", Height=1.5"
2: Length=2", Width=2", Height=35"
3: Length=60.997", Width=18.251", Height=30"
4: Length=27.225", Width=19.15", Height=11"
5: Length=27.225", Width=19.15", Height=7"
6: Length=12.871", Width=19.15", Height=5"

Create the foot stool model [see Fig. A5] using the **ChamferCyl** primitive.

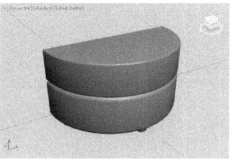

Dimensions:

1: Radius=14", Height=5.91", Fillet=0.32", Sides=24, and Fillet Segs=3
2: Radius=14", Height=7.5", Fillet=0.74", Sides=24, and Fillet Segs=3
3: Radius=1.104", Height=2.238", Fillet=0.276", and Fillet Segs=3

Hint

*Check **Slice On** for the cylinders and set **Slice To** to –180. Apply the **Taper** modifier to the legs of the stool.*

Activity 6: Creating a Sofa

Create the sofa model [see Fig. A6] using the **Chamfer Box** primitive. Assume the dimensions.

Activity 7: Creating a Wine Glass

Create the wine glass model [see left image in Fig. A7] using the **Line** primitive.

Hint

Create a shape [see right image in Fig. A8] and the use the **Lathe** *modifier to create the glass.*

Activity 8: Creating a Glass Rack

Create a model of a glass rack using the **Rectangle** spline, the **ChamferCyl** primitive, and the **Extrude** modifier [see the left image in Fig. A8].

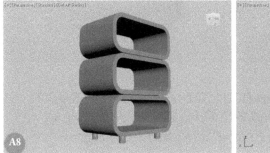 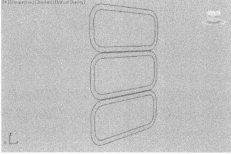

Hint

Create a **Rectangle** *spline, convert it to editable spline, give it some outline, and then apply the* **Extrude** *modifier [see the right image in Fig. A8].*

Appendix MA: Quiz Answers [Modeling]

Multiple Choice
1. A, **2.** B, **3.** D, **4.** A, **5.** B

Fill in the Blanks
1. Ctrl+N, **2.** RMB, **3.** Reset, 4.Ctrl+H, Alt+Ctrl+F, **5.** Ctrl+A, **6.** W, E, R,
7. Alt+Home, **8.** Ctrl+D, **9.** -, =, **10.** J, **11.** F3, **12.** F4

True/False
1. T, **2.** T, **3.** T, **4.** F, **5.** T, **6.** T, **7.** T

Multiple Choice
1. C, **2.** A, **3.** C, **4.** B

Fill in the Blanks
1. Clone, Edit, Ctrl+V, **2.** Spacing Tool, **3.** Reference, **4.** Select and Manipulate,
5. Shift+A, **6.** Normal

True/False
1. F, **2.** T, **3.** F, **4.** T, **5.** T, **6.** T

Unit M3 - Geometric Primitives and Architectural Objects

Fill in the Blanks
1. Tetra, Octa, and Icosa, **2.** Ctrl, **3.** Ace Templates.mat

True/False
1. T, **2.** T, **3.** T

Unit M4: Polygon Modeling

Multiple Choice
1. B, **2.** A, **3.** D, **4.** B

Fill in the Blanks
1. Vertex, Edge, Border, Polygon, and Element, **2.** triangular, **3.** Edit Poly, **4.** 1, 5, 6, **5.** Attach, **6.** Delete, Backspace

True/False
1. T, **2.** T, **3.** F

Unit M5: Graphite Modeling Tools

Multiple Choice
1. A, **2.** A, 3.B

Fill in the Blanks
1. Ribbon, **2.** Optimize

True/False
1. T, **2.** T

Unit M6: Spline Modeling

Multiple Choice
1. A, **2.** B, **3.** B

Fill in the Blanks
1, Splines, NURBS, **2.** Edit Spline, **3.** Rendering, Interpolation, **4.** Line, **5.** Helix, **6.** Section, **7.** Reset Tangents

True/False
1. T, **2.** T, **3.** F, **4.** T, **5.** F

Multiple Choice
1. C, **2.** B

Fill in the Blanks
1. Object Space Modifiers, World Space Modifiers, **2.** Transformation Matrix,
3. Perspective, Camera

True/False
1. T, **2.** T

This page is intentionally left blank

Index

W

Other Publications by
PADEXI ACADEMY

*Visit **www.padexi.academy** to know more about the books, eBooks, and video courses published by PADEXI ACADEMY.*

www.ingramcontent.com/pod-product-compliance
Lightning Source LLC
Chambersburg PA
CBHW062036050326

40690CB00016B/2960